Cisco WAN Quick Start

Ronald W. McCarty, Jr., Editor

Cisco Press
201 West 103rd Street
Indianapolis, IN 46290 USA

Cisco WAN Quick Start

Ronald W. McCarty, Jr.

Copyright© 2000 Cisco Systems, Inc.

Cisco Press logo is a trademark of Cisco Systems, Inc.

Published by:
Cisco Press
201 West 103rd Street
Indianapolis, IN 46290 USA

Printed in the United States of America 1 2 3 4 5 6 7 8 9 0

Library of Congress Cataloging-in-Publication Number: 99-67914

ISBN: 1-57870-104-x

Warning and Disclaimer

This book is designed to provide information about **Cisco wide-area networks**. Every effort has been made to make this book as complete and as accurate as possible, but no warranty or fitness is implied.

The information is provided on an "as is" basis. The author, Cisco Press, and Cisco Systems, Inc., shall have neither liability nor responsibility to any person or entity with respect to any loss or damages arising from the information contained in this book or from the use of the discs or programs that may accompany it.

The opinions expressed in this book belong to the author and are not necessarily those of Cisco Systems, Inc.

Trademark Acknowledgments

All terms mentioned in this book that are known to be trademarks or service marks have been appropriately capitalized. Cisco Press or Cisco Systems, Inc., cannot attest to the accuracy of this information. Use of a term in this book should not be regarded as affecting the validity of any trademark or service mark.

Feedback Information

At Cisco Press, our goal is to create in-depth technical books of the highest quality and value. Each book is crafted with care and precision, undergoing rigorous development that involves the unique expertise of members from the professional technical community.

Readers' feedback is a natural continuation of this process. If you have any comments regarding how we could improve the quality of this book, or otherwise alter it to better suit your needs, you can contact us through e-mail at ciscopress@mcp.com. Please make sure to include the book title and ISBN in your message.

We greatly appreciate your assistance.

Publisher	John Wait
Executive Editor	John Kane
Cisco Systems Program Manager	Jim LeValley
Managing Editor	Patrick Kanouse
Development Editor	Andrew Cupp
Project Editor	Marc Fowler
Copy Editor	Krista Hansing
Technical Editors	Danny Chami
	Stephen Kalman
	Au Nguy
Course Developers and Reviewers	Laurina Ferro
	Bob Martinez
	Peter F. Tunney
	Ken Zuhr
Team Coordinator	Amy Lewis
Book Designer	Gina Rexrode
Cover Designer	Louisa Klucznik
Production Team	Octal Publishing, Inc.
Indexer	Tim Wright

CISCO SYSTEMS

CISCO PRESS

Corporate Headquarters
Cisco Systems, Inc.
170 West Tasman Drive
San Jose, CA 95134-1706
USA
http://www.cisco.com
Tel: 408 526-4000
    800 553-NETS (6387)
Fax: 408 526-4100

European Headquarters
Cisco Systems Europe s.a.r.l.
Parc Evolic, Batiment L1/L2
16 Avenue du Quebec
Villebon, BP 706
91961 Courtaboeuf Cedex
France
http://www-europe.cisco.com
Tel: 33 1 69 18 61 00
Fax: 33 1 69 28 83 26

Americas Headquarters
Cisco Systems, Inc.
170 West Tasman Drive
San Jose, CA 95134-1706
USA
http://www.cisco.com
Tel: 408 526-7660
Fax: 408 527-0883

Asia Headquarters
Nihon Cisco Systems K.K.
Fuji Building, 9th Floor
3-2-3 Marunouchi
Chiyoda-ku, Tokyo 100
Japan
http://www.cisco.com
Tel: 81 3 5219 6250
Fax: 81 3 5219 6001

Cisco Systems has more than 200 offices in the following countries. Addresses, phone numbers, and fax numbers are listed on
the Cisco Connection Online Web site at http://www.cisco.com/offices.

Argentina • Australia • Austria • Belgium • Brazil • Canada • Chile • China • Colombia • Costa Rica • Croatia • Czech Republic
• Denmark • Dubai, UAE Finland • France • Germany • Greece • Hong Kong • Hungary • India • Indonesia • Ireland • Israel
• Italy • Japan • Korea • Luxembourg • Malaysia Mexico • The Netherlands • New Zealand • Norway • Peru • Philippines •
Poland • Portugal • Puerto Rico • Romania • Russia • Saudi Arabia • Singapore Slovakia • Slovenia • South Africa • Spain •
Sweden • Switzerland • Taiwan • Thailand • Turkey • Ukraine • United Kingdom • United States • Venezuela

About the Editor

Ronald W. McCarty, Jr., is a Senior Systems Engineer for one of the world's largest developers and manufacturers of communications equipment. His current responsibilities include presale design and support of carrier-class access network products and network system management. He is also CCNA certified. Before attaining his current position, Ronald supported global networks for Software Spectrum, a global supplier of call center support services. Earlier positions included maintaining edge and Internet services at FreiNet, an ISP in Freiburg, Germany, and handling internal network administration with the University of Maryland. Ronald earned his bachelor's degree in Computer Information Systems from the University of Maryland's international campus at Schwaebisch Gmuend, Germany. He has published articles on the RADIUS protocol, packet filtering with Cisco routers, IP security, and intrusion detection, and he currently has a monthly networking column with *Sys Admin* magazine.

About the Technical Reviewers

Danny Chami has held several technical positions in the internetworking industry since 1995, including jobs in the educational, service provider, and enterprise fields. He possesses solid technical and business understanding of enterprise and carrier internetworking challenges. Danny has advanced through several support, field implementation, and design positions specializing in LAN, WAN, MAN, access, VPN, and multiservice (Voice over IP, Voice over ATM, and Voice over Frame Relay) technologies. In his position at Cisco Systems, he was directly responsible for the development and growth of Cisco's network in the Asia Pacific theatre, and he oversaw infrastructure (LAN/WAN/access) rollout to 34 Cisco sites in the theatre. Currently, he is the Chief Network Architect for Cisco Systems IT (Information Systems) in Asia Pacific. He leads and oversees a team of Internetworking design specialists working on WAN/VPN/AVVID/multiservice/wireless and IP Technologies for IT. Danny achieved CCIE accreditation after merely two years of experience in the industry, and he runs regular Cisco internal and external customer training on a multitude of different technologies. He is also currently writing a book on Architecture for Voice Video and Integrated Data (AAVID).

Stephen Kalman is a data communications trainer. He is the author or technical editor of 12 CBT titles and is the author, technical editor, or trainer for eight instructor-led courses. He also is beginning a new distance-learning project as both author and presenter. In addition to these responsibilities, Stephen runs a consulting company, Esquire Micro Consultants, that specializes in data network design.

Au Nguy has worked in the internetworking industry for nine years. His experience includes LAN, WAN, and ISP-Dial network design, implementation, and support. He was certified as a CCIE in Routing and Switching and is near completion of the CCIE WAN Switching requirements. Au was involved in leading the design and implementation of one of the largest private LAN and WAN networks. He is currently working for Forsythe Solutions Group, a Cisco Gold Partner in Skokie, Illinois.

Dedications

I would like to thank my wife, Claudia, and my daughter, Janice, for their patience during the writing of this book. Claudia and Janice: Ich liebe Euch!

Also a big thanks to the rest of my family, especially Josef and Hildegard.

Acknowledgments

I would like to say thank you to the technical editors: Danny Chami, Steve Kalman, and Au Nguy. Danny, Steve, and Au spent a lot of dedicated time to ensure that we could bring you the quality of book that you are now reading and have come to expect of Cisco Press.

Thanks also goes to two other people who helped me throughout the project:

Andrew Cupp did an outstanding job of assisting me with all the work involved with this book. His professional attitude, friendly advice, and always-there-but-never-intruding presence ensured that work was (usually) timely and always fun.

John Kane is the editor that everyone should have. John provided motivation and humor throughout the last couple months while introducing me to some of the publishing industry's practices and guiding me to the completion of this book.

This book is the product of many contributors within Cisco Systems' Worldwide Training Department, including, but not limited to, Cisco course developers, course editors, and instructors. Cisco Press gratefully acknowledges the efforts of training developers Laurina Ferro, Peter F. Tunney, and Ken Zuhr.

Contents at a Glance

Table of Contents

Foreword

With the acquisition of StrataCom in July 1996, Cisco Systems, Inc., became a major player in ATM, augmenting its campus ATM portfolio with multiservice wide-area network ATM switching systems. Today, some of the largest and most sophisticated WAN networks in the world are based upon Cisco's WAN switching systems.

Recognizing the need for technical certifications extending beyond traditional routing and LAN switching disciplines, the Cisco Certified Internetwork Expert (CCIE) program was expanded in December 1997 to include a new standalone CCIE certification specific to WAN switching. More recently, Cisco has created two additional career certifications in this area: the Cisco Certified Network Associate (CCNA) and the Cisco Certified Network Professional (CCNP), addressing the needs of introductory and intermediate levels.

The range of the subject matter covered and the alignment to recommended courses in the career track make the *Cisco WAN Quick Start* coursebook an excellent study tool and an ongoing reference for those seeking WAN switching certification at the CCNA level. In a single, comprehensive reference, this coursebook covers WAN networking fundamentals and terminology while also providing a good introduction to the installation and basic configuration of Cisco WAN switching products.

I hope that you enjoy the *Cisco WAN Quick Start* coursebook as you pursue your certification and a better overall understanding of Cisco's WAN switching technologies.

Michael R. Clark
Consulting Systems Engineer
Cisco Systems, Inc.
CCIE #3503, WAN Switching

WAN Quick Start

CHAPTER 1

Overview of Cisco's WAN Switching Technology

Introduction

Cisco Press has published the *Cisco WAN Quick Start* coursebook to prepare you for the CCNA WAN Switching certification, one of Cisco's career certifications offered in its popular line of certification programs. The CCNA WAN Switching certification is the entry-level certification for wide-area networking professionals seeking network design or support positions. The introductory material provided in this book will introduce you to Cisco WAN switching so that you can prepare for CCNA WAN Switching certification and an entry-level WAN position.

Cisco's Web site (http://www.cisco.com) is the best resource for receiving the latest information concerning Cisco's career certifications. Of course, any of the numerous online job search engines shows the demand for Cisco professionals. The demand for Cisco career-certified individuals is high—if your interest is in the WAN field, this is your first step.

The *Cisco WAN Quick Start* coursebook is composed of two parts. Part I, "WAN Quick Start," presents the same information as the Cisco WAN Quick Start (WQS) self-paced course. The information covered is required to prepare for the Installation of Cisco WAN Switches (ICWS) course, which is covered in Part II, "Installation of Cisco WAN Switches," of this book.

As an added benefit, Part I also provides the prerequisite information to prepare for the Multiservice Switch and Service Configuration (MSSC) course, the BPX Switch and Services Configuration (BSSC) course, and the MGX ATM Concentrator Configuration (MACC) course.

Part I: WAN Quick Start

Part I gives a solid introduction to data communications and wide-area networking concepts.

Data communication terminology and technology are covered, including such topics as serial communications, narrowband and broadband communications, voice and data transportation, Frame Relay, and Asynchronous Transfer Mode (ATM). Each topic is covered within a context that can be further built upon as other technology is covered. Furthermore, data communications fundamentals apply to other areas of networking, including local-area networks, network access services (access routers and modem pools), and wide-area data networks.

Serial communications, covered in Chapter 2, "Serial Communication," have become predominant in private and business communications due to high modem sales, which have boomed based upon popularity of the Internet, the continually declining prices of T1 and E1 services in the business world, and the growing need for faster communication speeds in the business world. Point-to-point links and Frame Relay networks are the major uses of serial communications for business use, and Frame Relay is likely the most popular private WAN technology in the United States. Frame Relay can only lose market share through better tariffs in the ATM arena and the push for quality of services using ATM solutions.

Following serial communications, you receive an introduction to narrowband communication in Chapter 3, "Narrowband Transmissions," and broadband communication in Chapter 4, "Broadband Transmissions." Transmission types, line coding, and framing of E1 (Europe), J1/Y1 (Japan), and T1 (North America) serial links are covered, and time-division multiplexing (TDM) is addressed in the narrowband discussion. Chapter 4 also covers transmission types, line coding and framing of E3, DS-3 (T3), and SONET.

Digital voice and data concepts follow in Chapter 5, "Digital Voice Technical Concepts and Considerations." This chapter covers analog to digital conversion, bandwidth optimization, and signaling concepts.

Chapter 6, "Frame Relay," and Chapter 7, "Asynchronous Transfer Mode," cover application of the WAN switching concepts presented in Chapters 2 through 5.

Chapter 6 provides a thorough overview of Frame Relay concepts: frame format, addressing, signaling, the User-Network Interface (UNI), and the Network-to-Network Interface (NNI). Frame Relay is ideal for bursty data applications. Continual development of data applications, combined with the very competitive Frame Relay market in the United States, has often made this the technology of choice for data WANs.

Chapter 7 covers the physical interfaces supported by ATM and discusses the ATM layer and cell format, the ATM adaptation layer, ATM addressing, and the ATM UNI and NNI.

ATM has had an uphill battle for acceptance, but now it plays a role in many midsize and large organizations as a WAN solution. ATM LAN support will increase as hardware prices drop. Ethernet has a strong acceptance as the LAN of choice, and Gigabit has ensured that it will scale into the next century. ATM's major advantage over conventional LANs is its quality of service (QoS) guarantee—Ethernet and Token Ring have not provided similar QoS guarantees. QoS and class of service (CoS), therefore, also are covered in Chapter 7.

Chapter 8, "IP Addressing and Network Management," completes Part I of the book. This chapter presents the standards-based network management protocol: Simple Network Management Protocol (SNMP). Additionally, the chapter briefly covers IP addressing.

The knowledge gained from Part I is required to understand, configure, and troubleshoot Cisco-based switched wide-area networks, a topic that is covered in detail in Part II.

Part II: Installation of Cisco WAN Switches

Part II covers the actual WAN switch installation that is covered in the ICWS course. Although a study guide cannot provide the experience gained in the ICWS course or on the job, the guide does provide an excellent supplement to the four-day ICWS course. The technical details and reference material provide information covering WAN node functionality, card specifications and features, and power considerations needed to attain CCNA WAN certification.

Cisco WAN Switches

An objective of Part II is discussing interoperability and functionality of Cisco WAN switches. The WAN switching domain has traditionally belonged to large telecommunication carriers, but this distinction has eroded with the migration of WAN switches closer to the customer's campus. (Telcos typically refer to equipment placed on the customer's site as customer premises equipment [CPE].) The business need to provide integrated voice, video, and data has pushed this trend. Additionally, network designers continually seek to consolidate services into fewer devices and fewer channels to ease management and to create further demand for high port count and flexible WAN switching solutions. In other words, network designers want to add an additional card to an already existing piece of hardware that has proven performance and that has been designed with adequate redundancy and versatility. Integration with ATM networks, digital private branch exchanges (PBXs), Frame Relay, and point-to-point networks are business realities of today's networks. What was LAN-to-LAN connectivity has become integrated campus, WAN, and telephone networks.

The Cisco WAN product line comprises hardware and software products for the networking needs of private enterprises, WAN and Internet service providers, and telecommunication and carrier service providers.

Cisco's core WAN product line is cell-based switches: the IPX, IGX, BPX, and MGX platforms. Cell-based switching, covered thoroughly in Chapter 7, "Asynchronous Transfer Mode," is a technology based upon a fixed-length sequence of 53 bytes, referred to as a cell. Cell-based switching typically operates more efficiently than conventional time-division multiplexed (TDM) switching. This increase in performance is directly attributed to the fixed cell size (much of the switching logic can be placed in the hardware), known routes within the network (routing decisions are not made on the fly), and low latency of digital networks. Before the acceptance of the 53-byte size cell, Cisco developed the 24-byte cell, referred to as FastPacket for its IPX (and now IGX) switches.

The IGX 8400 series wide-area switch, the successor to the IPX switch, is a multiservice node with the flexibility of both narrow and broadband communication with transport rates up to 310 Mbps. The IGX switch is an expandable platform with a cellbus capacity of up to 1 gigabit per second (Gbps).

The IGX can interface with voice services, serial data services (E1, J1, and T1), High-Speed Serial Interface (HSSI) data services, Frame Relay (E1 and T1), and ATM (E1, T1, E3, T3, and OC3/STM-1).

The BPX 8600 series switch is a WAN switch designed as an ATM backbone node. The BPX switch is a broadband, multigigabit ATM switch with ATM interfaces that support 34 Mbps and higher. The BPX switch module offers 9.6 Gbps throughput. The BPX is typically used to create ATM core backbones where high throughput, low latency, and QoS are important. *Carrier class* is the term often used to describe ATM switches in this class because the services are high end.

The MGX 8220 (previously named the AXIS) and the MGX 8850 Concentrator are multiservice edge devices. MGX concentrators provide access for a variety of traffic passing data from the lower-speed interfaces (E1 and T1) directly to an ATM backbone (typically made up of BPX switches) over a 34 Mbps (E3), 45 Mbps (T3), or 155 Mbps (OC-3/STM-1) trunk.

In addition to discussing Cisco's hardware offerings, Part II also covers the software necessary to build, manage, and upgrade Cisco WAN switches.

Cisco WAN Features

The Stratm operating system (OS) comprises many software features that distinguish Cisco products and provide the capabilities to build integrated digital networks. These features include the following:

- **ForeSight**—The ForeSight feature is a closed-loop traffic-management and congestion-avoidance system that is used on Frame Relay and ATM traffic. The ForeSight feature continuously monitors available bandwidth on the trunks; it can make rate adjustments to avoid congestion and can dynamically use any spare bandwidth. Congestion avoidance plays a major role in avoiding delays often present in conventional networks during peak usage.

- **FairShare**—The FairShare feature is a virtual circuit queuing and rate scheduler that ensures that available bit rate (ABR) and ForeSight traffic is fairly allocated. Unlike some products that buffer all traffic together, the FairShare feature provides firewalls between connections, which helps prevent one connection from disrupting the performance of other connections.

- **OptiClass**—The OptiClass feature provides nine service classes by separating traffic types into queues throughout the network. The OptiClass queues prevent bursty, unpredictable traffic from affecting constant-rate and time-dependent traffic in the network.

- **AutoRoute**—The AutoRoute feature provides connection management that automatically routes and reroutes connection paths in the network. The AutoRoute feature enables use of alternative paths in case of trunk or switch failures. This feature helps provide reliability, lower operation complexity, and dynamic adjustments to network changes.

- **Repetitive pattern suppression (RPS) and voice activity detection (VAD)**—These two features provide bandwidth optimization on network trunks by eliminating unnecessary traffic in the network. RPS eliminates repeating patterns on data connections; VAD eliminates silence on voice connections. Chapter 5 covers bandwidth optimization methods in digital voice technology.

Part II also covers software and firmware upgrading, trunk configuration, verification of node interoperation, troubleshooting, and network operation and monitoring.

Getting Started

As mentioned, Part I covers data communication and networking technology, including Frame Relay and ATM. This is a great place to begin to build your general WAN switching knowledge base. Then you can move on to Part II. Chapter 9, "Cisco WAN Switch Product Overview," gives you a thorough overview of the WAN switches. Finally, Chapter 10, "Installing IGX 8400 Switches," through Chapter 19, "Upgrading Software and Firmware," cover installation, configuration, and management of Cisco WAN switches.

Good luck on your road to the CCNA WAN Switching certification.

Serial Communication

Data communications typically happen in one of two ways: serial or parallel.

Serial communication is a data transmission in which bits of data are transmitted over a single channel sequentially. For example, assume that an octet (8 bits) has the value 00101111, as shown in Figure 2-1. The left-most 0 bit is the most significant bit (MSB), and the right-most 1 bit is the least significant bit (LSB). The MSB is the bit that contains the highest value and is the bit to the farthest left when written. In computer systems, the data is not necessarily stored in the same order in which data is sent. If data is stored with the MSB first, the system is referred to as *big endian*. When the data is stored in memory by placing the LSB first, the system is referred to as *little endian*.

NOTE   The word *octet* is often preferred in data communications instead of the word *byte*. People commonly use the word *byte* to refer to 8 bits grouped together because the byte size used by PCs is 8 bits. Originally, a byte was the smallest amount of information that could be read with one read statement—its original definition had been lost. Often, the terms *octet* and *byte* are used interchangeably in this book.

The 8 bits are transmitted across the serial interface sequentially 1 bit at a time, starting with the MSB which happens to be a 0 in Figure 2-1.

Figure 2-1   *Serial Transmission*

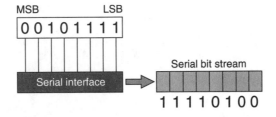

This sequential one-bit-at-a-time transmission contrasts with parallel data transmission, which passes several bits at a time, parallel, across multiple channels. Figure 2-2 shows the same octet being transmitted across a parallel interface. Instead of transmitting 1 bit at a time, the parallel bit stream can carry all 8 bits at a time. Keeping the parallel transmission of all 8 bits synchronized is successful over short distances and is typically used by devices located close to each other (for example, a PC and a local printer). In longer distances, bits might arrive at different times using parallel communications; therefore, additional overhead is required to synchronize the connection. This overhead usually outweighs any benefit from a parallel communication, so parallel communications have not become popular for longer distances.

Figure 2-2   *Parallel Transmission*

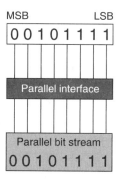

Because serial communication is more easily synchronized than parallel communication, WANs typically use serial transmission. To carry the energy to represent bits, serial channels use a specific electromagnetic or optical frequency range. Figure 2-3 shows that many media can move information across a WAN with serial transmission.

Figure 2-3   *Media That Support Serial Transmission*

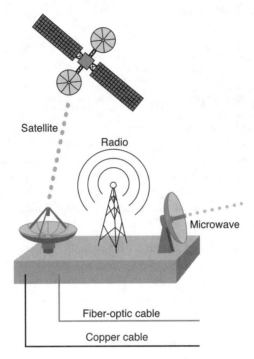

Serial data is often carried on copper cable for shorter distances—examples include the serial management cable between a PC and the console port on a router, or the serial cable used to connect a modem to a PC. Fiber optics has become the choice for new ground-based serial communications in which distance is a factor. Because of the initial high-capital investments required for satellite communications, satellites have only recently become feasible for some corporate campuses when used for transport of data that is not time-sensitive (such as NetNews) as well as backup links to the Internet. Low earth-orbiting satellites (LEOs) will expand the satellite market, and transport delays in satellite communications will decrease. Radio transmission is very popular in areas where fiber is not allowed to be installed, but this method of communication is subject to climate conditions. Microwave can also be used in areas where new fiber installation is not possible, but many governments heavily regulate its use. Microwave is also a military favorite.

This chapter includes the following sections:

* Asynchronous Serial Communication
* Synchronous Transmission Characteristics
* DTE and DCE
* DTE and DCE Control Leads

- Data Clocking
- Measuring Bandwidth
- Summary
- Review Questions

Asynchronous Serial Communication

When devices communicate with each other, they each must be capable of interpreting data sent to each other. Changes in voltage are easy enough to detect, but the stations must be capable of distinguishing the difference between two sequential bits that are the same (for example, 11) and simply a longer single bit that possibly has been corrupted by distortion on the path to the receiver. An agreed-upon timing or clock source can be used to make the distinction. As you will see in this section, the timing is determined by identifying start and stop bits within the data stream.

Asynchronous serial communication encapsulates individual characters (often 8 bits) within a frame that has a single start bit and, at a minimum, one stop bit. The amount of delay between frames is irrelevant to the communication. Figure 2-4 shows 3 bytes being transmitted in this way.

Figure 2-4   *Asynchronous—Character-Based Transmission*

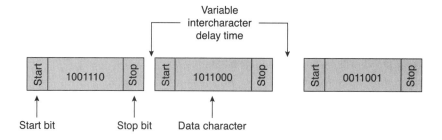

The major drawback to asynchronous communications is the overhead involved: Two bits required for every 8 bits of payload is very expensive in the data communications world.

Example applications of asynchronous communications include the following:

- Key strokes between a keyboard and a PC
- Modem transmissions
- Print code between a PC and a serial printer

Asynchronous Transmission Interfaces

The most commonly used asynchronous interface is EIA/TIA-232. The EIA/TIA-232 was formerly called RS-232 and is still often referred to in that way. This 25-pin interface standard has been in effect since 1969, when the U.S. Electronics Industry Association (EIA) published a specification describing how serial binary data could be interchanged at speeds below 20 kbps. The current specification calls for transmission rates of 56 kbps and less for distances up to 15 meters (50 feet). Figure 2-5 shows EIA/TIA-232 DB-25 connectors.

Figure 2-5   *DB-25 EIA/TIA-232 Connectors*

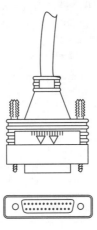

In Europe, the ITU-T adopted virtually the same specifications as the V.24 standard; V.24 describes the interchange circuits, V.28 covers electrical signals, and ISO 2110 on 25-pin assignments.

Synchronous Transmission Characteristics

Synchronous transmission uses clocking (synchronization) to operate at faster rates than asynchronous transmission. Synchronous transmissions also have larger payloads with lower overhead per frame than asynchronous character-based communication, thus offering further bandwidth improvements. (Remember that asynchronous communication has 2 overhead bits per octet.)

Each synchronous frame has the following components:

- **A header**—Addressing and control information.
- **The payload**—The information field that contains upper-layer protocol data (for example, data from the end-user application).

- **A cyclic redundancy check (CRC) field**—The result of an algorithm that generates a checksum based on the contents of the frame calculated with a polynomial value. At the receiving end, the included CRC can be checked against the CRC calculated by the receiver. If the results do not match, the whole frame can be dropped. With an ITU-T standard CRC test, devices at each end of a synchronous link can detect at least 99.997 percent of transmission errors.

- **Idle code**—Between synchronous frames, at least one instance of idle code (also called a flag) is inserted to delimit the frames. Unlike asynchronous transmissions, synchronous transmissions must always be active; in other words, bits must always be present. Multiple flags occur during idle periods. A commonly used idle flag is a hexadecimal 7E (binary 01111110). To avoid data being interpreted as the idle flag, a technique called *bit-stuffing* prevents six sequential 1 bits from occurring in the data. Bit-stuffing calls for the sender to add a 0 to the payload after the fifth 1, and for the receiver to remove that 0 before passing the data for interpretation.

Figure 2-6 gives a good view of synchronous transmission.

Figure 2-6   *Synchronous Transmission—Frame-Based Transmission*

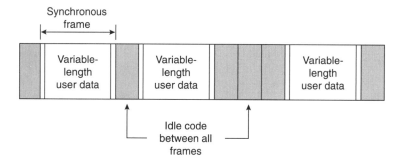

Some popular synchronous protocols include:

- SDLC
- HDLC
- X.25
- Frame Relay

Synchronous Transmission Interfaces

Synchronous serial interfaces use a physical cable with a connector for attaching two pieces of equipment. The most commonly used standards for synchronous serial interfaces include the following:

- EIA/TIA-232
- EIA/TIA-449
- X.21
- V.35

Figure 2-7 shows female and male versions of the serial connectors.

Figure 2-7   *Synchronous Serial Connectors*

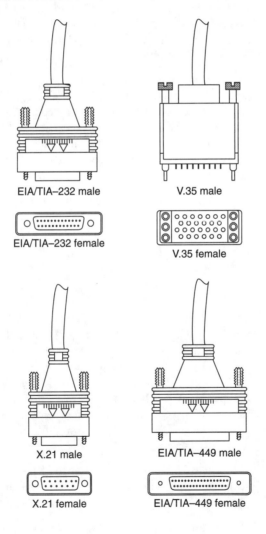

As mentioned in the section, "Asynchronous Transmission Interfaces," the EIA/TIA-232 interface is used for both asynchronous and synchronous transmission. The EIA/TIA-232 interface is intended for data rates less than 56 kbps and distances shorter than 50 feet (15 meters).

EIA/TIA-232 represents logical 1 bits with a negative voltage (less than –3V) and logical 0 bits with a positive voltage (greater than +3V).

The EIA/TIA-449 interface enhances EIA/TIA-232 for higher speeds (up to 2 Mbps) and longer distances. This cabling interface uses 37 pins in balanced mode. *Balanced mode* means the data signal is measured relative to a second signal rather than to the ground, which helps prevent the signal from decaying at higher data rates and longer distances. EIA/TIA-449 also uses additional timing and testing circuits for added functionality.

The X.21 interface standard defined by ITU-T employs a 15-pin connector and is often used for low- to mid-speed transmission. Unlike EIT/TIA-232 and EIA/TIA-449, X.21 uses a single clock lead and two control leads—one controlled by the data communications equipment (DCE), such as a WAN switch, and the other controlled by the data terminal equipment (DTE), such as a router. X.21 uses a differential signal. Each function (clock, data, or control) is supported by two wires, and the voltage difference is used to represent the logical 1s and 0s.

The ITU-T V.35 interface is becoming more common internationally (X.21 has been the most popular in Europe). This standard interfaces higher-speed modems (up to 19.2 kbps) and leased lines with balanced-mode wires (up to 2 Mbps). The cabling for V.35 uses 34 pins.

High-Speed Serial Interface

The High-Speed Serial Interface (HSSI) is a *de facto* industry standard developed by Cisco Systems and T3plus Networking (a manufacturer of DS-3/E3 DSUs and bandwidth managers). Functionally, HSSI serves the same purpose as lower-speed serial interfaces, such as V.35 and EIA/TIA-232, by providing the interface for serial communications. Classical serial interface standards, such as EIA/TIA-232 and V.35, cannot support T3 (a digital service that operates at 45 Mbps) or higher rates. HSSI is a serial interface developed to address the need for high-speed communication over WAN links. The ANSI EIA/TIA TR 30.2 committee has standardized HSSI: HSSI specifies both the electrical (no optical or other types of interfaces) and the physical interfaces.

HSSI supports speed up to 52 Mbps for lengths up to 15 meters (50 feet). As with X.21, HSSI uses differential signaling—two wires support each function (clock, data, or control), and the voltage difference is used to represent the logical 1s and 0s.

With speeds of up to 52 Mbps, HSSI can support 45-Mbps T3 as well as SONET and OC-1 (52 Mbps).

HSSI uses a 50-pin connector, which is smaller than the V.35 connector. To reduce the need for male-male and female-female adapters, HSSI cable connectors are specified as male. The HSSI cable uses the same number of pins and wires as the Small Computer Systems Interface 2 (SCSI-2) cable, but the HSSI electrical specification is tighter. Although the pin-outs of the two cables are the same, Cisco does not recommend the use of SCSI-2 cable for HSSI because the SCSI-2 cable has a lower impedance specification.

Bandwidth allocation is possible with HSSI at speeds ranging from 1.5 to 52 Mbps. The DCE controls the clock by changing its speed or by deleting clock pulses. In this way, the DCE can allocate bandwidth among applications. For example, a PBX might require a particular amount of bandwidth (4.5 Mbps), and a router might require another amount (for example, 20 Mbps). Bandwidth allocation is key to making T3 and other broadband services affordable and popular.

DTE and DCE

The interface connectors used for serial data have multiple pins that are used to carry various kinds of information between two attached devices. (The communication is still serial—the payload is never split across the control pins.) The most obvious type of information is the data that passes from one device to the other; clocking and control information is also passed between two devices. To facilitate the transmission and receipt of data, each device is identified as either data terminal equipment (DTE) or data communications equipment (DCE). The DTE is the end-user device that transmits and receives the data. The DTE could be a router, a terminal, or a PC. The DCE is the device responsible for transporting the data and providing clocking. The DCE could be a WAN switch or a modem.

The term DTE refers to any device that communicates directly to an end user or network, such as a network terminal, PC, or router. The DTE will have an interface to the DCE. Typically, in WANs, DTE is the router in which the packets are routed toward the receiver. The DCE is the device used to convert the user data from the DTE into a form acceptable to the WAN service facility. Figure 2-8 shows two examples of the relationship between DTE and DCE.

Figure 2-8 *DTE and DCE Examples*

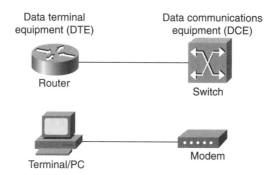

The DCE primarily provides the interface of the DTE into the communication link in the WAN cloud. The DTE/DCE interface acts as a boundary where responsibility for the traffic passes between the WAN subscriber and the WAN provider. The DTE/DCE interface uses one of the various protocols available for the codes that the devices use to communicate with each other.

This communication determines how call setup operates and how user traffic crosses the WAN.

Physical standards that specify the DTE/DCE interface include EIA/TIA-232, X.21, EIA/TIA-449, V.24, V.35, and HSSI, as discussed previously.

DTE and DCE Control Leads

DTE/DCE control leads and their logical grouping for an EIA/TIA-232 interface are shown in Figure 2-9.

Control leads provide the following interchange of signaling, control, and data between the DTE and the DCE:

- Power and grounding
- Control and testing
- Transmission circuits
- Reception circuits
- Variations on DTE/DCE control leads

Figure 2-9   *DTE and DCE Control Leads*

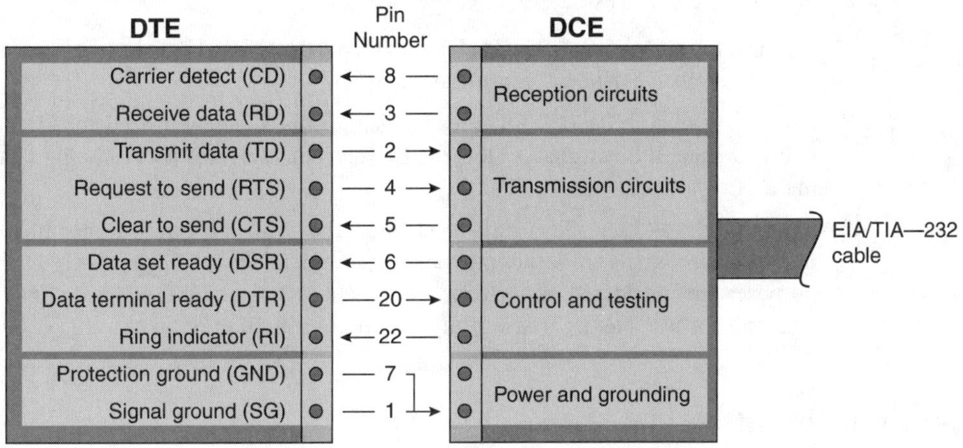

Power and Grounding

Protection ground (GND) and signal ground (SG) are the basic electrical grounds for the equipment chassis and for the other signal wires.

Control and Testing

The following are the control and testing leads (indicators):

- **Ring indicator (RI)**—This circuit indicates that a call has been received over the line (even if no ring is involved).

- **Data terminal ready (DTR)**—An ON condition means that the DTE is prepared to connect to the line; an OFF drops the line connection. The DTR enables the equipment to exert control over the connection.

- **Data set ready (DSR)**—ON tells the DTE that the data set (a telephone company term meaning modem) is connected to the facility and is ready for data. It is also used to indicate that a DCE self-test has been completed without an error.

Transmission Circuits

The following are the transmission circuit indicators:

- **Request to send (RTS)**—The DTE sends this to the DCE to indicate the DCE should prepare to receive data for transmission.

- **Clear to send (CTS)**—The DCE responds to the RTS indicating to the DTE that it is ready for data. If this signal is OFF, the DCE is indicating it is not ready for data from the DTE.

- **Transmit data (TD)**—This is the lead where the data itself can be transmitted. Data transmission signals are sometimes called in-band; all the other signals used for other purposes are considered out-of-band. If no data exists, the DTE can keep this circuit available for use later by transmitting a marking condition of all 1s.

Reception Circuits

The following are the reception circuit indicators:

- **Receive data (RD)**—Incoming data from the line to the terminal is demodulated by the DCE and then sent to the DTE over this circuit. When no data exists, the DCE can keep this RD circuit available for use later by transmitting a marking condition of all 1s.

- **Carrier detect (CD)**—This indicates that the line is providing the facility for data transmission by detecting a signal sent from the remote side of the link. Without carrier detect, no connection to the other side takes place.

Variations on DTE and DCE Control Leads

The relationship of DTEs to DCEs is a crucial consideration when setting up serial connections. The control leads described assume that the connection is from a DTE to a DCE. However, this is not always the configuration you will face. Figure 2-10 shows some of these DTE and DCE variations for an EIA/TIA-232 interface.

With common variations, you will need to be aware of when, how, and why the EIA signals from certain pins need to be crossed over to other different pins.

DTE-to-DTE or DCE-to-DCE

Sometimes a DTE connects to another DTE (for example, two routers connected through their serial interfaces in a lab environment) or to another DCE (for example, two modems connected directly to each other through their analog ports). The crossed serial cable used to connect two PCs (DTEs) is referred to as a *null modem cable*.

Under these circumstances, several pins must be crossed over for this control lead variation to work.

DTE-to-DTE, DCE-to-DCE, and DCE-to-DTE crossovers are shown in Figure 2-10.

Figure 2-10 *DTE-to-DTE, DCE-to-DCE, and DCE-to-DTE Crossovers*

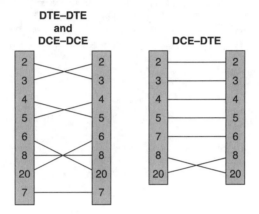

Data Clocking

Serial data transmission for most data communications uses synchronous clocking. Serial data transmission that is synchronous requires the data timing to be transmitted along with the data bits.

In general, the DCE is responsible for clocking the data. Some interfaces, including X.21, have only a single clock lead that is controlled by the DCE. Other interfaces, such as EIA/TIA-232 and V.35, have three clock leads: the transmit clock, the receive clock, and an external transmit clock. How these clock leads are controlled determines the device (DTE or DCE) responsible for defining the rate of the transmit and receive data.

The clocking between two devices can be configured in one of two ways:

- **Normal mode**—The DCE provides both the transmit and the receive clock. This is the most common clocking configuration and is often referred to as normal mode. In this case, the DCE is the clock master and the DTE is the clock slave.

- **DCE receive clock/DTE transmit clock**—The DCE provides only the receive clock, and the DTE provides the transmit clock. In this clocking configuration, each device appears to be independently clocking the data that it sends to the other device. In most cases, however, one of the devices is locking onto the clock from the other end and is recreating it as its own clock signal. In this way, one of the two devices (either the DCE or the DTE) is the clock master. This clocking configuration can be referred to as terminal, external, slave, or looped mode.

Measuring Bandwidth

Frequencies are described in terms of their cycles per second (or hertz) function as a band or spectrum for communications. For example, the signals transmitted over voice-grade telephone lines use 3.1 kHz (kilohertz, or thousand hertz). This band is called *bandwidth*.

Another way to express bandwidth is by the amount of data in bits per second (bps) that the serial channel can carry. In digital WAN communications, data is usually expressed in kilobits per second (kbps) or, on the high end, in megabits per second (Mbps). Figure 2-11 gives examples of various services and their bandwidth capabilities.

Figure 2-11   *Common Data Services and Their Associated Bandwidth*

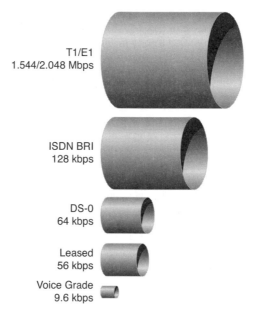

T1/E1
1.544/2.048 Mbps

ISDN BRI
128 kbps

DS-0
64 kbps

Leased
56 kbps

Voice Grade
9.6 kbps

To put bandwidth in perspective, this section contains some typical telecommunication service offerings and their applications.

Asynchronous-based services typically occur in the voice-grade range—300 bps minimum speed, and 19.2 to 38.4 kbps at the high end, with 56 kbps possible with V.90. Asynchronous connections are very popular for personal Internet use, remote router management, and even backup for low-speed leased lines.

With a leased line, a dedicated point-to-point connection is available for dedicated use. No call setup or need to dial any numbers to connect is required—the line is always up. Leased lines are typically E1, J1, or T1 lines (or fractions thereof), although leased ISDN lines are also available and popular in Europe. With fractional support, speeds in increments of

64 kbps are common. Leased lines are popular for Internet connectivity, private-to-private (ExtraNet) connectivity, and WAN connectivity in Europe. (In the United States, Frame Relay is usually chosen over leased point-to-point connections. Frame Relay is covered in Chapter 6, "Frame Relay.")

However, leased lines are not limited to rates more than 64 kbps. Fractional T1/E1 subrate transmission consists of multiple low-speed data logical connections that are submultiplexed into a single 64-kbps DS-0. DS-0 subrate data rates cover the range of 2.4, 4.8, 9.6, and 56 kbps, but they are not likely to be available from most carriers.

Standard ISDN lines have fast call setup and provide good response time for multimedia traffic, such as World Wide Web sessions. ISDN Basic Rate Interface (BRI) sends user traffic over one or two 64-kbps bearer (B) channels. An upper-level protocol, often Point-to-Point Multilink Protocol (MP), is used to bond the two channels. ISDN supports voice and data and is therefore very popular for small remote offices in which one B channel can be dedicated to voice and the other can be reserved for data.

Summary

Asynchronous and synchronous transmission are the two most common types of serial communications. Unlike parallel communications, serial communications send 1 bit at a time through a link. Because synchronous communications support longer distances, this is the serial communication of choice. Some common synchronous interfaces include EIA/TIA-232 (RS-232), EIA/TIA-449, X.21 (Europe), and V.35 (United States and international). To support the ever-increasing bandwidth, Cisco and T3plus developed the High-Speed Serial Interface (HSSI), which supports a speed of 52 Mbps and offers support for 45-Mbps T3, as well as SONET and OC-1 (52 Mbps).

Data communications equipment is identified as either data terminal equipment (DTE) or data communications equipment (DCE). The DTE is the end-user equipment (such as a PC or router); the DCE is the equipment that is responsible for formatting the data into a form that is understood by the WAN service facility. DCE examples include modems and WAN switch equipment.

DTEs and DCEs use signaling sent over dedicated leads to communicate with each other. The leads provide control and testing, transmission, and reception facilities. In addition, DTE-to-DCE communication requires timing synchronization. With normal mode, the DCE provides both transmit and receipt timing. The DCE might provide the receive clock and the DTE might provide the transmit clock; however, even in this mode, one of the devices listens to the other's clock signal and sets its timing to match.

Serial communication services are offered in a variety of flavors, from asynchronous to high-speed, multiservice capabilities. The bandwidth of these services can be measured in frequencies, but bandwidth is usually measured in bits per second.

Review Questions

The following questions test your retention of the material presented in this chapter. You can find the answers to the Review Questions in Appendix A, "Answers to Review Questions."

1 What is the minimum overhead of asynchronous communications?

A. 4 bits

B. 3 bits

C. None

D. 2 bits

E. Depends on the protocol being used

2 What do the start and stop bits in asynchronous communications provide?

A. Improved communications

B. Identification of octets within the data stream to avoid 2 individual bits from being identified as one

C. Priority synchronization

D. Framing

3 What overhead does synchronous communication have?

A. 2 bits and start and stop bits

B. Start and stop bits and CRC

C. Header and CRC

D. Header, payload, and CRC

4 Is a terminal a DTE or a DCE?

5 Is a modem a DTE or a DCE?

6 What is the maximum signaling rate of HSSI?

A. 1.54 Mbps

B. 45 Mbps

C. 52 Mbps

D. 2.048 Mbps

7 Which normally provides clocking, the DTE or the DCE?

CHAPTER 3

Narrowband Transmission

Narrowband transmission is a transmission that is made up of only one channel carried by a single media. Broadband, on the other hand, includes multiple channels carried on multiple frequencies on a single medium. Chapter 4, "Broadband Transmission," covers topics related to broadband transmission. Due to the low cost of narrowband facilities, narrowband is often the choice for businesses that have WAN communication needs of 2 Mbps and less.

In addition to narrowband transmission, this chapter covers the following four most common transmission types—T1, E1, J1, and Y1. For each transmission type, line coding, framing, signaling, and time-division multiplexing is covered.

This chapter includes the following sections:

- Transmission Types
- Cable Connectors
- Time-Division Multiplexing
- Line Coding, Framing, and Signaling
- T1
- E1
- J1 and Y1
- Summary
- Review Questions

Transmission Types

Four types of narrowband transmission facilities (line types) are available globally. Table 3-1 shows the breakdown of the facilities, where they are used, and particular implementation limitations of the technology.

Table 3-1   *Transmission Facility Characteristics*

Transmission Facility	Region	Implementation Limitations
T1	North America	—
E1	Africa, Asia (other than Japan), Australia, Europe, and South America	—
J1	Japan	PBX to switch interconnect
Y1	Japan	WAN switch to WAN switch interconnect

Of course, geographical location is not the only difference among the four facilities. Table 3-2 covers line type, signaling, number of time slots, and the maximum bit rate of each.

Table 3-2   *Transmission Facility Specifications*

Line Type	Signal Standard	Number of Time Slots[1]	Bit Rate (Mbps)
T1	DS-1	24	1.544
E1	2M	32	2.048
Y1	F-1	24	1.544
J1	Y-1	32	2.048

1.   Each timeslot within a DS-1 signal is referred to as DS-0.

Cable Connectors

Narrowband can be delivered to the DCE by a variety of different cable connectors, depending on the type of equipment that is being installed. Three popular connectors used for narrowband communication are the DB-15 connector, the RJ-48 connector, and the BNC connector.

DB-15 connectors have been very popular in the past for T1. However, RJ-48 connectors are used when a high density of interfaces in a small amount of space on hardware is required. Therefore, the RJ-48 connectors have become quite popular to save space. E1 systems can also use DB-15 or RJ-48 connectors, although a pair (one for transmit, one for receipt) of BNC connectors is also possible. Y1 and J1 facilities most often use DB-15 connectors.

Time-Division Multiplexing

Although narrowband is made up of only one channel, it seldom makes sense to dedicate the complete channel to one node. Time-division multiplexing (TDM) was originally designed to reduce the amount of cabling necessary to carry multiple voice channels. Rather than have 20 or 30 cables, TDM combines the information from different sources into the signal that is carried by the single line.

The foundation of TDM is built on the original 64-kbps channel created to carry voice traffic. When an analog voice signal is converted into a digital pulse code modulation (PCM) signal, a 64-kbps channel is created. Although many multiplexed facilities carry a variety of traffic (voice, data, video, and so on), the 64-kbps channel is the logical channel within the narrowband transmission.

TDM converts multiple parallel traffic streams into a single serial traffic stream, as shown in Figure 3-1. This is accomplished by taking an 8-bit byte from one 64-kbps input and following it serially with another 8-bit byte from a second 64-kbps input. This process continues until one 8-bit byte from each input has been sent onto the multiplexed line. The number of inputs (time slots) varies by line type, as mentioned previously. Regardless of the number of time slots, each time slot receives its data sequentially and must wait until the next iteration. If no data needs to be sent, the time slot is wasted.

Figure 3-1   *Time-Division Multiplexing*

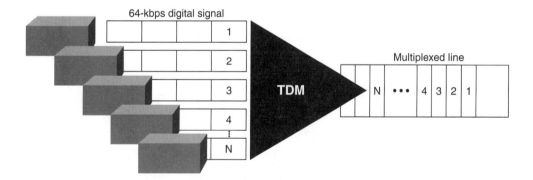

The portion of the multiplexed line that contains one 8-bit byte from each of the 64-kbps inputs is called a *frame*. The frame is the building block for all the line types covered in this chapter.

Upon receipt at the other end, the traffic must be re-created into its original form so the proper recipient receives each channel. This process is called *demultiplexing*. For example, assume that a T1 is used to connect your organization's two call center facilities. If John is talking to someone on channel 1 and Jane is speaking to someone on channel 2, their voices will be multiplexed onto the T1 and sent to the receiving PBX, which must then demultiplex (separate) the voice traffic so it can be sent to the proper telephone and recipient.

Line Coding, Framing, and Signaling

Each type of narrowband transmission facility has defined coding, framing, and signaling associated with it. Coding, framing, and signaling are required so those two-narrowband nodes can communicate with each other.

Line Coding

Line coding describes the way the logical bits (1 and 0) are represented on the transmission facility. For example, on a T1 line, a 0 bit is represented by a 0 voltage on the wire; with J1, however, a 0 bit is represented by a transition from a negative voltage to a positive voltage on the wire.

Another part of the coding definition of a line is the 1s density. Most transmission systems define a maximum number of consecutive 0 bits (therefore, a minimum density of 1 bit) that can occur on the line. The 1s density is necessary to maintain synchronization of the signal. Without creating bit errors, the facility must have a means of creating an acceptable 1s density. Both T1 and E1 systems have defined 1s density enforcement methods. Y1 and J1 do not require a 1s density method because the signal coding eliminates the need for additional 1s density enforcement.

When errors occur on a line, they can be the result of an error in the line coding, such as a bipolar or a line-code violation. It is important to understand how the facility is coded so you can easily determine the cause of these types of errors.

Line Framing

Line framing describes how the logical bits are organized when delivered to the transmission facility. Line framing provides synchronization, byte boundaries for multiplexing and demultiplexing, signaling bit locations, and alarm notification methods.

Each line type has one or more formally defined framing structures. Some line types have very similar framing structures, such as T1 and Y1. Figure 3-2 summarizes the number of channels or time slots, the framing bit(s), and the transmission rate of each of the four facility types—T1, E1, Y1, and J1.

Figure 3-2   *Line Framing Characteristics of T1, E1, Y1, and J1*

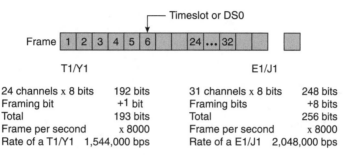

T1 frames occur at a rate of 8000 frames per second, or one frame every 125 microseconds.

Line Signaling

Line signaling describes how control or signaling information is passed between two devices, typically between PBXs transporting voice traffic. A typical application for signaling is to signal the seizure or the release (go off-hook or on-hook) of a voice channel. The transmission facility, depending on the type, reserves or borrows particular bits for signaling. The remainder of this chapter discusses line coding, framing, and signaling and other information for the four transmission types.

T1

As mentioned in Table 3-1, T1 is used in North America. AT&T originally developed the T1 standard, but it has since received ANSI approval. Much of what is used (and not used) in other countries is the direct result of the telecommunication industry's experience with T1.

T1 Line Coding

T1 uses alternate mark inversion (AMI) line coding. Electrically, the signal transmitted on a T1 line is a bipolar, return-to-zero (RZ) signal. This simply means that each logical 1 bit is transmitted as a positive or a negative pulse, after which the line voltage always returns to 0 volts. A 0 bit is transmitted as a 0 voltage on the line.

This format is known as alternate mark inversion because each logical 1 bit (pulse or mark) is of opposite polarity from the previous 1 bit sent. Figure 3-3 clarifies the concept.

Figure 3-3   *Alternate Mark Inversion*

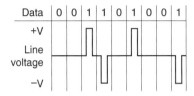

In AMI, no DC current flows through the circuit, and the frequency is half the line bit rate.

Bipolar Violation

One additional benefit of the AMI bipolar format is that it permits detection of line errors. If a line problem causes a pulse to be deleted or an unintended pulse to be transmitted, two consecutive pulses with the same polarity on the line results. This occurrence, called a *bipolar violation (BPV)*, is shown in Figure 3-4.

Figure 3-4   *AMI Bipolar Violation*

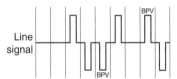

1s Density Enforcement for T1

The major disadvantage of the AMI format is that the transmission of a long sequence of 0s provides no activity on the line and is indistinguishable from a total loss of signal.

Because inactivity can be interpreted as a loss of signal that can trigger an alarm, care must be taken with lines that use AMI to ensure an adequate density of pulses on the line.

Two basic ways exist by which to ensure an adequate density of 1s. The first method is to ensure that the user equipment is incapable of generating a long sequence of 0s. This can be accomplished in voice-only systems, in which simply setting bit 7 to 1 would ensure a 1s density, and the user would never detect the difference because it cannot be heard by human ear.

With data systems, however, such a method corrupts data, so a method must be used to ensure a sufficient 1s density by carefully replacing long sequences of 0s with a special pattern that includes both 0s and 1s, which are unmistakably recognized at the remote end of the line. Upon receipt by the receiver, the substitution must be reversed—the original sequence of 0s must be replaced.

Bipolar 8-zero substitution (B8ZS) is a method that is widely used for enforcing 1s density on T1. B8ZS takes any sequence of eight consecutive 0s and replaces them with four 0s and four pulses (remember, 0s do not have pulses) in the following order: three 0s, an intentional BPV, a valid pulse, a 0, another BPV, and finally a valid pulse. This is shown in Figure 3-5.

Figure 3-5   *Bipolar 8-Zero Substitution (B8ZS)—1s Density Enforcement on T1 Lines*

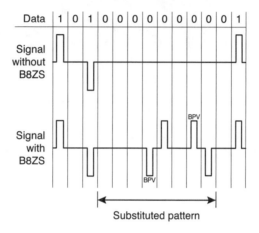

The B8ZS technique assumes that this particular sequence of pulses and bipolar violations is unlikely to occur naturally because of random transmission line errors. If the B8ZS substituted pattern does occur, the data on the line will be corrupted because the pattern will be assumed to be a string of eight 0 bits and will result in a loss of the original 8 bits.

T1 Framing

A T1 frame (see Figure 3-6) comprises 24 octets (8-bit bytes) and one additional bit for framing, making a total of 193 bits. The 24 octets are available to carry user traffic; the framing bit cannot be used for any other purpose. The specific sequence of framing bits in successive frames allows the receiving equipment to locate the beginning of each frame by locking on or synchronizing to the pattern. A T1 frame has 24 time slots per frame and 8000 frames per second.

Figure 3-6 *T1 Frame*

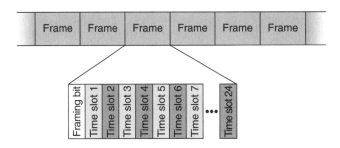

Two slightly different T1 framing bit sequences are in widespread use today. These are known as the D4 format and the Extended Superframe Format (ESF).

NOTE   In most systems, D4 framing is used without any 1s density enforcement; ESF framing is used with B8ZS.

D4 Framing

In the D4 framing format, the framing bits in 12 consecutive frames form a fixed pattern that receiving equipment is capable of detecting (100011011100, as shown in Figure 3-7). This sequence constitutes a *superframe*. The detection of this pattern locates the beginning of each individual frame and allows the receiver to distinguish individual frames from one other.

8DC

Figure 3-7 *D4 Framing for T1*

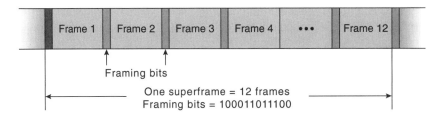

Extended Superframe Format

The Extended Superframe Format (ESF), as shown in Figure 3-8, differs from standard D4 format only in the total length of the superframe and its definition and use of the framing bits. The 24-frame ESF uses one-fourth of the framing bits (2000 bps) for actual framing using a frame bit pattern of 001011 in the frame bit positions in frames 4, 8, 12, 16, 20, and 24. In addition, the ESF also uses one-fourth of the framing bits (2000 bps) for CRC line error detection in the frame bit positions in frames 2, 6, 10, 14, 18, and 22. Finally, the other half of the framing bits (4000 bps) offer a nondisruptive diagnostic data channel for line maintenance and repair purposes. This data channel uses the frame bit positions in all the odd-numbered frames.

Figure 3-8   *ESF for T1*

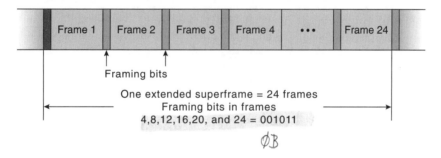

T1 Signaling

Most T1 systems transmit voice signaling information by specifying that certain bits, which would normally be used for actual user information, are used instead for signaling. Because these bit positions no longer can carry user information, this signaling technique is called *robbed bit signaling*.

Voice signaling is located in the least significant bit (LSB) position of every time slot in the 6th and 12th frame of every D4 superframe (as shown in Figure 3-9). If ESF framing is used, frames 18 and 24 also carry signaling bits.

Figure 3-9 *T1 Robbed Bit Signaling*

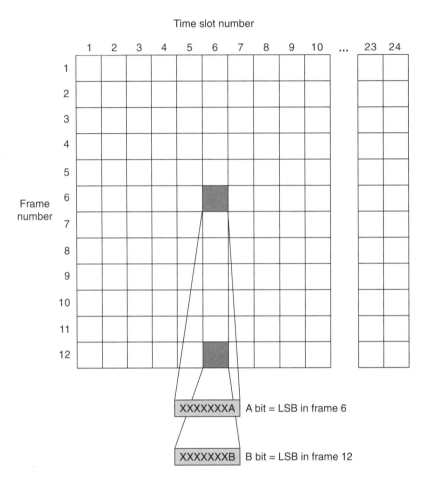

The signaling bit in frame 6 is called the A bit, and the signaling bit in frame 12 is called the B bit. Some devices can support four signaling bits—A, B, C, and D—on an ESF line where frame 18 carries the C bit and frame 24 carries the D bit. If only two signaling bits are needed on an ESF line, the A and B bits are simply repeated in frames 18 and 24, respectively.

In most cases, the corruption of a single bit in an 8-bit digital voice sample is negligible—it represents only 125 microseconds of the signal. However, it should be noted that a T1 system that uses robbed bit signaling can't carry 24 transparent data channels of 64 kbps each because, unlike voice transmission, every data bit is significant. Consequently, data transport services in North America historically carry some number of 56-kbps channels (that is, $N \times 56$ kbps), using only 7 bits in every octet to avoid the data corruption that would result from the insertion of the signaling bits. Most T1 systems today are flexible enough to eliminate the signaling bits if a channel is used for data, allowing for a full 64 kbps data rate.

E1

E1 is used throughout the world where T1 and Y1 are not used, including Europe and Asia. One difference with E1 is that it has a larger base of requirements than T1 where the vendors choose whether an option is supported. Although this often drives up development costs, better interoperability can be achieved because many options are built into E1.

E1 Line Coding

E1 lines use AMI line coding as described for T1 in the section "T1 Line Coding," earlier in this chapter.

1s Density Enforcement for E1

E1 transmission facilities use high-density bipolar 3 (HDB3) for 1s density enforcement, similar to the way that T1 facilities use B8ZS for the same purpose. Unlike B8ZS, HDB3 is standard for all E1s; it is not optional.

In HDB3, any sequence of four consecutive zeros is coded on the line as described here.

The first bit is coded as a valid pulse (according to the AMI rule) if there has been an even number of pulses (of either polarity) since the last intentional BPV. However, if there has been an odd number of pulses (of either polarity) since the last intentional BPV, then the first bit is coded as a 0. The next two bits are coded as 0 bits. The fourth bit is coded as an intentional BPV. HDB3 inserts bipolar violations in the fourth bit position in any sequence of four consecutive 0s to guarantee that intentional violations are of alternating polarity and that no DC component is introduced in the signal. Figure 3-10 depicts HDB3.

Figure 3-10 *High-Density Bipolar 3 (HDB3)—1s Density Enforcement on E1 Lines*

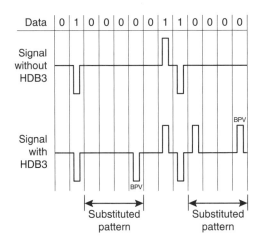

E1 Framing

An E1 frame, depicted in Figure 3-11, comprises 32 channels or time slots, one of which is reserved for framing. The remaining 31 octets in every frame are available to carry user traffic. Time slot 16 is reserved for signaling.

E1 frames occur at a rate of 8000 frames per second, or 1 frame every 125 microseconds.

Figure 3-11 *E1 Frame*

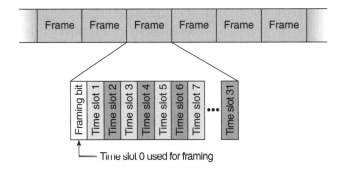

Time slot 0 also contains bits that support other functions besides framing. It contains framing information in a frame alignment signal (FAS), a remote alarm notification, 5 national bits, and optional CRC bits. Refer to Figure 3-12 to see the breakdown of the FAS within the frame.

Figure 3-12 *E1 Frame Alignment and CRC*

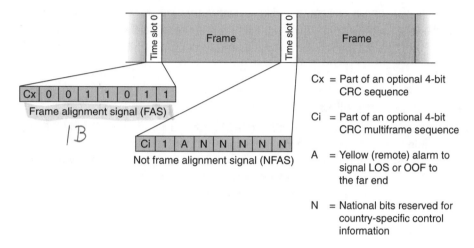

Figure 3-13 *E1 CRC Multiframe Structure in Time Slot 0*

To convey multiple frames, E1 uses a multiframe structure. Figure 3-13 shows how the structure implements the FAS and the optional CRC error checking.

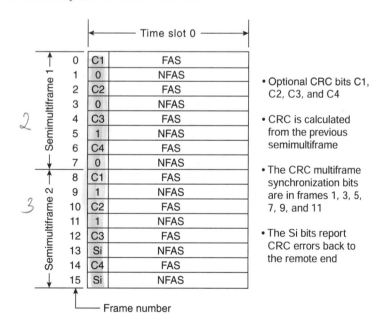

E1 Signaling

In the E1 format, one entire 64-kbps channel, time slot 16, is dedicated to carry the necessary signaling information for the other 30 information channels. Time slot 16 is typically used in one of two signaling formats: channel associated signaling (CAS) or common channel signaling (CCS).

Channel Associated Signaling

In the channel associated signaling (CAS) format, the available bandwidth in time slot 16 is allocated to the 30 information channels using the structure shown in Figure 3-14. In this structure, each channel is allocated a total of 2 kbps used to carry four signaling bits, known as the A, B, C, and D bits. For example, the four signaling bits for channel 23 are in bits 5, 6, 7, and 8 of frame 7 in time slot 16. The remaining 4 kbps are used for signaling, multiframing, and alarm reporting.

Figure 3-14 *E1 CAS Signaling Multiframe Structure in Time Slot 16*

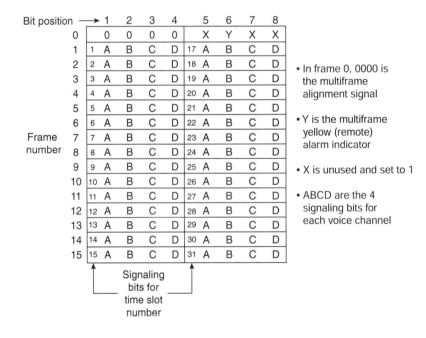

Common Channel Signaling

In the common channel signaling (CCS) format, the available bandwidth in time slot 16 is not preallocated to the 30 information channels. Instead, it is simply used as a transparent 64-kbps channel between the two end devices, which those devices can use to exchange signaling information of any type and in any format they choose. Typically, in CCS mode, signaling information is sent only for a particular channel when necessary.

J1 and Y1

This section examines the J1 and Y1 line characteristics used in Japan. J1 is the transmission type that uses a multiplexed 32-channel circuit line to a PBX. Similar to E1, J1 operates at 2.048 Mbps. J1 conforms to the Japanese TCC-JJ-20 circuit standard.

Y1 is the transmission type used for digital trunks (for example, between two remotely located switches). Similar to T1, Y1 operates at 1.544 Mbps. Y1 conforms to the Japanese Y circuit standard.

J1 and Y1 Line Coding

J1 and Y1 transmission facilities use coded mark inversion (CMI) for line coding. Electrically, the signal is a differential, nonreturn to zero (NRZ) signal, as illustrated in Figure 3-15.

Figure 3-15 *Coded Mark Inversion (CMI)*

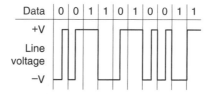

In this format, a logical 0 bit is transmitted with a low-voltage to high-voltage transition at the center of the bit time. A logical 1 bit is transmitted with no transition during the bit time. The line voltage might be high or low for the entire bit position. The logical 1 bit polarity is always opposite of the polarity of the previous logical 1 bit transmitted.

This CMI format provides two essential benefits: No DC current flows through the circuit, and there is no need for 1s density enforcement. Any data bit pattern (including long sequences of 0s or 1s) generates activity on the line.

An extended sequence of 0s on the line generates a signal with a fundamental frequency equal to the line bit rate. An extended sequence of 1s on the line generates a signal with a frequency equal to half the line bit rate.

Occasionally, the CMI coding rules are intentionally violated to identify significant bit positions in the overall data stream. The resulting coding rule violation (CRV) can be the illegal polarity for a 1 bit or an invalid high-to-low transition for a 0 bit. Each of these violation types is shown in Figure 3-16.

Figure 3-16 *Coding Rule Violations (CRVs)*

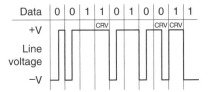

J1 Framing

Like E1 lines, J1 lines use time slot 0 for framing. The framing is accomplished by introducing an intentional CMI CRV on a 1 bit that occupies the first bit position of the octet in time slot 0. The remainder of each frame is made up of one octet from each of 31 channels. Consequently, there are 31 information time slots and one framing time slot in every J1 frame, as shown in Figure 3-17.

Figure 3-17 *J1 Frame*

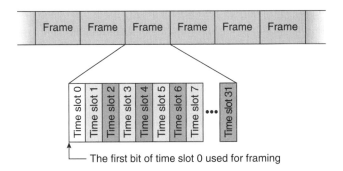

In time slot 0 of a J1 line, the third bit position carries the yellow (remote) alarm indication bit. The remaining bit positions either carry signaling information or are unused and set to 1. Like T1 and E1 frames, J1 frames occur at a rate of 8000 frames per second, or 1 frame every 125 microseconds.

Y1 Framing

Like T1, Y1 inserts 1 extra bit, a framing bit, at the beginning of every frame. (See Figure 3-18.) The framing bit is uniquely identified by introducing an intentional CMI CRV on a 1 bit that occupies the first bit position of the frame. The remaining 24 octets in every frame are available to carry user traffic. Like the T1, E1, and J1 counterparts, Y1 frames occur at a rate of 8000 frames per second, or 1 frame every 125 microseconds.

Figure 3-18 *Y1 Frame*

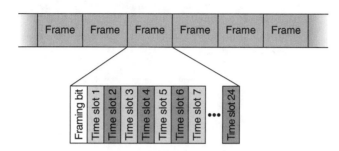

J1 Signaling

In Figure 3-19, you will notice that in the J1 format, the necessary signaling information for the other 31 information channels is included in time slot 0. J1 signaling is similar to E1 CAS signaling because each time slot signaling bit has a predefined position in time slot 0.

Figure 3-19 *J1 Structure in Time Slot 0*

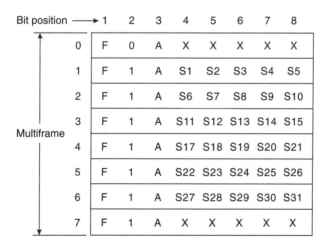

Bit position →	1	2	3	4	5	6	7	8
0	F	0	A	X	X	X	X	X
1	F	1	A	S1	S2	S3	S4	S5
2	F	1	A	S6	S7	S8	S9	S10
3	F	1	A	S11	S12	S13	S14	S15
4	F	1	A	S17	S18	S19	S20	S21
5	F	1	A	S22	S23	S24	S25	S26
6	F	1	A	S27	S28	S29	S30	S31
7	F	1	A	X	X	X	X	X

Multiframe

- F bits are CRVs for framing
- Bit 2 is for multiframe alignment
- X bits are unused and are set to 1
- A bits are for yellow (remote) alarm indication
- S1-S31 are signaling bits for channels 1 to 31
- There is no signaling bit for channel 16

Also note that no signaling bit is associated with time slot 16. In some systems, time slot 16 is used as an open 64-kbps signaling channel (as in E1 CCS signaling) instead of the defined bits in time slot 0.

Y1 Signaling

No signaling is defined for Y1 transmission facilities.

Summary

Narrowband transmission provides a single channel of communication across a single media. Narrowband is often used for WAN and telephone needs serviced by 2 Mbps and less. Four major narrowband line types exist: T1, E1, J1, and Y1. T1 is used throughout North America and parts of Asia. E1 is used in most of the rest of the world, and J1 and Y1 are used exclusively in Japan.

Each line type or transmission facility has its own characteristics that define the type of facility it provides. The most important characteristics are line coding, framing, and signaling. By covering line coding, framing, and signaling for T1, E1, J1, and Y1, you hopefully have gained an understanding of the technology as well as the capabilities and limitations of each.

Connection types, although important for actual implementation, do not determine the line type because all three types of connectors can often be ordered.

Review Questions

The following questions test your retention of the material presented in this chapter. You can find the answers to the Review Questions in Appendix A, "Answers to Review Questions."

1　Which of the following facilities are considered narrowband?

A. T1, DS-3, E1, E3

B. T1, E1, J1, Y1

C. E3, D3

D. OC-3, Ethernet, T1

2　How many time slots does T1 have?

3　How many time slots does E1 have?

4　True or false: T1 offers better performance than E1.

5 What type of multiplexing is used in narrowband transmission?

  A. Statistical multiplexing

  B. Time-division multiplexing

  C. Inverse multiplexing

  D. ATM inverse multiplexing

6 What is line coding?

  A. The number of bits that can be multiplexed per second

  B. The way logical bits are represented on the transmission facility

  C. The encoding used by the DCE to interpret the signal

  D. The decoding used by the DTE to interpret the signal

7 What type of line coding does T1 use?

8 What two types of framing does T1 support?

  A. B8ZS

  B. ESF

  C. AMI

  D. D4

9 True or false: Unlike T1, E1 does not use AMI for line coding.

10 Which E1 time slot is used for signaling?

  A. 0

  B. 4

  C. 8

  D. 16

11 What types of signaling does E1 support?

  A. Q.931

  B. CAS

  C. CCS

  D. AMI

CHAPTER 4

Broadband Transmission

This chapter describes the characteristics of broadband transmission facilities as well as transmission types, line coding, framing, and signaling. In addition, this chapter covers T3/DS-3, E3, SONET, OC-3, OC-12, STM-1, and STM-4.

This chapter includes the following sections:

- Transmission Types
- Line Coding, Framing, and Signaling
- DS-3
- E3
- DS-3 and E3 Cabling
- SONET
- Summary
- Review Questions

Transmission Types

The definition of broadband transmission has changed as the telecommunications industry has changed. Prior to the popularity of digital communications, *broadband* often referred to anything over the 3 kHz band (used by analog telephone). Broadband transmission also often meant that a transmission could support multiple channels, at different frequencies, carried on the same media. Cable television is a good example of this definition of broadband transmission—each channel you can view is sent at a different frequency. Cisco's (and others vendors') definition of broadband today usually refers to digital transmissions over 2.048 Mbps (E1) speeds used for wide-area networks. LAN technology, such as Ethernet and Token Ring, are still considered narrowband (baseband) despite their higher speed—they simply have retained their narrowband definition because they are single channels over one media.

These high-speed broadband WAN facilities are often used to transport traffic across a backbone network at LAN or better-than-LAN speeds. As the need for high-speed transmission increases, broadband rates have become more common between customer premises equipment (CPE) and the WAN.

Broadband facilities also are often used to transport ATM cells in the WAN. Therefore, this chapter covers ATM cell considerations and requirements.

Table 4-1 outlines the transmission hierarchy. Both narrowband and broadband rates are included.

Table 4-1 includes the following:

- Digital signal (DS)
- European digital transmission (E)
- Optical carrier (OC)
- Synchronous Transport Signal (STS)
- Synchronous Transport Module (STM)

Table 4-1   *Transmission Hierarchy*

Transmission	Line Bit Rate
DS-0	64 kbps
DS-1 (T1)	1.544 Mbps
E1	2.048 Mbps
DS-2	6.312 Mbps
E2	8.448 Mbps
E3	34.368 Mbps
DS-3	44.736 Mbps
OC/STS-1	51.840 Mbps
OC/STS-3 and STM-1	155.520 Mbps
OC/STS-9 and STM-3	466.560 Mbps
OC/STS-12 and STM-4	622.080 Mbps
OC/STS-18 and STM-6	922.120 Mbps
OC/STS-24 and STM-8	1244.160 Mbps
OC/STS-36 and STM-12	1866.240 Mbps
OC/STS-48 and STM-16	2488.320 Mbps

DS-0, DS-1 (T1), DS-2, and DS-3 represent the hierarchies used to describe digital transmission facilities. These transmission facilities are used in North America across copper or fiber cables. As you notice, DS-1 is the proper method to refer to T1s coding, framing, and signaling. T1 is actually the whole service and facility based upon telecommunication offerings of DS-1. The two are often used interchangeably. T2, T3, and so on do not exist as services, but users often use the terms incorrectly to identify DS-2, DS-3, and other broadband transmissions.

E1, E2, and E3 are used in most parts of Europe, Asia, and South America across copper or fiber cables.

OC-3, STS-3, OC-12, STS-12, and others are used in North America, usually across fiber-optic cables. The OC designator describes an optical transmission; the STS designator describes all characteristics except the optical interface.

STM-1, STM-4, and others are used throughout the world outside of North America. STM-1 is very similar to STS-3, with the only difference being a few bits in the frame structure.

Line Coding, Framing, and Signaling

Like narrowband lines, broadband lines require coding, framing, and signaling definitions. The details are described under each line type later in this chapter.

You should understand the significance of the coding, framing, and signaling on a line.

Line Coding

Line coding describes the way the logical bits are represented on the transmission facility. For example, on an E3 line, a zero voltage on the wire represents a 0.

The 1s density is also part of the coding definition of a line. Most transmission systems define a maximum number of 0s (therefore, a minimum 1s density) that can occur on the line. The 1s density is necessary to maintain synchronization of the signal. Like their narrowband counterparts, both DS-3 and E3 have defined methods for ensuring 1s density on the line.

Line Framing

Line framing describes how the logical bits are organized during transmission. The framing is responsible for line synchronization, control bit location, and alarm notification.

Each transmission facility has one or more defined framing structures, with additional frame structures possible for ATM services. For example, typically a DS-3 line is a facility that is formed by multiplexing multiple T1 lines together. If the DS-3 is transporting ATM cells, the DS-3 is not made up of multiplexed T1s; instead, additional framing is used within the one logical channel to delineate the ATM cells it carries.

Line Signaling

Line signaling describes how control and signaling information is passed between two devices. It should be noted that ATM signaling is carried in ATM cells, so line signaling need not be used.

DS-3

DS-3 is very popular for ATM implementations that require better-than-typical LAN speeds on the WAN backbone. DS-3 supports speeds up to 44 Mbps.

DS-3 Line Coding

Like a T1 or E1 line, a DS-3 line uses an alternate mark inversion (AMI) bipolar, return-to-zero (RZ) electrical signal to represent the 1 and 0 bits. Zero voltage on the line represents a logical 0. A positive or negative pulse on the line represents a logical 1 in a bit stream, after which the signal returns to 0 voltage. Figure 4-1 shows AMI. The pulses alternate in polarity so that a negative pulse follows a positive pulse, followed by a positive pulse, and so on. Any pulses that do not meet this requirement are called bipolar violations (BPVs). Figure 4-1 also shows a BPV.

Figure 4-1 *Bipolar Line Format with Bipolar Violation*

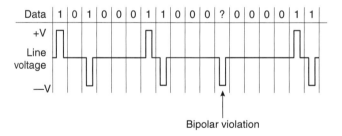

1s Density Enforcement for DS-3

If multiple 0 bits occur, line equipment will have difficulty remaining synchronized to the signal. To avoid synchronization problems, DS-3 lines use bipolar 3-zero substitution (B3ZS) to meet the required density of 1 bits. B3ZS is similar to B8ZS used on T1 lines or HDB3 used on E1 lines. However, unlike B8ZS on T1 lines, B3ZS is mandatory for DS-3.

Bipolar violations are used to substitute for strings of 0 bits. The substitution pattern is easily identified by the receiving equipment, which then replaces the substitution with the appropriate 0 bits.

In the B3ZS line-coding technique as defined in ANSI T1.102-1987, substitution of any three consecutive zeros on the line is as follows:

- The first bit is coded as a BPV (opposite polarity of the previous pulse) if there has been an even number of pulses of either polarity since the last intentional BPV. Otherwise, if there has been an odd number of pulses of either polarity since the last intentional (managed) BPV, the first bit is coded as a 0.

- The second bit is coded as a 0.

- The third bit is coded as an intentional BPV.

See Figure 4-2 to see B3ZS in action.

Figure 4-2   *Bipolar 3-Zero Substitution—1s Density Enforcement on DS-3 Lines*

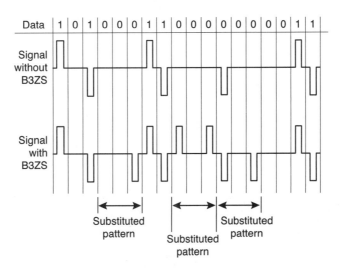

Assume an odd number of pulses not shown since
the last intentional bipolar violation

Line-Code Violations

A line-code violation is an error in which either of the following occurs:

- A pulse is the same polarity as the preceding pulse and is not part of a zero-substitution code.

- More than three consecutive 0s are on the line.

DS-3 Framing

The DS-3 frame format provides framing and control bits throughout the DS-3 frame. Because of this intermixing of bits, there is no fixed relationship between the standard DS-3 frame and any of the 53 octet ATM cells it carries. This situation requires special control bytes that will perform various control functions when the DS-3 frame carries ATM cells.

The Standard DS-3 Frame

In the ANSI T1.107-1988 standard, the DS-3 signal (44.736 Mbps) is partitioned into multiframes (M-frames) of 4760 bits each, or one every 106.4 microseconds. Note that the DS-3 is the only transmission facility that does not use a 125-microsecond frame time. DS-3 lines are designed to synchronously carry up to 28 DS-1 (T1) lines; that is, each T1 line is timed independently. For this reason, the DS-3 does not have the same frame time as a T1 to allow for timing flexibility. Figure 4-3 shows both the M-frame and the M-subframe format. As mentioned, when DS-3 is used for ATM, no multiplexing of DS-1s is performed—the transmission is treated as one logical channel.

Figure 4-3   *DS-3 Line Framing*

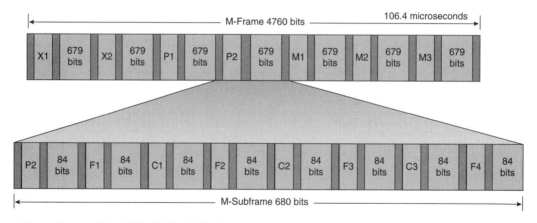

M-Frame Alignment Signal: M1 = 0, M2 = 1, M3 = 0
M-Subframe Alignment Signal: F1 = 1, F2 = 0, F3 = 0, F4 = 1
X1 and X2 bits: Yellow alarm signal to the far end
P1 and P2 bits: Parity for the preceding M-Frame
C1, C2, and C3: Embedded Operations Channel (EOC) or Far End Block Error (FEBE)

The DS-3 M-frames are subdivided into seven M-subframes of 680 bits each, and the M-subframes are further divided into eight blocks of 85 bits each, with 84 bits for user information and 1 bit for framing overhead. One M-frame includes a total of 4704 user information bits and 56 framing overhead bits.

Both the M-frame and the M-subframe have alignment signals (010 and 1001, respectively) that are used by the receiving equipment to track the frame structure. The P bits in the M-frame are used to check the parity of the line. The C bits in the M-subframes can be used in a format called C-bit parity, which copies the result of the P bits at the origin of transmission and rechecks the result at the far end. If there are errors in the C bits, a far-end block error (FEBE) is reported via the C bits back to the transmitting equipment. The C bit positions can also be used for an 84.6-kbps user channel if they are not used for C-bit parity.

The payload of a DS-3 is: (672 bits per M-subframe) × (7 M-subframes) ÷ (106.4 microseconds) = 44.21 Mbps

DS-3 PLCP Framing for ATM Transmission

ATM devices transport cells at the DS-3 rate using the Switched Multimegabit Data Service (SMDS) physical-layer convergence procedure (PLCP) framing structure, as specified in IEEE 802.6 and Bellcore TR-TSV-000773. Self-delineated cell framing is also supported as described in the "E3" section, later in this chapter.

The PLCP frame, which is used to delineate the ATM cells on a DS-3 line, is placed in the payload of the DS-3 frame. Notice that the PLCP overhead is an additional overhead to the DS-3 overhead described in the previous section. The framing, control, and overhead bytes are shown as A1, A2, Pn, Zn, and other bit designations. These bits perform the following framing control functions:

- The A1 and A2 bits identify the beginning of an ATM cell.
- The M, G, B, and F bytes provide operation and maintenance capabilities.
- The P byte helps distinguish among the various overhead bytes.
- The Z bytes are placeholders for future control purposes.
- A 52- or 56-bit trailer follows and is used to adjust the alignment of the PLCP frame within the DS-3 frame.

Figure 4-4 breaks down the PLCP framing.

Figure 4-4 *PLCP Framing—ATM Cells on a DS-3 Line*

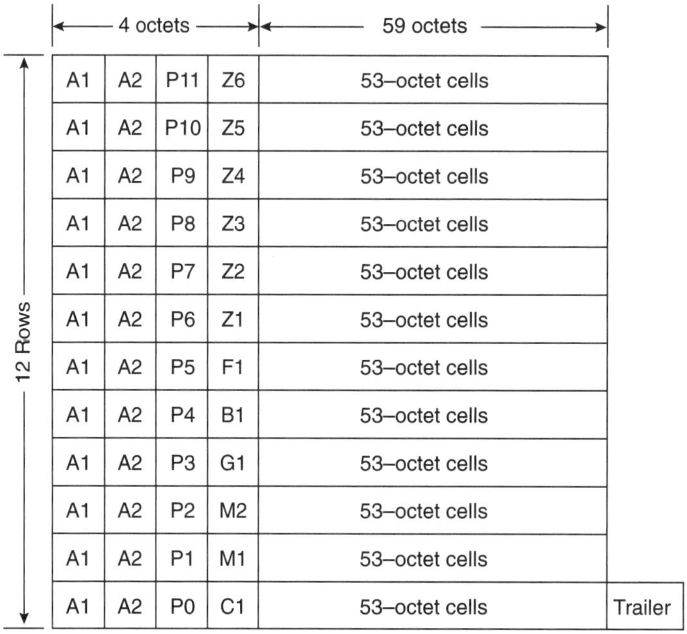

A1 = 11110110   Z1–Z6 = future use
A2 = 00101000   F1 = PLCP path user channel
B1 = BIP–8   G1 = PLCP path status
C1 = counter   M1–M2 = SIP L1 control info
Trailer = 13 or 14 nibbles (4 bits each) P0–P11 = path OH identifier

The PLCP frames occur at a frequency of 8000 frames per second, or once every 125 microseconds. Because one PLCP frame can carry twelve 53-octet ATM cells, the cells-per-second rate for a DS-3 with PLCP ATM framing is: (8000 frames per second) × (12 cells per frame) = 96,000 cells per second. The data rate of ATM cells on a DS-3 is: (96,000 cells per second) × (53 octets per cell) × (8 bits per octet) = 40.70 Mbps. The total overhead on a DS-3 using PLCP framing is approximately 9 percent.

E3

E3 provides 34.368 Mbps throughput and is often the choice for high-speed network WAN backbones outside North America.

E3 Line Coding

E3 lines use a bipolar, return-to-zero (RZ) format identical to DS-3 lines. A logical 1 in a bit stream is represented by a positive or negative pulse on the line, after which the signal returns to 0 voltage. Zero voltage on the line represents a logical 0.

1s Density Enforcement for E3

E3 uses high-density bipolar 3 (HDB3) to maintain the density of pulses on the line. HDB3 is also used on E1 lines and is similar to the B3ZS coding used on DS-3 lines, described previously.

Normally, every pulse is the opposite polarity of the previous pulse in the bipolar RZ format. However, with HDB3, when four consecutive 0s are detected in the bit stream, a bit pattern containing one purposeful BPV is substituted by the sending equipment for the four 0s. The receiver removes this BPV and restores end-to-end transparency.

ITU-T standard G.703, Annex A, defines the following method for 0 bit (four consecutive 0s) substitution:

- The first bit is coded as a valid bipolar pulse (opposite polarity of the previous pulse) if there has been an even number of pulses (of either polarity) since the last intentional BPV.

- Alternatively, the first bit is coded as a 0 if there has been an odd number of pulses (of either polarity) since the last intentional BPV.

- The second and third bits are coded as 0s.

- The fourth bit is coded as an intentional BPV (see Figure 4-5).

Figure 4-5   *HDB3—1s Density Enforcement on E3 Lines*

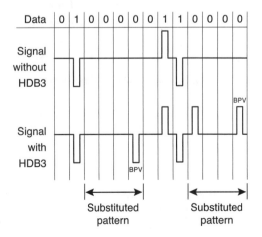

Therefore, whenever four 0s in a row are received, a line-code violation (LCV) has occurred. Any BPV that is not part of the HDB3 substitution pattern is also an LCV.

E3 Framing

Transport of ATM cells on an E3 facility conforms to ITU-T recommendations G.832 and G.804.

G.832 E3 Framing

The basic frame structure of G.832 has seven management octets and 530 payload octets, for a total of 537 octets, or 4296 bits per frame. E3 frames are sent every 125 microseconds (8000 frames per second). The G.832 frame includes two frame-alignment signals, referred to as FA1 and FA2, that are used to track or synchronize to the frame structure. Other control bits are used for error monitoring, remote alarm reporting, and network operations. The line rate of an E3 is: (4296 bits per frame) × (8000 frames per second) = 34.368 Mbps.

Figure 4-6 shows the 537-octet G.832 E3 frame structure.

Figure 4-6   *ITU-T G.832 E3 Framing*

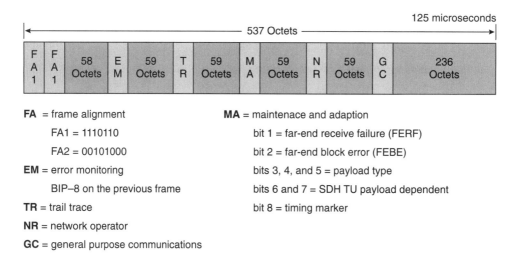

FA = frame alignment

    FA1 = 1110110

    FA2 = 00101000

EM = error monitoring

    BIP–8 on the previous frame

TR = trail trace

NR = network operator

GC = general purpose communications

MA = maintenace and adaption

    bit 1 = far-end receive failure (FERF)

    bit 2 = far-end block error (FEBE)

    bits 3, 4, and 5 = payload type

    bits 6 and 7 = SDH TU payload dependent

    bit 8 = timing marker

G.804 E3 Framing

An E3 that carries ATM cells employs G.804 framing. The G.804 frame structure is identical to that of the G.832 frame (same control fields, payload size, and line rate), except that the payload carries ATM cells. Unlike PLCP framing for DS-3s carrying ATM cells,

G.804 framing does not introduce additional overhead. ATM cells on an E3 line are self-delineated—the device receiving the cells is configured to recognize ATM and uses the cell structure (rather than the line structure) to determine where the cells begin and end.

The ATM cell 5-octet header comprises four octets of address and control, and an 8-bit cyclic redundancy check (CRC). The 8-bit CRC is called the header error control (HEC) field and is calculated on the bits in the header of the cell. Because every cell is a fixed length and has a header and an HEC field, the network equipment can use this structure to locate the cells on a line. By sampling a random cell, the network device can calculate the CRC and compare it to what it thinks is the cell header HEC field. If the CRC calculation is not correct, then the receiver shifts to the next cell and calculates again. Eventually, a header is found in the bit stream. If the calculation is correct, it is assumed that 53 octets later, there is another ATM cell whose header is also checked. This process continues until an appropriate number of cells (usually four) has passed the CRC check, at which time the cell framing is established. G.804 framing does not require the ATM cells to be aligned to the G.832 frame structure. G.804 E3 framing is shown in Figure 4-7.

Figure 4-7   *ITU-T G.804 E3 Framing*

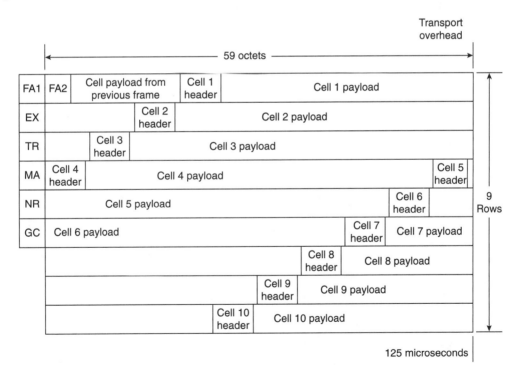

Based on the G.804 method, the E3 frame can transmit 10 ATM cells per frame, so the cells-per-second rate is: (8000 frames per second) × (10 cells per frame) = 80,000 cells per second. The data rate of ATM cells on an E3 line is: (80,000 cells per second) × (53 octets per cell) × (8 bits per octet) = 33.92 Mbps.

The total overhead on a G.804 E3 line carrying ATM cells is approximately 1 percent.

Other E3 Framing Methods

It is also possible to transmit ATM cells on an unframed E3 line by tracking the HEC field in the cell header. In this case, no overhead is associated with the line, and the cell rate is: (34,368,000 bits per second) ÷ (424 bits per cell) = 81,057 cells per second.

However, unframed E3 facilities are not widely available.

DS-3 and E3 Cabling

In most installations, DS-3 and E3 facilities are carried on a pair of 75-ohm coaxial cables with BNC connectors. One cable transmits, and the other receives.

SONET

A large percentage of high-speed broadband transmission facilities that must support speeds of more than 50 Mbps use fiber-optic technology. Synchronous Optical Network (SONET), as defined by Bellcore TR-NWT-000253, ANSI T1.105, and the ITU-T G.707, G.708, and G.709, provides a hierarchy of fiber-optic transmission facilities for use in the WAN.

Fiber Optics

Two types of optical transmission media exist: single-mode and multimode fiber.

Single-Mode Fiber

Single-mode fiber has an 8-micron fiber core for transport of a single coherent light wave. Single-mode fiber can be deployed in distances up to 45 km (28 miles). Single-mode fiber does not have any known speed limitations; therefore, it should support speeds up to the theoretical maximum of 12 Gbps. Single-mode fiber uses a laser for its light source. In single-mode fiber, only one bundle of light travels through the fiber (see Figure 4-8). Single-mode fiber usually costs much more than multimode fiber, but the price difference between the two has shrunk, as have prices for fiber in general. As a result, single-mode fiber is now an option for most companies seeking fiber solutions.

Figure 4-8   *Single-Mode Fiber*

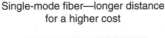

Multimode Fiber

Multimode fiber typically has a 62.5-micron fiber core for transport of different light waves at different angles (multiple light bundles bounce through the fiber, as shown in Figure 4-9). Multimode fiber is limited to a distance of 2 km (1.25 miles) and a maximum data rate of 155 Mbps. (The data rate is actually a limitation of the service being used, such as SONET. Gigabit Ethernet has been approved for multimode fiber.) Multimode fiber uses an LED for its light source. As mentioned, the price difference between multimode and single-mode has shrunk, but multimode is still very popular for connecting buildings within campus networks.

Figure 4-9   *Multimode Fiber*

Fiber Connectors

Two types of connectors are commonly used on fiber-optic SONET facilities. ST connectors have traditionally been used on single-mode fiber, and SC connectors have been used for multimode fiber. However, this is not a requirement of the standard, and SC connectors have actually become quite popular regardless of the fiber mode chosen.

STS, OC, STM, and Concatenated Services

SONET facilities, including T1, DS-1, DS-3, and T3, are referred to using different terms, depending on the installation or person describing the network. Often, these terms are incorrectly used interchangeably. The following shows how to accurately use these terms:

- **Synchronous Transport Signal (STS)**—This term is used to describe the facility characteristics (framing, signaling, and so on), but does not imply that the line is being transported across a fiber-optic media. STS-1 is the building block of the SONET hierarchy and is discussed later in this section. STS-3 comprises three STS-1 signals; STS-12 comprises 12 STS-1 signals. STS and OC often are used interchangeably.

- **Optical carrier (OC)**—This term is used to describe a facility identical to STS, except that the signal is being transported on a fiber-optic cable. So, OC-1 and STS-1 share the same coding, framing, and signaling characteristics. OC-3 comprises three OC-1 signals; OC-12 comprises 12 OC-1 signals.

- **Concatenated (STS-3c, OC-3c, STS-12c, OC-12c, and so on)**—The term *concatenated* describes a SONET facility that is not multiplexed. For example, an OC-3c line does not carry multiplexed OC-1 lines but is a single, independent, 155-Mbps bandwidth channel.

- **Synchronous Transport Module (STM)**—This term describes a SONET line as defined by ITU-T. STM facilities are used throughout the world outside North America. The building block of the STM hierarchy is the STM-1 signal, which is very similar to an STS-3c signal. In fact, the two have identical line rates and framing structure, although some of the control bits differ. An STM-4 line is equivalent to an STS-12c line. In most situations, SONET facilities are referred to as OC (OC-3, OC-12, and so on) in North America, and STM (STM-1, STM-4, and so on) around the world, regardless of the details described.

STS-1

The building block for North American SONET facilities is the Synchronous Transport Signal level 1 (STS-1). STS-1 defines a framing structure that consists of nine rows of 90 octets, for a total of 6480 bits per frame, as shown in Figure 4-10. Three octets per row are defined as transport overhead that is used for control information. The remaining 87 octets per row (a total of 6264 bits per frame) make up the envelope capacity or payload.

Figure 4-10 *STS-1*

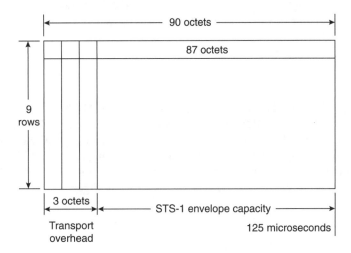

Each frame occurs 8000 times per second (once every 125 microseconds) on an STS-1 line. Therefore, the line rate of an STS-1 facility is: (6480 bits per frame) × (8000 frames per second) = 51.84 Mbps. Higher-rate SONET transmission facilities comprise multiple STS-1 facilities so that the rates are multiples of 51.84 Mbps. For example, an STS-3 line is three times faster than an STS-1 line, with a rate of 155.52 Mbps. STS-1 facilities are rarely chosen over DS-3 or E3 for ATM because there is not a large difference in the data rate and because the DS-3 or E3 is often priced better.

SONET Elements

In a SONET network, network elements are responsible for interpreting and generating the transport overhead. As the payload travels through the SONET network, network elements are classified as section-, line-, or path-terminating equipment (STE, LTE, and PTE). Note that these devices are not the WAN switches, but the transmission equipment in the SONET backbone most likely owned and operated by the carrier.

In general, an STS frame has the following parts:

- **Section overhead (SOH)**—The first three rows of the frame transport error information (and are considered overhead) between each STE.

- **Line overhead (LOH)**—The last six rows of the transport overhead are used for communications and synchronization between network elements.

- **Synchronous payload envelope (SPE)**—This data structure carries the payload of the SONET line. The SPE is not necessarily aligned in the payload of the SONET frame.

- **Path overhead (POH)**—The POH is the first octet in the SPE. The POH is generated at the point where the payload enters the SONET network, most likely at the WAN switch interface. The POH is removed at the SONET termination point, again at the WAN switch interface.

STS-3c

The STS-3c frame is made up of three STS-1 frames. The STS-3 and STS-3c frames are identical; the payload differentiates them. Remember that the STS-1 frame has nine rows of 90 octets, and frames transmit each 125 microseconds. The STS-3 frame has nine rows of 270 octets, three times the length of an STS-1 frame; like STS-1, the STS-3 frames also transmit frames every 125 microseconds. Each row of the STS-3 frame has 9 transport overhead octets and 261 payload octets, as shown in Figure 4-11.

Figure 4-11 *SONET STS-3c Framing*

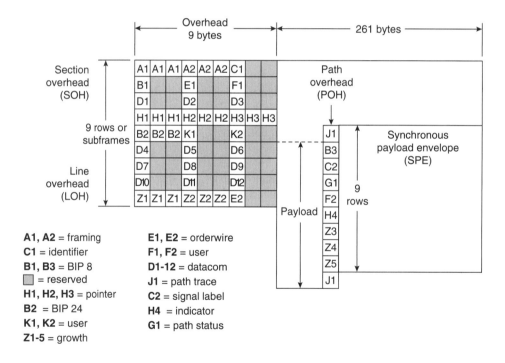

The line rate of an STS-3 facility is therefore: (270 octets per row) × (9 rows) × (8 bits per octet) × (8000 frames per second) = 155.52 Mbps.

The SPE carries ATM cells on a SONET facility without additional framing or overhead. On an STS-3c line, the cell rate can be calculated as follows:

(260 octets per row) × (9 rows per frame) = 2340 octets per frame (2340 octets per frame) ÷ (53 octets per cell) = 44.15 cells per frame (44.15 cells per frame) × (8000 frames per second) = 353,208 cells per second

The data rate of ATM is:

(353,208 cells per second) × (53 octets per cell) × (8 bits per octet) = 149.76 Mbps

The total overhead on an STS-3c line carrying ATM cells is approximately 4 percent.

STM-1 Characteristics

An STM-1 facility carrying ATM cells is very similar to the STS-3c facility described in the preceding section. ITU-T G.707 describes the framing structure of STM lines and the method for multiplexing a variety of facilities on STM lines. In the case of ATM cells, no multiplexing is required. The STM-1 frame structure is shown in Figure 4-12. Note the similarities to the STS-3c frame structure.

Figure 4-12 *STM-1 Framing*

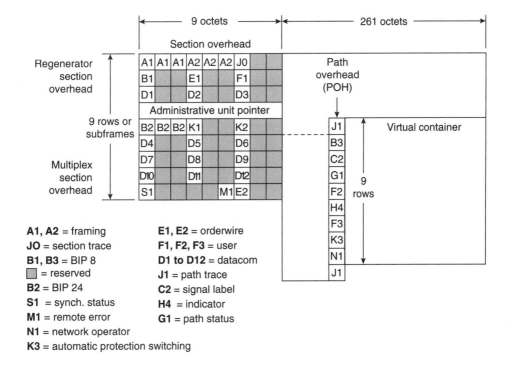

A1, A2 = framing
JO = section trace
B1, B3 = BIP 8
= reserved
B2 = BIP 24
S1 = synch. status
M1 = remote error
N1 = network operator
K3 = automatic protection switching

E1, E2 = orderwire
F1, F2, F3 = user
D1 to D12 = datacom
J1 = path trace
C2 = signal label
H4 = indicator
G1 = path status

STS-12c and STM-4

A STS-12 signal comprises 12 STS-1 or 4 STS-3 signals; an STM-4 signal comprises 4 STM-1 signals. The fields in the overhead sections are simply multiplied to accommodate for the additional signals that are multiplexed to create the line. However, STS-12c and STM-4 used to carry ATM cells are not multiplexed and therefore have a payload section available for ATM cells. Figure 4-13 shows the general structure of both STS-12c and STM-4.

Figure 4-13 *STS-12 and STM-4 Framing*

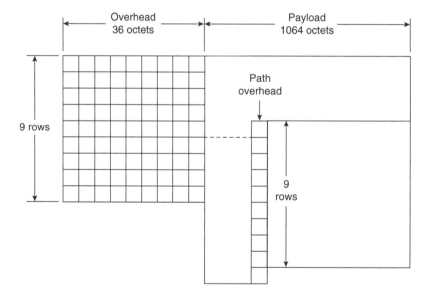

The STS-12c and STM-4 frame consists of nine rows of 1080 octets that occur every 125 microseconds. The overhead uses 36 octets of each row. The line rate is:

(77,760 bits per frame) × (8000 frames per second) = 622.08 Mbps

The cell rate of both an STS-12c and an STM-4 frame can be calculated as follows:

(1044 octets per row) × (9 rows per frame) = 9396 octets per frame (9396 octets per frame) ÷ (53 octets per cell) = 177.28 cells per frame (44.15 cells per frame) × (8000 frames per second) − 1,418,264 cells per second

The data rate of ATM cells is:

(1,418,264 cells per second) × (53 octets per cell) × (8 bits per octet) = 601.344 Mbps

The total overhead on an STS-12c or STM-4 line carrying ATM cells is approximately 3 percent.

Summary

Broadband transmission facilities are typically high-speed (above 2.048 Mbps) facilities suited for high-performance WAN implementations. Broadband includes digital services encompassing DS-*N*, E*N*, OC/STS-*N*, and STM-*N* facilities. DS is used within North America, with a very high concentration in the United States. E*N* is used outside the United States and provides similar speeds as DS-*N*. OC/STS-*N* and STM-*N* provide even higher speeds than DS-*N* and E*N*. OC/STS-*N* is used within North America, and STM-*N* is used in the rest of the world. Fiber optic is typically used for these higher-speed networks; however, the STS-*N* standard applies to cell framing, not the media—OC actually defines optical carrier specifications.

This chapter covered the framing of each facility and detailed framing requirements for ATM, where appropriate. Chapter 3, "Narrowband Transmission," and this chapter give you the fundamental knowledge of WAN switching facilities provided by carriers throughout the world needed to deploy and troubleshoot Cisco-based switched WANs.

Review Questions

The following questions test your retention of the material presented in this chapter. You can find the answers to the Review Questions in Appendix A, "Answers to Review Questions."

1 What line coding does DS-3 use?

A. None

B. Raw AMI

C. Alternate mark inversion bipolar, return to zero

D. Alternate mark inversion bipolar, return to one

2 What represents a logical 0 in DS-3 line coding?

3 How is 1s density enforced on DS-3?

A. HDB3

B. B8ZS

C. B3ZS

4 What line coding does E3 use?

A. Alternate mark inversion bipolar, return to zero

B. None

C. Raw AMI

D. Alternate mark inversion bipolar, return to one

5 How is 1s density enforced for E3?

   A. HDB3

   B. B8ZS

   C. B3ZS

6 Which two of the following are E3 framing methods?

   A. G.832

   B. H.323

   C. Q.931

   D. G.804

7 What cabling is typically used on customer premises for DS-3/E3?

   A. STP

   B. UTP

   C. CAT5 STP

   D. 75-ohm coaxial

8 SONET uses which medium for transport?

   A. STP

   B. Fiber

   C. UTP

   D. 75-ohm coaxial

9 Which is usually less expensive?

   A. Single-mode fiber

   B. Multimode fiber

CHAPTER 5

Digital Voice Technical Concepts and Considerations

Digital voice transmission is a key technology supported by Cisco WAN switches. This chapter covers digital voice concepts, including analog-to-digital conversion, bandwidth optimization, silence suppression, and voice signaling.

This chapter includes the following sections:

- Voice Services with the WAN
- The Voice Channel
- Bandwidth Optimization
- Signaling
- Echo
- Summary
- Review Questions

Voice Services with the WAN

The WAN has become the domain of integrated digital and voice facilities. This section looks at the voice services and how they are implemented in the public telephone network and a private telephone network.

Public and Private Telephone Networks

Most external telephone calls made usually use the public telephone network or Public Switched Telephone Network (PSTN). In the public telephone network, the local telephone company provides an analog circuit between the local exchange and the customer's home.

Organizations often have their own private telephone networks. These networks consist of a telephone switch (known as the private branch exchange [PBX]), internal circuits (analog or digital), and the users' telephones. The PBX connects to the local telephone company's transmission facility, such as a T1.

The internal circuits and the telco's transmission facility can be either analog or digital. The PBX then performs any conversion necessary. Most new deployments of private telephone networks use analog or digital circuits internally and digital transmission facilities externally.

Figure 5-1 shows a call being switched through a private or public telephone network.

Figure 5-1   *Call Switching in a Private or Public Network*

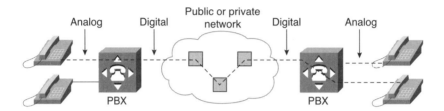

Organizations implement private telephone networks, as opposed to the public telephone network, for two basic reasons: cost effectiveness and business needs. A private telephone network is often much more feasible than the public telephone system to connect sites.

Cost-effectiveness is usually gained through integration of voice and data services. Organizations require both voice and data communications; therefore, simply adding additional bandwidth to a data link is often much more affordable than using the public data network for voice communications.

In addition to the savings of voice and data integration, the cost is a fixed cost that the company can easily plan for; in contrast, the variable cost associated with the public telephone system is hard to estimate accurately. The fixed monthly circuit charge and free internal network calls are a definite plus for most organizations.

Business needs also influence the choice of private telephone networks over the public telephone system. Businesses require internal flexibility to program internal features to support business needs such as call forwarding, voice mail, call groups, internal conferencing, simple extension dialing, reprogramming, and so on. Although all these services might be available from the local telephone provider, companies require that they determine for themselves the what, when, where, and how requirements in managing voice services for hundreds or thousands of employees.

Of course, the public telephone network is still available for smaller operations and also acts as a backup to the private telephone network. (The backup can be limited—the private and public networks can share common failure points within the telephone companies' networks.) Additionally, companies rely on the public network to supplement private networks in cases when capacity planning was not accurate and the current private network cannot support the user demand.

Analog-to-Digital Conversion

The human voice is a low-frequency analog signal with a frequency range of less than 4000 cycles per second (Hz). Analog telephone services have been designed to carry the voice frequency. Voice frequency circuits are also used to carry binary data that has been converted to analog using a modulator-demodulator (modem).

Prior to digital transmission, the analog voice must be converted to digital. Within a private telephone network, this function is handled by the coder-decoder (CODEC) within a channel bank or private branch exchange (PBX). Within the public network, the conversion to digital is performed by an analog-to-digital converter. (A digital-to-analog converter is used at the receiving end if the subscriber has an analog phone.)

Digital conversion is performed through pulse code modulation (PCM). A multiplexer (mux) then combines multiple digital voice signals onto channels. Each channel is given a time slot, and the voice conversations all go out over a single T1, E1, or J1 line. Figure 5-2 shows the conversion through a digital PBX.

Figure 5-2   *Digital PBX—Converting and Multiplexing Analog Voice Traffic*

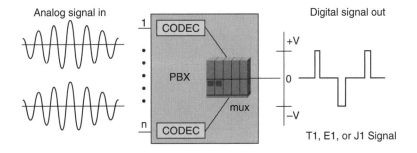

The Voice Channel

The voice channel (called a DS-0 in T1 systems) is the 64-kbps building block of time-division multiplexed (TDM) narrowband transmission facilities used to carry voice (as well as data) traffic. The first step in creating a digital voice channel from an analog voice signal is sampling.

Sampling looks at the waveform at designated intervals and measures the amplitude, or height, of the wave. The sampling rate, or how often the signal is sampled, determines the quality of the conversion. More frequent sampling results in more information stored about the signal and ultimately a better reconstruction of the signal at the receiving end.

The Nyquist theorem states that a minimum sampling rate of twice the frequency of the signal to be sampled will result in an accurate representation of the original signal. Because most human voice does not exceed 4000 Hz, and because telephone companies filter signals above 4000 Hz, a sampling rate of 8000 samples per second, or once every 125 microseconds, is used to ensure an accurate sampling of the original (after-filter) signal.

The conversion process begins by analyzing each sample and converting it into an 8-bit word, also called an octet. If there are 8 bits per sample and 8000 samples per second, then the product is 64,000 bits per second (64 kbps)—the digital voice channel.

Refer to Figure 5-3 for a summary of pulse code modulation.

Figure 5-3   *The 64-kbps Voice Channel from PCM*

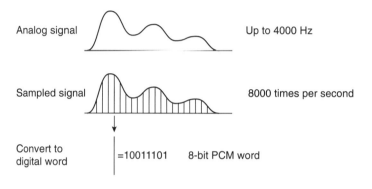

8 bits × 8000 samples = 64 kbps = a digital voice channel

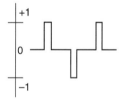

Companding Processes

Companding is the part of the PCM process that determines the digital bits used to represent the voice signal. With companding, the analog signal values are logically rounded to discrete scale-step values on a nonlinear scale. The process is reversed at the receiving terminal using the same nonlinear scale. In other words, the amplitude measurement of the analog wave is converted into a digital code representing the nearest discrete value, and then back again into an analog signal.

Companding consists of a matched compressor at the sending end and an expander at the receiving end. The purpose is to apply greater emphasis to low-level speech components rather than the high-level components. The trade-off is lower signal-to-noise ratios for high-amplitude signals. The two companding laws are shown here:

- **m-law (μ-law or mu-law) companding**—The standard for North America and Japan, which uses a logarithmic scale.

- **a-law companding**—The standard for Europe, Asia, South America, Australia, and elsewhere. This law uses a combination of linear at the lower levels and logarithmic at the higher input range.

An important point is that the two companding methods are incompatible. If a voice signal is coded into PCM samples using m-law, then it cannot be decoded using a-law. In fact, the resulting signal would be unintelligible. Therefore, international voice carriers must convert the digital signal from one companding method to the other.

Time-Division Multiplexing

As covered in Chapter 3, "Narrowband Transmissions," Time-Division Multiplexing (TDM) is the process of combining multiple voice channels into one line by assigning each channel a time slot for transmission.

Each narrowband facility has a set number of time slots. T1 supports 24 time slots, and E1 and J1 both have 32 time slots. (Remember that two time slots are used for framing and signaling on E1 and J1 facilities.) TDM can be improved upon using optimization methods.

Bandwidth Optimization

Ideally, bandwidth optimization maintains good voice quality while providing bandwidth savings. This section covers adaptive differential pulse code modulation (ADPCM), Code Excited Linear Prediction (CELP) coding, and silence suppression, which are all bandwidth-optimization methods supported by Cisco WAN switches.

Voice Compression with ADPCM

ADPCM encodes only the difference between one encoded voice sample and the following sample, not the actual value of the sample amplitude. Because the range of values for the difference is much smaller than the actual value of the sample, ADPCM requires fewer bits for encoding this difference. In general, the lower the data rate, the lower the voice quality. In many countries, ADPCM-compressed voice signals are not considered toll-quality services.

ADPCM is defined in the ITU-T G.726 recommendation. The following compressed rates are available:

- 40 kbps using 5-bit samples

- 32 kbps using 4-bit samples

- 24 kbps using 3-bit samples

- 16 kbps using 2-bit samples

With ADPCM, a formula is applied to the previous outgoing sample that predicts the range of values for the next sample. (See Figure 5-4.) The transmitter encodes the difference in level between the previous sample and the present sample, on a scale set by the prediction, and transmits this information to the far-end receiver. Because the receiver has the same data to work with as the transmitter has, it is capable of reconstructing the PCM data input to the transmitter.

Figure 5-4 *ADPCM Voice Compression—Compares the Sample to the Previous Sample*

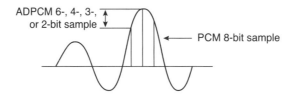

ADPCM uses neither a-law nor m-law and can be used as a common coding method between unlike systems.

High-speed modem and fax signals are distorted by ADPCM to the extent that operation above 4800 baud generally does not work reliably on ADPCM connections. A data-optimized 32-kbps ADPCM conversion exists to support modem and fax signals in some systems.

Voice Compression with CELP

At higher compression rates, ADPCM-compressed voice signals suffer from decreased quality. In an effort to increase bandwidth savings without decreasing voice quality, many voice systems have introduced Code Excited Linear Prediction (CELP) voice-compression methods. In general, a CELP-compressed voice signal is much better than an ADPCM-compressed voice signal at the same or even higher data rate.

Unlike PCM and ADPCM, CELP takes advantage of the known characteristics of human speech. A voice wave is not a random analog signal, and it has characteristics that can be mathematically predicted. By modeling the speech wave based on known factors, the information that is required to recreate the signal is reduced. This prediction result is sent to the receiving decoder to be used during the decoding.

A wide range of CELP compression methods exists; some (for example, ITU-T G.729 and G.729a CSA-CELP) are standard, and others are proprietary. Regardless of the specifics, CELP methods are based upon predicting the wave form to code and decode the voice signal. CELP popularity comes from its capability to reduce a 64-kbps voice signal down to 16 kbps (LD CELP, ITU-T G.728) or even 8 kbps (CSA-CELP, ITU-T G.729). CELP is commonly used in digital cellular systems because it provides acceptable quality while allowing for more concurrent users within the same bandwidth.

Silence Suppression

During a typical telephone conversation, only one person speaks at a time. During this time, the other person is silent and does not generate a voice wave to be transmitted. In fact, in the most extreme case where there is absolute silence, the digital signal sent from the silent end would be all 0s. More likely, the signal would contain some low level of noise due to background sounds and transmission noise. Regardless, the information coming from the silent end is negligible and need not utilize network bandwidth. Not transmitting this silence is appropriately called silence suppression and is displayed in Figure 5-5. In conjunction with PCM, ADPCM, or CELP voice coding, silence suppression can reduce the required bandwidth even more.

Figure 5-5   *Silence Suppression*

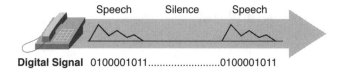

In most cases, any one person is speaking 50 percent of the time. In fact, the average utilization is less, depending on the language and speech patterns of those speaking. If no silence compression is used, then 50 percent of the bandwidth required for the conversation is wasted.

A silence suppression algorithm examines the voice signal and determines whether the signal represents speech or noise. The algorithm in the encoder recognizes defined characteristics of human speech, such as volume levels and frequencies, and does not transmit the data if the traffic is not speech.

As with the compression methods discussed in this chapter, silence suppression provides a trade-off between bandwidth usage and voice quality. If silence suppression is too aggressive, the voice might sound choppy, or the ends of words might even be cut off. However, savings of up to 60 percent bandwidth are not uncommon with silence suppression, so silence suppression is a very popular method of bandwidth optimization.

Signaling

In a voice network, signaling is used to set up a call or a connection. Both analog and digital voice interfaces have defined signaling methods and standards. Signaling occurs between a subscriber and a switch, as well as between switches (called *interswitch signaling*).

Signaling from the subscriber to the switch occurs whether the subscriber is calling from the public network or through a PBX. Examples of subscriber-to-switch signaling include on-hook and off-hook states, as well as dialing. An on-hook condition is indicated with an open loop (no current) and an off-hook condition is indicated with a closed loop (current flowing).

Interswitch signaling occurs between the local exchange carrier (LEC) and the interexchange carrier (IXC) in a public network to signal each other to complete a call. Interswitch signaling is also used between PBXs attached to a private or public network. Interswitch signaling can be either interpreted by network switches or passed transparently through the WAN. Interswitch signaling uses one of the following two methods:

- Channel associated signaling (CAS)
- Common channel signaling (CCS)

Channel Associated Signaling

CAS uses a well-known location for the signaling bits for each voice channel, which is sent on the same path with the voice traffic. CAS allows for interpretation of signaling bits by all network devices responsible for switching the call. The number of signaling states supported by CAS is limited by the number of bits used.

Common Channel Signaling

CCS uses an independent signaling channel that carries signaling information for the voice channels as needed. CCS allows for a wide range of signaling states. CCS is more complex than CAS, and network devices are typically incapable of interpreting the signaling states of the voice channels (for example, the signaling is transparent to the WAN). CAS and CCS distinctions are shown in Table 5-1.

Table 5-1 *CAS and CCS Distinctions*

Application/ Function	CAS	CCS
T1 signaling	Robbed bit signaling. Least significant bit of every sixth frame is robbed.	Time slot 24
E1 signaling	Time slot 16 carries 4 signaling bits per channel.	Time slot 16 as a clear channel
J1 signaling	Time slot 0 carries 1 signaling bit per channel.	Time slot 16 as a clear channel
Features	Limited.	Many features available
Signal versatility	Limited.	Wide variety of protocols available

Refer to Chapter 3, "Narrowband Transmissions," for more coverage of signaling.

Dialing Formats

Regardless of the type of circuit line (T1, E1, or J1), most voice switches recognize the following two types of dialing formats:

- Dual-tone multifrequency (DTMF)
- Pulse dialing

DTMF

In DTMF, digits are sent in-band to the switch from the telephone. Each number on a telephone keypad produces two tones that in combination uniquely identify the digit. After receiving an off-hook condition, a voice switch listens for DTMF tones and either interprets them or passes them through the network for interpretation upstream.

Pulse Dialing

In pulse dialing, bits are used to convey dialed digits. Usually, a transition from off-hook to on-hook and back again represents a single pulse. Each digit is represented by the same number of pulses as the digit. For example, a dialed 4 would create four pulses. The signaling bits change every 40 to 60 milliseconds (ms) within a dialed digit, with pauses between digits of greater than 100 ms. A voice switch must differentiate between a pulse-dialed digit and a series of independent signaling transitions based on the time between the pulses.

Echo

In a voice network, echo is a common problem that occurs because of impedance mismatches between two-wire and four-wire systems. A telephone is attached to a PBX or a switch using two wires, but the PBXs and switches use four wires. The impedance mismatch causes a portion of the original signal to be reflected to the source, as shown in Figure 5-6.

Figure 5-6 *Echo in a Voice Network*

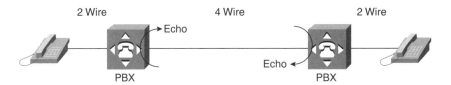

Echo is always present in a voice network, although it is not always a problem. Depending on the reflection delay and the strength of the reflection, the echo might be acceptable or unnoticeable.

For echo to be heard, there must be a noticeable delay between the original signal and the reflected signal, and the reflected signal must be audible. Echo is always present in a voice network, but not all echo is recognized by the listener. Figure 5-7 shows what is considered acceptable and unacceptable.

Figure 5-7 *Acceptable and Unacceptable Echo*

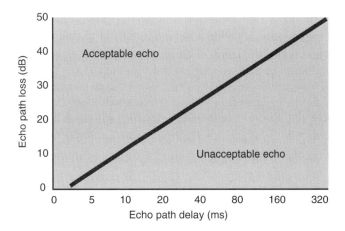

The primary cause of unacceptable echo in a voice network is delay. If two PBXs were installed side by side with a cable between them, the delay would be so short that the echo would go unnoticed. However, if you were to move one of the PBXs to a remote site with a private or public network between them, the delay might increase enough to make the echo noticeable. In addition, a packet-switched network adds more delay than a circuit-switched network.

Delays in Voice Networks

Limited delays in voice networks are acceptable to users; however, unnecessary long delays create poor service. Understanding where and how these delays occur is necessary to design and troubleshoot networks. The following are possible delays in a voice network:

- **Transmission**—The transmission itself requires a finite period of time. Longer distances require longer transmission periods.

- **Packetization**—A delay is created while queuing enough voice samples to create a packet.

- **Compression**—Compression requires computing processing and therefore adds additional delay.

- **Network congestion**—Network congestion is a problem only on packet-switched networks. Often there is a queuing delay at network nodes with the network.

- **Silence suppression**—Silence is often determined over a period of time, which requires that voice samples be compared to recognized characteristics and thus causes some delay from computations.

Echo is always present, so echo cancellers have been developed to minimize the effects of echo. Echo cancellers continuously monitor the digitized speech coming from the network (the receive direction) and compare it to the signal in the reverse direction. By comparing the two signals, the echo canceller can model the echo by determining the loss and the delay of the reflected signal. Based upon these measurements, the echo canceller then calculates the expected echo power level and subtracts it from the received signal.

Because the signal is being adjusted by the echo canceller, data communications are affected by echo cancellers. Therefore, many echo cancellers can be turned off for the duration of the call by using a 2100 kHz signal. Modems often include the signal during the call.

Summary

Voice communication must be converted from analog before transmission across digital networks. An encoder in the private branch exchange (PBX) typically handles this conversion before it is multiplexed and transmitted via a narrowband facility, such as T1, E1, or J1.

Pulse code modulation (PCM) is the common method used to sample analog voice to convert to digital.

Although a 64-kbps channel (or time slot) is the standard voice channel offered by telcos, additional voice communications can be carried within one time slot by using compression and silence compression. Two popular compression methods are adaptive differential pulse code modulation (ADPCM) and Code Excited Linear Prediction (CELP).

Voice signaling includes subscriber-to-switch and switch-to-switch signaling: channel associated signaling (CAS) and common channel signaling (CCS).

Finally, the chapter finished with the definition of echo and covered the major reasons for delays.

Review Questions

The following questions test your retention of the material presented in this chapter. You can find the answers to the Review Questions in Appendix A, "Answers to Review Questions."

1 What does PBX stand for?

2 What performs analog-to-digital conversion in a private network?

A. CODEC

B. Modem

C. a/d converter

D. D/C modulator

3 What is the available bandwidth of DS-0?

A. 56 kbps

B. 63 kbps

C. 64 kbps

D. 1.54 Mbps

4 What two companding standards are discussed in this chapter?

A. my-law

B. mu-law

C. a-law

D. pi-law

E. ILD-law

5 How does T1 support CAS signaling?

A. Time slot 16.

B. It does not support CAS.

C. Robbed bit signaling.

D. Time slot 0.

E. Time slot 4.

6   What are the two most common dialing formats supported?

A. Rotary dialing

B. Pulse dialing

C. Tone dialing

D. DTMF

7   Which of the following does not add delay to voice communication?

A. Compression

B. Companding

C. Network congestion

D. Silence suppression

CHAPTER 6

Frame Relay

Chapter 5, "Digital Voice Technical Concepts and Considerations," concentrates on technology applicable to transporting voice across the WAN. In this chapter and in Chapter 7, "Asynchronous Transfer Mode," much of the information will be related to data communications. Although Frame Relay and ATM have been very successful in connecting LANs, keep in mind that the technologies are used for data—their application as voice technology will only grow with the advancement of voice over technologies, such as Voice over Frame Relay (VoFR), Voice over ATM (VoATM), and Voice over IP (VoIP).

Frame Relay is a frame-based Layer 2 protocol that takes advantage of the low error rate of digital facilities. Frame Relay offers WAN solutions that provide higher bandwidth and lower costs than the older X.25 or point-to-point networks based upon HDLC or the Point-to-Point Protocol (PPP).

This chapter covers the Frame Relay frame format, data-link connection identifier (DLCI) and addressing options, signaling protocols, the User-Network Interface (UNI) and the Network-to-Network Interface (NNI). This chapter includes the following sections:

- Introduction to Frame Relay
- Signaling Protocols
- User-Network Interface
- Network-to-Network Interface
- Frame Relay Traffic Management
- Congestion Notification
- Summary
- Review Questions

Introduction to Frame Relay

Frame Relay is a service that has proven very popular in North America and other areas as an ideal solution to provide efficient data communications for high-speed, frame-oriented bursty data applications, such as those based upon the TCP/IP suite of protocols.

As such, Frame Relay is clearly a descendant of more traditional frame-oriented data services, such as X.25. Unlike X.25, however, Frame Relay services generally rely on the low error rates of digital high-speed data-carrying facilities available today, such as T1/E1, T3/E3, and higher-speed fiber-based technologies, to simplify the protocol and error-checking facilities required by X.25. Frame Relay has replaced most of the more complex, slower packet-switching services in North America and other countries and is the network solution of choice for most new installations. Frame Relay has not enjoyed as much popularity in all areas of the world—this will likely change as global communications companies compete locally to provide international and new national Frame Relay offerings.

Keep in mind that Frame Relay defines a data network interface standard on how data is formatted to be submitted to a Frame Relay network for transmission. In particular, the Frame Relay standards do not specify how the Frame Relay network must proceed to deliver the data from one point to another. The implementation details are left to the manufacturers of the Frame Relay network equipment, which is often supplied by a Frame Relay provider or, in many markets, the carrier.

A Frame Relay access device (FRAD) is equipment that is responsible for adapting data into Frame Relay frames. A router, switch, multiplexer, or concentrator that supports Frame Relay has integrated FRADs. In many of the figures in this chapter, routers are shown as the FRADs, but remember that FRAD functionality is not limited to routers and that FRADs are not routers by definition.

Meshed Networks with One Interface

One of Frame Relay's major advantages is that a physical interface is not required for each connection to a remote site within the network. This means that each remote site can communicate with the central location through a single interface at the central office. In fact, all nodes can communicate with all other Frame Relay nodes through each of their single interfaces (meshing). Without Frame Relay, each site with multiple connections requires a separate physical interface for each of the sites it needs to connect to.

These virtual connections to each site are appropriately called *virtual circuits*. Typically, the circuits are permanent virtual circuits (PVCs), which are static connections that do not require call setup after the PVC is provisioned. However, switched virtual circuits (SVCs) are supported by some providers for dynamic allocation sites not requiring a PVC. Due to aggressive pricing of PVCs, there is little demand for the SVC. Figure 6-1 shows a sample international Frame Relay network that is fully meshed.

Figure 6-1   *Frame Relay Full-Mesh Service with PVCs*

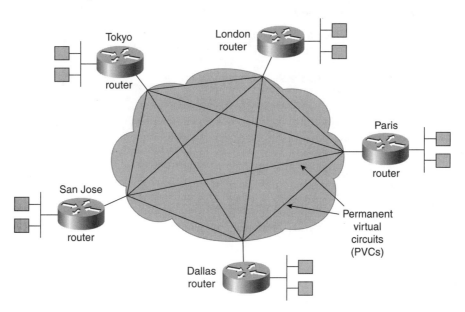

Although fully meshed topologies are possible, most Frame Relay tariffs are based upon the number of PVCs. In addition, most traffic flows to and from central locations where central services are available; therefore, partially meshed networks are much more common than fully meshed Frame Relay networks.

Frame Relay Terminology

As with most major networking protocols, Frame Relay uses many acronyms to define and describe key technical functions, which are covered in Table 6-1.

The frame in Frame Relay is a logical grouping of information sent as a data link layer unit over a transmission medium through a Frame Relay switch that performs the relaying function.

The frame contains bits designated for both control functions (for example, starting and ending flags, addressing, and other process-related fields) and a frame check sequence. The frame also contains the users' payload. Figure 6-2 shows a simplified view of the Frame Relay frame.

Table 6-1   *Frame Relay Terminology Reference*

Acronym	Description
Bc	Committed Burst rate
Be	Excess Burst rate
BECN	Backward explicit congestion notification
CIR	Committed information rate
DE	Discard eligible
DLCI	Data-link connection identifier
FECN	Forward explicit congestion notification
LMI	Local Management Interface
NNI	Network-to-Network Interface
UNI	User-Network Interface

Figure 6-2   *An Overview of the Frame Relay Frame*

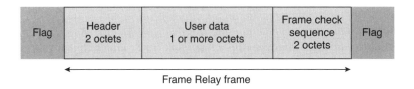

The Frame Relay Frame

The ITU-T Q.922 recommendation specifies the format of the frame and the fields included in the header. A frame consists of a two-octet header, a data field, and a two-octet CRC.

All frames are separated by flags (hexadecimal 7E) to delineate the beginning and end of the frame. The FRAD uses a technique called *bit-stuffing* to ensure that the flag is not contained inside the data portion of the frame. Figure 6-3 gives a more detailed view of the Frame Relay frame format.

A 10-bit DLCI identifies the path through the network to a specific destination. Because a 10-bit address can support only 1024 virtual circuits, Frame Relay network DLCIs have only local significance to allow carrier networks to have more than 1024 PVCs.

Figure 6-3   *Detailed Frame Relay Frame Format*

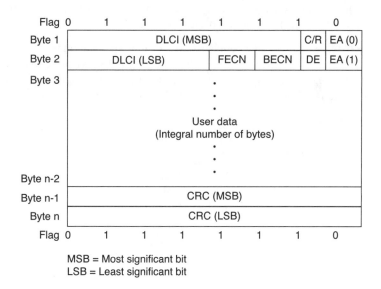

MSB = Most significant bit
LSB = Least significant bit

The forward explicit congestion notification bit (FECN) and backward explicit congestion notification bit (BECN) allow the Frame Relay network to inform the connected devices of congestion in the network. These two bits are covered more thoroughly later in this chapter.

The DE bit indicates to the network that a frame can be discarded, if necessary, in response to network congestion. The command/response (C/R) bit generally is not used. The extended address (EA) bit is the least significant bit of each header octet. Any header octet with the EA bit set to 0 is followed by another header octet. The last header octet has the EA bit set to 1. On a frame with a two-octet header, the EA bit is always 0 in the first octet and 1 in the second octet. The user data field (payload) can be used to carry any type of information.

The CRC is used to detect transmission errors and covers the header and data fields. Frames with transmission errors are discarded—upper layers then must request retransmission.

The overall frame length must be an integral number of octets with a minimum length of five octets. Frame Relay standards require a device to accept a frame size that is 4096 octets long, but larger frame sizes are supported by many vendors.

The Data-Link Connection Identifier

Of course, the Frame Relay format can be used to carry information between any pair of devices that adhere to the standard frame format. However, because of the capability of the Frame Relay network to deliver information to any number of destinations (based on the

DLCI), the predominant application of Frame Relay is in providing data WAN capabilities to multiple geographically dispersed LANs. However, voice over technology market growth ensures Voice over Frame Relay future growth.

The network and the device connected to it differentiate the multiple PVCs that share the same physical port using the DLCI. Thus, the DLCIs merely serve to distinguish the multiple virtual circuits that share a physical port. Refer to Figure 6-4 to see how frames entering the network are routed across the PVCs based upon their DLCIs.

Figure 6-4   *A DLCI Identifies Each PVC*

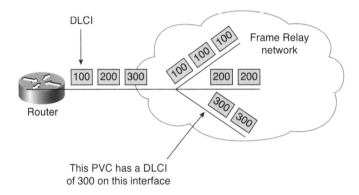

Because the DLCI serves to distinguish the multiple PVCs that share a port, each DLCI must be unique on that port. A DLCI is assigned to each end of a PVC. The DLCIs at each end of a particular PVC can be the same or different because most implementations of Frame Relay require only local significance of the DLCI. (Originally, the DLCI was designed to be globally unique within the frame cloud, but this idea has long since been abandoned.)

The only restriction is that the DLCIs fit within 10 bits. In other words, the DLCI must be in the range of 0 to 1023. In practice, DLCIs 0 to 15 and 1008 to 1023 are reserved for special functions; DLCIs typically are chosen to be in the range of 16 to 1007. The special functions include DLCI 0, which is reserved for standard signaling protocols defined by ITU-T and ANSI. DLCI 1023 is reserved for the Local Management Interface (LMI) signaling protocol. DLCIs 1019 to 1022 address multicast connections (one to several).

Assigning DLCIs

Every PVC that terminates at a Frame Relay port must have its own DLCI, distinct from the DLCIs associated with the other PVCs on the same port, so management of the DLCI numbering scheme is very important.

Because Frame Relay is usually offered as a public service in the data communication market, the Frame Relay provider often assigns the DLCIs.

As mentioned, a global addressing scheme for DLCIs is not required. DLCIs can have local-only significance, meaning that any locally available number can be provided by the Frame Relay service provider. The network administrator then maps the destination address to the local DLCI. For example, an administrator might map a DLCI to an IP address of the destination router interface. This mapping in the router points to a static route, which is the PVC to that remote router.

If you are setting up a Frame Relay network but do not get DLCI numbers assigned from a Frame Relay service provider, or if you can request DLCIs from the service provider, you may choose to use global addressing.

Valid DLCI numbers could be assigned nearly at random. Although such a numbering scheme is legal, it might become a difficult administrative situation as the number of ports and DLCIs in the network increases.

To prevent the potential network management difficulties, an orderly addressing convention, known as global addressing, is typically used in most Frame Relay networks.

Using the standard global addressing scheme, a unique identification number is assigned to each port in the network. Subsequently, PVCs are added with DLCIs chosen based on the port IDs at each end. As a result, the DLCI becomes globally significant, identifying the ID of the required destination.

Specifically, the DLCI assigned to each end of a PVC is made equal to the port ID of the port at the other end of the PVC. This numbering convention has the advantage that all frames submitted to the network with a given DLCI will always be delivered to the same port, regardless of their source. Figure 6-5 shows global addressing.

Figure 6-5 *Global Addressing—Using the DLCI as a Destination Address*

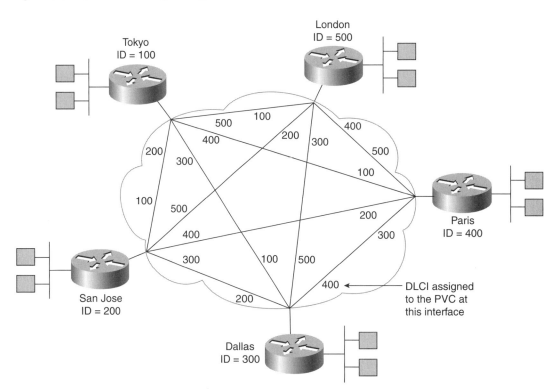

Automatic DLCI Association—Inverse ARP

In a router network, associating DLCIs with network addresses can be simplified through use of the Inverse Address Resolution Protocol (Inverse ARP). With Inverse ARP, the router needs to know only its own network protocol address on the nonbroadcast multiaccess (NBMA) Frame Relay network or subnet.

Figure 6-6 shows a simplified topology with two routers having Frame Relay interfaces configured and using Inverse ARP.

In Figure 6-6, the service provider specifies the DLCIs to use. The switches announce DLCI numbers for the router to use with a signaling protocol, such as LMI. The middle two boxes indicate the Frame Relay network providing a DLCI to Router B to use when attempting to reach the Frame Relay destination on Router A, and vice versa.

Figure 6-6   *Inverse ARP Automates the DLCI Discovery Process*

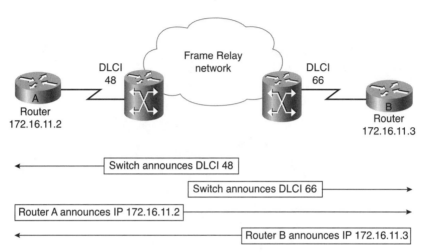

As the final piece of this Inverse ARP exchange, each router announces the network number the other side can resolve for the DLCI associated with getting to the destination over the Frame Relay network.

Signaling Protocols

A FRAD is responsible for sending and receiving frames and ensuring that the frames are free of errors; the WAN is responsible for transporting the frames across the network to the destination FRAD in a timely manner.

Frame Relay does not address outage situations. Therefore, a signaling protocol, the LMI, was developed to exchange keepalives and administrative information, such as the addition, deletion, or failure of a PVC.

The signaling protocol messages are exchanged between the FRAD and WAN Frame Relay interfaces. The signaling protocol messages are not passed through the network on a PVC (in-band) with the other traffic, as shown in Figure 6-7.

Figure 6-7 *Signaling Protocols in the Network*

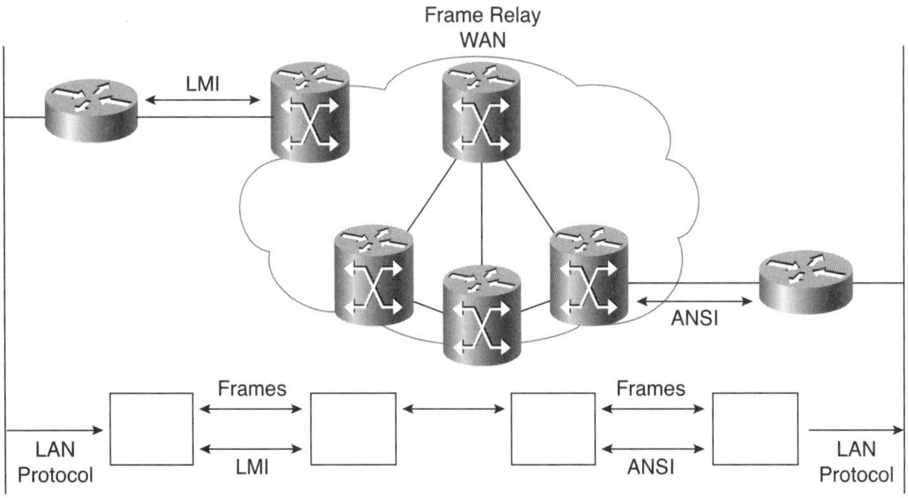

Available Signaling Protocols

LMI is not the only signaling protocol available today. In total, three signaling protocols are in widespread use. Each one is slightly different, but they all perform the same basic functions. The three common signaling protocols in use are:

- ANSI's Frame Relay signaling, defined in T1.617, Annex D
- ITU-T Frame Relay signaling, defined in Q.933, Annex A
- The original LMI as defined by the Gang of Four: Cisco, Digital Equipment Corporation, Northern Telecom, and StrataCom

When configuring a device for a signaling protocol, naming conventions might differ. For example, ANSI's version could be referred to as "ANSI," "Annex D," "T1.617," or a combination of these terms. The LMI is a specific signaling protocol, but keep in mind that Frame Relay signaling protocols are referred to generically as LMI, regardless of the type in use.

An administrator setting up a connection to a Frame Relay network can choose from these three alternatives to ensure proper Frame Relay operation.

The original LMI differs from ANSI and ITU-T in two ways:

- The number of connections for LMI is limited to 992. ANSI and ITU-T are limited to 976.
- LMI uses DLCI 1023, and ANSI and ITU-T use DLCI 0.

The choice of signaling protocols depends on the protocols supported by the FRAD and the WAN, as well as personal preference. The key to configuring a protocol is to ensure that both Frame Relay interfaces (the FRAD and the WAN) are configured for the same protocol. Some equipment has an autosensing feature so that only one side (usually the WAN) needs to be configured.

Such signaling protocols might not be a required feature on a Frame Relay port, especially from the perspective of a switch, or if the Frame Relay network is privately controlled end to end. However, many FRADs depend on the signaling protocol to ensure connectivity in the network.

Signaling Protocol Exchange

Each of the three signaling protocols uses the same basic handshake mechanism, consisting of a sequence of status query frames and response status frames. The FRAD is responsible for sending inquiries to the network. If the FRAD does not send an inquiry, the network will never transmits any signaling protocol messages.

Each status query frame contains a sequence number exchange and a request for either a short status frame or a long status frame. A status frame is sent in response to a status inquiry frame and is either short or long based upon the original status query.

Short status frames contain a sequence number exchange only. Short status frames are simply used as a keepalive between the two devices. Long status frames contain event notification. Each long status frame contains a sequence number exchange, as well as status and information for every PVC on the port.

The signaling protocol between a Frame Relay device and a Frame Relay network consists of regular short status exchanges with less frequent long status exchanges, as shown in Figure 6-8.

Note that an event in the network (such as the addition, deletion, failure, or modification of a PVC) will not be reported to the device until the next long status exchange.

Figure 6-8 *Frame Relay Signaling Protocol—Without Asynchronous Updates*

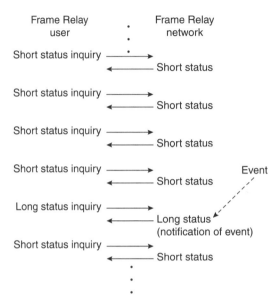

Defining Signaling Protocol Timers and Counters

This section covers how protocols and timers are defined and used to report Frame Relay problems.

Five parameters define the exchange of signaling information between two Frame Relay devices. Two of these parameters define how often a FRAD sends short and long status queries:

- T391 is the time interval, in seconds, between short status queries. This value is usually configured for 10 seconds.

- N391 is the multiplier that determines the frequency of long queries. In other words, every N391×T391 seconds a long status query will be performed. N391 is usually six cycles, which equates to a 60-second time interval when the standard 10-second T391 is used.

T391 and N391 define when the signaling exchange occurs, but parameters are also defined to determine when an alarm is triggered. Three parameters define when an alarm is declared by the WAN:

- T392 is the time interval, in seconds, between expected status inquires. This value is usually configured for 15 seconds and should be greater than T391 set on the FRAD. If the T392 timer expires and a status query frame has not been received, a timeout is counted.

- N392 defines the number of timeouts, out of N393 (covered next) expected queries that will cause an alarm to be generated.

- N393 is the number of expected queries that define a window for alarm declaration.

Signaling Protocol with Asynchronous Updates

As you probably noticed, the previously described frame status messages are subject to notification delay because there is a waiting period for the next long status exchange. Some Frame Relay devices and networks support asynchronous status updates that allow quicker intervention, more upper-layer routing protocols, and better network management.

Asynchronous updates are status frames that are immediately generated by the network in response to some critical event. This status update allows the event to be immediately reported to the Frame Relay device without waiting for the next long status query.

Refer to Figure 6-9 to see a network event being reported to the attached device using asynchronous updates.

Figure 6-9   *Frame Relay Signaling Protocol—With Asynchronous Updates*

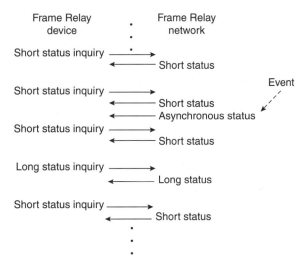

User-Network Interface

The signaling protocol described in the previous section (with or without asynchronous status updates) is strictly unidirectional. That means that only the FRAD can request information from the network. This method is appropriate to allow a Frame Relay DTE device (such as an edge router) to request information about the available PVCs from the Frame Relay network to which it is collected. Consequently, this unidirectional protocol defines a User-Network Interface (UNI) port.

A UNI applies signaling conventions on a local interface between the user equipment and the network, as shown in Figure 6-10.

Figure 6-10 *User-Network Interface*

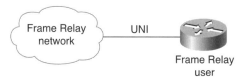

The FRAD can use this information to ensure that it is configured to accept or transmit frames with any DLCI defined on the network end of the port.

Unfortunately, this unidirectional protocol does not allow full configuration, administration, and control information between two peer devices, such as between two distinct Frame Relay networks that exchange information over a Frame Relay interface. This sort of communication requires a fully bidirectional protocol.

Network-to-Network Interface

To allow configuration, administration, and control information between two networks (possibly from different manufacturers), a bidirectional protocol is defined in ITU-T standard Q.933, Annex A, and ANSI standard T1.618, Annex D.

Typically, this bidirectional protocol is used to support signaling between two networks. Consequently, this protocol defines a Network-to-Network Interface (NNI) port. Figure 6-11 depicts two NNI ports—one between networks 1 and 2, and the other between networks 2 and 3.

In most cases, the hardware on a switch for an NNI is identical to that used for a UNI. The only difference between the two interface types is the signaling protocol in use. The NNI enables control information and traffic to pass at the border of two network nodes. The bidirectional signaling protocol used on the NNI simply consists of two independent unidirectional signaling protocols, one initiated from each network.

Figure 6-11 *Network-to-Network Interface*

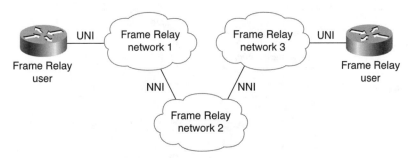

The status exchange between two networks is identical to that between a user and a network. The difference is that both networks send status query frames, and both networks respond with short or long response frames (see Figure 6-12). The signaling protocol timers are defined on each side of an NNI. The user values (T391 and N391) set on one network interface should correspond to the network timers (T392, N392, and N393) on the other network interface. Note that one network interface can be configured to send queries at a different frequency than the other network interface. Figure 6-12 shows the exchange of status frames on an NNI.

The NNI signaling protocol shown in Figure 6-12 lacks any asynchronous status updates; however, asynchronous status updates are supported on NNIs.

Figure 6-12 *Frame Relay NNI Signaling Protocol*

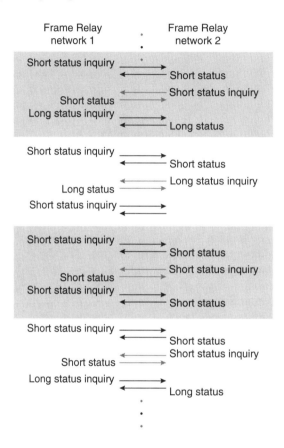

Frame Relay Traffic Management

Most Frame Relay networks provide a guarantee of throughput service to the application users. This guarantee applies as long as the user's rate of data input to the Frame Relay network falls below some established committed information rate (CIR).

If the user's rate of data input exceeds CIR for some period of time, the network can set the DE bit on the excessive frames. When the DE bit is set, the frame is then eligible for discard if congestion conditions occur within the network.

In many cases, the frames will successfully traverse the network without being discarded.

The key issue is how to provide flow control and avoid congestion and discarded frames in the network. This is an inherent problem with bursty LAN traffic using WAN serial lines.

In Figure 6-13, the PVCs on the right side (DLCIs 31 to 33) are assigned CIRs of 64 kbps, and the access rate (port speed) for each line is 128 kbps. The serial line connected to Router A can send at a 1.544 Mbps line rate and has a CIR of 512 kbps.

Figure 6-13 *The CIR*

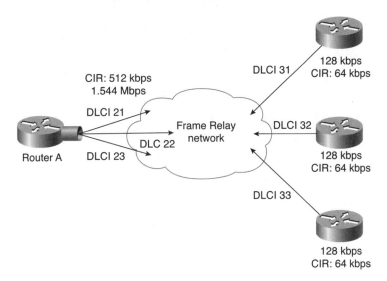

Within these subscription parameters, the potential is high that the router with the 1.54 Mbps port speed and 512 kbps CIR will attempt to transmit at a rate in excess of the maximum rate of the receivers.

By itself, the CIR does not provide much flexibility when dealing with varying traffic rates. However, if the FRAD is given the opportunity to burst up to higher speeds, then a very viable upgrade to the routers connected to DLCIs 31 to 33 in Figure 6-13 would be higher port speeds to more accurately match the subscription rate of the higher speed router.

Figure 6-14 gives an overview of the metrics (variables) involved with Frame Relay.

The Committed Burst (B_c) size and Excess Burst (B_e) size are amounts of data that a Frame Relay carrier agrees to transfer over time interval T. (B_c size is often referred to as Committed Information Burst Rate [CIBR] or Committed Burst Rate [CBR]. B_e size is often called Excess Burst Rate [EBR].)

B_c is the maximum amount under normal conditions, and B_e is the maximum amount in excess of B_c that the network will attempt to transfer under normal conditions. Notice how the B_c and B_e are applied over time.

Figure 6-14 *Frame Relay Traffic Metrics*

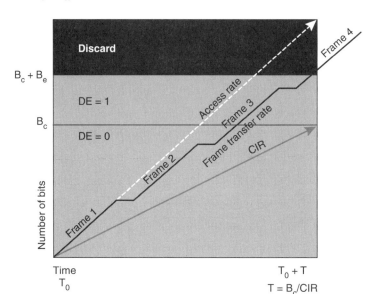

Also notice in Figure 6-14 that the actual frame transfer rate parallels the access rate; when a frame is being transmitted on a channel, that channel's access rate is affected by the transmission. (The access rate cannot be burst in this case because it is limited to the access speed.) The short horizontal lines in the frame transfer rate occur when no frames are being transmitted.

Notice that although the number of bits is less than the B_c, the frames enter the network unchanged. When the number of bits exceeds B_c, the frames are tagged with the DE bit set to 1. When the number of bits exceed $B_c + B_e$, the frames are discarded.

B_e determines a peak or maximum Frame Relay data rate (MaxR), measured in bits per second:

$$\text{MaxR} = [(B_c + B_e) \div B_c] \times \text{CIR}$$

For example, if $B_c = 32{,}000$, $B_e = 32{,}000$, and CIR = 64 kbps, then $[(32{,}000 + 32{,}000) \div 32{,}000] \times 64$ kbps = 128 kbps as the MaxR.

Congestion Notification

When congestion does occur, the Frame Relay network can set one of two control bits that signify the congested condition:

- Forward explicit congestion notification (FECN)
- Backward explicit congestion notification (BECN)

Figure 6-15 shows the FECN AND BECN.

Figure 6-15 *The FECN and BECN—Frame Relay Congestion Notification*

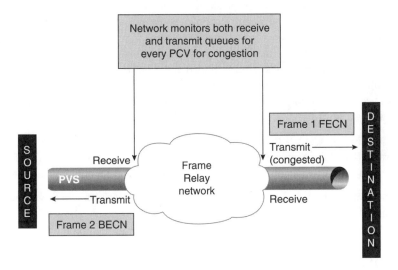

FECN is used to notify the destination or the receiver that congestion was encountered. Congestion occurs if a switch's buffers that queue traffic become full, or in other switch conditions. The FECN bit is set and placed on a frame sent to the destination to inform the destination that congestion is occurring in the network.

When the destination receives the FECN, it might be capable of indicating that a higher-layer process should invoke flow control or do some other remedial traffic adjustment. For example, a higher-layer transport function might slow its end-to-end acknowledgments. In practice, however, this rarely happens.

Likewise, BECN is used in the backward direction. The BECN bit is set and placed on a frame sent back to the traffic source to inform the source that congestion is occurring in the network. When the source receives the BECN, it might be capable of using flow control for its traffic transmission rate until the congestion problem is no longer occurring.

Remember that FECN-marked frames have experienced congestion. BECN-marked frames might not have experienced congestion but are used as messengers back to the source.

When troubleshooting congestion in a network, be sure to determine the congested traffic direction based on the FECN and BECN bits. Also keep in mind that although upper-layer protocols could take advantage of FECN and BECN, they rarely do, so FECN and BECN are mostly used for troubleshooting. They are also often monitored with network management systems for capacity planning.

Summary

Frame Relay is a popular Layer 2 protocol used in WANs. Frame Relay's major advantage over other technologies is its support of meshing networks with only one physical interface. This chapter covered the Frame Relay frame format and discussed that the frame includes a header, a payload, and a frame check sequence. The frame check sequence is checked only by the receiving Frame Relay and the frame is discarded if there is an error. Error correction and recovery are left to higher-layer protocols. The data-link connection identifier is used by the Frame Relay network to identify permanent virtual circuits (logical connections) within the network. DLCIs typically have only local significance within the Frame Relay cloud.

Frame Relay supports three signaling protocols: ANSI's Frame Relay signaling, the ITU-T Frame Relay signaling, and the original Local Management Interface (LMI). The term LMI is often used generically to mean any of the three Frame Relay signaling protocols.

The chapter also briefly covered Frame Relay traffic management as well as Frame Relay's support of congestion notification.

Review Questions

The following questions test your retention of the material presented in this chapter. You can find the answers to the Review Questions in Appendix A, "Answers to Review Questions."

1 True or false: Frame Relay is the digital version of X.25.

2 What is the major advantage of Frame Relay over point-to-point networks?

A. Frame Relay uses digital facilities.

B. One physical interface supports multiple virtual circuits.

C. Compression ratios on Frame Relay are much higher than point-to-point.

D. Frame Relay has no advantage over point-to-point networks.

3 How many bits in the Frame Relay frame are used by the DLCI?

A. 6

B. 8

C. 10

D. 12

4 True or false: The DLCI is globally unique within a Frame Relay network.

5 What is the Local Management Interface responsible for?

   A. Management features such, as dial-on-demand and routing updates

   B. Management features such, as dial backup and compression

   C. Management features such, as reporting failed PVCs and providing keepalives

   D. Management functions for the network layer

6 How does Frame Relay provide congestion notification?

   A. Frame Relay does not provide congestion notification.

   B. BECN and FECN

   C. FECN

   D. FECN and BFECN

CHAPTER 7

Asynchronous Transfer Mode

Asynchronous Transfer Mode (ATM) is a high-speed asynchronous, cell-based LAN and WAN technology. This chapter concentrates on ATM concepts, including the User-Network Interface (UNI), the Network-to-Network Interface (NNI), and the Broadband Integrated Services Digital Network (BISDN) reference model. The chapter also deals with the ATM adaptation layer (AAL) and the ATM layer, as well as cell format, the physical-layer ATM, signaling protocols, and ATM address formats. Finally, the chapter covers the Operation, Administration, and Maintenance (OAM) traffic management. The following is a list of the sections in this chapter:

- Introduction to ATM
- The ATM Cell
- The Broadband Integrated Services Digital Network Reference Model
- ATM Signaling Protocol
- Operation, Administration, and Maintenance
- Summary
- Review Questions

Introduction to ATM

ATM is a cell-switching and multiplexing technology that combines the benefits of circuit switching with those of packet switching. Circuit switching provides a constant transmission delay with guaranteed capacity, while packet switching gives flexibility and is efficient for intermittent traffic. ATM delivers important advantages over other LAN and WAN technologies, including scalable bandwidths at unprecedented price and performance points, and quality of service (QoS) guarantees that support applications that are time sensitive, such as multimedia. In addition, the international standards committee ITU-T also chose ATM as the transfer mode technology for the Broadband Integrated Services Digital Network (BISDN).

Figure 7-1 shows packet-switching and circuit-switching technologies. As you can see in the figure, ATM falls within the cell category of packet switching.

Figure 7-1 *Structure Overview of ATM Within Data Communications*

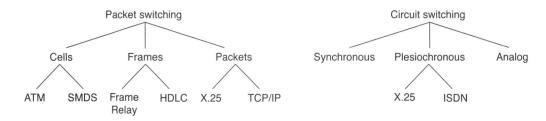

Asynchronous Alignment

The term *asynchronous* in ATM refers to the variable alignment of the cell headers to the actual line framing of the physical transport facilities (that is, DS-3, E3, and SONET/SDH).

Because ATM is an asynchronous mechanism, it differs from synchronous transfer-mode methods, as shown in Figure 7-2, in which time-division multiplexing (TDM) techniques are employed to assign users to time slots.

Figure 7-2 *Asynchronous and Synchronous Alignment*

Asynchronous alignment—the data is not aligned with the line framing

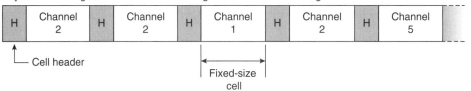

Synchronous alignment—the data is aligned with the line framing

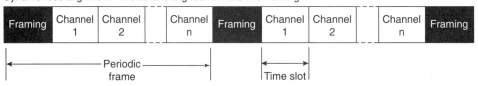

In ATM, bandwidth is made available on demand. TDM is inefficient relative to ATM because, if a station has nothing to transmit when its time slot comes up, that time slot is wasted. The converse situation, in which one station has much information to transmit, is also less efficient because the station will have to wait until its next time slot becomes available for continuing to transmit. With ATM, a device can send cells whenever necessary.

Refer to Figure 7-2 to contrast ATM's asynchronous transmission with synchronous alignment used for TDM as used with T1, E1, or J1 narrowband transmissions.

The ATM Cell

An ATM cell is 53 octets long and includes a 5-octet header and a payload of 48 octets, as shown in Figure 7-3. The payload can contain additional control information, which confuses many network professionals first learning about ATM. The five-octet ATM header is based upon the interface supported: User-Network Interface (UNI) or Network-to-Network Interface (NNI). Before covering the details of the ATM headers, though, this section contains a review of UNI and NNI.

Figure 7-3   *An Overview of the ATM Cell*

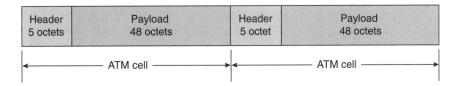

The UNI connects ATM end systems, such as hosts, routers, or switches, that are connected to an ATM switch. The NNI is used exclusively to connect two ATM switches. Like Frame Relay, ATM is offered as a public service by many carriers, so ATM interfaces are also classified as public or private:

- **Public UNI**—Typically is used to interconnect an ATM user with an ATM switch deployed in a public service provider's network.

- **Private UNI**—Typically is used to interconnect an ATM user with an ATM switch managed as part of the same private enterprise network.

- **Public NNI**—Specifies the connection between switches from two different ATM service providers. Issues of billing and traffic management are of major concern. A protocol known as the Broadband Inter-Carrier Interface (BICI) can be used to support multiple services on a single link between two public service providers.

- **Private NNI (PNNI)**—Specifies the connection between two private ATM switches and includes a signaling protocol for automatic call setup, QoS support, and dynamic routing. PNNI is more than an interface between two switches—it is a set of protocols. PNNI defines the protocols necessary between private switches or groups of switches to allow the construction of a scalable private ATM network comprising multivendor switches. The PNNI routing protocol is used to disseminate pertinent information, including topology and QoS characteristics, to all components in the network. The PNNI signaling protocol is also used to establish switched virtual circuits (SVCs) within the ATM network.

Refer to Figure 7-4 for an overview of the interfaces within an ATM network.

Figure 7-4   *ATM Interfaces*

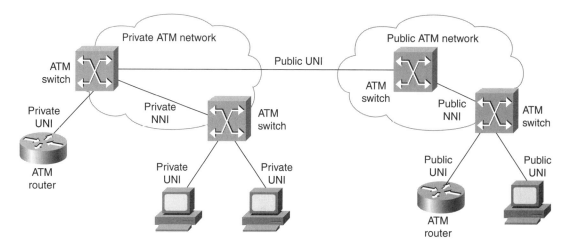

The ATM cell is a fixed 53-octet size. This fixed cell size allows switching to be performed in the hardware (as opposed to the software) within the ATM switch. Cells transit ATM networks by passing through ATM switches, which switch the cell to the appropriate output interface that connects the switch to the next appropriate switch. Then, at the application destination, the cells leave the ATM network and are reassembled into the original data format. In Figure 7-3, two ATM cells are shown, one following the other. The five-octet header contains address and control information, and the payload carries user data and sometimes additional control information.

On transmission facilities, an ATM cell always follows the preceding cell without a flag between them because the switch knows the size of the cell. During idle periods, one or more idle cells are inserted between data-carrying cells. Idle cells are also 53 octets with all 0 bits in the header portion of the cell and an idle pattern in the payload.

The Broadband Integrated Services Digital Network Reference Model

The BISDN reference model shown in Figure 7-5 illustrates the organization of ATM functionality and the interrelationships among the layers of functionality.

Figure 7-5   *The Broadband Integrated Services Digital Network Reference Model*

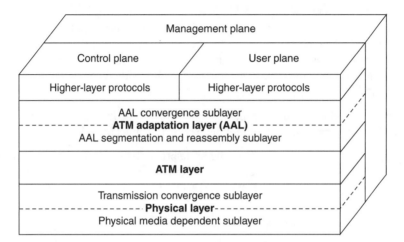

As you likely surmised, the ATM layer and the ATM adaptation layers are roughly equivalent to the data link layer of the Open System Interconnection (OSI) reference model, and the ATM physical layer is analogous to the physical layer of the OSI reference model. However, unlike in the OSI reference model, the z-axis is made up of the control, user, and management planes. The z-axis shows that features or control functions of the control, user, and management planes are found in each of the ATM layers. The management, user, and control planes each have specific functions:

- **Management plane**—The management plane is used for monitoring and controlling all layers. Notice that the management plane, unlike the control and user planes, is not layered and is not as standardized as the others, leaving many options open to vendor-specific support.

- **User plane**—The user plane manages the transfer of data through the ATM switch.

- **Control plane**—The control plane handles signaling requests, such as call setup.

Higher-Layer Protocols

Higher-layer protocols include all non-ATM information that is encapsulated for ATM transport. Examples include digital voice, Frame Relay, SNA, and IP. IP and ATM's growth have made ATM very popular as a data link protocol for IP. Except for brief examples, however, this section does not cover higher-layer protocols because they are outside the scope of this book.

ATM Adaptation Layer

The ATM Adaptation Layer (AAL) accommodates data from various sources and performs the conversion to and from ATM payloads. It translates between the larger service data units (SDUs), such as video streams and packet data, of upper-layer processes and ATM cells. In the receive direction, AAL adapts the services provided by the ATM layer to those services required by the higher layers, such as circuit emulation, video, audio, Frame Relay, and so on.

The AAL receives the data from the upper-level protocols or applications and converts it to 48-byte segments that will fit into the payload of an ATM cell.

The adaptation layer also defines the basic principles of sublayering. In addition, it describes the service attributes of each layer in terms of constant or variable bit rate, timing transfer requirement, and whether the service is connection-oriented or connectionless.

The AAL has two major sublayers: the convergence sublayer (CS) and the segmentation and reassembly (SAR) sublayer. Furthermore, the CS is then divided into a common part convergence sublayer (CPCS) and a service specific convergence sublayer (SSCS). The CPCS provides error detection, and the upper sublayer SSCS provides specific error recovery to the AAL service in use.

In the transmit direction, the AAL convergence sublayer processes the higher-layer protocols from the control plane and the user plane, and delivers them to the AAL SAR in the form of variable-length units called *convergence sublayer protocol data units (CS-PDUs)*.

In the receive direction, the AAL convergence sublayer receives the data from the AAL SAR sublayer and then processes and delivers it to the appropriate higher-layer protocol plane (either the control plane or the user plane).

The SAR sublayer is the lower of two sublayers (CS and SAR) that make up the AAL. In the transmit direction, the AAL SAR sublayer receives data from the AAL convergence sublayer and segments the data into 48-octet groups called *segmentation and reassembly protocol data units (SAR-PDUs)*. This is the fixed-size 48-octet portion of the cell. As SAR delivers these fixed-size segments to the ATM layer, they become the payload of the ATM cells.

In the receive direction, the AAL SAR sublayer receives data in fixed-size 48-octet segments from the ATM layer. SAR reassembles the data from the cells and delivers the data to the AAL convergence sublayer.

The format of CS-PDUs and SAR-PDUs depends on the type of traffic coming from the higher-layer protocols. Before covering the different AALs, it is important to note that the ITU-T created and recommended classes based upon service requirements. Four different service classes were created to support a variety of traffic that is categorized based on the following criteria:

- **Connection mode**—Connection-oriented traffic has two defined endpoints (like a telephone connection). This implies that communications are acknowledged. Connectionless traffic does not require an acknowledgment—either acknowledgments are not required by upper-layer protocols (such as with a voice application, in which waiting for resend of dropped packets causes more of an interruption than simply dropping the packets), or error detection and recovery are provided by a higher-level protocol.

- **End-to-end timing**—End-to-end timing defines whether the traffic is time sensitive and must have a constant clock rate.

- **Bit rate**—The bit rate can be either a constant bit rate or variable.

The ITU-T's four classes of services are named Class A, B, C, and D:

- Class A services require a connection-oriented, end-to-end timing connection with a constant bit rate.

- Class B services require a connection-oriented, end-to-end timing connection with a variable bit rate.

- Class C services require a connection–oriented connection with a variable bit rate. End-to-end timing is not required.

- Class D services are connectionless, with a variable bit rate. End to end timing is not required.

AAL protocols have been developed to support these four types of services. (Note that there is not a one-to-one mapping—the classes are ITU-T recommendations. Also note that AAL2 has not received wide vendor support.) The ATM network must also manage AAL protocols. To guarantee these classes of services, ATM uses traffic shaping and policy either to provide the class of service for the duration of the connection or to not provide the connection. (ATM is not a best-effort protocol.)

Traffic Shaping and Policing

When an ATM end station connects to the ATM network, it is essentially making a contract with the network based on QoS parameters. This contract specifies values for peak bandwidth, average sustained bandwidth, and burst size. An ATM connection set up with specified traffic descriptors constitutes a traffic contract between the user and the network. The network offers the type of guarantee appropriate to the service class, as long as the user keeps the traffic on the connection within the envelope defined by the traffic parameters.

Traffic shaping is used to control and reduce congestion within a network, for instance, by limiting the peak rate of a connection to that of the slowest link along the path. Traffic shaping involves the use of queues to constrain data bursts, limit peak data rate, and smooth jitters so that the traffic will fit within the promised envelope.

The network can enforce the traffic contract by a usage parameter control (UPC) mechanism known as *traffic policing*. ATM switches have the option of using traffic policing to enforce the contract. *UPC* is a set of algorithms performed by an ATM switch upon the receipt of cells within a connection that determines whether the cell stream is compliant with the traffic contract. The switch can measure the actual traffic flow and compare it against the agreed-upon traffic envelope. If the switch finds that traffic falls outside the agreed-upon parameters, it can set the cell loss priority (CLP) bit or discard the offending cells. Setting the CLP bit makes the cell discard eligible, which means that the switch, or any other switch handling the cell, is allowed to drop the cell during periods of congestion.

Now that you know that the traffic can be managed, the remainder of this section covers the various AAL protocols. Table 7-1 lists the AAL protocols with their characteristics.

Table 7-1   *AAL Protocols and Characteristics*

Characteristics	AAL1	AAL2	AAL3/4	AAL5
Timing required between source and destination	Yes	Yes	No	No
Data rate	Constant	Variable	Variable	Variable
Connection mode	Connection-oriented	Connection-oriented	Connection-oriented and connectionless	Connection-oriented and connectionless
Traffic types	Voice and circuit emulation	Voice (telephone-quality) with compression support	Data (such as Switched Multimegabit Data Service)	Data (such as IP and LAN emulation)

AAL1

AAL1 carries payloads for constant bit rate (CBR), a connection-oriented service that requires timing transfer (synchronous). The payload data consists of a synchronous sample. AAL1 is appropriate for transporting telephone traffic (uncompressed voice) and uncompressed video traffic.

The use of the convergence sublayer function depends on the services using the AAL1 and is not needed in every case. When the service does not require a CS-PDU, AAL1 traffic is sent down to the SAR sublayer and is segmented into SAR-PDUs. The SAR-PDU format is shown in Figure 7-6. For proper support of various video applications, encoding in either AAL1 or AAL5 is important to match the application: AAL1 for H.320-compliant videoconferencing equipment, and AAL5 for most other compressed video streams.

Figure 7-6   *AAL1 SAR-PDU Format*

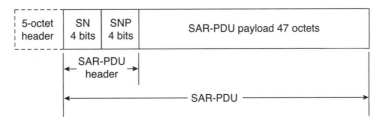

Sequence number (SN) and sequence number protection (SNP) fields provide the information that the receiving AAL1 needs to verify that it has received the cells in the correct order. The 4-bit SN is divided in two subfields: a 1-bit convergence sublayer indication (CSI) field and a 3-bit sequence count (SC) field.

The SC is used to detect a gap (missing cells) or misinsertion of cells in the stream of cells. The 1-bit CSI is used to carry timing recovery information or to indicate the existence of structured data. AAL1 provides a time stamp known as Synchronous Residual Time Stamp (SRTS). AAL1 is used for CBR traffic when a time stamp is needed for precise transmission clocking. The remaining 47 octets of the payload field are filled with the user data.

AAL2

AAL2 is designed to provide services to low bit–rate, delay-sensitive applications, such as telephone-quality voice services. The traffic in these types of applications is of variable length, so logical link controls (LLCs) were designed to provide virtual point-to-point connections that use the LLC field and the length field to assemble the smaller variable-length packets into ATM cells. AAL2 has not yet received wide vendor support.

AAL3/4

AAL3/4 was designed for network service providers and is closely aligned with Switched Multimegabit Data Service (SMDS). AAL3/4 is used to transmit SMDS packets over an ATM network.

The CS creates a PDU by placing a beginning/end tag header to the frame and appending a length field as a trailer, as shown in Figure 7-7.

Figure 7-7 *AAL3/4 CS-PDU Format*

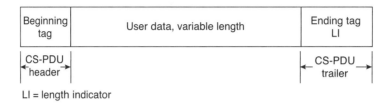

LI = length indicator

The SAR sublayer fragments the CS-PDU and prepends to each SAR-PDU a header that includes the type (beginning, end, or continuation of a message), the sequence number, and the multiplexing identifier (MID), as shown in Figure 7-8.

Figure 7-8 *AAL3/4 SAR-PDU Format*

ST = segment types (see chart at right)
MID = multiplexing identifier

Segment type identification	MSB	LSB
Beginning of message (BOM)	1	0
Continuation of message (COM)	0	0
End of message (EOM)	0	1
Single segment message (SSM)	1	1

The SAR sublayer also appends a CRC-10 trailer to each SAR-PDU. The completed SAR-PDU becomes the payload field of an ATM cell to which the ATM layer prepends the standard ATM header.

AAL5

AAL5, the most popular AAL, is the adaptation layer used to transfer most types of data, such as signaling messages; RFC 1577 classical IP over ATM, "LAN Emulation (LANE)"; and RFC 2684, "Multiprotocol Encapsulation over ATM Adaptation Layer 5."

Figure 7-9 shows how AAL5 prepares a cell for transmission. First, the convergence sublayer of AAL5 appends a variable-length pad and an 8-byte trailer to a frame. The padding is long enough to ensure that the resulting PDU falls on the 48-byte boundary of the ATM cell. The trailer includes the length of the frame and a 32-bit CRC computed across the entire PDU, which allows AAL5 at the destination to detect bit errors and lost or missing cells that are out of sequence.

Figure 7-9   *CS-PDU and SAR-PDU Structure for AAL5*

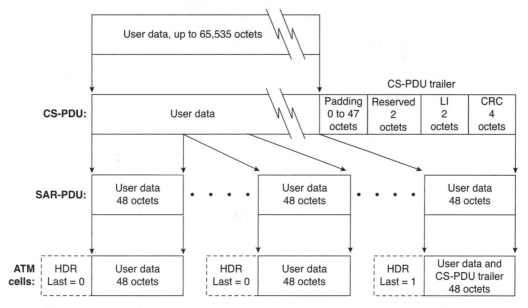

Last = bit 3 in the PTI field

Next, the segmentation and reassembly segments the CS-PDU into 48-byte blocks. The SAR-PDUs have no additional overhead associated with them. The ATM layer places each block into the payload field of an ATM cell. For all cells except the last cell, a bit in the payload type identifier (PTI) field is set to 0 to indicate that the cell is not the last cell in a series that represents a single frame. For the last cell, the bit in the PTI field is set to 1. AAL5 is often referred to as the simple and efficient AAL (SEAL). AAL5 is the adaptation layer most widely adopted in ATM networks.

ATM Layer

The ATM layer is responsible for establishing connections and passing cells through the ATM network by using the information contained in the header of each ATM UNI and NNI cell, as shown in Figure 7-10. Given the fixed-size 48 octets from the AAL layer above it, the ATM layer's key function is to add four of the five octets of the fixed-size cell header. The fifth octet of the cell header is an 8-bit CRC that is added by the TC sublayer of the physical layer.

Figure 7-10 *ATM Cell Format—The UNI and NNI Cell*

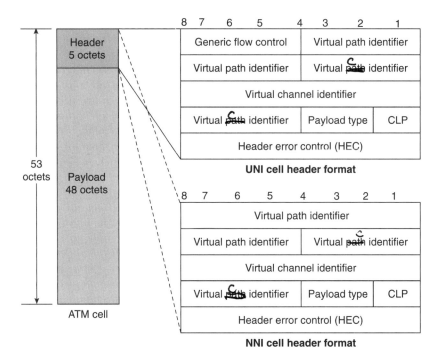

The ATM layer uses the structural components in the ATM cell header to provide cell multiplexing and demultiplexing, end-to-end connection information (virtual paths and circuits), cell header generation and extraction, and generic flow control.

Virtual Path Identifiers and Virtual Circuit Identifiers

One primary function of both header types is to identify virtual path identifiers (VPIs) and virtual circuit identifiers (VCIs, sometimes known as virtual channel identifiers) as switching identifiers for ATM cells. VCI and VPI identify the path of a virtual connection. A VCI is a logical identification for a virtual channel between two ATM entities. A VPI is a logical grouping of VCIs, like a larger pipe containing smaller pipes, as shown in Figure 7 11. A VPI allows an ATM switch to perform operations on groups of VCIs.

When a cell arrives in the ATM network, the VPI and VCI are used to identify which PVC the cell is transported across. VPIs and VCIs have local significance only to each interface. These fields may change as the cell moves through the network, depending on the routing and addressing needs of the network.

Figure 7-11 *Virtual Paths and Virtual Circuits*

Multiple virtual channels can be combined into a single virtual path when necessary, to simplify routing and switching of cells with the same endpoints. Virtual paths may also be switched as single entities.

Figure 7-12 shows an ATM UNI with three terminating connections. Two of the connections are identified by both a VPI and a VCI (in the form VPI/VCI). The remaining connection is identified by a VPI only and can carry multiple channels transparently through the network.

Figure 7-12 *The VPI and VCI Identify Each PVC*

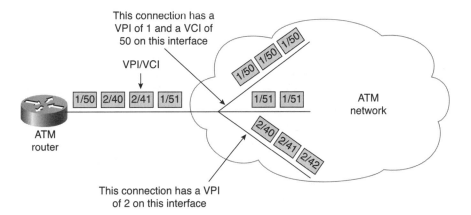

The VPI/VCI pair identifies the next connection segment that a cell transits on its way to a final destination. As shown in Figure 7-13, a switch receives a cell from the router with a VPI/VCI pair of 6/40. The switch table indicates that this cell should be sent out with a VPI/VCI pair of 2/90. That VPI/VCI connects the cell to the other switch. The other switch assigns a new VPI/VCI (8/30) for the next ATM hop.

Figure 7-13 *The VPI and VCI Change as the Cells Move Through the Network*

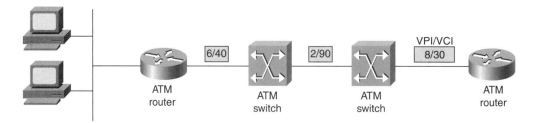

A *virtual path connection (VPC)* is a service that is a collection of virtual channels that share the same VPI. Sometimes this type of connection is referred to as a virtual path (VP) tunnel because it provides a tunnel for multiple channels in a network. VPCs are often used to switch traffic between two ATM switches through a public ATM cloud. Virtual path switching is shown in Figure 7-14.

Figure 7-14 *Virtual Path Switching*

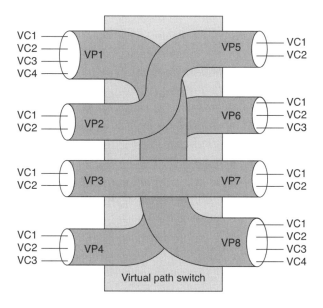

In most instances, *virtual channel connections (VCCs)* identify end-to-end ATM connections. A VCC is a connection that depends on both the VPI and the VCI to determine a cell's path through the network. Virtual channel (VC) switching is the term used to describe this process. Figure 7-15 shows virtual channel switching and how it interacts with virtual path switching. The VPCs may change both the VPI and VCI as they pass through the switch. Note that in many switches, both VP and VC switching is supported.

Figure 7-15 *Virtual Channel and Virtual Path Switching*

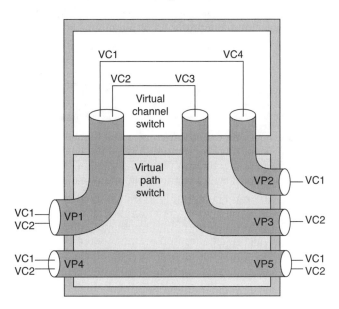

The UNI and NNI cell headers differ in the number of addressable PVCs that may terminate on an interface, as shown in Table 7-2.

Table 7-2 *Number of Addressable PVCs*

Cell Header	VPIs	VCIs	Total Connections
UNI	256	65,535	16,776,960
NNI	4,096	65,535	268,431,360

VCIs 0 to 15 have been reserved by the ITU-T, and VCIs 16 to 31 have been reserved by the ATM Forum for management and signaling messages.

Payload Type Field of the ATM Header

The Payload Type (PT) is a 3-bit field that characterizes the information in the payload of the cell—either data or management information. The first bit defines whether the cell carries user data or connection-management information.

If the cell is carrying user data, bit 2 is the Explicit Forward Congestion Indication (EFCI) bit. The EFCI is set to 1 if the cell experienced congestion in the network. Bit 3 is used if the cell was segmented using AAL5. This bit determines whether the cell is the last cell in a frame or a message.

If the cell is carrying connection-management information, bit 2 defines whether the cell is an OAM cell or a resource management (RM) cell. Bit 3 defines whether an OAM cell is for a segment or an end-to-end flow.

A complete listing of payload types is shown in Table 7-3.

Table 7-3 *Payload Types*

Value	Description
000	A user data cell, with no congestion, that is not the end of an AAL5 frame
001	A user data cell, with no congestion, that is the end of an AAL5 frame
010	A user data cell, with congestion, that is not the end of an AAL5 frame
011	A user data cell, with congestion, that is the end of an AAL5 frame
100	A segment-flow OAM cell
101	An end-to-end-flow OAM cell
110	An RM cell
111	Undefined

Cell Loss Priority Bit

The goal of a cell loss priority (CLP) bit is to respond to congestion situations that threaten data loss. CLP determines whether the cell is of normal or low priority. A low-priority cell (one with the CLP bit set to 1) is discarded if congestion occurs in the network, as shown in Figure 7-16.

Figure 7-16 *Cell Discard Based Upon Congestion and CLP Bit Set*

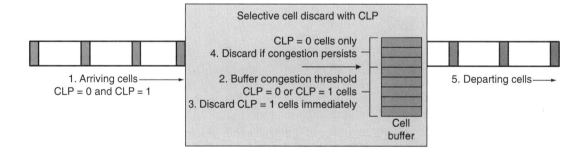

Header Error Control Field

The Header Error Control (HEC) field is an 8-bit result of a CRC generated on the cell header. It provides an optional bit-by-bit error correction.

The HEC is calculated and inserted after the other four header octets are inserted. The HEC can also be used to identify and track cell header locations for transmission on unframed digital facilities, as discussed in Chapter 4, "Broadband Transmissions." The HEC, however, is generated at the physical layer.

Physical Layer

The ATM physical layer controls transmission and receipt of bits on the physical medium. It also keeps track of ATM cell boundaries and packages cells into the appropriate type of frame for the physical medium being used.

The ATM physical layer is divided into two parts: the transmission convergence (TC) sublayer and the physical medium dependent (PMD) sublayer. The PMD sublayer is responsible for sending and receiving a continuous flow of bits with associated timing information to synchronize transmission and reception. Because it includes only physical medium dependent functions, its specification depends on the physical medium used.

ATM can use any physical medium capable of carrying ATM cells. Existing standards that can carry ATM cells include SONET/SDH, DS-3/E3, 100-Mbps local fiber, 155-Mbps local fiber, and various data rates over twisted-pair wire. For more information on the facilities that carry ATM cells, refer to Chapter 4, "Broadband Transmissions."

The TC sublayer is responsible for HEC generation and extraction, cell delineation (cell boundary maintenance), decoupling (idle cell maintenance), and management of the physical-layer frame structure.

The PMD sublayer defines the characteristics of the transmission facility. These characteristics include connector definitions, cable impedance, 1s density enforcement, framing, transmission rates, clocking, line error detection, and line alarm reporting.

ATM Signaling Protocol

ATM provides two virtual circuit communications services: PVCs and SVCs. PVCs are similar to dedicated private lines because the connection is set up on a permanent basis. Users establish PVCs by requesting them either from a public carrier providing the ATM service or from the WAN administrator of the private network. SVC connections require signaling (call setup and teardown).

ATM signaling protocols vary by link type. ATM UNI signaling is used between an ATM end system and an ATM switch across an ATM UNI. ATM NNI signaling is used across NNI links.

Signaling requests are carried on a well-known connection that uses a VCI of 5 (within the range reserved by ITU-T). The current ATM Forum standard for ATM UNI signaling is based on Q.2931 developed by the ITU-T. Two fundamental types of ATM connections exist:

- Point-to-point
- Point-to-multipoint

Point-to-point connections connect two ATM end systems. Point-to-point connections can be either unidirectional or bidirectional.

Point-to-multipoint connections connect a single source end system to multiple destination end systems. Cell replication is done within the network by the ATM switches in which the connection splits into two or more branches. Such connections are unidirectional. These connections are often called *multicast connections*.

When an ATM device (the sender) wants to establish a connection with another ATM device (the receiver), the sender sends a signaling request packet to its directly connected ATM switch. This request contains the ATM address of the desired ATM endpoint (receiver) as well as any QoS parameters required for the connection.

The signaling packet is reassembled by the switch and is examined. If the switch has a switch table entry for the receiver's address, and if it can accommodate the QoS requested for the connection, the switch sets up the virtual connection on the input link and forwards the request out the interface specified in the switching table for the ATM address the receiver.

The PNNI routing protocol then routes ATM signaling requests between ATM switches. (Some ATM switches may use proprietary routing mechanisms within the bounds of the network.)

Every switch along the path to the endpoint reassembles and examines the signaling packet and forwards it to the next switch. The QoS parameters can be supported while setting up the virtual connection as the signaling packet is forwarded. If any switch along the path cannot accommodate the requested QoS parameters, the request is rejected and a rejection message is sent back to the originator of the request.

When the signaling packet reaches the receiver at the endpoint, it is reassembled and evaluated. If the endpoint can support the desired QoS, it responds with an accept message. As the accept message propagates back to the originator of the request, the switches set up a virtual circuit. The originator of the request receives the accept message from its directly connected ATM switch, as well as the VPI/VCI value that the originator should use for cells destined for the endpoint.

A simplified view of the setup process between two ATM devices is shown in Figure 7-17.

Figure 7-17 *ATM Signaling Protocol—Establishing a Connection*

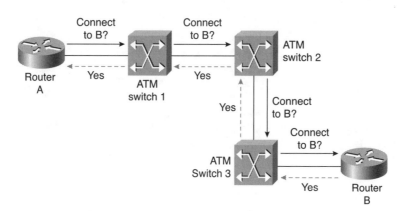

ATM Address Formats

The ATM signaling protocol requires an addressing scheme to allow the signaling protocol to identify the source and destination of connections. The ITU-T has long settled on the use of telephone-like E.164 numbers as the addressing structure for public ATM/BISDN networks. Several ATM address formats have been developed—one for public networks and three for private networks.

ATM End Station Addresses (AESAs) are designed for use within private ATM networks. Three formats of private ATM addressing exist:

- Data Country Code (DCC)
- International Code Designator (ICD)
- Encapsulated E.164 addresses

Figure 7-18 summarizes these three formats.

The first octet of each address format identifies the address type—DCC, ICD, or E.164. DCC numbers are administered by various authorities in each country. For example, ANSI has this responsibility in the United States. The DCC identifies the authority that is responsible for the remainder of the routing fields. ICDs are administered on an international basis by the British Standards Institute. E.164 addresses are essentially telephone numbers (ISDN) that are administered by telephone carriers.

The routing field can be thought of as an address space. The term *routing field* implies that there is more to the field than a simple address. In particular, the addressing mechanism will probably be hierarchical to assist in the routing. In the E.164 option, the use of the routing field is left undefined.

Figure 7-18 *ATM Address Formats*

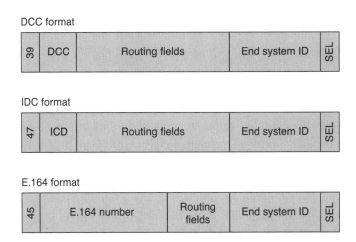

The first 13 octets of the address (up to and including the routing field) are used to identify a switch and are assigned by the ATM network. The six-octet end system ID is used to identify the destination end-user device. The selector (SEL) byte is not used by the ATM network and is passed through the network as a user information field. The SEL can be used to identify elements in the terminal—for example, a protocol stack.

Integrated Link Management Interface

The Integrated Link Management Interface (ILMI) protocol uses Simple Network Management Protocol (SNMP) format packets across the UNI (and across NNI links) to access an ILMI Management Information Base (MIB) associated with the link, within each node. Chapter 8, "IP Addressing and Network Management," covers SNMP thoroughly. The ILMI messages are encapsulated in AAL5 and use VPI 0 and VCI 16.

The ILMI allows adjacent network elements to determine various characteristics of each other—for instance, the size of each other's connection space, the type of signaling used (for example, UNI 4.0 versus UNI 3.1), hooks for network management autodiscovery, and so on. One of its most useful features is address registration, which facilitates the administration of ATM addresses. This feature allows an ATM end system (such as a router) to inform an ATM switch across the UNI of its Media Access Control (MAC) address and to receive in return the remainder of the node's full AESA. ATM address registration is similar to the DHCP protocol used for IP address assignments on LANs.

To summarize, the ILMI service provides data on the physical layer as well as ATM-layer VP connections, VC connections, and address registration information.

Operation, Administration, and Maintenance

Operation, Administation, and Maintenance (OAM) cells carry standard management information between ATM devices. Many different functions of OAM take place in an ATM network. This section focuses on the fundamental principles of OAM messaging within the ATM layer.

There are two types of OAM messages to consider: F4 and F5. These flows are carried within the ATM cell. F4 OAM cells are used for virtual path monitoring; F5 OAM cells are used for virtual circuit monitoring.

OAM traffic flows occurs end to end or on a single segment for either F4 or F5 messages. End-to-end flows are between terminating equipment such as routers and are not interpreted by the intermediate network elements. Segment flows are between two adjacent network elements, such as a router and a switch. End-to-end and segment flows are shown in Figure 7-19.

Figure 7-19 *OAM Cells—End-to-End and Segment Flows*

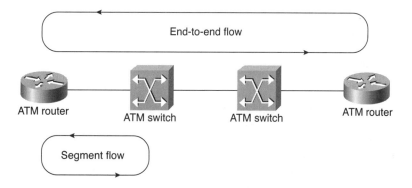

For the F4 flow, reserved VCIs 3 and 4 identify the segment and end-to-end flows, respectively. The F5 OAM cell flow uses the PTI field in the cell header to identify the flow type. When coded as 100, PTI is a segment flow; the 101 value identifies an end-to-end flow.

OAM cells typically are not present during normal network operation. OAM cells travel with the user data in the ATM network and provide local and remote alarm notification to upstream and downstream network elements. OAM also provides loopback requests and continuity checks.

Summary

This chapter covered introductory material on ATM. ATM's popularity comes from its QoS characteristics as well as the fact that it is both a LAN and a WAN protocol. The BISDN reference model was used to discuss ATM layers and planes. The chapter also covered the management, the user, and the control planes, as well as the ATM adaptation layer (AAL), the ATM layer, and the physical layer. In addition, the chapter overviewed the four classes of services upon which the various AAL protocols are based.

Review Questions

The following questions test your retention of the material presented in this chapter. You can find the answers to the Review Questions in Appendix A, "Answers to Review Questions."

1   How many octets make up an ATM cell?

2   How large is the ATM header?

   A. 5 cells

   B. 5 octets

   C. 8 bytes

   D. ATM has no headers.

3   What is the function of the UNI?

   A. To connect legacy network hosts to ATM networks

   B. To connect ATM switches with the ATM network

   C. To connect ATM nodes (user nodes) to the ATM network

   D. To translate between legacy networks and ATM

4   What is the purpose of the ATM adaptation layer (AAL)?

   A. To provide cell switching to the network

   B. To convert upper-layer protocols and larger service data units to ATM cells

   C. To translate synchronous services to ATM

   D. To provide network-management capability to the ATM network

5   What is the ATM layer responsible for?

   A. Converting upper-layer protocols and larger service data units to ATM cells.

   B. Converting the cells to a transmission understood by the physical media.

   C. Establishing connections and passing cells through the ATM network based upon the ATM header.

   D. There is no ATM layer.

6   What role does the physical layer provide?

A. It controls transmission and receipt of bits on the physical medium.

B. It converts cells to a format understood by the AAL.

C. It functions as a TDM for the ATM network.

D. The physical layer is not important for the functionality of ATM.

7   Which protocol provides ATM with management capabilities?

A. Link Management Interface

B. Integrated Local Management Interface

C. Private Network-Network Interface

D. B-ISDN AAL (I.362)

CHAPTER 8

IP Addressing and Network Management

This chapter covers network management technology and IP addressing. An understanding of IP addressing is required to integrate WAN switches into LANs for management and, in some cases, to provide routing capabilities. An understanding of network management and the Simple Network Management Protocol (SNMP), the most popular protocol for network management, is required to support and troubleshoot Cisco WAN switches.

This chapter includes the following sections:

- An Overview of Classful IP Addressing
- Classless IP Addressing
- Variable Length Subnet Mask
- Prefix Notation
- Network Management Defined
- Simple Network Management Protocol
- SNMP Operation
- SNMP Message Format
- SNMPv2 Security
- Summary
- Review Questions

An Overview of Classful IP Addressing

The official description of Internet addresses is found in RFC 1166, "Internet Numbers." Internet addresses are currently assigned by three organizations: American Registry for Internet Numbers (ARIN), Asia Pacific Network Information Center (APNIC), and the Réseaux IP Européennes (RIPE) Network Coordination Center. Address assignment for IP addresses is generally geographically based. IP, the Layer 3 protocol in the Internet suite, provides routing, fragmentation, and reassembly of datagrams. The addressing scheme is integral to routing IP datagrams through an internetwork. An IP address is 32 bits in length.

IP Address Classes and Formats

As described in RFC 1020, the IP address space is divided into five classes: Class A, Class B, Class C, Class D, and Class E. Classes A, B, and C are used for unicast traffic; Class D is reserved for multicast traffic; and Class E is reserved for future use. These classes differ in the number of bits allocated to the network and the host portions of the address. (In an IP networking environment, all network-attached devices are referred to as *hosts*.) An IP address is 32 bits in length, divided into either two or three parts. The first part designates the network address; the second part (if present) designates the subnet address; and the final part designates the host address. Subnet addresses are present only if the network administrator has decided that the network should be divided into subnetworks.

The lengths of the network, the subnet, and the host fields are all variable but should be applied uniformly within organizations using classful-based implementations or using routing protocols that are limited to classful networking, such as RIP version 1.

As mentioned, IP addressing (IP version 4 [IPv4]) supports five different network classes (the far-left bits indicate the network class):

- **Class A**—Class A networks are intended mainly for use with a few very large networks because 8 bits are dedicated to the network, which gives a theoretical total of 128 Class A networks. However, 24 bits are dedicated to hosts, which means that each Class A network can support almost 17 million hosts. The first bit in all Class A networks is set to 0.

- **Class B**—In Class B networks, the two highest-order bits are 10. Class B networks allocate 16 bits to the network field and 16 bits to the host address field. More than 16,000 Class B networks can exist, and each Class B network can have more than 65,000 hosts. Within the classful model, this address class offers a good compromise between network and host address space.

- **Class C**—Class C networks allocate 24 bits for the network address field and only 8 bits for the host field. The first 3 bits in a Class C address are always 110. More than two million Class C networks can exist, and each Class C network can have up to 254 hosts. The number of hosts per network could be a limiting factor.

- **Class D**—Class D addresses are reserved for multicast groups. Unlike Class A, B, and C addresses, the last 28 bits of a Class D address have no further structure. In Class D addresses, the 4 highest-order bits are set to 1110.

- **Class E**—Class E addresses are also defined but are reserved for future use. In Class E addresses, the 4 highest-order bits are all set to 1.

Figure 8-1 shows the class portion of the network bits, the network bits, and the host bits for Class A, B, and C addresses.

Figure 8-1   *Class A, B, and C IP Addressing*

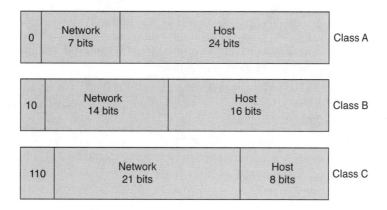

Internet Address Notation

The notation for Internet addresses is four base-10 integer numbers separated by dots. Each number, written in decimal, represents an 8-bit octet. When strung together, the four octets form the 32-bit Internet address. This notation is called *dotted decimal*. The following examples show 32-bit values expressed as Internet addresses:

- 192.31.7.19
- 10.7.0.11
- 255.255.255.255 (global broadcast address)

Note that 255, which represents an octet of all 1s, is the largest possible value of a field in a dotted decimal number.

To refer to a specific network, the bits in the host portion of the address are all 0. For example, the Class C address 192.31.7.0 refers to a particular network because no host is specified in the fourth byte.

If you want to send a packet to all hosts (broadcast) on the network specified in the network portion of the address, the local address must be all 1s. For example, the Class B address 128.1.255.255 refers to all hosts on network 128.1.0.0. Because of these conventions, you cannot use an Internet address with all 0s or all 1s in the host portion of any host address (including routers).

Internet Addresses with Specific Purposes

Some Internet addresses are reserved for special uses and cannot be used for host, subnet, or network addresses. Reserved and available Internet addresses are as follows:

- 0.0.0.0. is used as a default gateway. It should not be used, and most equipment will not allow the address to be configured.

- 127.0.0.0 is the local loopback network, and 127.0.0.1 is the local loopback address. This IP address is used for access resources on the local host as if the requests were coming through the network.

- 255.255.255.255 is the local broadcast.

IP Subnetting

IP networks can also be divided into smaller units, called subnets. *Subnetting* is a scheme for imposing a simple two-level hierarchy on host addresses, allowing multiple, logical networks to exist within a single Class A, Class B, or Class C network. This scheme provides extra flexibility for network administrators. The usual practice is to use a few left-most bits in the host portion of the network addresses for a subnet field. For example, assume that a network has been assigned a Class B address and that all the nodes on the network currently conform to a Class B address format. Then assume that the dotted decimal representation of this network's address is 128.10.0.0 (all 0s in the host field of an address specifies the entire network). Subnetting borrows bits from the host portion of the address, as shown in Figure 8-2.

Figure 8-2   *Subnet Addressing*

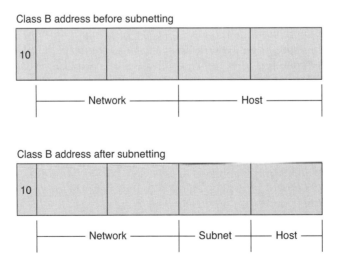

If a network administrator uses 8 bits of subnetting, the third octet of a Class B IP address provides the subnet number. For example, address 128.10.1.0 refers to network 128.10, subnet 1; address 128.10.2.0 refers to network 128.10, subnet 2; and so on. Refer to Figure 8-2 to see which parts are assigned to the subnet. As with the host portion of an address, do not use all 0s or all 1s in the subnet field with older equipment. (The all 0s and all 1s rule is no longer a requirement of most equipment, and its support is often configurable on routers.)

Subnet Mask

A subnet mask identifies the subnet field of network addresses. The number of bits borrowed from the network for the subnet address is variable. To specify how many bits are used, IP provides the subnet mask. With classful networking, all subnets of a given Class A, Class B, or Class C must use the same subnet mask.

Subnet masks use the same format and representation technique as IP addresses. Subnet masks have 1s in all bits except those bits that specify the host field. This mask is a 32-bit Internet address written in dotted decimal notation with all 1s in the network and the subnet portions of the address. For example, the subnet mask that specifies 8 bits of subnetting for Class A address 34.0.0.0 is 255.255.0.0. The subnet mask that specifies 12 bits of subnetting for Class A address 34.0.0.0 is 255.255.240.0. Figure 8-3 shows these examples.

Figure 8-3   *Using Subnets with IP Addressing*

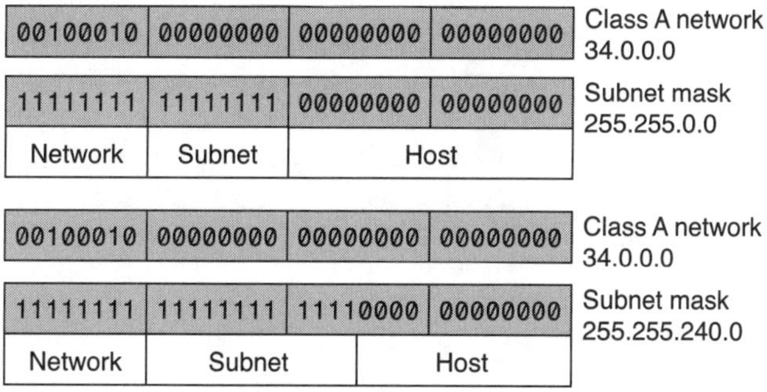

00100010	00000000	00000000	00000000	Class A network 34.0.0.0
11111111	11111111	00000000	00000000	Subnet mask 255.255.0.0
Network	Subnet	Host		

00100010	00000000	00000000	00000000	Class A network 34.0.0.0
11111111	11111111	11110000	00000000	Subnet mask 255.255.240.0
Network	Subnet	Host		

The subnet field can consist of any number of the host field bits; you need not use multiples of four or eight.

As mentioned, the subnet mask must be the same for all interfaces connected to subnets of the same network within a classful environment.

Classless IP Addressing

Much of the information covered under classful IP addressing applies to classless IP addressing. Networks are still made up of hosts with individual IP addresses that are located on subnets or networks. The major difference is that the environment (or, more specifically, the equipment and the protocols) is not limited to the requirements of classful addressing and routing.

Prior to the deployment of classless IP addressing, Class B networks were the most-requested size of address space because of the number of hosts a Class B network supports. The demand for Class B networks created a shortage of address space as well as large, unmanageable routing tables on backbone routers (each class network required a routing entry).

Instead of assigning a complete Class B network, an organization can now receive a block of addresses with 1024 addresses that gives the equivalent address space of four Class C networks within a larger address space allocated to the Internet service provider (ISP). This gives the organization the required number of addresses and simplifies routing.

This can be clarified with an example. Assuming that your ISP receives the classless interdomain routing (CIDR) block 192.168.0.0 through 192.168.255.255, this block can be routed as 192.168.0.0 255.255.0.0. (This network is actually reserved for internal use as defined in RFC 1918 and is being used as an example here.) The upstream provider of your ISP has one routing entry for the whole network; under the class system, each organization received an independent network that had to be entered in all central routers. From the network 192.168.0.0 255.255.0.0, you can then be assigned a block with 1,024 addresses, such as 192.168.8.0 255.255.252.0. Your address space would then be 192.168.8.0 through 192.168.11.255. In addition, your ISP would require only one routing entry instead of four for the four Class C networks. For example, assuming a T1 serial connection from your ISP and static routing, without CIDR, the ISP router's routing entry would appear as this:

```
ip route 192.168.8.0 255.255.255.0 serial 0/1
ip route 192.168.9.0 255.255.255.0 serial 0/1
ip route 192.168.10.0 255.255.255.0 serial 0/1
ip route 192.168.11.0 255.255.255.0 serial 0/1
```

That differs from the following for CIDR:

```
ip route 192.168.8.0 255.255.252.0 serial 0/1
```

Although only three routing entries are saved here, this same principal is applied to all upstream providers with all ISPs, which greatly reduces the number of routing entries required in the backbone.

Variable Length Subnet Mask

With many implementations of classful addressing, and with routing protocols based upon classful addresses, subnets are required to all have the same masks. Requiring the same subnet mask within an organization is simply not flexible enough for today's enterprise.

With Variable Length Subnet Mask (VLSM), various sizes of subnets can be defined based upon the size of the subnet, or for management purposes. For example, an overseas organization can receive a block of 512 addresses from its headquarters and can subnet as business needs require locally.

Due to the inflexibility of global subnet masks, RFC 1009, "Requirements for Internet Gateways," specifies that VLSM subnets are allowed. Although VLSM was supported before CIDR, it was not popular outside of very large organizations until CIDR became popular. For this reason, CIDR and VLSM are often considered the same technology, but this is not the case.

Prefix Notation

When describing networks thus far, the network and netmask have been given. A common method to identify networks is to use the prefix notation (also known as slash notation). The prefix notation lists the network, followed by a forward slash and then the number of bits assigned to the network. For example, 192.168.1.0 with a netmask of 255.255.255.0 can be written as 192.168.1.0/24. 255.255.255.0=11111111.11111111.11111111.00000000 in binary. Because only the 1s belong to the network, there are 24 mask bits in this case.

Network Management Defined

Network management is the process of managing and controlling a network, often using purpose-built software tools. Network management includes monitoring alarms and events; provisioning network elements (including trunks, lines, ports, and connections); troubleshooting and testing; collecting and analyzing network statistics; accessing configuration information; storing configuration information (backups); and reporting performance and capacity.

Network management is often used to generically describe any tasks involved in any of the listed tasks, such as monitoring alarms and events. Both definitions are accurate and useful depending on the context.

Network management is often defined as in-band or out-of-band. *In-band* means that the management information is passed through the WAN (or other network) alongside the user data. *Out-of-band* means that the management information travels over circuits outside the network and can often be used even in the case of a network failure. There are no requirements that a device must support only one method of management; in fact, ideally, both methods are supported.

In many cases, network management tools are run on workstations or PCs that access the WAN across a LAN using management software based on Simple Network Management Protocol (SNMP). SNMP is a protocol designed specifically for management of network devices. These devices must have IP addresses assigned so that they can communicate with the network management platform.

Other methods besides SNMP are also used for network management. Furthermore, it is not uncommon for both proprietary and standard methods to be combined to increase the capabilities of a network management tool.

Simple Network Management Protocol

Simple Network Management (SNMP) is an application-layer protocol designed to aid in the management of network devices. It has become the most popular protocol for managing internetworks.

By using SNMP to access management information data (such as packets per second and network error rates), network administrators can more easily manage network performance and find and solve network problems.

Two versions of SNMP are widely supported: version 1 and version 2. SNMP version 1 (SNMPv1) is the initial version of SNMP. SNMP version 2 (SNMPv2) incorporates security features and improvements in protocol operations and management architecture. SNMP is part of a larger architecture called the Internet Network Management Framework (NMF). Additional versions of SNMP have not yet gained wide industry support.

SNMPv1 NMF is defined in RFCs 1155, 1157, and 1212, and SNMPv2 NMF is defined by RFCs 1441 through 1452.

SNMP Management Model

As specified by the SNMP RFCs, a network management system is comprised of several parts, as shown in Figure 8-4.

Figure 8-4   *The SNMP Management Model*

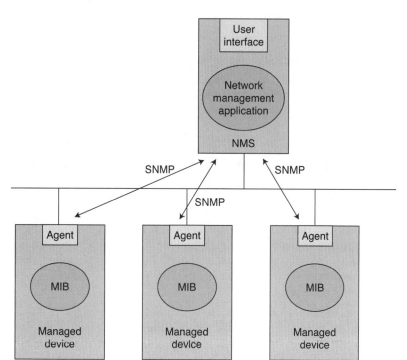

Network Elements

Network elements, also sometimes called managed devices, are hardware devices or systems such as switches, computers, routers, and terminal servers that are connected to the managed networks.

Agents

Agents are software modules that reside in network elements. They collect and store management information, such as the number of error cells received by a network element. Agents have access to information about the managed devices in which they run and make this information available to network management systems (NMSs) via SNMP. An agent might keep track of the following:

- ATM virtual circuits
- Error messages
- Number of bytes, cells, and packets in and out of attached interfaces

- Maximum output
- Queue length
- Number of broadcast messages sent and received
- Network interfaces status (up or down)
- Any other information that is useful for network management, including troubleshooting, statistical analysis, and alarm report

Managed Object

A *managed object* is any attribute of a network node that can be managed. For example, a list of currently active circuits in a particular switch is a managed object. Managed objects differ from variables, which are particular object instances within the managed object. Using this example, an object instance is a single active circuit in a particular switch. Managed objects can be scalar (defining a single object instance) or tabular (defining multiple, related instances).

Management Information Base

Management Information Base (MIB) is a collection of managed objects residing in a virtual information store. Collections of related managed objects are defined in specific MIB modules. All managed objects are contained in the MIB, which is essentially a database of objects. A MIB is depicted as a tree, with individual data items as leaves.

Object identifiers (OIDs) uniquely identify or name MIB objects in the tree. Object IDs are like telephone numbers—they are organized hierarchically with specific digits assigned by different organizations. Top-level MIB object identifiers are assigned by the International Organization for Standardization (ISO)/International Electrotechnical Commission (IEC). Lower-level object IDs are allocated by the associated organizations.

The current Internet-standard MIB, MIB-II, is defined in RFC 1213. These objects are grouped by protocol (including TCP, IP, User Datagram Protocol [UDP], SNMP, and others) and other categories, including system and interfaces. Several prominent branches of the MIB tree are shown in Figure 8-5. Figure 8-5 not only shows the logical name of the objects, it also shows their integer equivalents that are used by management software.

The MIB tree is extensible by virtue of experimental and private branches (not shown in Figure 8-5). For example, vendors can define their own private branches to include instances of their own products. MIBs that have not been standardized are typically positioned in the experimental branch.

Figure 8-5   *Branches of the Management Information Base Tree*

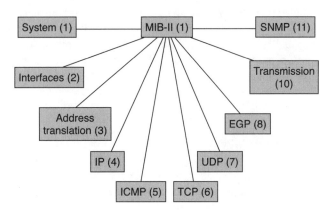

Syntax Notation

A *syntax notation* is a language used to describe a MIB's managed objects in a machine-independent format. Consistent use of a syntax notation allows different types of computers to share information. Internet management systems use a subset of the ISO's Open System Interconnection (OSI) Abstract Syntax Notation 1 (ASN.1) to define both the packets exchanged by the management protocol and the objects that are to be managed.

Structure of Management Information

The Structure of Management Information (SMI) defines the structure of the MIB and the rules for defining MIBs. The SMI allows the use of standard ASN.1 data types: integers, octet strings, and object identifiers. It also defines the following data types:

- **Counters**—Counters are positive integers that increase until they reach a maximum value, when they wrap back to 0. The total number of bytes received on an interface is an example of a counter.

- **Gauges**—Gauges are nonnegative integers that can increase or decrease, but that retain the maximum value reached. The length of an output packet queue (in packets) is an example of a gauge.

- **Time ticks**—Time ticks measure hundredths of a second since some event. The time since an interface entered its current state is an example of a time tick.

- **Opaque**—An opaque is an arbitrary encoding used to pass arbitrary information strings outside the strict data typing used by the SMI.

Network Management System

Network Management System (NMS), sometimes called consoles, execute management applications that monitor and control network elements. Physically, network management systems are usually engineering workstation-caliber computers with fast CPUs, megapixel color displays, substantial memory, and abundant disk space. At least one NMS must be present in each managed environment.

Parties

A *party* is a logical SNMPv2 entity (and SNMPv2 only) that can initiate or receive SNMPv2 communication. Each SNMPv2 party comprises a single, unique party identity; a logical network location; a single authentication protocol; and a single privacy protocol. SNMPv2 messages are communicated between two parties. An SNMPv2 entity can define multiple parties, each with different parameters. For example, different parties can use different authentication or privacy protocols.

Management Protocol

A *management protocol* is used to convey management information between agents and NMSs. SNMP is the Internet community's *de facto* standard management protocol.

SNMP Command Types

A NMS can control a managed device by sending a message requiring the managed device to change the value of one or more of its variables. Interactions between the NMS and the managed devices can be any of four different types of commands:

- **Reads**—To monitor managed devices, NMSs read variables maintained by the devices.

- **Writes**—To control managed devices, NMSs write variables stored within the managed devices.

- **Traversal operations**—NMSs use these operations to determine which variables a managed device supports and to sequentially gather information from variable tables (such as IP routing tables) in managed devices.

- **Traps**—Managed devices use traps to asynchronously report certain events to NMSs. The other three command types are initiated by the NMS, whereas a trap is generated by the managed device.

SNMP Operation

The SNMP protocol consists of several types of operations used to manipulate management information. These operations are shown in Figure 8-6.

Figure 8-6 *SNMP Operations*

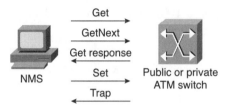

The following is a brief explanation of each operation:

- **Get**—Get retrieves specific management information. Get could be used to get the number of dropped packets by a particular interface, for instance.

- **GetNext**—GetNext is used to retrieve management information via traversal of the MIB. It allows the NMS to retrieve the next object instance from a table or a list within an agent. In SNMPv1, when an NMS wants to retrieve all elements of a table from an agent, it initiates a Get operation, followed by a series of GetNext operations. GetNext can be used to get the routing table of a router.

- **GetBulk (SNMPv2)**—The GetBulk operation was added to make it easier to acquire large amounts of related information without initiating repeated GetNext operations. GetBulk was designed to virtually eliminate the need for GetNext operations.

- **Set**—Set is used to alter management information. For example, it can be used to change configuration information, such as the IP address of a serial interface.

- **Trap**—Trap asynchronously informs the NMS of some event. Unlike the Get, GetNext, and Set operations, Trap does not elicit a response from the receiver. An example of a Trap event is when an ATM switch notifies the NMS that the switch's power supply has failed and that the switch is running on the backup power supply.

- **Inform (SNMPv2)**—The Inform operation was added to allow one NMS to send Trap information to another NMS. This feature can be useful in environments where management is decentralized, but major events should be reported to a central NMS.

The SNMP Message Format

SNMPv1 messages (packets) contain two parts. The first part contains the version and the community name, and the second part contains the actual SNMP protocol data unit (PDU). The version field is used to ensure that all network elements are running software based on the same SNMP version. The community name serves two functions. First, the community name defines an access environment for a set of NMSs using that community name. Second, because devices that do not know the proper community name are precluded from SNMPv1 operations, network managers have also used the community name as a weak form of authentication.

The second part of the SNMPv1 messages contains the actual SNMP PDU specifying the operation to be performed (Get, Set, and so on) and the object instances involved in the operation.

The SNMPv1 PDU message format is shown in Figure 8-7. All the fields are variable in length, as prescribed by the ASN.1 encoding rules.

Figure 8-7   *SNMPv1 PDU Message Format*

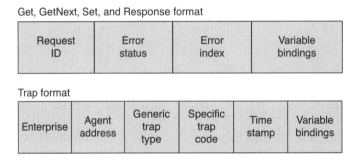

Get, GetNext, Set, and Response format

Request ID	Error status	Error index	Variable bindings

Trap format

Enterprise	Agent address	Generic trap type	Specific trap code	Time stamp	Variable bindings

SNMPv1 Get, GetNext, Response, and Set PDUs include a request ID, which associates requests with responses, and an error status, which indicates the error and the error type. Additionally, variable bindings, which comprise the data of an SNMPv1 PDU, are included. Each variable binding associates a particular variable with its current value (with the exception of Get and GetNext requests, for which the value is ignored).

Trap PDUs are slightly different from the Get, GetNext, Response, and Set PDUs. Trap PDUs include an enterprise identifier, which identifies the type of device sending the Trap; an agent address, which specifies the address of the object generating the Trap; a generic Trap type; and a specific Trap code. The time stamp provides the amount of time that has elapsed between the last network reinitialization and generation of this Trap. Variable bindings provide a list of variables containing interesting information about the Trap.

Like SNMPv1 messages, SNMPv2 messages contain two parts. The second part of the SNMPv2 message (the PDU) is virtually identical to that of an SNMPv1 message. The first part of the SNMPv2 message contains the majority of the differences between SNMPv1 and SNMPv2.

To simplify PDU processing, all SNMPv2 operations except the GetBulk operation use the same PDU format as SNMPv1. The PDU format is used by the Get, GetNext, Set,

Response, and Trap operations, as well as the new Inform operation. In addition to the fields in the SNMPv1 PDU, the SNMPv2 PDU includes a PDU type field. The PDU type identifies the SNMP operation included in the message (Get, GetNext, Set, Response, or Trap).

The GetBulk request operation uses the PDU format shown in Figure 8-8.

Figure 8-8   *SNMPv2 GetBulk Message Format*

PDU type	Request ID	Nonrepeaters	Max-repetitions	Variable bindings

In the GetBulk operation, the PDU type, the request ID, and the variable bindings fields all serve the same function as the PDU for Get, GetNext, Set, Response, and Trap operations. Nonrepeaters specify the number of variables in the variable bindings list for which a single lexicographic successor is to be returned. Max-repetitions specify the number of lexicographic successors to be returned for the remaining variables in the variable bindings list.

Originally, SNMPv1 specified that SNMP should operate over the User Datagram Protocol (UDP) and IP. SNMPv2 defines implementations of SNMP over other transport protocols, including OSI Connectionless Network Protocol (CLNP), AppleTalk Datagram Delivery Protocol (DDP), and Novell Internet Packet Exchange (IPX). Multiprotocol support has made SNMP the protocol of choice for many vendors, regardless of network protocol.

SNMPv2 Security

The first part of a SNMPv2 message is often called a *wrapper*. The wrapper includes authentication and privacy information in the form of destination and source parties. A party includes the specification of both an authentication and a privacy protocol. In addition to a destination and a source party, the wrapper includes a context. A context specifies the managed objects visible to an operation.

The authentication protocol is designed to reliably identify the integrity of the originating SNMPv2 party. It consists of authentication information required to support the authentication protocol used. The privacy protocol is designed to protect information within the SNMPv2 message from disclosure. Only authenticated messages can be protected from disclosure. In other words, authentication is required for privacy.

The SNMPv2 specifications discuss two primary security protocols: one for authentication and one for privacy. These protocols are the Digest Authentication Protocol and the Symmetric Privacy Protocol.

The *Digest Authentication Protocol* verifies that the message received is the same one that was sent. Data integrity is protected using a 128-bit message digest calculated according to the Message Digest 5 (MD5) algorithm. The digest is calculated at the sender and is enclosed with the SNMPv2 message. The receiver verifies the digest. A secret value, known only to the sender and the receiver, is prefixed to the message. After the digest is used to verify message integrity, the secret value is used to verify the message's origin.

To help ensure message privacy, the *Symmetric Privacy Protocol* uses a secret encryption key known only to the sender and the receiver. Before the message is authenticated, this protocol uses the Data Encryption Standard (DES) algorithm to effect privacy. DES is a documented National Institute of Standards and Technology (NIST) and American National Standards Institute (ANSI) standard.

Summary

IP addressing is important for WAN switch integration into the LAN to provide network management and initial integration. IP connectivity provides the initial connections required to provision the switch so that inband management can also be used in the future. An IP address includes the network, the subnet (if applicable), and the host addresses. Class addressing is the original standard defined by the Internet community, but due to a shortage of address space, addresses are no longer assigned using the class model. Some environments still have class requirement, so issues related to class-based networks are still very important to know.

Classless interdomain routing (CIDR) is the current standard and the best practice for IP addressing. Due to CIDR, VLSM has become very popular—it allows organizations to exercise much more flexibility in address assignment.

Network management is often based upon the SNMP protocol. Many network devices and practically all enterprise management software support versions 1 and 2 of SNMP. SNMP can be used to gather information as well as to configure network devices. Version 2 adds security measures because version 1 is not considered secure enough for many environments.

Review Questions

The following questions test your retention of the material presented in this chapter. You can find the answers to the Review Questions in Appendix A, "Answers to Review Questions."

1 How many bits are assigned to the network in a Class C network?

  A. 6

  B. 8

  C. 24

  D. 32

2 What Class A network is reserved for loopback?

  A. 10.0.0.0

  B. 127.0.0.0

  C. 1.0.0.0

  D. 192.168.1.0

3 How many classes does CIDR support?

  A. 3

  B. 4

  C. None

  D. 8

4 What does SNMP stand for?

  A. Slow Node Management Protocol

  B. Simple Node Management Protocol

  C. Simple Network Management Protocol

  D. Synchronous Network Management Protocols

5 Which SNMP operation allows objects to be configured?

  A. Write

  B. Read

  C. SNMP Set

  D. SNMP Write

6 What mechanism allows a node to report problems to the NMS?

  A. Trap

  B. Get

  C. SNMP Set

  D. Not supported with SNMP

P A R T II

Installation of Cisco WAN Switches

CHAPTER 9

Cisco WAN Switch Product Overview

Chapters 1 through 8 covered general data, communication, and network principals that are required to support Cisco WAN switches and to integrate Cisco WAN switches into wide-area networks (WANs) and local-area networks (LANs). This chapter introduces the Cisco WAN switch product line, which is the focus of the second part of this book. In addition to the product overview, Part II, "Installation of Cisco WAN Switches," covers installation and configuration, system troubleshooting, and network integration. Step-by-step instructions are provided where appropriate, and command syntax and parameters used for installation, configuration, troubleshooting, and networking are covered.

The key features of the individual Cisco WAN switch devices, as well as user services and management software, are covered in this chapter.

This chapter includes the following sections:

- Cisco WAN Switch Product Family
- Service Types
- Advanced Network Features Supported by Cisco WAN Switches
- Cisco WAN Switch Network Topologies
- Network Management
- Cisco WAN Manager
- Summary
- Review Questions

Cisco WAN Switch Product Family

The current Cisco WAN switch product range that this book covers consists of the following families of WAN switches:

- IGX 8400 series
- BPX 8600 series
- MGX 8850 edge switch
- MGX 8220 edge concentrator

As mentioned, hardware installation and integration of these switches is covered in this part, as are the appropriate associated commands. The commands covered later in the book are specific to the particular switch being covered. Additionally, specific hardware installation and configuration for each of the switches is covered. Finally, the chapters in this part discuss network interfaces supported, management module specification, and system integration issues, such as redundancy and software configuration and updates.

IGX 8400 Series

The IGX 8400 series comprises three models: IGX 8410, IGX 8420, and IGX 8430, with 8, 16, and 32 card slots, respectively. Figure 9-1 shows these models. Each IGX system can be rack-mounted; the IGX 8420 switch is also available as a standalone unit.

IGX switches provide access for multiple user services, including voice, data, Frame Relay, and ATM. IGX switches can also support a backbone network interconnected by trunks ranging in speeds from 256 kbps to OC-3/STM-1.

Figure 9-1   *IGX 8400 Series*

The Cisco IGX switch uses a 1.2-Gbps redundant cellbus to switch cells between optionally redundant user and trunk interface modules. A wide range of service modules offers various port densities for ATM, Frame Relay, voice, and circuit data interfaces. (In addition, IGX switch technology is integrated in the Cisco 3810 switch. The 3810 is often used to extend the backbone to a branch location.)

IGX systems support trunk speeds from 256 kbps to OC-3/STM-1. The IGX switch is a midplane design with front cards that perform processing and switching functions, and back cards that provide interfaces for physical connectivity and adaptation function. This design architecture enables most system maintenance to be performed at the front cards, without disconnecting interface cables. Hardware, firmware, and software are designed for maximum service availability during maintenance and upgrades: all user and trunk interface modules can be configured redundantly to achieve the required level of node reliability, and all cards are hot-swappable.

In enterprise WANs, the IGX switch can form the network core, connecting headquarters and regional sites. It also can be used to concentrate traffic from geographically dispersed branch offices. Service providers often deploy IGX switches to deliver multiple services on a single platform in areas where traffic volumes or service demands do not justify placement of a higher-capacity WAN switch, such as a BPX 8600 series switch. IGX nodes also can be configured to operate in feeder mode to another IGX or a BPX node.

BPX 8600 Series

This book covers two models of the BPX 8600 series: BPX 8620 and BPX 8650. The BPX 8620 switch is a single-rack chassis with 15 card slots and is optimized for broadband ATM services and for operation as a backbone ATM switch. Port and trunk interfaces range from E3/DS-3 to OC-12/STM-4.

The BPX 8650 switch expands the capabilities of the BPX 8620 through the inclusion of a Label Switch Controller (LSC). The LSC provides Layer 3 routing services and enables Multiprotocol Label Switching (MPLS), an open standard protocol that provides Layer 3 services and a Virtual Private Networks (VPNs) solution on top of Layer 2 ATM and Frame Relay. Today, LSC is an external 7200 IOS router connected to the BPX switch via an ATM interface. In the future, the LSC functionality will be provided via a native BPX switch card. The BPX 8600 series switch offers up to 19.2 Gbps of high-throughput switching.

The BPX node consists of a single shelf with 15 card slots. Three of these slots are reserved for common equipment cards, and the other 12 are general-purpose slots used for network trunk cards or service interface cards. Each of the 12 slots has access to 800 Mbps (with the BCC-32 and the BCC-3-32 broadband controller cards) or 1600 Mbps (with the BCC-4V) of dedicated bandwidth. The cards are provided in sets, consisting of a front card and an associated back card. The BPX node can be mounted in a Cisco rack enclosure, which provides mounting for co-located MGX interface shelves.

The BPX node provides DS-3, E3, OC-3/STM-1, and OC-12/STM-4 port and trunk interfaces.

MGX 8850 Edge Switch

The MGX 8850 edge switch shown in Figure 9-2 provides a variety of narrowband (less than 2 Mbps) and high-speed (up to E3/DS-3) interfaces into an ATM backbone network. The MGX 8850 is capable of switching traffic between service modules, or between a service module and the backbone trunk. In future releases, the MGX 8850 will support multiple trunk interfaces and will be capable of switching between these trunks.

Figure 9-2   *MGX 8850 Edge Switch*

The MGX 8850 switch has two card shelves, which are referred to as upper and lower shelves (bays), and can have up to 32 card slots. These are termed *single-height slots* and are designed to accommodate many of the existing card module sets from the MGX 8220. Some slot positions are reserved for double-height cards. For example, slot 7 on the upper shelf and slot 23 on the lower shelf form one of the reserved double-height slots. In total,

24 single-height or up to 12 double-height slots are available for service modules. Double-height cards are unique to the MGX 8850 in the MGX series. Dividers must be removed from slot pairs 1 to 2, 3 to 4, 5 to 6, 9 to 10, 11 to 12, or 13 to 14 for the addition of double-height cards.

The MGX 8850 edge switch is a recent addition to the Cisco WAN switching product range. This device builds on the capabilities of the MGX 8220 edge concentrator by supporting local switching and, in future releases, remote switching. This is in addition to the traditional feeder shelf function performed by the MGX 8220 concentrator.

The MGX 8850 has two card shelves, or bays, each of which consists of 16 slots. Service module interfaces range from narrowband (T1/E1) to broadband (E3/DS-3). Available trunk interfaces are E3, DS-3, OC-3/STM-1, and OC-12/STM-4.

The MGX 8850 edge switch is designed for carrier-class reliability. Every system component can be configured for full redundancy, and all MGX 8850 switch controller modules can be removed and reinserted without impacting service delivery or affecting the performance of other modules. Background diagnostics continually monitor switch functions on active as well as standby modules, ensuring fault-tolerant operation.

MGX 8220 Edge Concentrator

The MGX 8220 edge concentrator was formerly named the AXIS shelf. The MGX 8820 provides a variety of interfaces into an ATM backbone network. The MGX 8220 is not capable of switching traffic between service modules, and it has a single backbone trunk.

The MGX 8220 edge concentrator is an interface shelf (sometimes called a feeder shelf) for the BPX 8600 switch. It provides various narrowband and/or broadband ATM and non-ATM service interfaces without consuming BPX switch slots.

In addition, the MGX 8220 edge concentrator can operate as a standalone unit that aggregates traffic for transmission to and from an ATM network.

To support the various interfaces and services, two types of cards can be installed in the MGX shelf: core group cards and service interface cards.

Core group cards provide shelf control, broadband network connections, and interface card redundancy. Service interface cards provide Frame Relay, ATM, and circuit emulation connections.

The MGX 8220 edge concentrator is a self-contained rack-mountable unit. The shelf chassis has 16 slots; each slot can accommodate a front and a back card. Six slots are reserved for common equipment modules; the other 10 slots are available for any service (I/O) module.

Service modules provide a range of interfaces from T1/E1 to E3/DS-3, for a variety of different service types. The single trunk interface to the BPX 8600 or other ATM switch can be E3, DS-3, or OC-3/STM-1.

A 1:1 redundancy is supported for the core modules, and 1:N redundancy is supported for the service modules (where N is the number of modules used for redundancy, which may not be more than the number of free slots for service modules).

Service Types

IGX, BPX, and MGX nodes support a variety of traffic connections on either permanent or switched virtual circuits (PVCs or SVCs), as summarized in Table 9-1. Each connection is defined as a particular service type, with further parameters, such as data rate, compression, traffic policing, and management characteristics.

Table 9-1 *Supported Traffic Services*

Service Type	IGX	BPX	MGX 8850	MGX 8220
Synchronous Data Stream	X			
Frame Relay	X		X	X
Circuit emulation			X	X
ATM constant bit rate (CBR)	X	X	X	X
ATM variable bit rate (VBR), nonreal time	X	X	X	X
ATM variable bit rate (VBR), real time	X	X		
ATM standards–based available bit rate (ABR)	X	X		
ATM ForeSight available bit rate (ABR)	X	X	X	X
ATM unspecified bit rate (UBR)	X	X	X	X
ATM-Frame Relay	X	X	X	X
Inverse Multiplexing for ATM (IMA)	X		X	X

The remainder of this section provides a review of the service types in Table 9-1.

Voice

As discussed in Chapter 5, "Digital Voice Technical Concepts and Considerations," digitized voice is supported by IGX. Bandwidth optimization, including compression and silence suppression/voice activity detection (VAD), and conversion from a-law to mu-law also are supported.

Data

Synchronous data streams of up to 1.3 Mbps may be transported between IGX nodes. A variety of physical interfaces are provided on the low- and high-speed data modules, enabling the transparent interconnection of many user devices, including cluster controllers, front-end processors, and host gateways.

Frame Relay

IGX and MGX nodes provide standards-based Frame Relay services at port speeds up to E1 rate (2.048 Mbps). The MGX 8220 supports High-Speed Serial Interface for Frame Relay. Additionally, the MGX 8850 node provides broadband E3, DS-3, and High-Speed Serial Interface (HSSI) interfaces for Frame Relay. Both User-Network Interface (UNI) and Network-to-Network Interface (NNI) traffic are supported, allowing connection to user customer premises equipment (CPE) and carrier Frame Relay networks. Refer to Chapter 6, "Frame Relay," for a review of Frame Relay.

Circuit Emulation

MGX nodes support circuit emulation services (CESs), which convert circuit data into ATM cells using ATM adaptation layer 1 (AAL1). All data on the line, including signaling and framing, is encapsulated into ATM cells for transport across the ATM backbone network as point-to-point constant bit rate (CBR) traffic.

Asynchronous Transfer Mode

As shown in Table 9-1, the following ATM services are supported:

- **Constant bit rate (CBR)**—CBR traffic is used for time-dependent, constant-rate traffic, such as uncompressed voice, video, or synchronous data. ATM specifications make no allowances to accommodate bursting on CBR connections.

- **Variable bit rate (VBR)**—VBR traffic is used for bursty traffic that may have a time dependency, such as compressed voice, video, or synchronous data. Traffic is permitted to burst within set limitations.

  IGX and BPX nodes will support real-time VBR and nonreal-time VBR services on BXM, ASI, and UXM lines with Release 9.2 of the system software.

- **Available bit rate (ABR)**—ABR traffic is a variation on VBR and is most commonly used for LAN-WAN services, such as router traffic. ABR connections use either a standards-defined mechanism or the ForeSight feature for congestion avoidance, which increases or decreases the traffic rate, depending on network availability.

- **Unspecified bit rate (UBR)**—UBR traffic is not offered a guaranteed service rate. If there is congestion or no available bandwidth, a UBR connection is not given bandwidth in the network. UBR connections are used for variable-rate traffic that is tolerant of zero-transmission periods.

ATM-Frame Relay

All the products support ATM-Frame Relay. However, it is important to note that the BPX has been designed for the core switching, whereas Frame Relay and ATM access is provided at the edge by the MGX (or IGX). Therefore, the BPX node does not participate in the conversion of ATM traffic to Frame Relay traffic. The BPX simply transports the ATM cells as required to and from the other nodes; therefore, the Frame Relay network is transparent to the BPX node.

Inverse Multiplexing for ATM

Inverse Multiplexing for ATM (IMA) takes cells from a broadband ATM line (E3/DS-3) and transmits the cells on a cell-by-cell basis across multiple narrowband (T1/E1) lines. IMA enables ATM traffic to be carried over less expensive facilities, while also providing resiliency on the narrowband lines.

Figure 9-3 shows an example topology with an IGX, a BPX, an MGX 8220, and an MGX 8850 and with various services that have been covered up to this point.

Figure 9-3   *Wide-Area Network Using Cisco Switches*

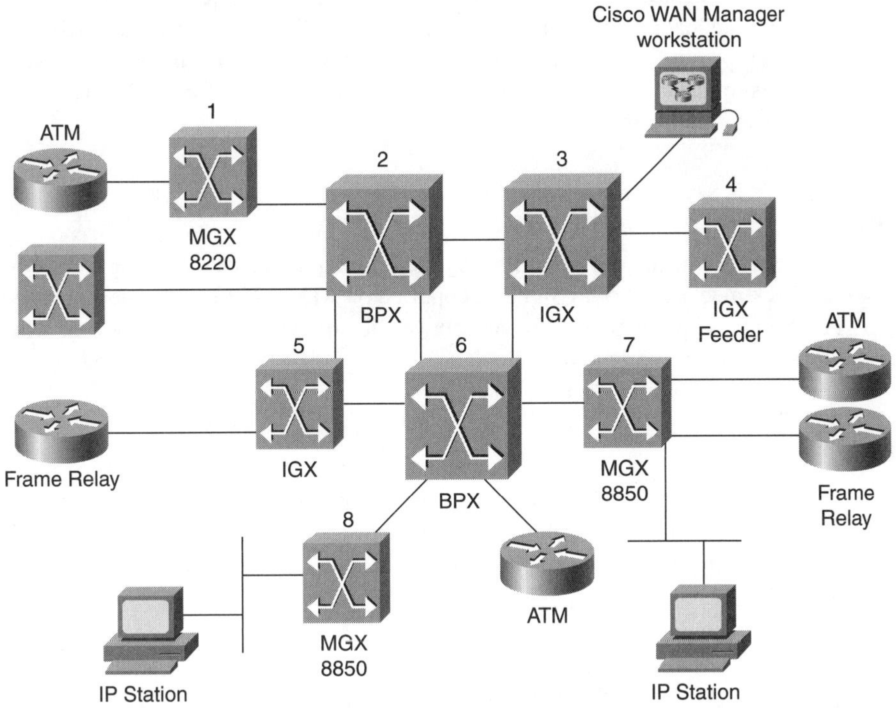

Advanced Network Features Supported by Cisco WAN Switches

In addition to standards-based features required of the various services supported, Cisco WAN switches support additional, proprietary features that ensure that WAN switches provide the services necessary to stay very competitive in the WAN switch market. These features include AutoRoute, OptiClass, ForeSight, and FairShare.

AutoRoute

The AutoRoute feature supports automatic connection routing. When a connection is first added to the network, or in the event of network trunk failure, the initiating node automatically determines the best available path through the network for the connection.

OptiClass

OptiClass is an independent queue servicing a variety of traffic types, including IGX native traffic (voice, data, and Frame Relay) and ATM traffic (CBR, VBR, and ABR/UBR). OptiClass prevents dissimilar services from competing for bandwidth on network trunks. OptiClass bypasses the four broad classes of services defined for ATM and offers 32 classes of service.

ForeSight

Congestion avoidance is performed by the ForeSight mechanism using a closed-loop feedback mechanism. ForeSight is supported on ATM ABR and Frame Relay services. ForeSight also permits users to burst above CIR for extended periods of time when there is unused network bandwidth available.

FairShare

FairShare provides per-VC queue management on ingress. To guarantee a minimum throughput for each connection, ingress queues are used for Frame Relay and ABR connections to prevent one connection from overrunning the other connections on the same interface.

Cisco WAN Switch Network Topologies

Cisco switched WAN topologies are classified as one of the following:

- Flat
- Tiered
- Structured

This classification is used both to integrate additional nodes and to manage the network. Each topology requires closer examination.

Flat

A flat network consists of nodes attached to each other using trunks. All nodes are aware of each other and can communicate with the entire network. This book primarily focuses on flat network topologies. An example flat network is shown in Figure 9-4.

Figure 9-4   *Flat WAN Network*

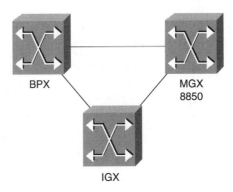

Tiered

A tiered network consists of routing nodes and interface shelves (feeder nodes). Routing nodes behave like nodes in a flat network. Interface shelves are single-trunk devices and do not route or switch traffic; instead, they interface with user devices and forward all the traffic to the attached routing node. Interface shelves do not have contact with other network nodes. IGX and MGX 8850 nodes may be configured as either routing nodes or interface shelves; a BPX node is always a routing node. An MGX 8220 edge concentrator is always an interface shelf. An example of a tiered network is shown in Figure 9-5. The MGX 8850s are acting as an interface shelf and have contact only with the BPX, not the IGX.

Figure 9-5   *Tiered WAN Network*

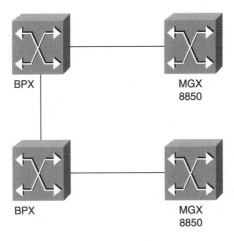

Structured

A structured network is a large network comprising multiple flat or tiered networks called *domains*. Each domain is a subnetwork and attaches to other domains through nodes identified as junction nodes. Junction nodes limit capabilities and are responsible for communication across domains. Non-junction nodes have limited contact with nodes beyond the local domain.

Tiered and structured networks are not supported in all software releases. Tiered networks were introduced in Release 8.1 system software.

Structured networks were introduced in Release 6.3 system software, but because they are not supported after Release 7.3 system software, they are not shown here.

Network Management

Switched WAN management requires an understanding of the topologies just covered, as well as an understanding of the network-management principles covered in Chapter 8, "IP Addressing and Network Management." The remainder of this chapter examines some of the specifics involved in managing WAN switches.

Command-Line Interface

A command-line interface (CLI) allows the network manager to enter commands that the switch understands. The CLI is typically required to initially configure WAN switches. Multiple command-line access allows several network administrators to access the same node at once. CLI access is available through the following methods:

- Control and auxiliary ports on IGX and BPX nodes, control port on the MGX 8850 switch, or maintenance port on the MGX 8220 concentrator. Serial EIA/TIA-232 interfaces provide access using a VT100 terminal or a PC with terminal emulation.

- The maintenance port on the MGX 8850 switch, or the control port on the MGX 8220 concentrator. A Serial Line Internet Protocol (SLIP) port enables access through Telnet from a PC running SLIP.

- The LAN. All nodes have an Ethernet attachment unit interface (AUI) operating at 10 Mbps that enables access to the CLI using Telnet from a LAN-attached PC or workstation. Capability for multiple Telnet sessions is built in.

- The virtual terminal. When node-to-node communication has been established via the network trunking, and when access to one node has been accomplished, a virtual terminal (VT) function can be used to access other nodes across the trunks. Multiple VT sessions (up to 6) are an optional feature. VT is not supported on MGX nodes.

- With LAN access at one node in the network, other nodes can be accessed in-band via Telnet using the optionally configurable IP Relay addressing, which creates an IP relay or management network within the WAN.

Cisco WAN Manager and CiscoView can also be used to manage the network and are typically the interface of choice in complicated networks. CiscoView can act as a front end to Cisco WAN Manager.

Cisco WAN Manager

The Cisco WAN Manager (formerly known as StrataView Plus) is a network- and element-management system that addresses operations, maintenance, and management of multiservice networks. Core features include topology management via real-time topology displays, connection-management graphical user interface (GUI-based provisioning of end-to-end connections), performance management (for real-time and historical statistics data collection), and element management (for configuration and monitoring of network elements). Cisco WAN Manager and CiscoView run on Sun Solaris and IBM AIX systems.

Topology Management

The Cisco WAN Manager automatically discovers the network and displays a graphical topology map. Standalone topology map displays as well as HP OpenView, CiscoWorks, and IBM NetView maps are supported. Multicolored map displays are updated in real time, in response to events occurring in the network, such as node alarms or trunk failure, giving the network manager both a global view of the network and local problem reporting.

Connection Management

The Cisco WAN Manager provides a GUI to provision connections in the wide-area multiservice network. Connection templates also are available to minimize the effort required for provisioning large numbers of connections. ATM, Frame Relay, ATM-Frame Relay internetworking, voice, and legacy data connections are supported.

Performance and Accounting Data Management

The Statistics Collection Manager application is used to program the network elements with the types of statistics to be collected and the statistics collection policies to be used. Historical performance data is stored in an Informix relational database that can be accessed using the built-in Report Generator application, or by Structured Query Language (SQL).

The Report Generator application queries the SQL database and produces performance and utilization reports in a wide selection of graphical formats. The reports also can be converted to ASCII text file or other spreadsheet formats.

Element Management

As mentioned, Cisco WAN Manager integrates with CiscoView, which provides graphical front and back panel displays, extensive equipment configuration capabilities, and real-time monitoring and troubleshooting features.

Events from the network also can be automatically forwarded to the HP OpenView or IBM NetView event browser. Searching, sorting, and filtering operations can be performed, and events can be tied to extensible actions—for example, you could page someone when a certain type of Simple Network Management Protocol (SNMP) trap is received.

The WAN Manager also supports software and firmware download and distribution using the TFTP protocol. Node configuration information can be downloaded and restored if a node fails.

Summary

The IGX, BPX, MGX 8550, and MGX 8220 switches offer narrowband and broadband services, including serial, Frame Relay, and ATM services. Cisco WANs are defined as flat, tiered, and structured, and can be managed using the CLI or Cisco WAN manager. The CLI can be accessed via local and LAN ports, as well as IP relays through other switches.

Review Questions

The following questions test your retention of the material presented in this chapter. You can find the answers to the Review Questions in Appendix A, "Answers to Review Questions."

1 What are the two principal functions of the IGX node?

A. A multiservice concentrator

B. A time-division multiplexer

C. A Frame Relay access device

D. A wide-area node for backbone applications

2   What is a BPX node?

A. An ATM switch

B. An ATM access device

C. A multiprotocol access device

D. A multiprotocol packet switch

3   Which of the following best describes the MGX 8220 edge concentrator?

A. A multiprotocol router

B. An ATM-only access device

C. A multiservice access device

D. An ATM switch with ATM interfaces

E. An ATM switch with multiservice interfaces

4   Which of the following best describes the MGX 8850 edge switch?

A. A multiprotocol router

B. An ATM-only access device

C. A multiservice access device

D. An ATM switch with ATM interfaces

E. An ATM switch with multiservice interfaces

5   Which one of the following is not an IGX function?

A. Supports analog voice

B. Supports Frame Relay

C. Can be a feeder node for a BPX node

D. Can be a feeder node for another IGX node

E. Supports CBR, VBR, and ABR ATM traffic

6   Which three of the following functions does the BPX node perform?

A. Switches ATM cells

B. Can be a feeder node in a tiered network

C. Segments and reassembles Frame Relay frames

D. Supports CBR, VBR, ABR, and UBR ATM traffic

E. Communicates with a Cisco WAN Manager network-management station

7 Which two of the following functions do both MGX devices perform?

A. Route ATM traffic

B. Perform ADPCM voice compression

C. Provide a feeder function to an IGX routing node

D. Segment and reassemble Frame Relay traffic into ATM cells

E. Communicate with a Cisco WAN Manager network management station

8 Match the service type in the table with its definition.

A. ATM cells that carry Frame Relay traffic

B. Traffic without a service guarantee

C. Serial bit stream up to 1.344 Mbps

D. Time-dependent, variable-rate, traffic-compressed voice, data, and video

E. Variable-rate traffic with congestion avoidance-router LAN-WAN traffic

F. Time-dependent, constant-rate, traffic-uncompressed voice, data, and video

Service Type	Definition
CBR	
VBR-rt	
ABR	
UBR	
ATM-Frame Relay	
Synchronous data	

9 Match the networking feature in the table with its definition.

A. Routing and rerouting of network connections

B. Per-PVC ingress queuing for Frame Relay and ABR connections

C. A closed-loop congestion-avoidance mechanism used on Frame Relay and ABR connections

D. Per-traffic type queuing to prevent unlike traffic types from competing for trunk bandwidth

Networking Feature	Definition
AutoRoute	
OptiClass	
ForeSight	
FairShare	

10 Match the network type in the table with its definition.

A. A network of routing and feeder nodes

B. A large network made up of multiple domains

C. A network of peer nodes that communicate with all other nodes

Network type	Definition
Flat	
Tiered	
Structured	

11 Which two of the following are not a function of the Cisco WAN Manager?

A. Provisioning user services

B. Performing network monitoring of cell payload

C. Collecting statistics from a single node or network-wide

D. Downloading software and firmware images to network nodes

E. Providing SNMP management support for Cisco routers and LAN switches

F. Providing real-time indication of network alarms on the topology map

CHAPTER 10

Installing IGX 8400 Switches

Chapter 9, "Cisco WAN Switch Product Overview," introduces Cisco WAN switches, including the IGX 8400 switches. This chapter builds on that by providing detailed information on the physical, mechanical, and electrical installation of the IGX 8400 series switches. A functional description is also provided for each of the card module sets supported with system software Release 9.2.

This chapter includes the following sections:

- IGX Hardware Overview
- IGX 8410 Installation
- Power Considerations—IGX
- Installing the IGX 8420/8430
- Card Module Installation
- Control Modules Card Group
- Attaching IGX System Peripherals
- Trunk Modules Card Group
- Services Modules Card Group
- Frame Trunk Module Card Module
- Voice Card Group
- Serial Data Card Group
- ATM Service Card Module
- Frame Relay Card Group
- Summary
- Review Questions

IGX Hardware Overview

Currently, three types of IGX chassis exist:

- IGX 8410
- IGX 8420
- IGX 8430

The primary difference is in the number of card slots available, as shown in Table 10-1.

Table 10-1 *IGX Chassis and Number of Card Slots*

IGX Model	Number of Slots
8410	8
8420	16
8430	32

Node and card functionality, bus architecture, throughput, and management are identical among the three node types, but cooling and power distribution might vary.

Components

IGX chassis' can be grouped into two types: single-shelf (8 and 16 slots, IGX 8410 and 8420, respectively) and two-shelf (32 slots, IGX 8430).

The single-shelf models contain the following:

- One 8-slot card shelf, or one 16-slot card shelf, depending on the model
- A backplane for plugging in the front and back cards
- A fan tray with four or six fans
- An exhaust plenum
- Power connections
- An optional AC power tray that holds up to four (8-slot) or six (16-slot) power supplies

The IGX 8430 (two-shelf) chassis differs from the IGX 8410 and IGX 8420 in the following respects:

- Two 16-slot card shelves
- Two front doors with tool-operated latches
- Two backplanes into which plug the front and back cards
- A main (lower) fan tray with six fans
- A booster (upper) fan tray

- Power connections for each shelf
- An optional AC power tray that holds up to six power supplies

System status LEDs are visible on all IGX nodes with the front door open or closed, and indicate the current node alarm status, as shown in Table 10-2.

Table 10-2   *System Status LEDs*

Alarm	Status
Green	Operational (no alarm)
Yellow	1+ minor alarm(s), 0 major alarms
Red	1+ major alarm(s), possible minor alarms

Power Considerations

The IGX power supply is a –48V DC supply that provides power to all card modules in the nodes. All installed power supplies share the total load and adjust for removed power supplies, allowing for removal of power supplies without disrupting service as long as minimal power requirements are met. The following list summarizes the power considerations:

- **DC power**—DC power does not require a separate power tray or power supplies. A DC Power Entry Module (PEM) is installed in the node, and the DC input is directly wired to the PEM.
- **AC power**—AC power may be used to power an IGX node. The AC power supplies require an AC power tray to hold the supplies. The IGX 8430 and IGX 8420 AC power tray is a separate shelf installed below the node fan assembly that holds up to six power supplies. The IGX 8410 AC power tray is installed vertically next to the card shelf.

The DC output from the AC power tray is plugged into the DC PEM that is installed on the right side of the back card shelf. All necessary PEM internal wiring and installation are completed at the factory.

AC input between 180V and 264V is supported.

System Bus Backplane

The system bus backplane on the IGX node supports the following four buses:

- **Cellbus**—The cellbus consists of four 256-Mbps paths referred to as *lanes*. Each lane operates as a time-division multiplexed (TDM) bus. The cellbus is used by all cards except the ARM, and it transports FastPackets or ATM cells from one card to another. Only data transfers between two Universal Switching Module (UXM) cards use ATM cells on the cellbus; all other transfers use FastPackets, even when one of the cards involved is a UXM. ATM transfers (UXM to UXM) use all four cellbus lanes, whereas FastPackets use a single lane. A fifth cellbus lane is available as a redundant standby in case an active lane fails.

- **Control bus**—The Nodal Processor Module (NPM) uses the control bus to configure and to communicate with all the other cards in the node.

- **Timing bus**—The timing bus distributes synchronization signals to all cards in the node.

- **Power bus**—The power bus provides –48V DC and ground to all cards in the node.

Card Module Sets

The IGX card module sets, like the BPX model, consist of a front card and a back card. In general, the front card contains the functional intelligence of the card set, resident in the firmware. The back typically is concerned with physical-layer and electrical interfacing to the attached customer equipment or to the carrier trunk equipment.

Both front cards and back cards have faceplates with indicator LEDs; some front cards have push-button controls. In addition, back card faceplates have the cable connectors. In slots where no back card exists, a blank faceplate must be present to minimize electromagnetic interference (EMI) and radio frequency interference (RFI), and to ensure correct airflow to avoid heat problems.

Different card sets have different arrangements of LED indicators, which provide a visual means of identifying operational status and failure conditions. The LEDs for particular card sets are discussed later in this chapter; however, most front and back card faceplates include at least a green Active LED and a red Fail LED.

The backplane sits in the upper part of the card cage and connects up to 16 front cards. Figure 10-1 shows an IGX 8420 backplane. Except for having eight fewer card slots, the IGX 8410 card cage looks the same as the IGX 8420 backplane.

The system bus resides beneath the NPM slots at the left. Also shown in Figure 10-1 are the card guides in the front and the rear. Each front card plugs into the backplane at the upper connector. In addition to the physical connectors for the cards, the backplane also contains the system bus.

The IGX 8410 backplane has eight 216-pin connectors. Each IGX 8420/8430 backplane has sixteen 216-pin connectors and occupies more than half the height of the card cages.

In the IGX 8430 node, the upper and lower card cages are slightly different. The upper card cage has a utility bus beneath the backplane for the NPMs and the System Clock Module (SCM). The lower card cage in the IGX 8430 node has a backplane with no utility bus because only service cards exist on the lower shelf.

Some IGX card sets are created from hardware originally designed for the now-discontinued IPX switch. These IGX front cards consist of an IPX front card, an Adapter Card Module (ACM), and a new faceplate. These cards are listed in Table 10-3.

Figure 10-1 *IGX Backplane*

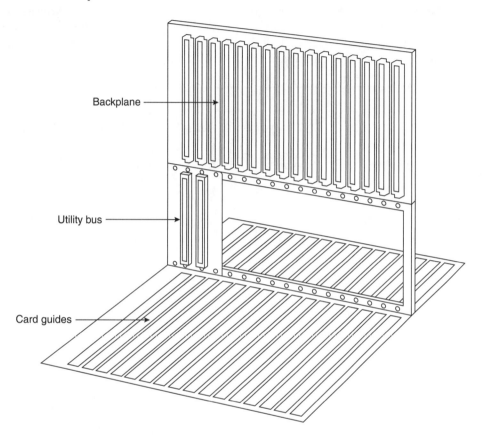

Table 10-3 *IPX Legacy Cards Supported on IGX*

IGX Back Card	IPX Front Card
Network Trunk Module (NTM)	IPX Network Trunk Card (NTC)
Broadband Trunk Module (BTM)	IPX ATM Internetworking Trunk (AIT)
FastPAD Trunk Module (FTM)	IPX FastPAD Trunk Card (FTC)
Channelized Voice Module (CVM)	IPX Channelized Data PAD (SDP)
Low-Speed Data Module (LDM)	IPX Low-Speed Data PAD (LDP)
Frame Relay Module (FRM)	IPX Frame Relay PAD (FRP)

One primary difference between the IGX node and the IPX node, initially, is the system backplane. The ACM, shown in Figure 10-2, creates the correct interface between the IPX front card connectors and the IGX system backplane connectors. New card modules, such as the UXM, are designed exclusively for the IGX to take advantage of its higher-speed system bus and ATM capabilities.

Figure 10-2 *Card Architecture with ACM*

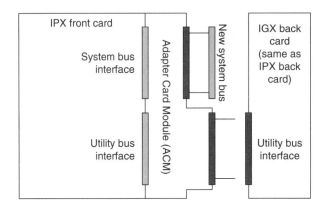

An overview of IGX card groups is shown in Figure 10-3.

Figure 10-3 *IGX Card Groups*

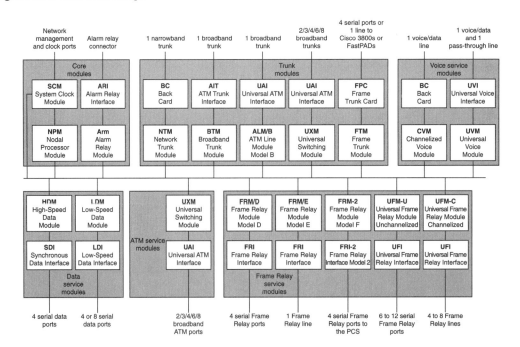

A brief summary of the modules in Figure 10-3 follows:

- **Nodal Processor Module**—The Nodal Processor Module (NPM) is the central processor for the IGX node and stores system software and all configuration information. The NPM also communicates with network management platforms.

- **Alarm Relay Module**—The Alarm Relay Module (ARM) is an optional card group that provides a visual indication of an alarm status on the node. The ARM includes a set of relays that can be used to signal a node or network alarm condition to an external apparatus.

- **Network Trunk Module**—The Network Trunk Module (NTM) supports a single T1, E1, Y1, or subrate (X.21, V.35, EIA/TIA-449) FastPacket trunk.

- **Broadband Trunk Module**—The Broadband Trunk Module (BTM) supports a single E1, E2, T3, E3, or High-Speed Serial Interface (HSSI) ATM trunk and converts FastPackets into ATM cells.

- **ATM Line Module Model B**—The ATM Line Module Model B (ALM/B) supports the same functions as the BTM at full T3 or E3 rates. The UAI back card is available for T3 or E3 trunk formats.

- **Universal Switching Module**—The Universal Switching Module (UXM) supports four or eight E1/T1, three or six E3/T3, or two or four OC-3/STM-1 ATM trunks. The UXM transports a full range of ATM service types, including constant bit rate (CBR), variable bit rate (VBR), available bit rate (ABR), and unspecified bit rate (UBR). A UXM card can be configured to operate in either trunk or line (port) mode.

- **Frame Trunk Module**—The Frame Trunk Module (FTM) attaches a FastPAD or Cisco MC3810 concentrator to the IGX network, and converts Frame Relay frames into FastPackets for transport across the network. V.35, X.21, T1, and E1 interfaces are available.

- **Channelized Voice Module**—The Channelized Voice Module (CVM) supports a single T1, E1, or J1 line and is used to bring in multiplexed digital voice traffic. The CVM can also be used to support transparent data traffic or a combination of voice and data. The CVM also packetizes voice and data traffic.

- **Universal Voice Module**—The Universal Voice Module (UVM) supports a single channelized digital voice line in T1 or E1 format. In addition to optional adaptive differential pulse code modulation (ADPCM) and voice activity detection (VAD) compression, voice connections terminating on the UVM can be configured for low-delay Code Excited Linear Predictor (LDCELP) or Conjugate Structure Algebraic Code Excited Linear Predictor (CS-ACELP) compression. Back cards for the UVM include the UVI-2T1, UVI-2E1, and UVI-2J1.

- **High-Speed Data Module**—The High-Speed Data Module (HDM) supports four high-speed serial data ports and creates FastPackets from the incoming transparent data. EIA/TIA-232, V.35, and EIA/TIA-449 interfaces are available.

- **Low-Speed Data Module**—The Low-Speed Data Module (LDM) supports four or eight low-speed serial data ports, much like the HDM. EIA/TIA-232 and Digital Data Service (DDS) interfaces are available.

- **Frame Relay Module Model D**—The Frame Relay Module Model D (FRM-D) converts Frame Relay data into FastPackets and supports four serial ports (V.35 or X.21). The FRM takes Frame Relay frames from multiple end-user devices (typically routers) and segments them into FastPackets. Frame Relay connections terminating on the FRM can be configured to use the ForeSight algorithm to take full advantage of the end-to-end congestion avoidance provided by ForeSight. A FRI-V.35 or FRI-X.21 back card is used with the FRM/D front card.

- **Frame Relay Module Model E**—The Frame Relay Module Model E (FRM/E) provides support for a single T1 or E1 channelized Frame Relay line. The FRM takes Frame Relay frames from multiple end-user devices (typically routers) and segments them into FastPackets. Frame Relay connections terminating on the FRM can be configured to use the ForeSight algorithm. A FRI-T1 or a FRI-E1 back card is used with the FRM/E front card.

- **Frame Relay Module Model F**—The Frame Relay Module Model F (FRM-2) is used to support up to 44 serial Frame Relay ports with the Port Concentrator Shelf (PCS).

- **Universal Frame Relay Module Channelized**—The Universal Frame Relay Module Channelized (UFM-C) supports all the same features as the FRM. In addition, the UFM supports service interworking (Frame Relay to ATM interworking) and either four or eight channelized lines. The UFI back card is available in either a T1 or an E1 format.

- **Universal Frame Relay Module Unchannelized**—The Universal Frame Relay Module Unchannelized (UFM-U) supports all the same features as the FRM. In addition, the UFM supports service interworking and either 6 or 12 serial lines. The UFI back card is available with a choice of V.35, X.21, or HSSI interfaces.

IGX 8410 Installation

This section deals with the physical installation of the eight-slot IGX 8410 switch. The IGX 8410 is shown in Figure 10-4.

Apart from the number of slots, the main difference between the IGX 8410 and the other models in the IGX 8400 series is the number and the arrangement of the AC power supplies.

The first item is to determine whether the switch is a standalone unit or a rack-mounted unit.

The IGX 8410 rack-mounted system is mounted in a standard 19-inch rack, such as the Cisco-supplied Stratm cabinet. This installation uses standard EIA rail spacing.

Figure 10-4 *IGX 8410 Components*

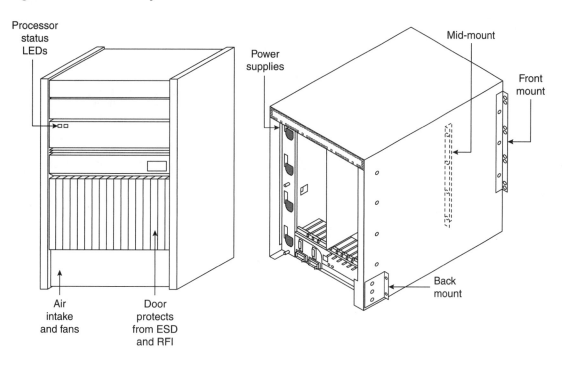

Front view

Back view

The IGX 8410 standalone system, shown in Figure 10-5, comes in a freestanding enclosure with a tool-operated front door latch. Side panels attach to the unit on vertical mounting rails at each corner of the unit. The four wheels at the base of the standalone unit allow the unit to roll into position. The unit also includes levelers. With the unit at the appropriate location, the height of the levelers can be adjusted so that the unit is immobile. The wheels and feet can also be removed, allowing the IGX system to be secured to the floor with four 1/4-20 fasteners.

All IGX 8410 systems include a backplane with eight usable slots, a fan tray with four fans, an exhaust plenum, and power connections for the shelf. An optional AC power tray can hold an additional four power supplies.

Cisco standalone WAN switch systems are shipped with cards, cabling, and power supplies installed in the cabinet. Field installation consists of placing the unit at its operational location, unpacking it, and verifying the structural and power connection integrity before turning on the power.

Figure 10-5 *IGX 8410 Standalone System*

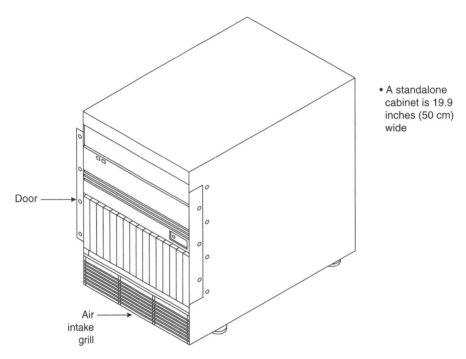

The rack-mounted IGX 8410 system fits in a rack with a minimum of 17.75 inches (45 cm) between rails. When mounting the chassis in a rack, brackets are attached to the front of the chassis. A pair of mounting brackets is attached at the back of the chassis after the chassis is placed in the rack. Brackets for a midrack mounting also come with the kit.

To provide some protection against seismic activity, the feet and the wheels of the IGX standalone cabinets can be removed to permit the cabinet to be bolted to a concrete floor.

Cisco-supplied cabinets also provide seismic anchoring. Holes are provided in the lower front and rear corners through which 5/8-inch (15-mm) bolts can be placed into an existing structural member.

Stability Plate Installation

Alternatively, an optional stability plate, shown in Figure 10-6, can be ordered and attached to the Cisco cabinet. The stability plate is bolted to the floor, and then the Cisco cabinet is bolted to the stability plate for seismic anchoring. Complete the following steps to set up the Cisco cabinet with the stability plate:

Step 1   Use the dimensions provided in the template included with the stability plate kit to drill the holes for installing the stability plate.

Figure 10-6 *Stability Plate*

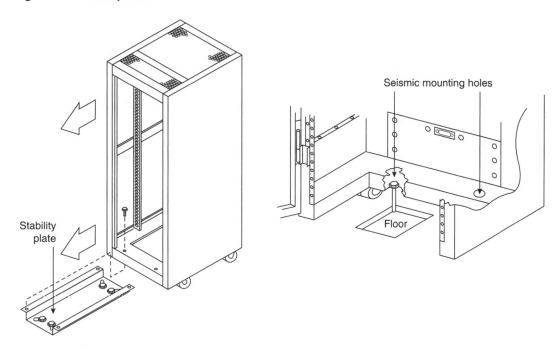

Step 2   Remove the stability plate from the base of the Cisco cabinet. Save the nuts and bolts.

Step 3   With the user-provided anchoring bolts, attach the stability plate to the floor.

Step 4   Roll the Cisco cabinet over the stability plate.

Step 5   Using the nuts and bolts from the shipping setup, secure the cabinet to the stability plate.

Temporary Mounting Brackets Installation

Because of the weight of the IGX 8410 system, Cisco includes two temporary spacer brackets and a temporary mounting bracket to help with the installation, as shown in Figure 10-7. These pieces are removed after installation. The temporary spacer brackets stabilize the rack, and the temporary mounting bracket together with the spacer brackets creates a partial shelf onto which the installers can slide the node. These pieces support the system, and the installers secure the permanent front- and back-mounting brackets to the rack.

Figure 10-7 *Temporary Mounting Brackets*

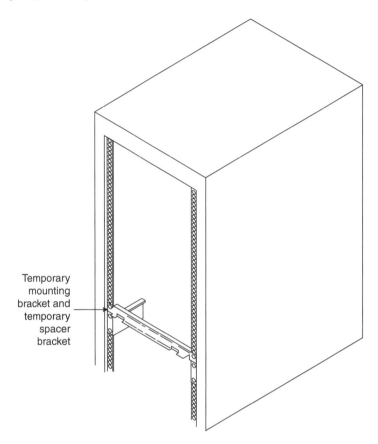

Temporary
mounting
bracket and
temporary
spacer
bracket

To install the IGX 8410 switch in a rack using these rails, perform the following steps:

Step 1 Decide where the IGX 8410 system should reside in the rack. Take into account the space required for the AC power unit (if any) and any other equipment that will share the rack.

Step 2 At the front of the rack, attach the temporary spacer bracket and temporary mounting brackets so that the uppermost face of each bracket is just under the intended location of the IGX 8410 switch.

Step 3 Position the IGX 8410 system in front of the cabinet so that the back of the IGX card cage faces the front of the rack. If you have not already done so, remove the foam strips from the sides, the front, and the back.

Step 4 Remove the rack-mounting rails from the packaging along with the package of mounting hardware.

Step 5 Remove the attached mounting brackets (filler plates) for the standalone version. If an IGX 8410 switch is ordered with the rack-mounting hardware, it comes with two rack-mounting rails strapped to the top packing plate.

Step 6 Locate the tapped holes on the side of the IGX 8410 cabinet. One set of holes is for front-mounting the cabinet; the other set is for midmounting.

Step 7 Attach the rails to the cabinet by using the #10-32 machine screws.

Step 8 Identify the locator studs provided with the kit (threaded on one end and smooth on the other end).

Step 9 Secure the locator studs into the rack holes that correspond to the top holes in the rack-mounting rails.

A fully loaded IGX 8410 system can weigh up to 175 pounds (78 kg). A second person is required to assist with the following steps.

Step 10 This step requires one person on each side of the IGX card cage. Lift and slide the card cage into the rack at the front of the rack. Slide the IGX 8410 switch to the back, and rest the rear of the system on the temporary mounting brackets and spacer.

Step 11 Secure the front bracket (or midmount bracket) to the rack. The midmount brackets require the threaded rolling screws, included in the IGX 8410 kit. Attach the IGX 8410 switch to the rack with eight #10-32 machine screws.

Step 12 Remove the temporary mounting brackets and temporary spacer bracket. The electrical power and grounding requirements shown in the figure cover installations at central office (CO) and private enterprise locations.

Power Considerations—IGX

AC or DC power can be used to power the IGX switch. In addition to AC and DC power requirements of the IGX, this section also covers bonding, grounding, and power redundancy.

AC Power

An AC power source must be available within 6 feet (1.8 m) of the system and must be easily accessible. Before turning on the power, verify that the power supplied to the node comes from a dedicated branch circuit.

The dedicated branch circuit should be protected by a two-pole circuit breaker with a long trip delay—15A for the IGX 8410, and 20A for the IGX 8420/8430.

The receptacle must include grounding. The grounding conductor that connects to the receptacle should connect to protective earth at the service equipment.

DC Power

Only a –48 VDC dedicated branch supply that complies with the Safety Extra Low Voltage (SELV) requirements of EN 60950 can connect to the IGX switch DC input.

Each dedicated branch supply should be protected by a single-pole 25A circuit breaker with a long trip delay.

Consult local or national codes for proper conductor sizing. The conductors must be suitable for 20A—10 to 12 AWG (4 square mm) is adequate.

Bonding and Grounding

To limit EMI, the unit must be bonded to an integrated ground plane or an isolated ground plane network. A frame bonding connection is provided on the Cisco-supplied cabinet for rack-mounted systems and on the Cisco standalone cabinets. This is illustrated in Figure 10-8.

Except for the AC power supply module, every module in a rack-mounted system relies on the rack itself for grounding. Therefore, the rack must be properly connected to protective earth before operating the system.

A DC-powered IGX node must have grounding conductors that connect at two separate locations:

- The grounding conductor provided with the supply source must connect to the Safety Ground terminal of the PEM.
- A grounding conductor must connect to the appropriate terminal of a rack assembly or to the chassis of an IGX node. Frame-bonding connections are provided on both types of Cisco cabinets: the Cisco rack cabinet and the standalone cabinet.

Cisco cabinets come with attached grounding studs at the top and bottom of the cabinet for securing the grounding conductors. Hardware for securing a ground conductor to the studs is included with the cabinet. The standalone cabinet has captive nuts on the vertical rear mounting rails, to which a grounding conductor can be attached. The nuts require a screw size of 1/4 inch with 20 threads per inch.

The ground attachment points in the Cisco and standalone cabinets are indicated by a ground symbol on the cabinet near the point of attachment.

In cases where a switch is mounted in a non-Cisco cabinet, the switch housing has provisions for mounting grounding conductors on the chassis by screws. This provision is a pair of captive nuts (threaded holes 1/4 × 20) for the screws that attach the user-provided ground cable. Figure 10-8 shows the frame-bonding connection on an IGX 8410 switch.

Figure 10-8 *IGX 8410 Frame-Bonding Connection*

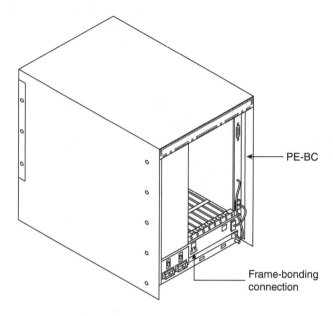

Cisco recommends the following stacking order for attaching a ground conductor to the frame:

- External tooth star washer placed first onto the stud
- The grounding conductor terminated with a closed-loop ring or two-hole compression fitting
- A second external toothed star washer or lock washer
- The nut

Power Redundancy

The IGX support power redundancy for both AC and DC power supplies. AC power redundancy can include both redundant power supply modules and redundant AC power sources.

For DC-powered systems, power redundancy is limited to dual DC sources. There is no DC equivalent of the AC power supply module in the switch.

AC Redundancy

An AC-powered system may include up to four internal power supplies, each of 400W rating. The IGX power supplies convert the incoming AC voltage to –48 VDC that is distributed inside the switch on the system power bus.

The power supplied to the IGX 8410 switch can be either AC or DC. Both systems require a Power Entry back card (PE-BC), pictured in Figure 10-9 with an AC power source.

Each system comes with a factory-installed PE-BC. In both AC-powered and DC-powered systems, the PE-BC connects the –48 VDC primary power for the system to the backplane. It also routes power to the fan tray. Because of its shape, the PE-BC is also called the E card. In an AC-powered system, a cable from the AC power supply module plugs into the PE-BC. In a DC-powered system, the PE-BC has at least one factory-installed PEM, which terminates the building's –48 VDC supply.

Figure 10-9 *Power Entry Back Card (PE-BC)*

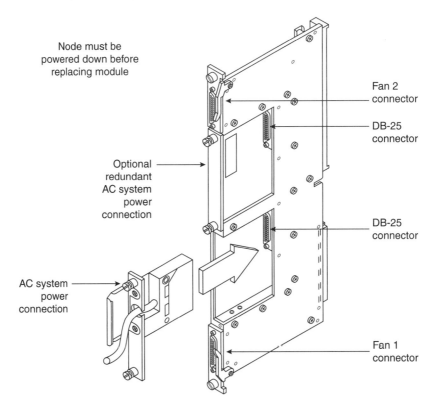

A PE-BC slot has no number; it resides between back card slot 1 and the side of the cabinet, as shown in Figure 10-10. Figure 10-10 shows a PE-BC for an AC-powered system. In normal use, the cable guard conceals the PE-BC.

Figure 10-10 *Power Entry Back Card Location*

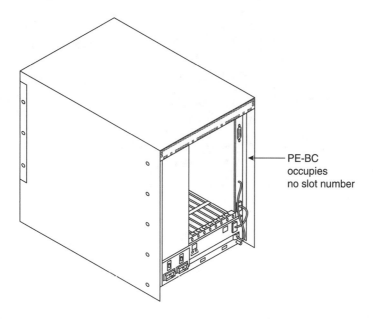

PE-BC
occupies
no slot number

Figure 10-11 shows the main components of the AC power supply system. The AC power supply housing is located vertically between the card cage and the side wall of the node.

Up to four 400W power supplies may be installed. The AC system provides the system with –48 VDC from the 100 to 240 VAC input.

One or two AC sources may be connected at the IEC power receptacles, which have associated circuit breakers. Adjacent to the power receptacles is the frame-bonding connection, used when a Cisco cabinet is not used.

Figure 10-11 *Power Supply Area AC System*

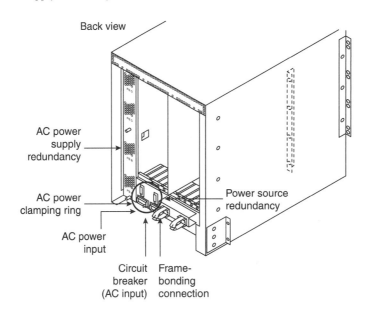

AC Power Connections

Figure 10-12 shows the rear view of the AC power connection panel.

Figure 10-12 *AC Power Connection*

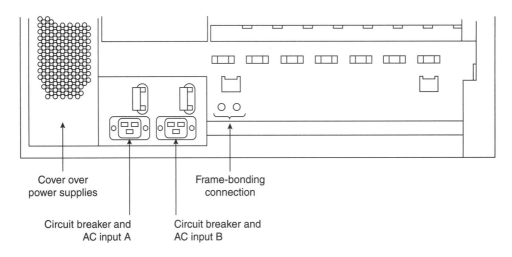

To make AC power connections to the IGX switch, complete the following steps:

Step 1 Ensure that all AC and system power circuit breakers are in the off position.

Step 2 Plug the power cord into the IEC connector, and tighten the screw on the clamping ring. An 8-foot (3-meter) power cord is supplied with each AC power supply assembly.

Step 3 Plug the IGX switch power cord into a single-phase wall outlet rated for a nominal voltage from 200 to 240 VAC or 100 to 120 VAC. The outlet must also be capable of supplying up to 12A (13A in the United Kingdom).

Step 4 For the dual power feed version, plug the second power cord into a receptacle that connects to a separate building circuit to provide backup if one building circuit fails.

Step 5 Verify that the ground (green) wire of the AC power cord is connected to the IGX switch for safety ground. Each AC receptacle in the building must be grounded.

Step 6 In addition to the preceding, Cisco recommends that an AC power strip with at least four outlets be available. Place the strip near the IGX node to supply optional modems, CSUs, DSUs, or test equipment. Be sure to connect this power strip to an AC source voltage that is standard for the region (for example, 115 VAC in North America or 230 VAC in Europe).

The minimum requirement for an AC-powered system is one AC source and one power supply. One supply is adequate for up to four IGX card modules unless power supply redundancy is specified.

Figure 10-13 shows the four power supply slot designations A through D, and the correspondence between the individual slots and the AC input (A or B) from which they are supplied.

Figure 10-13 also shows a dual input system. In a dual input system, input A supplies power supply slots A and B. Input B supplies power to slots C and D. A single AC input system does not have these distinctions: The single input supplies AC power to slots A through C.

In supporting single and dual AC inputs, power supply arrangements differ. When a system uses two AC inputs, the number of supplies that receive power from AC input A must be the same as the number of supplies that receive power from AC input B. But when a system uses one AC source, the input connection has no alphanumeric designation.

Figure 10-13 *Power Supply Slot Designations*

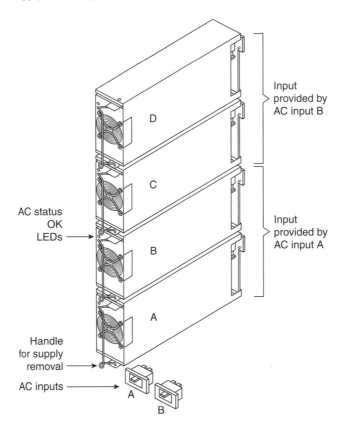

Table 10-4 shows the minimum number of 400W AC power units required for different IGX systems, based on the number of card modules installed.

Table 10-4 *Minimum Number of AC Power Units*

System	Number of Cards	N+1 Supply Redundancy	A	B	C	D
One AC Input	Four or fewer	No	X			
	Four or fewer	Yes	X	X		
	More than four	No	X	X		
	More than four	Yes	X	X	X	
Two AC Inputs	Four or fewer	No	X		X	
	More than four	Yes		X	X	X

As seen in Table 10-4, the factors that determine the number of supplies are the number of AC inputs, number of cards (one supply can power four cards), and redundancy.

The System column shows the number of AC inputs. The Number of Cards column shows the number of cards at the cutoff point for more supplies. The N+1 Supply Redundancy column indicates whether the configuration includes a redundant supply for backup. For columns A through D, an X shows that the corresponding slot in the power supply housing must have a power supply to meet the configuration requirements.

DC Power Connection

The DC Power Entry Module (PEM) is a small, factory-installed card that plugs into a connector on the PE-BC. The PEM plugs into the same connector, as would a cable from the AC power supply module in a system using an AC source, as shown in Figure 10-14.

Figure 10-14 *DC Power Entry Module*

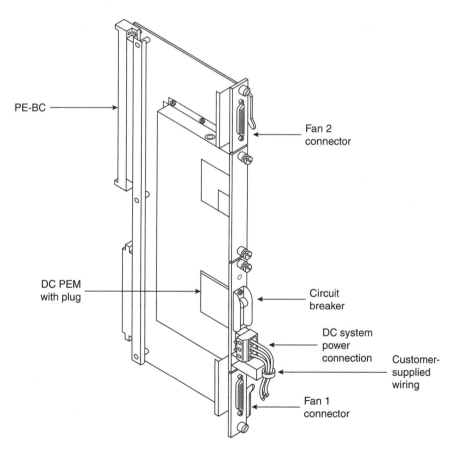

The PEM takes the DC power directly from the DC power source in the building, filters it, and passes it to the PE-BC. A PEM also has a circuit breaker for turning the power on and off, and a strain-relief clamp for the DC power cable. The illustration shows a PEM plugged into a PE-BC in a nonredundant system. It also shows the blank plate that covers the unused connection in a nonredundant system.

The redundancy of DC sources and PEMs allows continued system operation if one of the two independent DC branch circuits fails. DC-powered systems support either a single or a dual power source.

Wiring is connected from one or two –48 VDC power sources to one or two DC PEMs. These wires should be capable of carrying 20A using 10- or 12-AWG wire. DC power cabling is not included with the switch.

Installing DC power consists of attaching the three wires of the DC power source to a removable wiring block, and then plugging that block into the connector on the PEM. The PEM is plugged into the PE-BC. Figure 10-15 shows a PE-BC removed from the card cage with the PEM wired up and plugged into it. Note that this shows a nonredundant DC power configuration. Note also the blank plate that covers the unused connection.

Figure 10-15   *DC Power Supply*

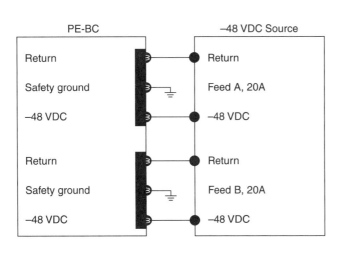

Wiring diagram for
redundant DC power source

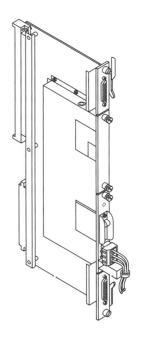

PE-BC and DC PEM with
plug (nonredunant
configuration shown)

A DC-powered system makes no distinction between a primary and a redundant PEM (unlike the redundancy scheme in an AC-powered system). However, you should label the PEM to indicate the branch circuit to which it is connected.

A closer view of the terminal assignments on the pluggable terminal block is shown in Figure 10-16.

Figure 10-16 *DC Power Connection*

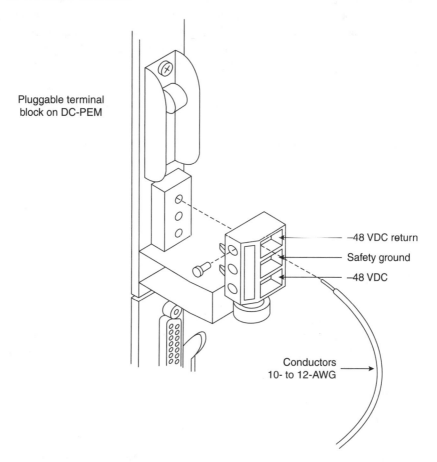

Pluggable terminal
block on DC-PEM

−48 VDC return

Safety ground

−48 VDC

Conductors
10- to 12-AWG

Complete the following steps to make a DC power connection:

Step 1   Ensure that the polarity of the DC input wiring is correct. Under certain conditions, connections with reversed polarity can trip the primary circuit breaker or damage the equipment. Remember that this is a positive ground system.

Step 2   Make sure that the circuit breaker is in the off position.

Step 3   For both rack-mounted and standalone systems, the cable guard (located at the right edge of the chassis) remains off until the system is ready to power up. Remove the cable guard by loosening the captive screw at its base and swinging it away from the chassis (do this latter movement by holding the top of the cable guard in place while moving the bottom of the cable guard away from the chassis).

Step 4   Insert and secure the stripped ends of the supply cable in the wiring block. The numbers start with 1 at the bottom and go to 3. The connection at the top is for the –48 VDC wire. The middle wire is safety ground. The connection at the bottom is for the positive return wire (for the –48 VDC).

For personal safety, the green or green/yellow wire must connect to safety (earth) ground at both the equipment and the supply side of the DC wiring.

Step 5   Attach the pluggable terminal block to the receptacle on the PEM.

Step 6   Loop the DC wiring through the strain-relief clamp.

Step 7   Connect the DC input wiring to a DC source capable of supplying at least 20A (typical). The –48 VDC power source in the building should have a 25A DC circuit breaker. The building's wiring should include an easily accessible disconnect device. Make sure that the ground wire connects to a reliable building (earth) ground using 10- or 12-AWG wire.

Step 8   Leave the cable guard off until the power is on.

Step 9   Check the supply voltage with a voltmeter. Use the screws at positions 1 and 3 on the pluggable terminal block as a convenient measuring point. Also, check the impedance between the safety ground (screw at location 2 on the pluggable terminal block) and the chassis. It should be approaching 0 ohms.

Step 10 Do not power on the system at this point.

Fan Tray Assembly

In an IGX 8410 switch, the fan tray is installed from the front of the cabinet and slides immediately below the card cage, as shown in Figure 10-17. Each fan tray contains four fans.

Figure 10-17 *Fan Tray Assembly*

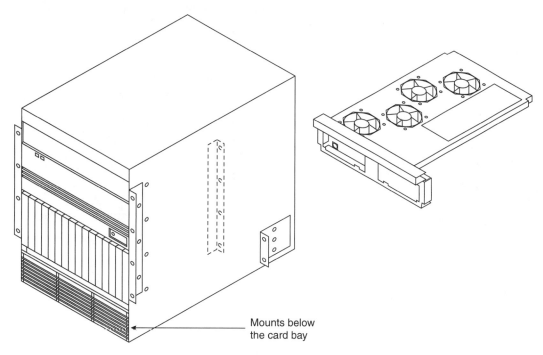

Mounts below
the card bay

When the power supply installation and fan tray assembly are complete, the next step is to install or reinstall the card modules in the switch. Card module installation is covered after the following "Installing the IGX 8420/8430" section.

Installing the IGX 8420/8430

This section describes the physical installation of IGX 8420 and IGX 8430 nodes. The overall process is very similar to that for the IGX 8410 system, although there are mechanical differences between the model types that will be highlighted at appropriate points.

IGX 8420/8430 systems are available in the following model variations:

- IGX 8420 standalone, 16-slot, single-shelf unit in a freestanding cabinet
- IGX 8420 rack-mounted, 16-slot, single-shelf rack-mountable unit
- IGX 8430 standalone, 32-slot, dual-shelf unit in a freestanding cabinet
- IGX 8430 rack-mounted, 32-slot, dual-shelf rack-mountable unit

The IGX 8420 and IGX 8430 are shown in Figure 10-18.

Figure 10-18 *IGX 8420 and 8430 Systems*

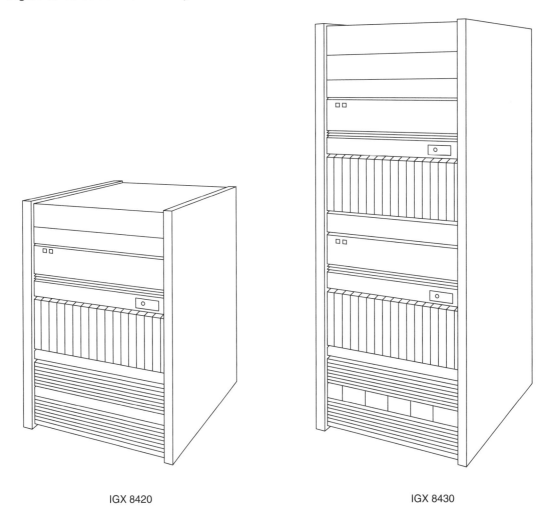

IGX 8420   IGX 8430

As with the IGX 8410 system, IGX 8420 and IGX 8430 support AC or DC power.

The IGX 8420 rack-mounted system is mounted in a standard 19-inch rack, such as the Cisco Stratm cabinet.

The IGX 8420 standalone system comes in a freestanding enclosure with a tool-operated front door latch. Side panels attach to the unit on vertical mounting rails at each corner of the unit. The four wheels at the base of the standalone unit allow the unit to roll into position. The unit also includes levelers. With the unit at the appropriate location, the height of the levelers can be adjusted so that the unit is immobile. The wheels and feet can also be removed, allowing the IGX system to be secured to the floor with four 1/4-20 fasteners.

All IGX 8420 systems include the following:

- 16-slot card shelf
- A backplane into which front cards, back cards, and PE-BCs plug
- A main (lower) fan tray with six fans
- An exhaust plenum
- Power connections for the shelf
- An optional AC power tray that holds the power supplies

These components are identified in Figure 10-19.

Figure 10-19 *IGX 8420 Components*

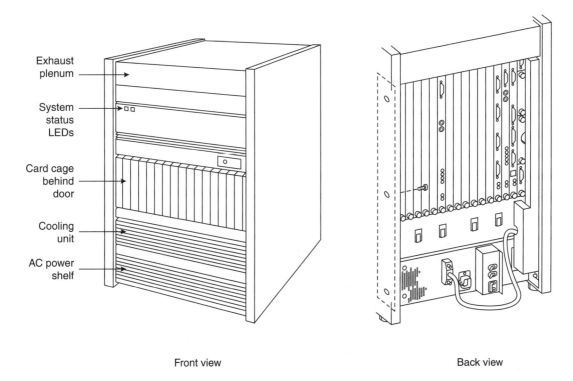

Exhaust plenum

System status LEDs

Card cage behind door

Cooling unit

AC power shelf

Front view   Back view

As shown in Figure 10-20, the IGX 8430 system includes the following:

- Two 16-slot card shelves
- Two backplanes, into which front cards, back cards, and PE-BCs plug
- A main (lower) fan tray with six fans
- A booster (upper) fan tray

- An exhaust plenum
- Power connections for each shelf
- An optional AC power tray that holds up to six power supplies

Figure 10-20 *IGX 8430 Components*

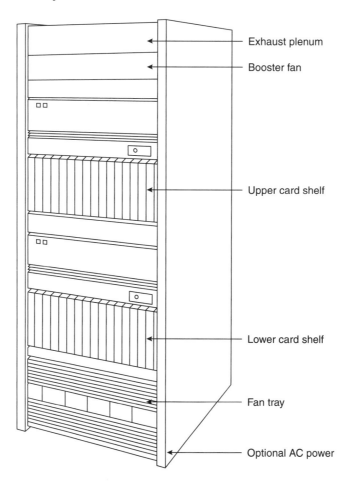

The back view of an IGX 8430 standalone unit is shown in Figure 10-21. The cable guards, which normally conceal the fan and the system power cables, have been removed for clarity.

Figure 10-21 *IGX 8430 Standalone System*

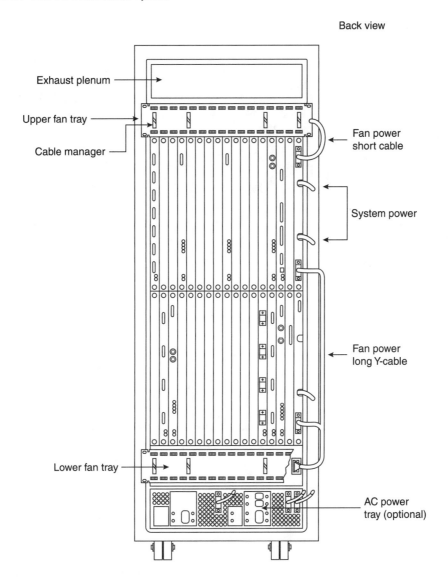

Back view

Exhaust plenum

Upper fan tray

Cable manager

Fan power
short cable

System power

Fan power
long Y-cable

Lower fan tray

AC power
tray (optional)

IGX 8420 Rack Mount Installation

The IGX 8420 rack-mounted system, shown in Figure 10-22 is mounted in a standard 19-inch rack. If an IGX is mounted in a non-Cisco cabinet, ensure that a front-to-back free flow of air in and out of the enclosure is possible.

Figure 10-22 *IGX 8420 Rack-Mounted System*

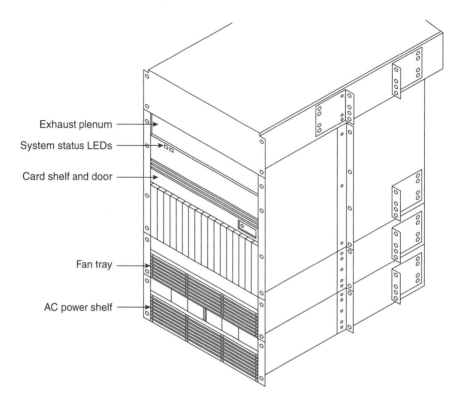

Exhaust plenum

System status LEDs

Card shelf and door

Fan tray

AC power shelf

Complete the following steps to rack-mount the IGX 8420 switch:

Step 1 Decide where the IGX 8420 switch should be located.

Step 2 Install the optional AC power supply kit. Refer to the "AC Power Installation" section, later in this chapter.

Step 3 Install the fan tray. Refer to the "Fan Tray Assembly" section, later in this chapter.

Step 4 Position the card cage in front of the cabinet so that the back of the IGX 8420 card cage faces the rack. Remove the foam strips from the sides, front, and back.

Step 5 A fully loaded IGX 8420 system can weigh up to 250 pounds (113 kg). Three people are required to assist with the following steps.

Step 6 With one person on each side of the IGX card cage, lift and slide it into the rack.

Step 7 Make sure that mounting the equipment does not create a hazardous condition due to uneven mechanical loading. The equipment rack should be securely supported.

Step 8 Attach the cabinet to the rack with eight #10-32 machine screws.

Step 9 Install the exhaust plenum.

Step 10 For an AC-powered system, connect the AC source to the switch. Refer to the "AC Power Connections" section, later in this chapter.

Step 11 For a DC-powered system, connect the DC source to the switch. Refer to the "DC Power Connections" section, later in this chapter.

IGX 8430 Rack Mount Installation

The rack-mounting procedure for an IGX 8430 switch, as shown in Figure 10-23, is similar to that for an IGX 8420 unit, with a few additional steps.

After installing the lower card cage as for the IGX 8420, the upper card cage must be installed for the IGX 8430 switch. Note that the two cages must be aligned so that a plate in the upper portion of the lower cage couples with a plate in the lower portion of the other card cage to form the EMI tunnel.

This tunnel provides a means of routing the intershelf ribbon cables, which are installed next. Refer to the "Backplane Interconnect" section, later in this chapter.

After installing the two card cages and the ribbon cables, the upper fan tray assembly is installed next, followed by the exhaust plenum.

For an AC-powered system, connect the AC source to the switch. Refer to the "AC Power Connections" section, later in this chapter.

For a DC-powered system, connect the DC source to the switch. Refer to the "DC Power Connections" section, later in this chapter.

Figure 10-23 *IGX 8430 Rack-Mounted System*

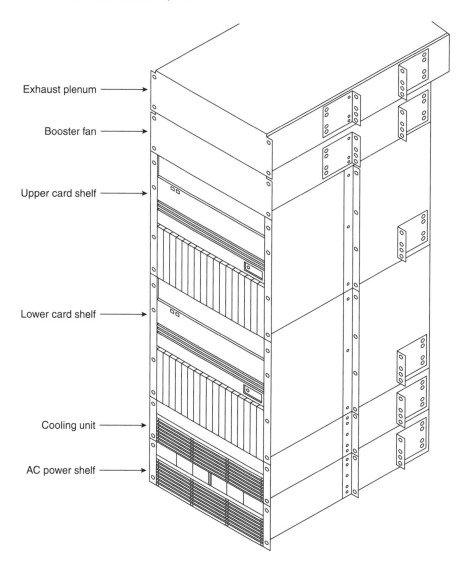

IGX 8420 and 8430 Power Redundancy

The power redundancy options for IGX 8420/8430 systems are similar to those for an IGX 8410 node. IGX 8420/8430s, however, can have up to six AC power modules installed, each of which is rated for 875W. The AC power modules are grouped in two sets of three modules, and 110 VAC power is not an option for the IGX 8420/8430 systems—a 230 VAC (nominal) source is mandatory.

Figure 10-24 shows the slot designations for the maximum number of six AC power modules that can be installed in an IGX 8420 or IGX 8430 switch.

Figure 10-24 *Power Supply Slot Designations*

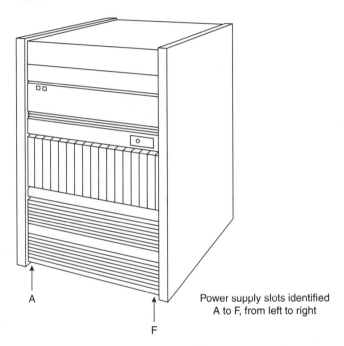

AC powered systems include the following components:

- Power supplies (up to six)
- Power supply tray
- Power and sense cables between the AC power module and the PE-BC
- Dummy cover panels for unused power supply slots
- Mounting brackets
- Air inlet bezel

The actual number of power supplies required, and their physical placement in the power tray, depends on the number of AC power inputs, the IGX model, and the number of cards in the system. Table 10-5 shows possible options. In the table, X = presence of supply and 0 = optional supply.

The minimum configuration is one AC source and one supply. This minimum number applies to the IGX 8420 switch; with 12 or fewer cards, one supply is adequate.

Table 10-5   *IGX 8420 and IGX 8430 Power Requirements*

System	A	B	C	D	E	F	Kit Part No.
IGX 8420 One AC Input No redundancy	X	0					IGX8420-AC-1
IGX 8420 One AC Input Redundancy	X	X	0				IGX8420-AC2-1
IGX8420 Two AC Inputs No redundancy	X	0		X			IGX8420-AC2-2
IGX8430 One AC Input No redundancy	X	X	0				IGX8430-AC2-1
IGX8430 One AC Input Redundancy	X	X	X	0			IGX8430-AC4-1
IGX8430 Two AC Inputs	X	X	0	X	X	0	IGX8430-AC4-2

AC Power Installation

For standalone systems, the AC power supplies are already installed. For a rack-mounted system, complete the following steps:

Step 1   Attach the power tray mounting brackets to the rack frame. Figure 10-25 shows brackets for both midframe and rear mounting (unlikely to require both). In this view of the cabinet, the bracket shown is labeled with –00 on its edge. Brackets on the other side of the system are labeled with –01.

Step 2   With the support of either another person or an inanimate object at the rear of the IGX switch, slide in the power supply tray.

Step 3   Install the mounting screws at the rear of the cabinet through the holes in the tray and the mounting brackets. Note that for a midmount rack only, the head of each mounting screw goes on the inside of the tray, and each associated nut goes on the outside. If this arrangement is reversed, the power supplies at the outer walls of the tray cannot fit.

Figure 10-25 *AC Power Installation, Rack-Mounted Unit*

Step 4   Secure the front of the power supply tray with the front screws. When tightening each of the front screws, hold the adjacent front flange of the tray slightly to the outside so that the hinged door can freely open and close. The space between the right-angle edge of the flange and the edge of the hinged door should be at least 1/2 inch (13 mm).

Step 5   Install the power supplies. When a power supply almost reaches the end of the slot in the tray, a slight resistance is encountered. Push the power supply slightly farther in to achieve the final position.

Step 6   At the front of each supply, secure the supply to the tray by tightening the captive screw at the bottom front of the supply.

Step 7   Close the hinged door and secure it with the screw at the top-center of the door. For each slot without a power supply, the hinged door has a dummy panel.

Step 8   Connect the system power cables and the AC source power, as described in the "AC Power Connections" section, covered next.

An 8-foot (3-m) power cord is supplied for a single-feed AC power supply assembly, and two power cords are supplied for a dual-feed AC power supply assembly. For a dual-feed system, make sure that a separate branch circuit is available for each power cord; otherwise, the purpose of having redundant sources for AC power is defeated.

AC Power Connections

Complete the following steps to make AC power connections to the IGX switch:

Step 1   Make sure that all AC and system power circuit breakers are in the off position.

Step 2   With the correct number of AC supply modules in place, connect the system power cables as shown in Table 10-6.

Table 10-6   *AC Power Cable Connections*

Switch	Power	Connection
IGX 8420	Single AC	From connector A 1–16 on power supply shelf to connector A on PE-BC.
IGX 8420	Dual AC	First cable from connector A 1–16 on power supply shelf to connector A on PE-BC. Second cable from B 1–16 on power supply to B on PE-BC.
IGX 8430	Single or dual AC, three or fewer supplies	First cable from connector 17–32 on power supply shelf to connector A on the lower PE-BC. Second cable from A 1–16 to connector A on the upper PE-BC.
IGX 8430	Single or dual AC, four or more supplies	From connector 17–32 on power supply shelf to connector A on the lower PE-BC. Second cable from A 1–16 to connector A on the upper PE-BC. Third cable from B 1–16 to connector B on the upper PE-BC.

Step 3   Plug each power cord into the IEC connector, and tighten the screw on the clamping ring.

Step 4   Plug each AC power cord into a single-phase wall outlet rated for a nominal voltage of 200 to 240 VAC. Each outlet must also be capable of supplying up to 16A (13A in the United Kingdom, where the plug has a built-in 13A fuse). The ground (green) wire of each AC power cord is connected to the IGX switch for safety ground. Also ensure each AC receptacle is grounded.

Step 5   Place a power strip with at least four outlets near the IGX node to supply optional modems, CSUs, data service units (DSUs), or test equipment. Be sure to connect this power strip to an AC source voltage that is standard for the region (for example, 115 VAC in North America).

DC Power Connections

See the "DC Power Connection" section, earlier in this chapter, for a description of the DC-PEM and the procedure for connecting a DC power source to the switch. The procedure is similar for the IGX 8410 and 8420 units.

Figure 10-26 shows how to connect the source power to the preinstalled PEMs in both redundant and nonredundant configurations.

Figure 10-26 *IGX 8420 Power Connections*

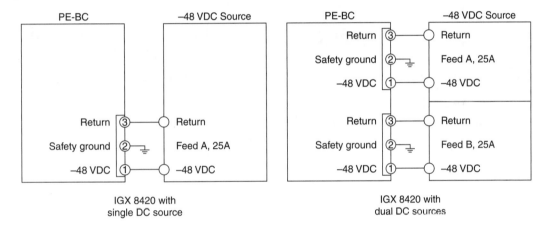

The DC power connection for an IGX 8430 system differs from that for an IGX 8420 system. The IGX 8430 has a PE-BC installed in both the upper and lower card shelves. For the IGX 8430 system, two scenarios are possible, as illustrated in Figure 10-27.

Figure 10-27 *IGX 8430 Power Connections*

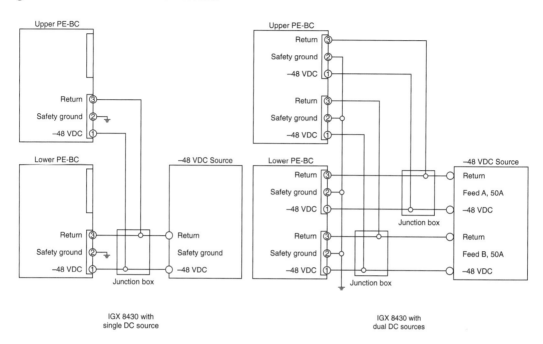

Cooling Unit Installation

The IGX 8420 has a single cooling unit, whereas the IGX 8430 node has two. The units are functionally identical, with some differences in the mounting method. Figure 10-28 shows the fan tray assembly.

Two cables are provided for supplying power to the fans: a short cable, which is used in both the IGX 8420 and 8430 nodes, and a longer Y-cable, which is used on the IGX 8430 only.

Complete the following steps to install the cooling unit assembly or assemblies:

Step 1   Examine the front and the back of the fan tray to familiarize yourself with the setup. Note that for the lower fan tray, the captive screws that secure it are in the front. For the booster fan tray in the IGX 8430 node, the captive screws are located at the back of the cabinet.

Figure 10-28 *Fan Tray Assembly*

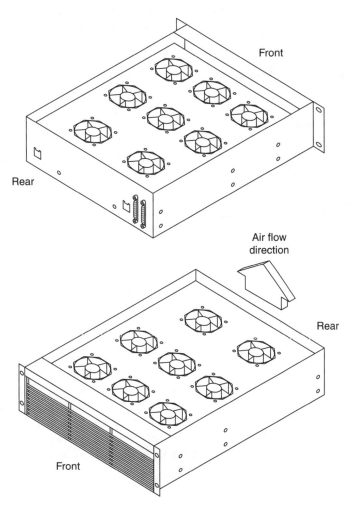

Step 2 On the PE-BC card(s), plug the D-connector of the appropriate fan power cable into the appropriate PE-BC connector:

— **IGX 8420 node**—Short cable to connector fan 1

— **IGX 8430 node**—Short cable to connector fan 2 on upper PE-BC; long branch of Y-cable to fan 1 on upper PE-BC; shorter branch of Y-cable to fan 1 on lower PE-BC

Step 3   Plug the power connectors on the other end of the cables into the fan trays. At the power receptacles on each fan tray, the power connector is a latched housing. Plug P1 into connector P1; plug P2 into connector P2.

Step 4   Attach the clamp for the fan power cord to the chassis.

Step 5   For lower fan tray installation, attach the air intake bezel.

Backplane Interconnect

In the case of the IGX 8430 node only, the backplanes in the upper and lower card shelves are connected through two ribbon cables that attach to the extension connectors on the backplane in front of the PE-BC. The intershelf ribbon cables provide interconnectivity between shelves.

As shown in Figure 10-29, the two folded ribbon cables that connect the upper and lower backplanes pass through a cutout space in the card cages. The cables connect to two 100-pin connectors that reside on the front side of each backplane.

Complete the following steps to install the ribbon cables:

Step 1   Connect the cable from the upper connector in the upper backplane to the upper connector in the lower backplane.

Step 2   Connect the cable from the lower connector in the upper backplane to the lower connector in the lower backplane.

Step 3   A two-piece conduit fits together around the ribbon cables and is placed in the cutout space of the card cages. This conduit is the EMI tunnel. Fit the pieces of the EMI tunnel around the ribbon cables, and screw this combined piece into the cutout space between the upper and lower card cages. The illustration shows the EMI tunnel in place in the normal-scale drawing and prior to assembly in the highlighted area.

Step 4   Slip the ribbon cables through the fastener clamps, and then attach the fastener clamps (which include self-adhesive bases) to the side of the card cage.

Figure 10-29 *IGX 8430 Backplane Connector Cables*

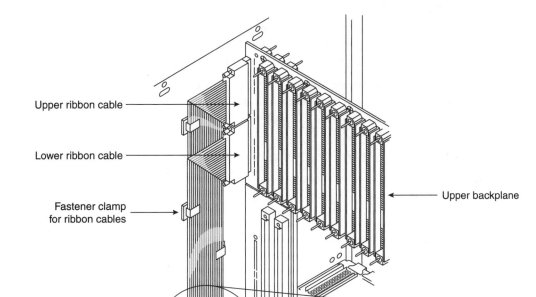

Upper ribbon cable

Lower ribbon cable

Fastener clamp
for ribbon cables

Upper backplane

Card cage tunnel

EMI
gasket

EMI
gasket

Card Module Installation

As part of the process of installing the card modules in a rack-mounted IGX 8420 or 8430 system, you must configure the SCM for operation in one of the two switch types. This step is not required with a standalone system because the configuration is done at the factory before shipment. It is also unnecessary with an IGX 8410 system.

First locate the W6 jumper on the SCM card. The jumper is located above component U7P (near the top of connector P2).

To configure the SCM for operation in an IGX 8430 switch, remove the jumper. For an IGX 8420 switch, leave the jumper in place on the card. Make a record that this step is complete so that removing and checking the card at powerup is unnecessary.

The locations of the system cards in an IGX switch depend on the hardware configuration. Except for the reserved slots, cards can reside in any slot on the appropriate side of the backplane.

The locations for the Nodal Processor Modules (NPMs) and System Clock Modules (SCMs) in IGX 8410, 8420, and 8430 switches are shown in Table 10-7.

Table 10-7   *NPM and SCM Redundancy and Slot Locations*

Switch	NPM Redundant	NPM Location (Front Slot)	SCM Location (Back Slot)
IGX 8410	No	1	1
IGX 8410	Yes	1 and 2	1
IGX 8420	No	1	1
IGX 8420	Yes	1 and 2	1
IGX 8430	No	1	1
IGX 8430	Yes	1 and 2	1

When slot 2 is unused, insert a blank card panel in both the front and the back card slots. Do not put spare cards in slot 2 because this can inhibit proper bus communication.

This chapter provides a description of each of the card module sets supported in IGX systems. The components comprising each card module—usually a front card set and a back card set—are covered. The physical interfaces on each back card, and the status indicators that are located on both front and back cards, are also described. A brief functional description of each card module, including the user services supported, is included as well.

The card modules for IGX systems are categorized into card groups:

- Control Modules Card Group
- Trunk Modules Card Group
- Service Modules Card Group

Control Modules Card Group

The control modules card group consists of the Nodal Processor Module (NPM) front card, the System Clock Module (SCM) back card, the Alarm Relay Module (ARM) front card, and the Alarm Relay Interface (ARI) back card.

The NPM front card is the central processor for the IGX switch and stores system software and all configuration information. In addition, the NPM is responsible for communicating with network management platforms.

The NPM is available in two basic models: 32-MB and 64-MB Dynamic RAM (DRAM). The later B version of each model has +5 VDC flash memory.

The NPM is a microprocessor-based system controller that contains the software for controlling, configuring, and monitoring the IGX node.

The NPM does the following:

- Functions as a CPU running the IGX node and the network administration software in DRAM
- Stores a nonvolatile but downloadable copy of the system software in Flash EEPROM
- Stores all user-provided node configuration information in nonvolatile BRAM
- Manages the flow of FastPackets and ATM cells on the cellbus by allocating bus bandwidth
- Configures and controls other cards in the node using the control bus (CBus)
- Communicates with other nodes in the network
- Communicates with network-management devices, such as terminals, PCs, and workstations, including the Cisco WAN Manager station

As shown in Figure 10-30, the view of the NPM front panel indicates the following:

- **System status indicator**—An LED that indicates the highest current alarm condition on the node: major (red), minor (yellow), or none (green). This LED is visible through a small window when the IGX cabinet door is closed.
- **Fail and Active indicators**—The NPM monitors its own activity. If a failure is detected, the Fail LED is lit. If the node has redundant NPMs, the online NPM is indicated by the lit Active LED, while the standby NPM has no lit indicators.

Figure 10-30 *NPM Front Panel*

All IGX front cards and back cards have at least Fail and Active indicator LEDs. Some card modules have additional front panel indicators, described later in this chapter.

The SCM, shown Figure 10-31, is a back card that plugs directly into the NPM card in slot 1. The NPM controls and monitors the SCM control buses. A single SCM supports redundant NPMs. The major functions of an SCM are the following:

- Regulates and monitors the clock used by the node for backplane timing, trunk timing, and line timing. Duplicate circuits are included for critical timing and control functions.
- Provides the necessary external interfaces for network management access.
- Measures cabinet temperature.

Figure 10-31 *SCM Rear Panel*

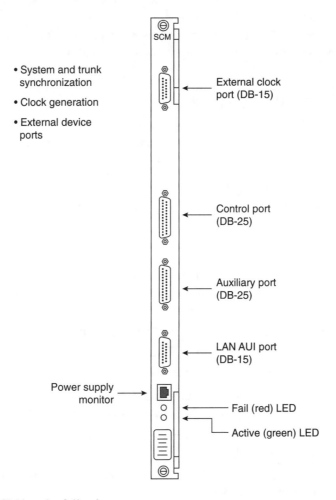

The SCM has the following ports:

- **15-pin external clock input port**—The external clock input port accepts network synchronization signals from an external clock source. This external timing reference signal must be EIA/TIA-422 at 1.544 MHz or 2.048 MHz.

- **Control port**—The control port is a 25-pin EIA/TIA-232 DCE port that is used to attach a VT100 terminal or a PC running terminal emulation for command line interface (CLI) access.

- **Auxiliary port**—The auxiliary port is a 25-pin EIA/TIA-232 DCE port that can be configured as a secondary CLI port, a network event log printer, or other functions.

- **LAN port**—The LAN port is a 15-pin 802.3 LAN attachment unit interface (AUI) port that provides StrataView Plus access for network management, and Telnet access for other LAN devices to the CLI.

- **Power supply monitor port**—The power supply monitor port is factory-wired to measure power supply voltages and cabinct temperature.

Attaching IGX System Peripherals

One of the functions of the SCM is to provide a means to connect a network-management station and other peripheral equipment to the IGX system. The next several sections detail how these devices are connected physically to various ports on the SCM card. Software configuration on the IGX node is also needed to support these devices, as covered in Chapter 12, "Establishing Initial Access to BPX and IGX Switches," and Chapter 13, "Initial Configuration of IGX and BPX Systems."

Control Terminal Configuration

As a preliminary to the node configuration phase of the installation process, you must have access to the system for a control terminal. This can be a dumb terminal (VT100 or equivalent) or a PC running a terminal program.

The control terminal is connected to the SCM using either the control port or the auxiliary port. The connection can be either local or direct, as shown, or via a modem connection.

Complete the following steps to attach the control terminal to the SCM:

Step 1 From the back of the cabinet, run a straight-through EIA/TIA-232/V.24 cable through the opening at the bottom and up to the SCM card in back slot 1.

Step 2 Locate the control port connector on the SCM, and attach the control terminal EIA/TIA-232/V.24 cable to it, as shown in Figure 10-32.

Step 3 Tighten the EIA/TIA-232 connector screws to firmly attach the cable to the control port connector.

Step 4 Plug the control terminal power cord into the appropriate wall receptacle.

Step 5 Configure the terminal for the following communication parameters, which are the default for an IGX control port: 9.6 kbps, no parity, 8 data bits, 1 stop bit, and XON/XOFF flow control.

Figure 10-32 *Connecting a Control Terminal*

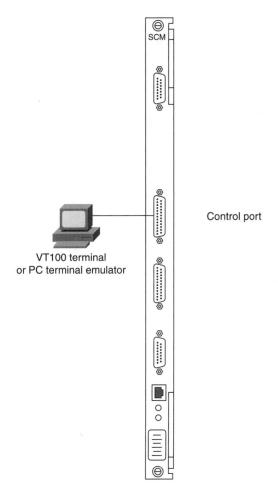

Step 6 Leave the terminal in place for use in node configuration. An Ethernet AUI port is provided on the SCM part to facilitate a LAN connection. If the Cisco WAN Manager station will be connected to this IGX node, it must be connected via the SCM LAN port. This connection can be either direct, as shown in Figure 10-33, or via intermediate switches or routers. (If a direct connection is used, then a crossover cable is required.)

Physical connectivity is implemented by connecting an AUI-to-RJ45 transceiver to the 15-pin AUI connector on the SCM LAN port, and from there to the LAN connection point (hub, router, or switch, for example).

Figure 10-33 *LAN Connection for the Network-Management Station*

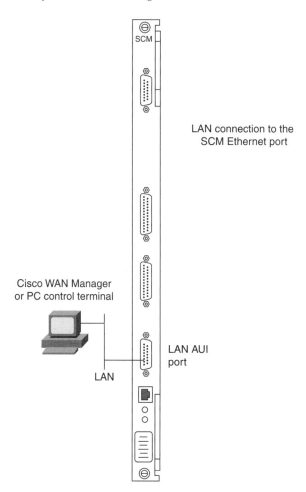

Printer Connection

At least one node in the network should have a printer connected. The printer connects to the auxiliary port on the SCM. Complete the following steps to attach the printer to the IGX switch:

Step 1   Check the printer EIA/TIA-232/V.24 cabling pinout and, if required, adjust the DIP switches to the settings indicated for the type of printer to be connected to the IGX switch. The printer must emulate an Okidata 182 printer and have a straight-through serial cable attached.

Step 2 At the back of the cabinet, run the printer EIA/TIA-232/V.24 cable through the opening at the bottom and up to the SCM card in back slot 1.

Step 3 Locate the auxiliary port connector, as shown in Figure 10-34, on the SCM and attach the printer EIA/TIA-232/V.24 cable to it.

Figure 10-34 *Connecting a Printer*

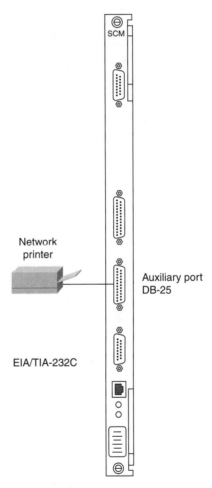

Step 4 Tighten the EIA/TIA-232/V.24 connector screws to firmly attach the cable connector to the auxiliary port connector.

Step 5 Plug the printer power cord into the appropriate wall receptacle.

Modem Connection

Two modems can be connected to any IGX switch, as shown in Figure 10-35, in the network to provide access for configuration, remote troubleshooting, and remote alarm logging. Each connection between the SCM and a modem requires a special cable and setup procedure.

Figure 10-35 *Connecting a Modem*

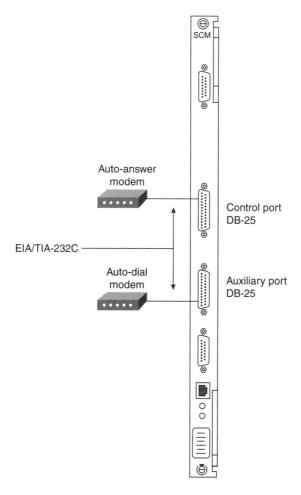

The modem used to provide access for remote troubleshooting is connected to the control terminal port on the SCM. Typically, the modem connects to the telephone wall jack with a direct-dial line.

The modem used to provide remote alarm logging is connected to the auxiliary port on the SCM. This modem connects to a wall jack using a standard telephone line.

A crossover cable must be used in both cases.

Chapter 13, "Initial Configuration of IGX and BPX Switches" covers control and auxiliary port configuration for modem connection.

Alarm Relay Module

The Alarm Relay Modules (ARM), shown in Figure 10-36, provides indicator LEDs and dry contact relay switch points for visual and audible major and minor alarm indications for the node.

Figure 10-36 *Alarm Relay Module*

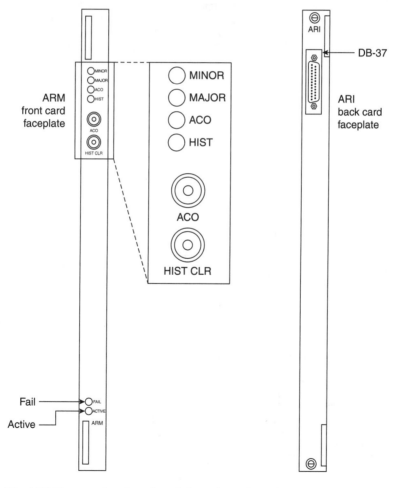

The ARM is an optional card module and consists of an ARM front card and an ARI back card. It provides local node major and minor alarms through the use of LEDs, as well as dry contact relays for external visual or audible alarms to indicate local or network major and minor alarms.

The ARM provides visible indicators to local personnel concerning the alarm condition of the node. Table 10-8 shows the alarm indicators.

Table 10-8   *Alarm Indicators*

Alarm	Indicates
Minor (yellow)	Local minor alarm.
Major (red)	Local major alarm.
Alarm Cut Off (ACO)	Alarm has been silenced by pressing the ACO button on the ARM.
History	Indicates that an alarm has an alarm or that one has been present. This alarm remains on until the major or minor alarm condition clears and the HIST CLR button is pressed.

The Alarm Relay Interface (ARI) is the back card for the ARM and provides the 37-pin connector for the external alarm wiring. The connector provides access to the relays for major and minor, audible and visual network alarms. Table 10-9 lists important pins and their functions.

Table 10-9   *Alarm Relay Interface Pins*

Pin	Function
1	Chassis ground
3	Network major alarm—normally open
4	Network major alarm—common
10	Node minor visual alarm—normally open
12	Node minor visual alarm—common
16	Node minor visual alarm—common
17	Node minor visual alarm—normally open
23	Network minor alarm—normally open
25	Network minor alarm—common
29	Node major audible alarm—normally open
31	Node major audible alarm—common
35	Node major visual alarm—common
36	Node major visual alarm—normally open

Trunk Modules Card Group

The trunk modules card group supports narrowband and broadband communications and consists of the following modules, as shown in Figure 10-37:

- Network Trunk Module (NTM) front card (narrowband) and BC back card
- Broadband Trunk Module (BTM) front card and ATM Trunk Interface (ATI) back card
- ATM Line Module (ALM/B) front card and Universal ATM Interface (UAI) back card
- Universal Switch Module (UXM) front card and Universal ATM Interface (UAI) back card
- Frame Trunk Module (FTM) and Frame Port Card (FPC) back card

Figure 10-37 *Trunk Modules Card Group*

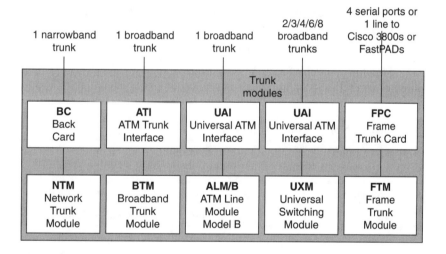

NTM Card Group

The NTM card group provides a single narrowband trunk that transports FastPackets between two IGX nodes in a network. Narrowband in the Cisco WAN switching context means transmission rates up to E1 or 2.048 Mbps.

The NTM card exists in two forms. One uses an ACM1 adapter, and the other is a single-card or native version. Functionally, they are identical, but their firmware is not interchangeable.

The NTM card module consists of the following:

- A front card (NTM)
- A back card (BC) that may be any one of the following:
    - T1 format back card (BC-T1).
    - E1 format back card (BC-E1). DB-15 or BNC connectors are available.
- Y1 format back card (BC-Y1); used in Japan.
- Subrate format back card (BC-SR). Includes X.21, V.35, or EIA/TIA-449 interfaces on a single card. The subrate interface is for a serial line with separate data, control, and timing leads.

The NTM card module performs the following:

- Receives FastPackets from the cellbus and queues them for transmission across the trunk
- Receives and performs a cyclic redundancy check (CRC) on the header field of incoming FastPackets from the trunk
- Provides all necessary line and packet framing for the trunk
- Monitors the trunk for alarms and errors

The BC-T1 and BC-Y1 back cards are shown in Figure 10-38. Table 10-10 shows the status indicators of the BC-T1 and BC-Y1 cards.

Table 10-10   *Status Indicators of BC-T1 and BC-Y1 Cards*

Status Indicator	Purpose
Card status	Indicates cards status: active or fail
Loss of Signal (LOS)	LOS at local end
Red alarm	Loss of local packet alignment
Yellow alarm	Loss of remote packet alignment
Alarm Indication Signal (AIS)	Indicates presence of all 1s on the line

Figure 10-38 *NTM Interfaces—T1 and Y1*

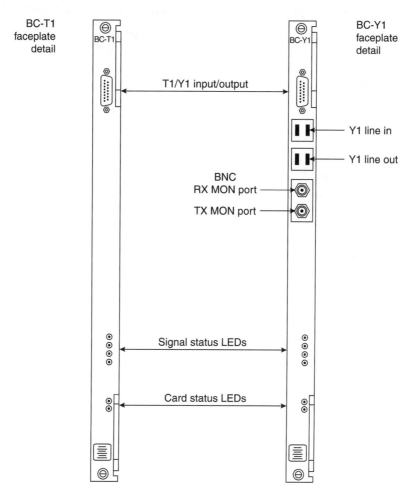

Trunk Connection

Complete the following steps to make a T1 or Y1 trunk connection:

Step 1   Bring each T1/Y1 trunk cable through the opening at the bottom of the cabinet (if applicable) and up the back of the unit.

Step 2   Use the cable management feature to help route the cables.

Step 3   Attach the trunk cable to the DB-15 15-pin connector on the back card.

Step 4 Record the IGX card slot number of each trunk. This information is
necessary for configuring the system after installation is complete.

Figure 10-39 shows the BC-E1 and BC-SR cards. Status indicators for the BC-E1 and BC-SR cards are shown in Table 10-11.

Figure 10-39 *NTM Interfaces—E1 and Subrate*

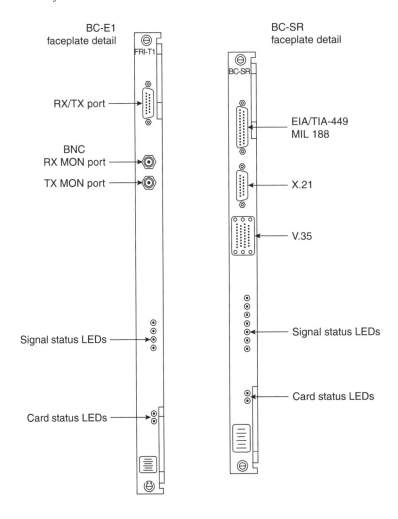

Table 10-11 *Status Indicators of BC-E1 and BC-SR Cards*

Card	Status Indicator	Purpose
BC-E1	Card status	Active and Fail LEDs.
BC-E1	E1 signal status	Two LEDs: MRFA and MFYA. MRFA (red) indicates a loss of local multiframe alignment. MFYA (yellow) indicates a loss of remote multiframe alignment.
BC-SR	Subrate signal status	Two LEDs: LOS (red) at local end. Bad CLK (red) indicates loss of clock or clocking error.
BC-SR	Yellow alarm	Loss of remote packet alignment.
BC-SR	Data Set Read (DSR)	DSR (green) lead is high (ON).
BC-SR	Data Terminal Ready (DTR)	DTR (green) lead is high (ON)
BC-SR	Receive Data (RXD)	RXD (green) shows receive activity.
BC-SR	Transmit Data (TXD)	TXD (green) shows transmit activity.

The procedure for adding an E1 or subrate trunk cable is similar to that used for a T1 or Y1 trunk. In the case of E1, you must connect to either the 120-ohm DB-15 connector, or to the 75-ohm BNC coaxial connectors.

A subrate trunk is terminated on the IGX using one of the three interfaces on the BC-SR back card: X.21, V.35, or EIA/TIA-449.

Y-Cable Redundancy

Many IGX and BPX card modules support Y-cable redundancy for trunks or lines, as shown in Figure 10-40. After the appropriate cables have been attached, Y-cable redundancy is configured using a control terminal or Cisco WAN manager. Refer to the Cisco WAN Switching Command Reference on your documentation CD-ROM for command details. Both cards must be active and available before you set up redundancy.

Figure 10-40 *Y Redundancy—Lines and Trunk Cards*

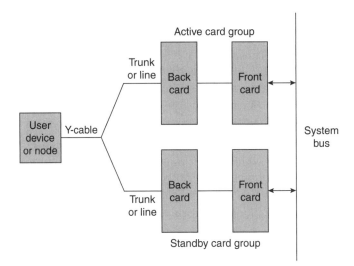

Switchover to a Redundant Card

If the card fails, a switchover occurs to a Y-cabled, redundant card set if one is available. If the switchover occurs, the primary card acquires failed status, and the red Fail indicator lights. If Y-cable redundancy is not available and the failed card is a network clock source, the node switches to another clock source and marks the line as a failed clock source.

The UXM features hot standby as part of its Y-cable redundancy capability. With hot standby, the redundant card receives the configuration information as soon as you finish specifying redundancy. The standby card also receives updates to its configuration as the active card configuration changes. Hot standby lets the backup card go into operation as soon as necessary rather than waiting for the NPM to download the configuration.

Broadband Trunk Module Card Group

The Broadband Trunk Module (BTM) card group provides an ATM trunk for transport of IGX traffic across an ATM network. The BTM creates ATM cells from FastPackets and provides a high-speed trunk from one IGX node to another IGX node, or from an IGX node to a BPX node.

The BTM card module consists of a BTM front card and of the following back cards, each of which supports a single trunk:

- T3 format back card (ATI-T3)
- E3 format back card (ATI-E3)

- E2 format back card (ATI-E2)
- High-Speed Serial Interface format back card (ATI-HSSI)
- E1 format back card (Broadband Trunk Interface, BTI-E1)

A logical view of the BTM card group trunk support is shown in Figure 10-41.

Figure 10-41 *Broadband Trunk Module*

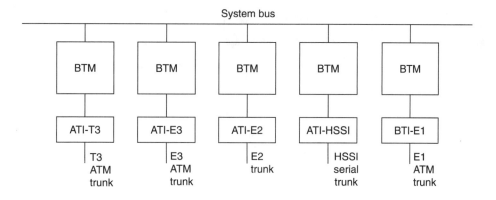

The BTM card group performs the following:

- Implements cell queuing for cells being transmitted and received on the ATM trunk
- Performs simple and complex gateway functions to convert FastPackets into ATM cells (standard UNI or StrataCom Trunk Interface [STI] cells)
- Checks header error control/header check sum (HEC/HCS) on incoming cells from the trunk
- Provides all necessary line and cell framing for the trunk
- Monitors the trunk for alarms and errors
- Extracts timing, if required, for use as a network clock source
- Support the bidirectional flow of up to 16 Mbps of ATM cells

Figure 10-42 shows the faceplates on the five back cards that are available for the BTM.

Figure 10-42 *BTM Interfaces*

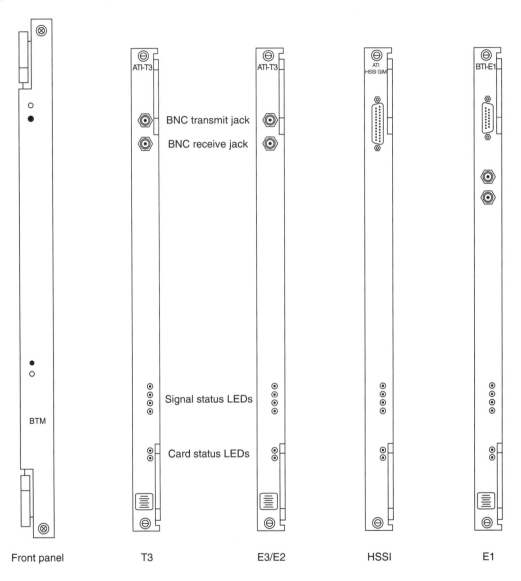

Status indicators for the BTM back cards are shown in Table 10-12.

The E1, E2, E3, and DS-3 back cards provide 75-ohm BNC interfaces; the E1 also has the alternative 120-ohm DB-15 interface. The HSSI back card has the 50-pin interface.

Table 10-12 *Status Indicators of BTM Back Card*

Status Indicator	Purpose
Card status	Active and Fail LEDs
Loss of Signal (LOS)	LOS (red) at local end
Red alarm	Loss of local frame or cell alignment
Yellow alarm	Loss of remote frame or cell alignment
Alarm Indication Signal (AIS)	AIS (green) indicates the presence of all 1s on the line

ATM Trunk Module Card Group

The ATM Trunk Module (ALM/B) card group provides an ATM trunk for transport of IGX traffic across an ATM network. The ALM/B creates ATM cells from FastPackets and provides a high-speed trunk from one IGX node to another IGX node, or from an IGX node to a BPX node. Its functions are listed here:

- Receives and transmits cells
- Segments and reassembles FastPacket to cell traffic
- Services truck queues
- Frames line and cell traffic
- Extracts timing from trunk (optional)
- Monitors trunk errors, alarms, and statistics
- Functions like BTM with full DS-3 throughput

The ALM/B card module is made up of an ALM/B front card and an ALM/B card, which is either a DS-3(T3) (UAI-1T3) or E3 (UAI-1E3).

The ALM/B functionally is similar to the BTM, with the additional capability of sustaining full E3 or T3 throughput, up to 50 Mbps.

The card and signal status indicators, shown in Figure 10-43, on the UAI back card are identical to those on the ATI back card for the BTM. The UAI back card provides 75-ohm BNC coaxial interfaces for both E3 and DS-3 trunks.

Figure 10-43 *ALM/B Interfaces*

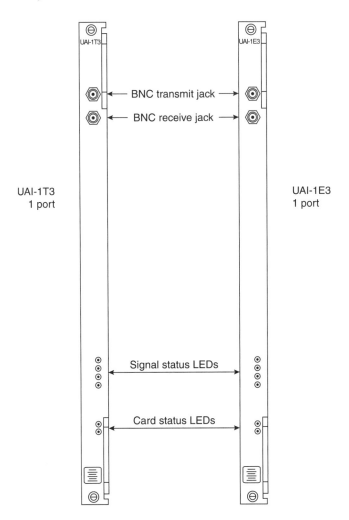

Universal Switch Module

The Universal Switch Module (UXM) card modules are recent additions to the IGX product line and require Switch Software Release 9.1. The UXM transports ATM cells to and from the cellbus at a maximum rate of 310 Mbps in either direction.

The UXM communicates only in ATM cells to either the network or the CPE. On the cellbus, however, the UXM communicates in either ATM cells or FastPackets, according to the card type. When communicating with another UXM, it communicates only in ATM cells. However, when communicating with other cards, the UXM communicates in FastPackets. Through its gateway functionality, the UXM translates between FastPackets and ATM cells so that it can transport voice, data, or Frame Relay traffic that other cards have converted to FastPackets.

The UXM can function in one of two modes. In trunk mode, the UXM supports trunks in the network. In port mode, it has either an ATM User-Network Interface (UNI) or a Network-to-Network Interface (NNI) for attachment of user equipment. With Release 9.1, the entire card must be configured for either trunk mode or port mode. Release 9.2 will provide the capability to configure individual interfaces on a single card as a trunk or port.

In trunk mode, the UXM transmits and receives standard UNI or NNI cells. The UXM does not support the Cisco proprietary STI cell header format that is supported on the BTM and ALM/B. The UXM also transports both ATM cells and traffic originating in FastPacket-based cards.

A common UXM card module configuration consists of a UXM front card and a back card that is either a T1 format back card with four ports (BC-UAI-4-T1-DB15) or eight ports (BC-UAI-8-T1-DB15), or an E1 format back card with four ports (BC-UAI-4-E1-DB15 or BC-UAI-4-E1-BNC) or eight ports (BC-UAI-8-E1-DB15 or BC-UAI-8-E1-BNC). Additional back card options are shown in Table 10-13.

Table 10-13 *UXM Back Cards, Interfaces, and Ports*

Back Card	Interface	Ports
BC-UAI-3-T3	T3	3 (DB15)
BC-UAI-6-T3	T3	6 (DB15)
BC-UAI-3-E3	E3	3 (DB15 or BNC)
BC-UAI-6-E3	E3	6 (DB15 or BNC)
BC-UAI-2-155-MMF	OC-3/STM-1	2 (Multimode fiber ports)
BC-UAI-4-155-SMF	OC-3/STM-1	4 (Single-mode fiber ports)

Front panel status indicators on the UXM, shown in Figure 10-44, are the same as on previously discussed IGX cards, with the addition of a third card status LED, the Standby LED. This LED is lit if the card is in standby mode, and it blinks to indicate that the card is in self-test mode.

Figure 10-44 *UXM Front Panel*

The narrowband UXM back cards do not have separate card status and line signal status indicators. Instead, they have a single, tricolor status LED next to each physical interface. Table 10-14 lists the three possible colors and their status.

Card failure is signaled by all LEDs turning red.

Figure 10-45 shows the T1 and E1 UXM interface.

Table 10-14 *UXM Tricolor Status Indicators*

Color	Status
Green	Card is in service and is active
Yellow	Line is active, but a remote alarm is detected
Red	Line is active, but a local alarm is detected

Figure 10-45 *UXM Interfaces—T1 and E1*

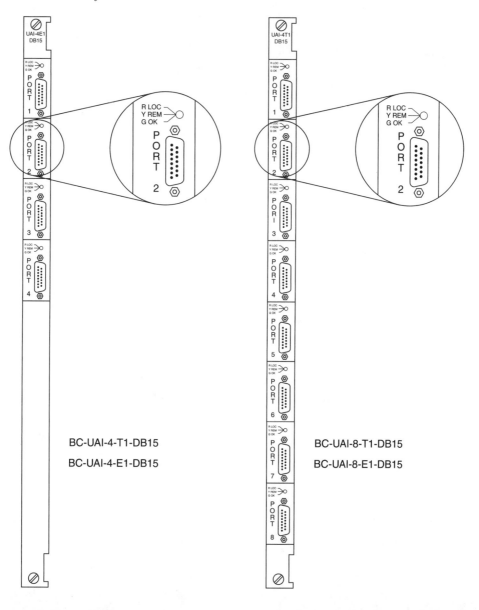

BC-UAI-4-T1-DB15

BC-UAI-4-E1-DB15

BC-UAI-8-T1-DB15

BC-UAI-8-E1-DB15

Figure 10-46 shows the 75-ohm subminiature BNC (SMB) coaxial interfaces, which provide an alternative physical interface type for E1 only. There are four or eight pairs of SMB connectors, depending on the back card type.

Figure 10-46 *UXM Interfaces—E1 BNC*

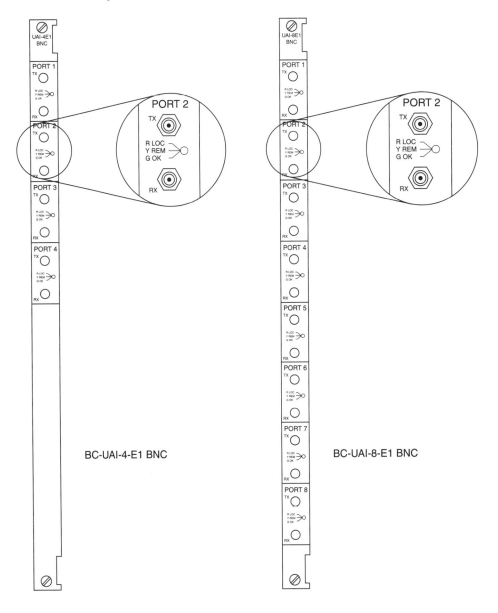

Figure 10-47 shows the T3 and E3 back cards.

Figure 10-47 *UXM Interfaces—T3 and E3*

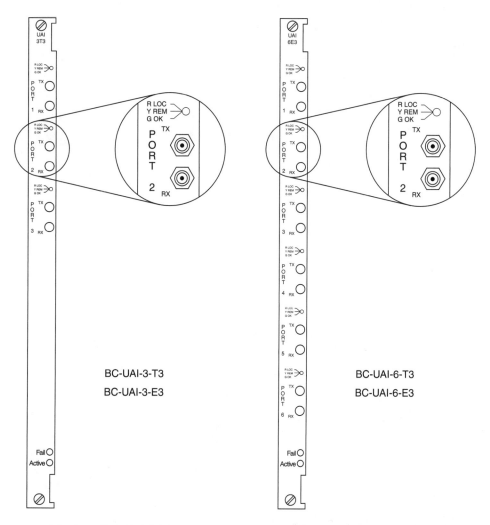

BC-UAI-3-T3

BC-UAI-3-E3

BC-UAI-6-T3

BC-UAI-6-E3

The broadband UXM back cards have separate card status LEDs at the lower end of the faceplate. Each physical interface has a tricolor LED; green indicates that the line (not the card) is active and has no alarms.

Figure 10-48 shows the fiber-optic SC interfaces for the OC-3/STM-1 back cards.

Line and card status indicators are the same as the narrowband card (refer to Table 10-14).

Figure 10-48 *UXM Interfaces—OC-3/STM-1*

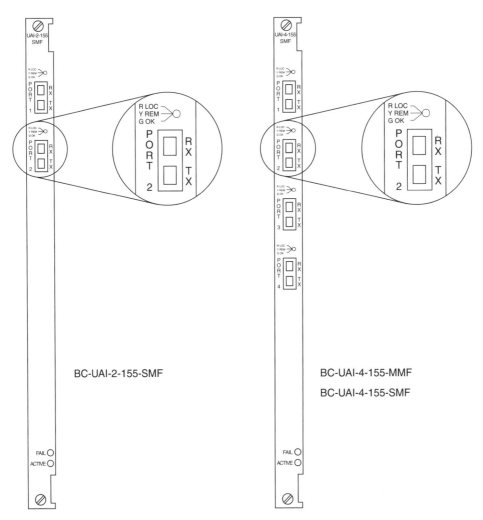

Services Modules Card Group

The services modules card group provides access to Frame Relay, serial, and voice networks. The services modules card group includes the following:

- Frame Trunk Module card module
- Voice card group
- Serial data card group

- ATM service card module
- Frame Relay card group

Frame Trunk Module Card Module

The Frame Trunk Module (FTM) card module is designed to interface with access devices, such as Cisco MC 3810 and FastPADs. The access device concentrates user traffic, such as analog voice, data, or Frame Relay, and forwards the traffic as Frame Relay frames. The FTM packetizes frames for transport across the IGX network.

The FTM card module consists of an FTM front card and one of the following FTP back cards:

- Four-port V.35 serial (FPC-V.35)
- Four-port X.21 serial (FPC-X21)
- Single-line T1 format (FPC-T1)
- Single-line E1 format (FPC-E1)

The FTM assembles and disassembles Frame Relay data packets for each of its ports. The FTM also multiplexes and demultiplexes channels from a T1 or E1 line (with a FPC T1 or an E1 back card).

In addition, the FTM regulates the flow of packets into the network to prevent and control congestion using the ForeSight feature.

As mentioned, the FTM card module is designed to interface with an MC 3810 or FastPAD and, as such, supports intelligent communication via signaling protocols. The FTM also provides management and control functions for the attached MC 3810 or FastPAD.

The FTM includes two configurable clock modes for serial (V.35 or X.21) interfaces and provides line framing for the T1 and E1 line formats. Like other card groups, the FTM monitors lines for alarms and errors, and extracts timing, if required, for use as a network clock source (with an FPC T1 or E1 back card).

Voice Card Group

The voice card group is made up of two voice groups:

- Channelized Voice Module (CVM), which includes the CVM front card and a back card
- Universal Voice Module (UVM) front card and Universal Voice Interface (UVI) back card

Channelized Voice Module Card Group

The Channelized Voice Module (CVM) card group performs packet assembly and disassembly (PAD) for channelized digital voice or transparent data traffic. In addition, it performs voice compression and any necessary voice signaling processing. The CVM card module supports various services:

- Front cards

  — CVM without echo cancellation

  — CVM with integrated echo cancellation for T1 (CVM-T1EC)

  — CVM with integrated echo cancellation for E1 (CVM-E1EC)

- Back cards

  — T1 format back card (BC-T1)

  — E1 format back card (BC-E1) with DB15 or BNC connectors

  — J1 format back card (BC-J1)

The CVM T1 and E1 back cards are identical to those used for the NTM. Table 10-15 summarizes the CVM functions.

Table 10-15   *Channelized Voice Module Functions*

Function	Description
Multiplexing/demultiplexing	The CVM multiplexes and demultiplexes 64-kbps voice and data channels on to the T1 or E1 line
Assembly/disassembly	The CVM assembles and disassembles voice and data packets.
Voice Activity Detection (VAD)	VAD is performed for bandwidth optimization.
ADPCM compression	This compression format converts 8-bit PCM voice samples (64 kbps) to ADPCM voice samples. (Supports 4 bit/32 kbps, 3 bit/24 kbps, and 2 bit/16 kbps.)
Echo cancellation (when supported)	This function performs echo cancellation on each voice channel.
mu-law/a-law conversion	This function performs mu-law to a-law or a-law to mu-law conversion on individual channels.
Tone detection	Tone detection identifies modem and fax usage, and disables compression for these circuits.
Alarms and errors	This function monitors lines for alarms and errors.

Universal Voice Module Card Group

The Universal Voice Module (UVM) card group performs packet assembly and disassembly (PAD) for channelized digital voice or transparent data traffic. In addition, it performs voice compression and any necessary voice signaling processing.

The UVM card module consists of a UVM front card and either a T1 (UVI-2T1EC) or an E1 (UVI-2E1EC) back card, as seen in Figure 10-49. Both the T1 and E1 cards have integrated echo cancellers. The T1 back card has two DB-15 interfaces; the E1 back card has two DB-15 and two 75-ohm BNC coaxial interfaces. There is no J1 interface for the UVM.

Figure 10-49 *UVM Interfaces—T1 and E1*

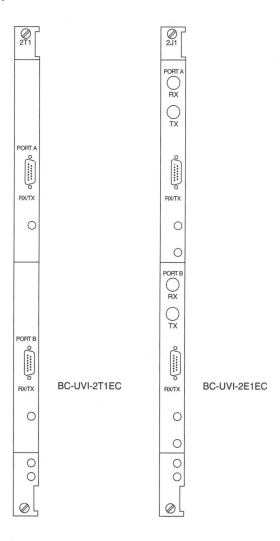

Although the UVI back card has two physical interfaces (port A and port B), only one is normally used to terminate a line from the customer equipment. The second interface might be needed to support line pass–through, as shown in Figure 10-50, for certain types of voice compression.

Figure 10-50 *UVM Pass-Through*

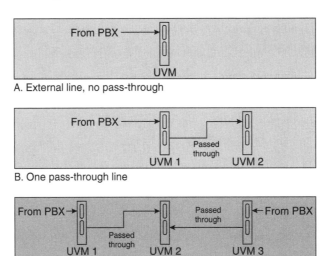

A. External line, no pass-through

B. One pass-through line

C. Two pass-through lines

Example A in Figure 10-50 shows an external line with no pass-through configuration.

Example B in Figure 10-50 shows a one–pass-through line configuration. For example, this might be a T1 line with 24 LDCELP channels, 16 processed on the primary (UVM1) and 8 passed through to the secondary (UVM2).

Example C in Figure 10-50 shows a two–pass-through line configuration. Here, the two T1 lines terminating on primaries UVM1 and UVM3 are each passing through up to eight LD-CELP channels to a secondary UVM2. Note that in this case, the two pass-through lines each use a separate physical line on the secondary.

If the number and types of connections exceed the capacity of the UVM, a second UVM is necessary to handle the additional channels. This approach is called pass-through. In this scheme, a primary UVM connects through an external cable to a secondary UVM. The primary UVM passes the unprocessed channels to the secondary UVM. The UVM's status indicators are shown in Table 10-16.

Pass-through configuration requires the pass-through cable as well as software configuration.

Table 10-16 *Universal Voice Module Status Indicators*

Status	LEDs	Indicator
Card status	Active and Fail LED	Indicates card either is operational or has failed.
Line status	Tricolor	Red—Line is active, but a local alarm was detected.
		Yellow—Line is active, but a remote alarm was detected.
		Green—The card is active and in service.
E1 line status—A second LED next to each interface	Bicolor	Red (RMFRA)—Loss of multiframe alignment has occurred.

The UVM performs the same functions as the CVM; however, there are additional features supported, such as integrated echo cancellation and additional voice compression schemes. Additional voice compression schemes include LDCELP and CS-ACELP. LDCELP provides a 4:1 compression ratio with better voice quality than ADPCM, and CS-ACELP provides an 8:1 compression ratio. Two variants of CS-ACELP are supported: G.729 and G.729a.

Both LDCELP and CS-ACELP might require implementation of the line pass-through feature to take advantage of additional processing power.

The UVM card includes hardware that supports ADPCM, LDCELP, or CS-ACELP compression. Up to 32 ADPCM or G.729a CS-ACELP channels, or up to 16 LDCELP or G.729 CS-ACELP channels can be supported on a single UVM. A mix of connection types is permitted, although not generally recommended. For example, you could add 12 connections that use ADPCM and 6 that use LDCELP. Any combination is possible as long as the configuration does not exceed the capacity of the card.

Serial Data Card Group

The serial data card group consists of the following modules:

- High-Speed Data Module (HDM) and Synchronous Data Interface (SDI) back card
- Low-Speed Data Module (LDM) and Low-Speed Data Interface (LDI) back card

High-Speed Data Module

The HDM card module performs packet assembly and disassembly for low-speed or high-speed transparent serial data traffic. The HDM operates at speeds from 1.2 kbps up to

1344 kbps on all four ports while performing link error monitoring. The HDM card module consists of the following:

- An HDM front card
- An SDI back card with one of the following serial interfaces:
    - Four-port EIA/TIA-232D
    - Four-port EIA/TIA-449
    - Four-port V.35
    - X.21 (requires EIA/TIA-449 plus an adapter cable)

The HDM card module performs the following functions:

- Assembles and disassembles data packets for each of its four ports
- Supports data rates of up to 1344 kbps per port
- Performs Data Frame Multiplexing (DFM), a protocol-independent data-compression scheme using a repetitive pattern suppression (RPS) algorithm
- Implements one of three configurable clock modes, as well as isochronous clocking (nonnetwork synchronized clock)
- Provides loopback capabilities for testing
- Performs control lead processing, including configurable end-to-end control lead mapping

Each port on the SDI back card can be configured as either a DTE or a DCE interface using a jumper board, as shown in Figure 10-51.

Figure 10-51 *SDI DCE/DTE Port Configuration*

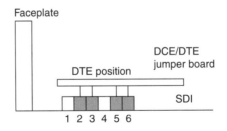

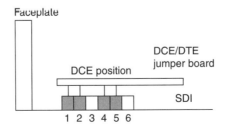

The factory-set, default mode of a four-port SDI card is DCE, DTE, DCE, and DTE. Although this is the default, verify it before starting up the system.

Two versions of the jumper card are available, with impedance of either 100 or 200 ohms. For higher port speeds, this impedance is important when Y-cable redundancy is specified. With Y-cable redundancy on a higher-speed connection, use the 200-ohm jumper card. Without Y-cable redundancy or when the port speed is relatively low, the 100-ohm jumper card is adequate.

To change the mode on a port to DTE, position the jumper card for that port as follows:

Step 1   To prevent damage to the SDI card, wear a wrist strap and clip the strap to the enclosure.

Step 2   At the back of the IGX switch, remove the SDI card.

Step 3   Unscrew the captive mounting screws on both ends of the faceplate.

Step 4   Using the card extractors, slide out the card.

Step 5   If a port is in DTE mode and needs to be changed to DCE, plug the jumper card into the connector receptacle pin rows closest to the SDI faceplate. Reverse this if changing the port from DCE to DTE.

Low-Speed Data Modules

The Low-Speed Data Modules (LDM) card performs packet assembly and disassembly for low-speed transport data traffic up to 56 kbps. The LDM card group is made up of an LDM front card and a low-speed data interface (LDI) that is either a four-port EIA/TIA-232C or an eight-port EIA/TIA-232C interface. The LDM card performs the following functions:

- Assembles and disassembles data packets for all ports

- Supports data rates of up to 56-kbps (for a four-port LDI) or 19.2 kbps (for an eight-port LDI) per port

- Performs DFM, a protocol-independent data-compression scheme using an RPS algorithm

- Provides loopback capabilities for testing

- Performs control lead processing, including configurable end-to-end control lead mapping

The remaining indicators on the LDM are the same as those on the HDM front card. The LDI back card provides Fail and Active LED indicators. Each port on an LDI card uses an adapter cable, which defines the configuration as DCE or DTE, as shown in Figure 10-52.

Figure 10-52 *LDI DCE/DTE Port Configuration*

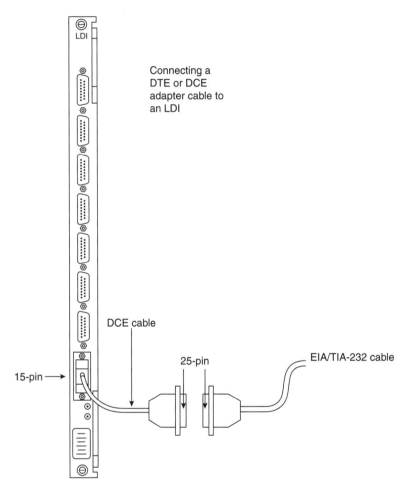

The cable is responsible for the following actions:

- Determining whether the port operates in DCE mode or DTE mode
- Connecting the port's 15-pin connector to a 25-pin D connector
- Converting to either a male or a female pin-out

Loopbacks on HDM and LDM

Figure 10-53 shows the faceplate of the HDM and LDM front cards. Several of the indicators and the push-button controls are associated with the manual setting of loopbacks on the card modules.

Figure 10-53 *Using a Data Card Faceplate for Loopback Control*

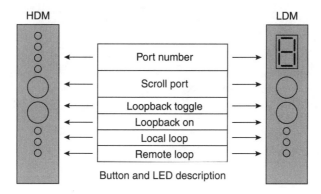

The HDM and LDM can add and delete local and remote loops using the pushbuttons on the faceplate of the card modules. The loopback is a useful feature when troubleshooting user connections.

In addition to the pushbuttons, the faceplates include LEDs that identify the current test status (if any) and the port under test, as well as specific control lead status, as previously described. The HDM and LDM faceplates provide the same controls and information, although the number of ports under test is displayed differently. The additional reporting supported by the LEDs is covered in Table 10-17.

Table 10-17 *HDM and LDM Status Indicators*

Component	Status	Indicator
Card	Card status	Active or failed card.
Line status	LL (yellow)	Local loopback is set on a port.
	RL (yellow)	Remote loopback is present on a port.
	DTR (green)	Data Terminal Ready (DTR) signal is on at the selected port.
	TXD (green)	Transmit Data (TXD) signal is on at the selected port.
	DCD (green)	Data Carrier Detect (DCD) signal is on at the selected port.
	RXD (green)	Receive Data (RXD) signal is on at the selected port.

Table 10-18 gives a comparison of the HDM and LDM features.

Table 10-18 *HDM and LDM Feature Comparison*

Feature	HDM	LDM
Data rate	Up to 1344 kbps per port	Up to 56 kbps per port (four-port module)
		Up to 19.2 kbps per port (eight-port module)
Number of ports	Four per card	Four or eight per card
DFM	Up to 128 kbps	Up to 56 kbps
Clock modes	Configurable	Not configurable
Isochronous clocking	Supported	Not supported
Control leads connector	All	Limited by 15-pin maximum
Fast EIA	Supported	Not supported
Embedded EIA	Not supported	Supported
DTE/DCE selection	Jumper board on SDI	Cable on LDI

ATM Service Card Module

The ATM UNI card module consists of the following:

- Universal Switching Module (UXM) front card
- Universal ATM Interface (UAI) back card

The UXM can be configured to operate in two modes: trunk mode and port mode. Trunk mode operation is discussed in the "Universal Switch Module (UXM)" section, earlier in this chapter. In port mode, the UXM performs the following functions:

- Provides a narrowband or a broadband network interface for user devices supporting the UNI or NNI cell format
- Provides an interface for the following types of ATM service: CBR, VBR, standard ABR with and without virtual source/virtual destination (VS/VD), ABR with ForeSight, and UBR
- Supports ATM to Frame Relay service interworking (SIW) and network interworking (NIW)
- Provides 10 ATM connection classes to facilitate the provisioning of user connections
- Performs traffic policing at ingress to and egress from the network, with per-connection queue management
- Supports either of two signaling protocols: Local Management Interface (LMI-ITU-T standard) and Integrated Local Management Interface (ILMI-ATM Forum standard)

Refer to the "Universal Switch Module (UXM)" section, earlier in this chapter, for details of the physical interfaces and status indicators.

Frame Relay Card Group

The Frame Relay card group consists of the following modules:

- Frame Relay Module, Model D (FRM/D) front card and Frame Relay Interface (FRI) back card
- Frame Relay Module, Model E (FRM/E) front card and FRI back card
- Frame Relay Module, Model F (FRM/F) front card and Frame Relay Interface, Model 2 (FRI-2) back card
- Universal Frame Relay Module, Channelized (UFM-C) front card and Universal Frame Relay Interface (UFI) back card
- Universal Frame Relay Module, Unchannelized (UFM-U) front card and UFI back card

The major functions of the FRM card group are as follows:

- Assembles and disassembles Frame Relay data packets for each of its ports
- Multiplexes and demultiplexes channels from the T1 or E1 line (Model E only)
- Regulates the flow of packets into the network to prevent and control congestion using the optional ForeSight feature
- Supports intelligent communication with the user equipment using one of several supported LMI signaling protocols
- Provides two configurable clock modes for serial interfaces (Model D only)
- Provides all necessary line framing (Model E only)
- Extracts timing, if required, for use as a network clock source (Model E only)
- Monitors the line for alarms and errors (Model E only)

Frame Relay Module, Model D

Frame Relay Module, Model D (FRM/D), unchannelized, supports four serial ports with V.35 or X.21 interfaces.

The FRM/D card module consists of the following:

- An FRM/D front card
- One of the following back cards:
    — 4-port V.35 (FRI-V.35)
    — 4-port V.21 (FRI-X.21)

Frame Relay Module, Model E

Frame Relay Module, Model E (FRM/E), channelized, supports a single T1 line or a single E1 line.

The FRM/E card module consists of the following:

- An FRM/E front card
- One of the following back cards, each of which supports a single line:
  - T1 format (FRI-T1)
  - E1 format (FRI-E1)

The FRM/D and FRM/E front cards are not interchangeable. The firmware on the front card must match the type of interface on the back card. For example, revision D firmware on the FRM supports X.21 and V.35 protocols, and revision E firmware on the FRM supports T1 and E1 interfaces.

Frame Relay Interface Cards

Both the Model D and Model E cards use the Frame Relay Interface (FRI) cards shown in Figure 10-54. The interfaces and the connectors are summarized in Table 10-19.

Table 10-19 *Interfaces And Connectors*

Interface	Connector
T1	DB-15 subminiature connector
E1	75-ohm unbalanced BNC or 120-ohm balanced BNC
V.35	34-pin female MRAC
X.21	Female DB-15 subminiature connectors

The status indicators of the FRI are shown in Table 10-20.

Table 10-20 *Frame Relay Interface Indicators*

Component	Status	Indicator
Card	Card status	Active or failed card
Line status T1/E1	LOS (red)	Loss of signal on local end
	Red alarm (red)	Loss of local frame alignment
	Yellow alarm (yellow)	Loss of remote frame alignment
	AIS (green)	Alarm Indication Signal, which indicates all 1s on the line
E1	MRFA (red)	Loss of local multiframe alignment
	MFYA (yellow)	Loss of remote multiframe alignment

Figure 10-54 *Frame Relay Interface Cards*

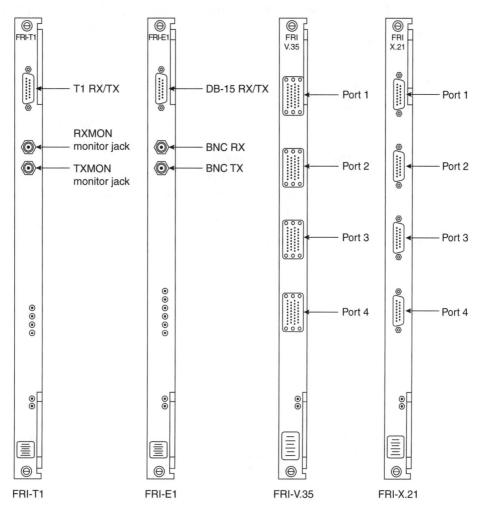

On the unchannelized FRI back cards (V.35 and X.21 interfaces), you can configure each port as either a DCE or a DTE, using onboard jumpers as described for the HDM card module.

FRM-2

The FRM-2 card module is specifically designed to provide a network interface for the IGX Port Concentrator Shelf (PCS). The PCS is an external device that acts as an access concentrator for up to 44 low-speed Frame Relay devices. Up to four modules with the necessary interface cards can be installed in the PCS for IGX connectivity.

The FRM/F card module consists of FRM/F front card and a FRI/F back card with an X.21 interface. FRM/F ports perform the same functions as the Frame Relay ports supported by the FRM/D card module previously discussed. The FRM/F also supports additional features, including these:

- Port rates from 9.6 to 384 kbps
- Aggregate of 1.792 Mbps across 44 Frame Relay ports
- V.35, V.11, and V.28 serial interfaces

Universal Frame Module Channelized

The Universal Frame Module Channelized (UFM-C) performs similar to the FRM/E, except that instead of a single T1 or E1 line, the UFM-C supports four or eight lines, depending on the type of front card purchased. All back cards for the UFM-C contain eight physical interfaces, although only four of these are activated unless a front card with support for the full eight ports is installed. Table 10-21 summarizes the possible front and back cards.

Table 10-21 *Universal Frame Module Channelized Card Ports and Interfaces*

Front Cards	Back Cards
Four-port (UFM-4C)	T1 format back card with 8-DB15 interfaces (UFI-8T1-DB15)
Eight-port (UFM-8C)	E1 format back card with 8-DB15 interfaces (UFI-E1-DB15)
	E1 format back card with 8-BNC interfaces (UFI-8E1-BNC)

Universal Frame Module Unchannelized

The Universal Frame Module Unchannelized (UFM-U) performs a similar function to the FRM/D, with higher port density, or an HSSI interface, which is not available for the FRM/D. The UFM-U card module consists of a UFM-U front card and one of the following back cards:

- 12-port V.35 (UFI-12 V.35)
- 12-port X.21 (UFI-12 X.21)
- 4-port HSSI (UFI-4 HSSI)

The major functions of the UFM are these:

- The front card maps, segments, and reassembles Frame Relay data streams to and from FastPackets.
- The UFM-C is configurable for 1 to 24 (T1) or 31 (E1) Frame Relay data streams.
- UFM-U provides serial line clocking to attached devices.

- Individual ports are configurable as a Frame Relay UNI or a Frame Relay NNI.
- The UFM cards support the following Frame Relay signaling protocols: Enhanced Local Management Interface (ELMI), Cisco LMI, T1.617 Annex D, and CCITT Q.933 Annex A.
- The UFM generates CLLM messages for congestion notification across NNIs and UNIs.
- The UFM supports traffic policing and per-connection queues in the ingress direction.
- The UFM supports the optional ForeSight congestion management feature.

Universal Frame Relay Interface

The T1 and E1 UFI back cards have eight physical interfaces, as shown in Figure 10-55. In the figure, the UFI-8E1 back card on the right is identical to the IFI-8E1 on the left except for the physical interfaces: One has BNC connectors, and the other has DB-15 connectors. The four-port version (UFM-4C) of the card set with a T1 DB-15 connection (UFI-8T1-DB-15) has eight ports, but only four ports are enabled.

The narrowband UFI back cards do not have separate card status and line signal status indicators. Instead, they have a single, tricolor status LED adjacent to each physical interface. The status indications are shown in Table 10-22.

Table 10-22 *Universal Frame Relay Interface Tricolor Status Indicator*

Color	Indicator
Red	The line is active, but a local alarm is detected.
Yellow	The line is active, but a remote alarm is detected.
Green	The card is active and in service.
No color or light	The line is inactive.

Figure 10-55 *UFI Interfaces—T1 and E1*

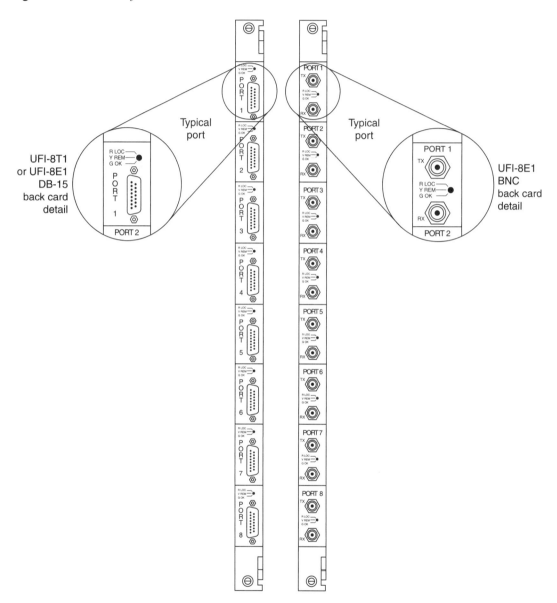

As shown in Figure 10-56, the V.35 and X.21 UFI back cards have six physical interfaces, and the HSSI back card has four interfaces.

Figure 10-56 *UFI Interfaces—Unchannelized*

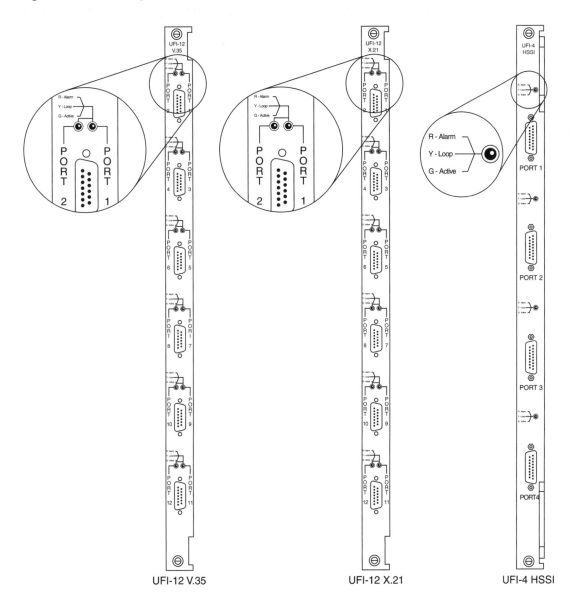

UFI-12 V.35   UFI-12 X.21   UFI-4 HSSI

With the V.35 and X.21 back cards, each physical connector supports two Frame Relay ports, and special two-port hydra cables are required to connect user devices. Different cables are available for V.35 and X.21, and both come in DCE or DTE versions.

These serial UFI back cards do not have separate card status and line signal status indicators. Instead, they have a tricolor status LED for each port adjacent to each physical interface. The V.35 and X.21 interfaces have two LEDs, as shown in Figure 10-56. The status indications for the serial cards are the same as for the T1/E1 cards, shown in Table 10-22.

Summary

This chapter covered the installation of the IGX switch and the card groups and interfaces that the IGX supports. The IGX consists of a chassis that contains 8, 16, or 32 card slots; a backplane (midplane); a fan assembly; and a power supply. Additionally, the IGX offers services through card modules, which are made up of a front and a rear card. The front card typically provides the intelligence, whereas the back card provides the interfaces. The IGX card modules can interface with narrowband and broadband services.

Review Questions

The following questions test your retention of the material presented in this chapter. The answers to the Review Questions can be found in Appendix A, "Answers to Review Questions."

1 Which two of the following statements apply to the IGX 8410 node?

A. A booster fan assembly is required.

B. The system can operate on 110 VAC power.

C. The AC power tray holds six power modules.

D. The AC power tray holds four power supplies.

E. The backplane includes the utility bus as installed on the IPX switch.

2 When installing an IGX in a rack, which of the following two steps are always required?

A. Install the DC-PEM.

B. Install the AC power modules.

C. Install the temporary mounting brackets.

D. Remove the card modules (if installed) from the card cage before lifting it into place.

E. Install the multishelf ribbon cable between the upper and lower backplanes.

3 Mark the following statements as true or false.

A. SCMs should be installed in slot 1.

B. For an IGX 8410 with six cards, three power modules are required.

C. In an IGX 8430 node, redundant NPMs are installed in slots 1 and 17.

D. An IGX 8430 needs at least three power modules for N+1 redundancy.

E. When installing an SCM in an IGX 8410, the W6 jumper must be removed.

4 Which two cards support ATM trunks?

A. NPM

B. NTM

C. UXM

D. UFM-U

E. UFM-C

F. ALM/B

5 How many E1 ports are there on a UXM?

A. 2 or 4

B. 1 or 2

C. 4 or 8

D. 3 or 6

6 How many physical connectors are there on a UFM-U with a V.35 back card?

A. 4

B. 6

C. 12

D. 6 or 12, depending on the front card type

7 Which two devices could you attach to a CVM or a UVM card?

A. A digital PBX

B. A Cisco LightStream 1010 ATM switch

C. A Cisco 7000 router with a serial interface

D. An IGX switch with a BTM or ALM/B trunk card

E. A front-end processor with a synchronous interface

8 Match the card module in the table with its function in the list that follows.

Card Module	Answer
NPM	
SCM	
NTM	
UFM/U	
UXM	

A. Support for lines attached to ATM end-user equipment

B. IGX to IGX trunks transporting FastPackets

C. Central processor, software storage, and network management

D. Serial lines, traffic policing, and ForeSight feature

E. Local alarm notification, LAN port, and external clock port

CHAPTER 11

Installing BPX 8600 Switches

Chapter 9, "Cisco WAN Switch Product Overview," gives an introduction to the BPX 8600 switches. This chapter builds upon the information provided in that chapter and provides detailed information on the physical, mechanical, and electrical installation of the BPX 8600 series switches. In addition, this chapter provides a description of each of the card module sets that are supported with System Software Release 9.2.

This chapter includes the following sections:

- BPX Hardware Overview
- BPX 8620 Chassis Installation
- Power Requirements and Installation
- Card Installation
- Broadband Control Card
- Management Connections
- Additional Configuration for BPX 8650
- Summary
- Review Questions

BPX Hardware Overview

The BPX, like the IGX, is made up of a chassis and card modules placed within the chassis.

Chassis

The BPX node is housed in a rack-mounted (19- or 21-inch rack) chassis with 15 card slots on one shelf. It has a backplane with connectors on the front and back to attach the front and back card modules. The backplane is also referred to as a *midplane*. Several bus systems are supported by the backplane that allow the cards to communicate with each other and the processor card.

Each BPX node has a fan assembly that is used to cool the chassis. Three fans on the back of the chassis draw air through a vent in the front of the chassis, through the card modules and out the back of the cabinet. The performance of these fans and the cabinet temperature can be monitored using software commands that will be covered in Chapter 12, "Establishing Initial Access to IGX and BPX Switches."

The BPX node can be powered from either an AC or a DC source. One or two power supplies can be used to power the node, depending on the need for redundancy. The DC power supplies are mounted directly into the chassis; the AC power supplies require a separate power distribution shelf to be mounted below the chassis.

The primary power for a BPX node is –48 volts of direct current (VDC), which is bused across the backplane for use by all card slots. An optional AC power supply is also available. The BPX switch can use either one or two power feeds. For true redundancy, each feed must be connected to different electrical circuits.

A fan assembly with three 6-inch –48 VDC fans is mounted on a tray at the back of the BPX shelf. Air for cooling the cards is drawn through an air intake grill located at the bottom front of the enclosure. Air passes up between the vertically mounted cards and exhausts at the top rear of the chassis. All unused slots in the front are filled with blank faceplates to properly channel airflow.

Backplane

The BPX backplane supports the following bus structures:

- **Crosspoint switch paths**—The crosspoint switch paths are used to carry data among all cards and the crosspoint switch, which is on the processor card in slot 7 or 8. The crosspoint switch creates multiple temporary connections between cards transmitting cells and cards receiving cells. Each crosspoint switch path is serial and is serviced at a rate of 800 Mbps.

- **Arbiter polling bus**—The arbiter polling bus carries the crosspoint switch-polling signal. The arbiter polls each card in the BPX node to determine the next configuration of the crosspoint switch.

- **Communications bus**—The communications bus carries internal communications between the processor card and the other card modules. Status information, statistics, and configuration details are exchanged across the communications bus. The communications bus does not carry user data.

- **Timing bus**—The timing bus carries timing signals between the processor card and the other card modules. The cards use the timing signals to clock the lines and trunks that they support.

- **Control bus**—The control bus provides a signal to the cards in the node that defines which processor card is active, either A (slot 7) or B (slot 8).

- **Power bus**—The power bus provides –48 VDC to all cards in the BPX node.

Card Modules

As with IGX card groups, a front and back card pair create a *card group*. Each card group performs a specific function on the BPX node. In general, the front card has the intelligence to run the software or firmware and to perform the features and functions for the card group. The back card is responsible for interfacing with the attached equipment using a variety of connectors. In most cases, the back card has little, if any, intelligence and is responsible for only physical-layer functions.

On each front card, LEDs report card conditions. The card status also can be viewed via system commands or network-management software. Different card sets have different arrangements of LED indicators, which provide a visual means of identifying operational status and failure conditions. The LEDs for particular card sets are discussed later in this chapter; however, most front card faceplates include at least a set of card status LEDs that indicate whether the card is in an active, standby, or failed condition.

A blank faceplate must be present in empty slots to minimize electromagnetic interference (EMI) and radio frequency interference (RFI). Faceplates also should be inserted when equipment is removed to ensure correct airflow.

Figure 11-1 gives an overview of the card groups supported by the BPX.

Figure 11-1 *BPX Card Module Groups*

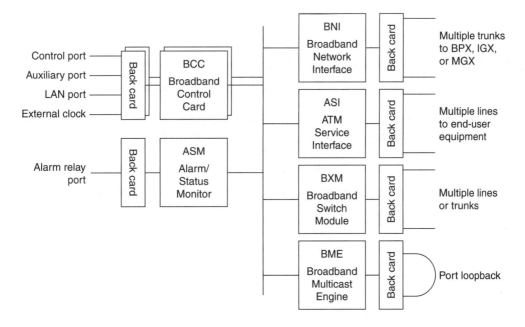

The following list offers a brief discussion of each card group:

- **Broadband Control Card**—The Broadband Control Card (BCC) is the central processor for the BPX node, and stores system software and all configuration information. The BCC also contains the crosspoint switch and communicates with network management systems.

- **Alarm/Status Monitor**—The Alarm/Status Monitor (ASM) is responsible for measuring local environmental conditions and reporting local and network errors.

- **Broadband Network Interface**—The Broadband Network Interface (BNI) card provides two or three network trunks with T3, E3, or OC-3/STM-1 interfaces.

- **ATM Service Interface**—The ATM Service Interface (ASI) card provides two ATM line interfaces to accept user traffic from an attached user device with DS-3, E3, or OC-3/STM-1 interfaces.

- **Broadband Switch Module**—The Broadband Switch Module (BXM) provides 8 or 12 DS-3/E3, 4 or 8 OC-3/STM-1, or 1 or 2 OC-12/STM-4 interfaces. A BXM card can be configured to operate in either trunk or line (port) mode. Starting with Software Release 9.2, individual interfaces on a BXM card can be configured in trunk or port mode.

- **Broadband Multicast Engine**—The Broadband Multicast Engine (BME) supports multicast connections on the BPX switch. The BME is an adaptation of the BXM with an OC-12/STM-4 two-port back card.

BPX 8620 Chassis Installation

The BPX switch, shown in Figure 11-2, is designed for mounting in a standard equipment rack. A minimum space between rails of 17.75 inches (44.5 cm) is required. Mounting flanges are attached permanently to the front edge of the chassis. It is recommended that the chassis be mounted with all plug-in cards temporarily removed to lessen the weight. (A fully loaded BPX chassis can weigh up to 215 lbs [97 kg]—a second person is required to assist with the rack-mounted installation.)

A temporary support bracket and a temporary spacer bracket are included with the installation kit, as shown in Figure 11-3. The wooden pallet tray on which the BPX chassis is shipped can be used to lift, to align, and to install the chassis in a rack.

Figure 11-2 *BPX 8600 Components*

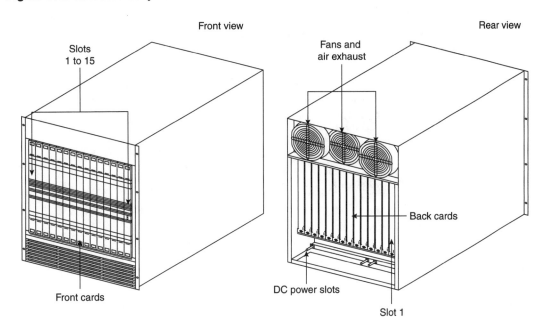

Figure 11-3 *Rack-Mounting the Chassis*

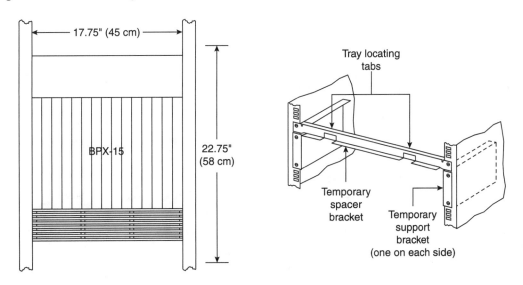

If an AC power supply assembly is also mounted in the same rack, install the switch chassis first and then install the shelf for the AC power supply assembly.

The BPX AC power shelf requires a minimum vertical space of three rack-mount units (RMUs), equivalent to 5.25 inches (13.4 cm).

BPX 8620 chassis installation follows this process:

Step 1   To begin, position the shipping container and pallet in front of the cabinet, with the rear of the chassis toward the cabinet. Remove the foam strips on the sides, front, and rear.

Step 2   Remove the card-retaining bracket from the front of the chassis by unscrewing the four Phillips screws. This bracket is used to retain the boards during shipping.

Step 3   Remove the air intake grill and all front and rear cards from the shelf, and temporarily set them aside.

Ground yourself before handling BPX cards by placing a wrist strap on your wrist and clipping the strap lead to the cabinet.

Step 4   Install the temporary support bracket and spacer bracket. Use four mounting screws to attach the support bracket and two screws to attach the spacer bracket to the rack.

Step 5   With one person on each side of the BPX chassis, lift the pallet tray and BPX chassis, positioning the slots at the rear of the pallet tray over the locating tabs on the spacer bracket, as shown in Figure 11.4.

Figure 11-4   *Installing the Chassis*

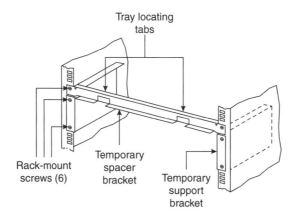

Step 6   Slide the chassis back over the support brackets and into place.

Step 7   Attach the cabinet to the rack with eight #10-32 machine screws and flat washers.

Step 8   If desired, remove the temporary support bracket and spacer bracket.

Step 9   Do not reinstall the system cards until after you install the power supply.

Power Requirements and Installation

The electrical power and grounding requirements shown in Table 11-1 cover installations at central office and private enterprise locations.

Table 11-1   *Power Requirements*

Power	Requirements
220 VAC	Power must be available within 6 feet (1.8 m).
–48 VDC	Supply must comply with the Safety Extra Low Voltage (SELV) of EN 60950.
Grounding	The chassis frame must be bonded to protective ground, per ITU-T recommendation K.27 or Bellcore GR-1089.

AC

General requirements for AC power for the BPX are listed here:

- An AC power source must be available within 6 feet (1.8 m) of the system and must be easily accessible. Before turning on the power, verify that the power supplied to the node comes from a dedicated branch circuit.

- The dedicated branch should be protected by a 20A two-pole circuit breaker with a long trip delay.

- The receptacle into which the node connects must be of the grounding type. The grounding conductor that connects to the receptacle should connect to protective earth at the service equipment.

DC

General requirements for DC power are listed here:

- Only a –48 VDC dedicated branch supply that complies with the Safety Extra Low Voltage (SELV) requirements of EN 60950 can connect to the BPX switch DC input.

- Each dedicated branch supply should be protected by a single-pole 50A circuit breaker with a long trip delay.

- Consult local or national codes for proper conductor sizing. The conductors must be suitable for 20A; 10 to 12 AWG (4 square mm) is adequate.

Bonding and Grounding

To maintain the full integrity of the equipment, it must be bonded to an integrated ground plane or an isolated ground plane network. A frame-bonding connection is provided on the Cisco-supplied cabinet for rack-mounted systems.

Except for the AC power supply module, every module in a rack-mounted system relies on the rack itself for grounding. Therefore, the rack must be properly connected to protective earth before operating the system.

A DC-powered BPX node must have grounding conductors that connect at two separate locations, as follows:

- The grounding conductor provided with the supply source must connect to the safety ground terminal of the DC Power Entry Module (PEM). See the section "DC Power Integration," later in this chapter, for information on how to make this connection.

- A grounding conductor must connect to the appropriate terminal of a rack assembly or to the chassis of a BPX node.

The primary power for a BPX node is –48 VDC, which is bused across the backplane for use by all card slots. The DC power supply comes preinstalled in the BPX chassis. For applications requiring operation from an AC power source, an optional AC power supply assembly and shelf are available. The AC power shelf converts the 208/240 VAC input to –48 VDC.

DC-to-DC converters on each card convert the –48 VDC to logic voltages for use on each card. The –48 VDC input connects directly to the DC PEM. The DC PEM provides a circuit breaker and a line filter for the DC input.

In a DC configuration, nodes can be equipped with either a single PEM or dual PEMs for redundancy. The PEMs are mounted at the back of the node below the backplane. A conduit hookup box or an insulated cover plate is provided for terminating the conduit or a wire at the DC power input.

Rear Support Bracket Installation

Although the DC power supplies come factory-installed in the BPX chassis, you must secure them from the rear of the rack using rear support brackets. These same brackets also must be installed for a BPX switch with optional AC power. Refer to Figure 11-5 when completing the following rear support bracket installation steps:

Step 1 Locate the two rear support brackets and adjustable plates in the miscellaneous parts kit.

Figure 11-5 *Installing the Power Supply Rear Support Brackets*

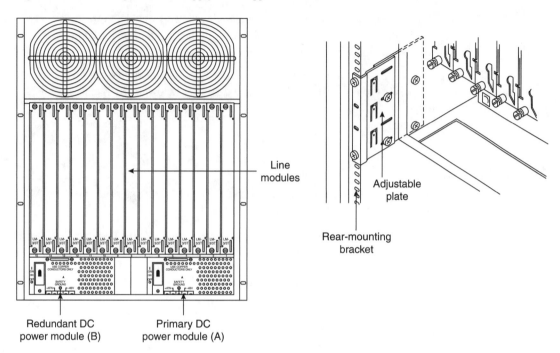

Step 2 Align the tabs in the three punch-outs facing up, and slide one of the adjustable plates between the vertical rail at the rear of the enclosure and the rear side of the BPX chassis.

Step 3 Align the top and bottom holes in the adjustable plate with the corresponding holes in the side panel of the BPX chassis. The bottom of the plate should be approximately aligned with the bottom of the BPX switch.

Step 4 Secure the plate to the BPX switch using two #10-32 screws and flat washers.

Step 5 Attach a support bracket to the adjustable plate with two #10-32 screws and flat washers. Do not tighten them yet.

Step 6 Secure the support bracket to the rack using two #10-32 screws. You might have to lift the chassis slightly to align the holes in the bracket to the holes in the rack.

Step 7 Tighten the screws attaching the support bracket to the adjustable plate.

Step 8 Slide a cable strap over each of the three tabs on the support bracket.

Step 9   Repeat Steps 2 through 8 to mount the bracket for the other side.

Step 10   Before continuing, check that the source power is 180 to 264 VAC or –42 to –56 VDC. If it is not, do not continue with the installation until you resolve the power problem.

In an AC BPX configuration, a separate shelf houses one or two optional AC power supplies. This shelf is mounted directly below the BPX chassis in the rack and is secured by a rear support bracket, as described previously.

AC Power Supply

When the rear support bracket is installed, complete the following steps to install an AC power supply:

Step 1   Install the temporary support bracket and spacer bracket in a rack 5.25 inches (13.4 cm) below the bottom of the BPX chassis. Use four mounting screws to attach the support bracket, and two screws to attach the spacer bracket to the rack.

Step 2   Remove the air intake grill by doing the following:

Locate the small access hole in the top center of the front air intake grill on the power supply shelf. Insert a slotted-blade screwdriver (0.25 inch [6 mm] or smaller) into the access hole until it stops (approximately 1 inch [2.5 cm]). Carefully rotate the screwdriver approximately 90° in either direction. The top of the air intake grill should spring out. Figure 11-6 shows this step.

Remove the air intake grill.

Step 3   Insert and secure the shelf by doing the following:

Slide the AC power supply shelf in the rack between the BPX chassis and the support bracket. If cables are attached, use care to avoid damaging them.

Install screws and washers to loosely secure the power supply assembly to the rack. Align the front flanges of the power supply assembly with the flanges on the BPX chassis and tighten the screws. There should be approximately 1/16-inch (2 mm) clearance between the BPX shelf and the AC power supply shelf to provide sufficient clearance for inserting power supplies.

Figure 11-6 *Installing the AC Power Supply*

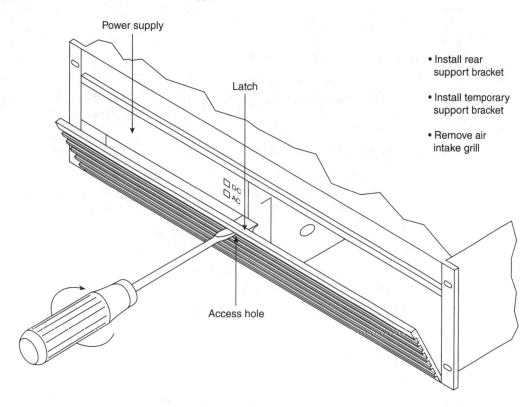

Removing the air intake grill

Secure the rear support brackets to the power supply shelf using one #10-32 screw and one flat washer on each side. Use the lower hole in the brackets.

Before continuing, ensure that the source AC power is not connected to the IEC power receptacle(s) at the rear of the BPX node.

Step 4   Connect the cables by doing the following:

Connect and secure a power supply interconnect cable (cable A) between the primary AC power supply (P1 PSI plug end) and the BPX backplane power connector (J1 BSB jack end).

If a second, redundant AC supply is installed, connect and secure a second power supply interconnect cable (cable B) between the redundant AC power supply and the BPX backplane power connector.

Remove the temporary support bracket and the spacer bracket.

Step 5   Set the circuit breaker(s) at the back of the AC power supply assembly to off.

Step 6   Insert the power supplies as follows:

Loosen the captive screw in the center of the power supply retainer, and rotate the retainer down. Align the power supply assembly in the left (A) slot at the bottom of the AC power supply shelf, and gently slide it in part of the way.

Continue to slide the assembly in until it mates with the rear connector.

If the power supply is seated completely in its connector, the pin plunger on the left side of the supply engages with a hole in the tray. If not, push firmly on the front edge until the power supply assembly seats in the connector.

Screw in the thumbscrew on the right, and tighten it using your fingers.

When a second power supply is provided, install it in the PS-B slot in the same manner after removing the blank panel from slot B.

Rotate the power supply retainer up, and tighten the center captive screw.

Step 7   Check that the input power is within the range of 180 to 264 VAC.

If it is not, do not continue with the installation until you resolve the power problem.

Step 8   Install the air intake grill. Press on the top center until the latch snaps into place.

AC Power Integration

This section covers three possible AC power configurations:

- Single power supply, single AC power feed
- Dual power supplies, single AC power feed
- Dual power supplies, dual AC power feeds

An 8-foot (3-meter) power cord is supplied with each AC power supply assembly. Complete the following steps to make AC power connections to the BPX chassis:

Step 1   Plug the power cord(s) into the applicable IEC connector(s), and tighten the cord retainers. A separate power cord connects to each of one or two IEC connectors, depending on the version of power supply shelf provided.

Step 2 Plug the BPX cord into a 220 to 240 VAC, single-phase wall outlet capable of supplying 15A. The building circuit should be protected with a 20A circuit breaker.

Step 3 For the dual power feed version, plug each power cord into receptacles on separate building circuits to provide maximum protection against power feed failure. Each building circuit should be protected with a 20A circuit breaker.

Step 4 The ground (green/yellow) wire of the AC power cord should be connected to the BPX chassis for safety. Make sure that the building AC receptacle also is adequately grounded.

Step 5 Provide an additional AC outlet strip, with at least four outlets, near the BPX node to power optional modems, CSUs or DSUs, test equipment, and so on. There is no accessory AC outlet supplied on the BPX chassis. This outlet strip should be connected to a source of AC voltage normal for the region—for example, 115 VAC for North America.

Before installing power connections, make sure that all source power is turned off at the building circuit breaker.

DC Power Integration

Two versions of the DC-powered BPX cabinet exist:

- Single DC PEM, for single power feed
- Dual DC PEM, for dual power feed

DC wiring is connected from a –48 VDC power source to one or both DC power entry modules. This wiring is not provided as part of the normal Cisco installation. A metallic conduit box that meets all U.S. electrical codes for attaching electrical conduit is factory-installed at the DC PEMs.

Use conduit if required by local electrical code.

An alternate connection scheme entails the use of a Cisco-supplied plastic cover for the input power leads. This method is appropriate for installations in locations where conduit protection is not required.

Follow these steps to make DC power connections to the BPX chassis:

Step 1 Locate the conduit terminating box shipped with the node. Remove the two cover screws and lift off the cover, as shown in Figure 11-7.

Figure 11-7 *Making DC Power Connections*

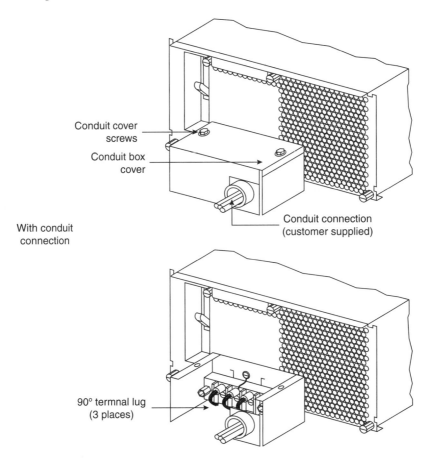

Step 2 If the conduit is not required, remove the conduit box by removing the two screws, one above the terminal block and one below it. The DC terminal block is visible then, as shown in Figure 11-8.

Step 3 Run three wires from the DC terminal block to a source of –48 VDC. Use 8 AWG wire (or the metric equivalent). Use a #10 screw ring lug designed for 8 AWG wire (90° terminal lug if using the conduit box) to terminate the wires.

Step 4 Ensure that the polarity of the DC input wiring is correct. Connections with reversed polarity might trip the primary circuit breaker or damage the equipment.

Figure 11-8 *DC Terminal Block*

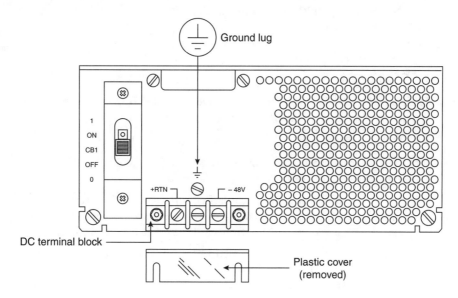

Without conduit connection

Step 5 Remember that this is a positive ground system. Connect the positive lead to the +RTN terminal. Connect the negative lead to the –48V terminal. Connect the earth ground to the middle terminal labeled SAFETY GROUND.

Step 6 For personal safety, the green/yellow wire must be connected to the safety (earth) ground both at the equipment and at the supply side of the DC wiring.

Step 7 Terminate the DC input wiring on a DC source capable of supplying at least –48V at 40A. A 40A DC circuit breaker is required at the –48 VDC facility power source. An easily accessible disconnect device should be incorporated into the facility wiring. Be sure to connect the ground wire/conduit to a solid earth ground.

Step 8 Primary overcurrent protection is provided by the building circuit breaker. In North America, this breaker should protect against excess currents, short circuits, and earth faults. A new electrical circuit would require an installation of a circuit breaker by a qualified electrician.

Step 9 If the system is equipped with dual power feed, repeat Steps 2 through 8 for the second power feed.

Step 10 Either replace the cover on the conduit terminating box, or attach the plastic cover plate to the terminal block with screws into the two terminal block standoffs.

Card Installation

There are 15 vertical slots in the front and the rear of the BPX enclosure for card modules. When installing cards in the BPX, keep these guidelines in mind:

- Use slot 7 for the BCC front card and the BCC-BC back card.

- If the node includes redundant BCCs, use slot 8 for the standby BCC and its back card. If there is a single BCC, leave slot 8 empty.

- Use slot 15 for the ASM front card. If you are using the LM-ASC back card, install it in back slot 15. If you are not using an ASM, leave both front and back slots 15 empty. If you are using only an ASM front card, leave the back slot empty.

- Use slots 1 through 6 and 9 through 14 for network interface and service interface cards. Where cards are Y-cabled for redundancy, plan to locate those cards in adjacent slots. (Cards using Y-cable redundancy must be placed in adjacent slots.)

The front cards slide into the BPX node from the front of the chassis. They are held in place by the air intake grill, which must be removed before you can insert or remove front cards. There are extractor levers on the top and bottom of the cards; hold these as you insert the card.

Figure 11-9 identifies the card placement with a front and rear view of the chassis.

Figure 11-9 *Card Slot Conventions*

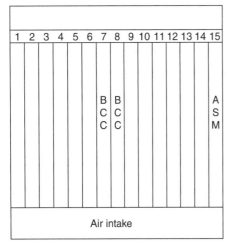

Front view

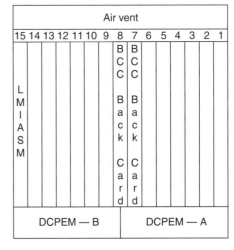

Rear view

Front Card Installation

Complete the following steps to install a front card. Refer to Figure 11-10 during the front card installation steps:

Step 1   Ground yourself using the antistatic strap.

Figure 11-10 *Installing Front Cards*

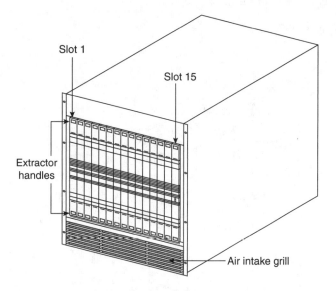

Step 2   Examine the backplane and card cage guides for any signs of loose or misplaced EMI gaskets (seals).

Step 3   Examine the backplane connectors for bent or damaged connection or power pins.

Step 4   Remove the air intake grill.

Step 5   Position the card into the locating guide slots at the top and bottom of the card cage.

Step 6   Gently slide the card all the way to the rear of the slot.

Step 7   You should feel only slight friction as you insert the card. Stop and investigate any binding, which probably indicates misalignment.

Step 8   Seat the board by fully seating both extractor handles.

Step 9   The handles should snap back to a vertical position when seated.

Step 10 Install cover plates over empty card slots to eliminate RFI and EMI, and to ensure correct airflow through the card cage.

Step 11 Replace the air intake grill.

Back Card Installation

It is recommended that you install the front cards first and then install the back cards. Making the connection between the two cards is easier from the back card. Figure 11-11 gives a back view for the back card installation.

Figure 11-11 *Installing Back Cards*

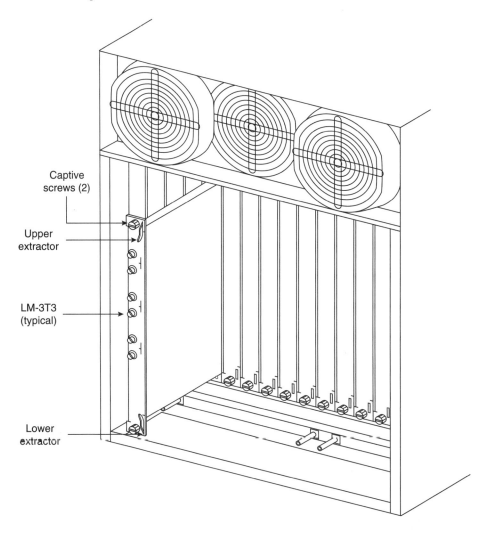

Complete the following steps to install a back card:

Step 1   Ground yourself.

Step 2   Locate the corner edges of the card into the appropriate guide slots at the top and bottom of the card cage.

Step 3   Gently slide the card all the way to the rear of the slot, and push to seat the card in the connector. The card should slide in easily. Investigate any binding—do not use excessive force.

Step 4   Tighten the two captive screws.

BNC and Subminiature BNC Connections

The BNI and ASI back cards have three pairs of BNC connectors for T3 and E3 interfaces. The BXM back cards have either 8 or 12 pairs of subminiature BNC (SMB) "posi-lock" connectors for T3 and E3.

Complete the following steps to make single T3/E3 connections to each port:

Step 1   Bring each cable through the opening at the bottom of the cabinet at the back, and route it up the side.

Step 2   The BPX chassis has tie-downs inside the cabinet to hold cabling in place. Pull them apart as applicable, place the routed cable in position, wrap the ties around the cable, and remake the loops by pressing the two sections together.

Step 3   Connect the cables to the BNC or SMB connectors on the back card. Connectors marked RX are for inputs to the BPX node; TX indicates an output. The ports are numbered from top to bottom, as shown in Figure 11-12.

Step 4   The maximum distance from the BPX chassis to a DS-3 crossconnect point is approximately 450 feet (150 meters).

Step 5   Record which slot and port numbers are used for each trunk or line. You will need the information later when configuring the network.

Figure 11-12 *Making T3 or E3 Connections*

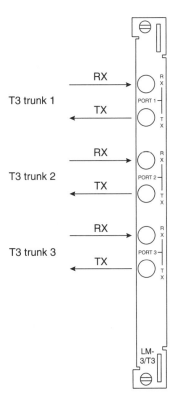

BNC and SMB Y Connections

You can connect two adjacent identical cards to a single trunk or line for redundancy using a Y-cable, as shown in Figure 11-13.

To install the Y-cable, follow these steps:

Step 1 Locate a three-way BNC or SMB Y-cable adapter for each port that is so ordered.

SMB cables supplied for the BXM are terminated with a BNC connector for attachment of the external cabling.

Step 2 As an alternative to the Y-cable, use a BNC "T" and two short BNC-BNC cables (or SMB equivalents).

Step 3 Ensure that there are two appropriate line modules located in adjacent slots.

Figure 11-13 *Using a Y-Cable for T3/E3 Connections*

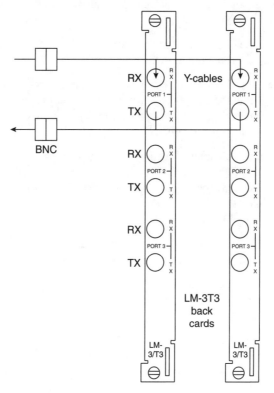

Step 4   Connect two legs of the Y-cable to the TX T3 or E3 connectors on the same port on each of the two line modules. Do the same with the two RX T3 or E3 connectors.

Step 5   Connect the third leg of the TX and RX Y-cable adapters to the TX and RX trunk cable.

Fiber Optic Connections

The OC-3/STM-1 and OC-12/STM-4 back cards support fiber optic interfaces using SC connectors for multimode fiber, SC connectors for Y-redundancy single-mode fiber (SMF) connectors, and FC connectors for single-mode fiber.

The following cabling outline applies to all fiber back cards, except that Y-cable redundancy is supported only on the SMF back cards. Complete the following steps to make connections:

Step 1   Bring the cables through the opening at the bottom of the cabinet at the back, and route them up the side.

Step 2   The BPX chassis has tie-downs inside the cabinet to hold cabling in place. Pull the tie-downs apart as applicable, place the routed cable in position, wrap the ties around the cable, and remake the loops by pressing the two sections together.

Step 3   Connect the cables to the applicable connectors on the back card, as shown in Figure 11-14. The SC connectors are keyed to facilitate correct placement. SC connectors are marked RCVR for an input to the BPX, and XMTR for an output from the BPX node. The ports are numbered from top to bottom.

Step 4   Record which slot and port numbers are used for each trunk or line. You will need the information later when configuring the network.

Step 5   For card redundancy, make sure that there are two appropriate line modules equipped in adjacent slots.

Step 6   Y-cable redundancy is supported only for the SMF back cards. Connect two legs to the XMTR connectors on the same port on each of the two line modules. Do the same with the two RCVR connectors.

Figure 11-14 *Making Fiber Optic Connections*

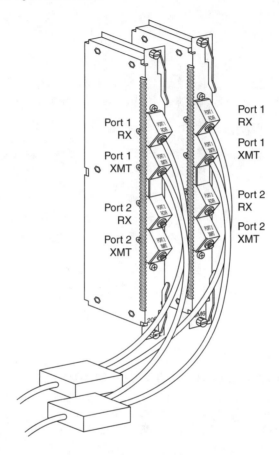

BME OC-12 Port Loop

The two ports on the OC-12 back card for the BME multicast card are set up by connecting the transmit of port 1 to the receive of port 2, and the receive of port 1 to the transmit of port 2, thus looping the two ports together. Signal attenuators are required in the loop cables, as shown in Figure 11-15; 10 decibel (dB) and 15 dB versions are available from Cisco.

Figure 11-15 *Making a BME OC-12 Port Loop*

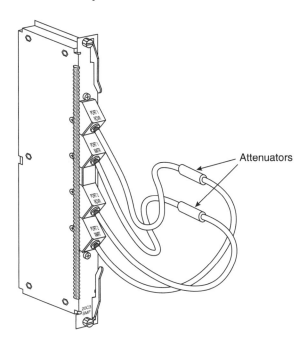

Attenuators

Automatic Protection Switching Connections

Automatic protection switching (APS) provides a standards-based line redundancy for BXM OC-3 and OC-12 cards. With Release 9.2, the BXM OC-3 and BXM OC-12 cards support the SONET APS 1+1 and APS 1:1 standards for line redundancy, as shown in Figure 11-16.

Figure 11-16 *SONET Automatic Protection System (APS)*

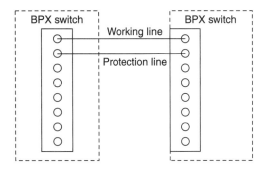

APS 1:1 redundancy   APS 1+1 redundancy

APS provides the capability to configure a pair of SONET lines for line redundancy so that the hardware automatically switches from the active line to the standby line when the active line fails.

Each redundant line pair consists of a working line and a protection line. The hardware is set up to switch automatically. Upon detection of a signal fail or a signal degrade condition, the hardware switches from the working line to the protection line.

The following APS types of redundancy are supported:

- APS 1:1
- APS 1+1
- APS 1+1 (Annex B)

To support line redundancy only (APS 1:1), no additional hardware is required other than cabling. To support card and line redundancy, APS 1+1 requires a new-paired back card.

APS 1+1 redundancy, which provides both card and line redundancy, uses the standard BXM OC-3 and OC-12 front cards, but requires a special APS redundant backplane and APS redundant back cards. With earlier card cages, because of the positioning of mechanical dividers, the APS card pairs can be inserted only in certain slots. These are slots 2 through 5 and 10 through 13. With current card cages supported from Release 9.2, this limitation is removed, and the APS card pairs can be located anywhere, except BCC cards slots 7 and 8, and ASM card slot 15. An APS 1+1 redundant card pair must be in adjacent slots (2, 3 or 4, 5 and so on). Complete the following steps while referring to Figure 11-17 to install APS redundant frame assembly and back cards:

Step 1   If not already in place in the APS redundant frame assembly, slide the two APS back cards into the APS redundant frame assembly.

CAUTION   Nylon standoffs on the APS redundant frame assembly must be in place to prevent shorting against –48 VDC pins and ground pins on the BPX midplane.

Step 2   Verify that the nylon standoffs are securely installed on the APS redundant frame assembly.

Step 3   Carefully slide the APS redundant frame assembly and APS cards into selected side-by-side slots at the back of the BPX shelf. Slide the APS redundant frame assembly and cards into the BPX shelf until they are snug against the BPX midplane.

Step 4   Going back and forth between the screws, gradually tighten the retaining screws at the top and bottom of the APS back cards until they are secure.

Figure 11-17 *APS Hardware*

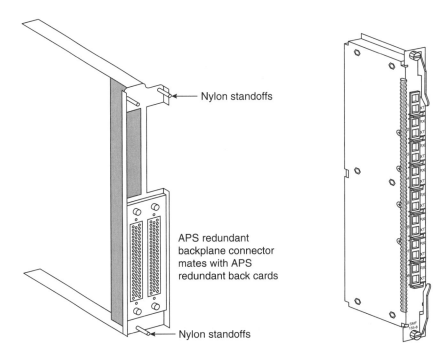

Nylon standoffs

APS redundant
backplane connector
mates with APS
redundant back cards

Nylon standoffs

Broadband Control Card

The *Broadband Control Card (BCC)* is the central processor for the BPX node, and it stores
system software and all configuration information. The BCC also contains the crosspoint
switch.

The BCC communicates with other nodes in the network and network-management
platforms, such as the Cisco WAN Manager station.

Most BPX nodes have redundant BCCs installed in card slots 7 and 8. One BCC is always
active, and the other is a hot standby. All information, including configurations, statistics,
and event logs, is passed between the two BCCs so that they are both up to date. The BPX
node can run on a single BCC, but if it fails, the node fails.

Four BCC models are supported by Release 9.2 system software:

- BCC-32 (model B)
- BCC-3-32 (model C)
- BCC-3-64 (model D)
- BCC-4 (model E)

One of the functions of the BCC back card is to provide a means to connect a network-management station and other peripheral equipment to the BPX system. Figure 11-18 shows the connection ports and BCC LEDs. Software configuration on the BPX node also is needed to support these devices. Configuration is covered in Chapter 12, "Establishing Initial Access to IGX and BPX Switches," and Chapter 13, "Initial Configuration of IGX and BPX Switches."

Figure 11-18 *BCC LEDs and Interfaces*

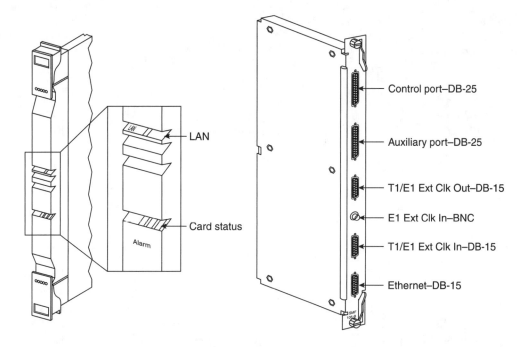

If you already connected peripherals to the IGX node(s) in your network, you might not need to repeat this step for your BPX node(s). Attachment and configuration for BPX peripherals follow the same procedures that are used with the IGX node, with the exception that the BPX might have redundant back cards for the controllers. This enables Y-cable redundancy to be used on the control, auxiliary, and LAN ports.

Management Connections

Network nodes require management connections to provide an initial configuration interface. In addition, management connections allow a node to be configured out of band through a local-area network connection, through a console cable, or a modem. The management port also can be used for node alarms, and the output can be sent to a printer.

Control Terminal

As a preliminary to the node configuration phase of the installation process, you must have access to the system for a control terminal. This can be a dumb terminal (VT100 or equivalent) or a PC running a terminal emulation program.

The control terminal is connected to either the BCC back card using the control port, as shown in Figure 11-19, or the auxiliary port. The connection can be either local or direct or via a modem connection.

Figure 11-19 *Connecting a Control Terminal*

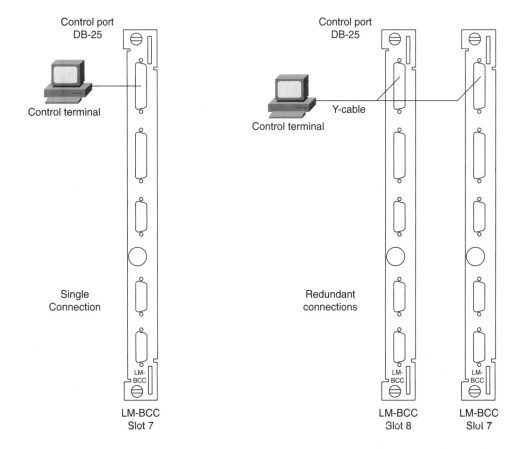

Complete the following steps to attach the control terminal to the back card:

Step 1   From the back of the cabinet, run a straight-through EIA/TIA-232/V.24 cable through the opening at the bottom and up to the back card in slot 7 or 8. If Y-cable redundancy is required, the Y-cable must be connected to both back cards in slots 7 and 8.

Step 2   Locate the control port connector on the back card, and attach the control
terminal EIA/TIA-232/V.24 cable to it (or both).

Step 3   Tighten the EIA/TIA-232 connector screws to firmly attach the cable to
the control port connector.

Step 4   Plug the control terminal power cord into the appropriate wall receptacle.

Step 5   Configure the terminal for the following communication parameters,
which are the default for a BPX control port: 9.6 kbps, no parity, 8 data
bits, 1 stop bit, and XON/XOFF flow control.

Step 6   Leave the terminal in place for use in node configuration.

Ethernet AUI Port

An Ethernet AUI port is provided on the BCC back card to facilitate a LAN connection. If
the Cisco WAN Manager station is connected to this BPX node, it must be connected via
the LAN port. This connection can be either direct or via intermediate switches or routers.
(If the node is connected directly to the Cisco WAN Manager, as shown in Figure 11-20,
then a crossover Ethernet cable, such as a Category 5 twisted-pair cable, is required.)

Physical connectivity is implemented by connecting a suitable cable with a 15-pin AUI
connector to the BCC-LM LAN port, and from there to the LAN connection point (hub,
router, or switch, for example).

Figure 11-20 *LAN Connection for the Network-Management Station*

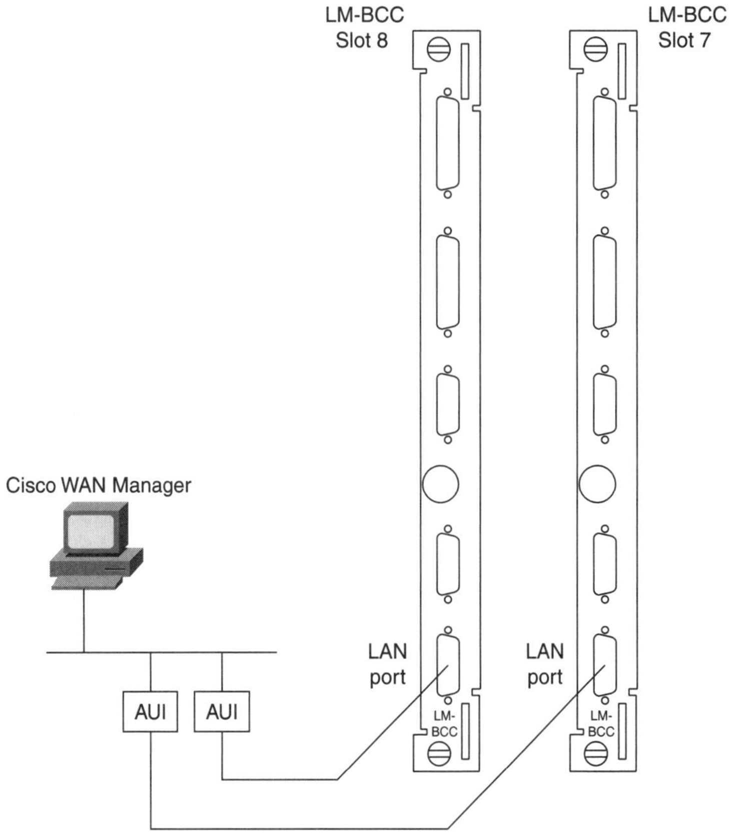

Printer

Printed output might be helpful during the initial network installation phase and during troubleshooting. The printer is connected to the auxiliary port, as shown in Figure 11-21.

Complete the following steps to connect the printer directly to the BCC:

Step 1 Check the printer EIA/TIA-232/V.24 cabling pin-out. If required, adjust the DIP switches to the settings indicated for the type of printer to be connected to the BPX switch. The printer must emulate an Okidata 182 and be attached by a straight-through serial cable.

Figure 11-21 *Connecting a Printer*

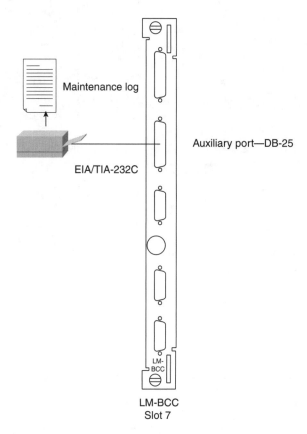

Step 2 For nodes with single BCC, connect the EIA/TIA-232/V.24 printer cable to the auxiliary port on the LM-BCC back card.

Step 3 For nodes with redundant BCCs, a Y-cable is required for this application. Connect one leg of the Y-cable to the auxiliary port connector on the LM-BCC in slot 7, and connect the other leg to the auxiliary port connector on the LM-BCC in slot 8.

Step 4 Plug the printer power cord into the appropriate AC outlet (115 VAC or 240 VAC).

Modem Support

One or two modems can be connected to each BPX node, as shown in Figure 11-22, to provide for remote access and remote alarm reporting.

Figure 11-22 *Connecting a Modem*

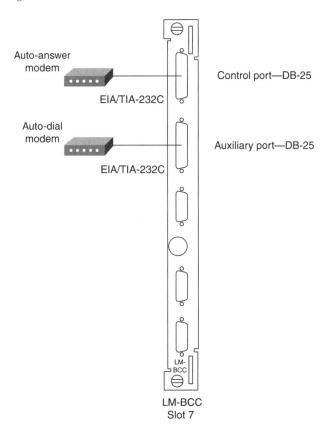

An auto-answer modem is used to provide access for remote access. It is connected to the control bidirectional port connector.

An auto-dial modem is used to provide remote alarm logging or remote statistics gathering. It is connected to the auxiliary port connector on the LM-BCC. This is a unidirectional transmit-only port. These modems connect to a standard telephone line wall jack. The modem connections require null modem cables and special setup procedures, which are described in the installation manual for the BPX switch. If the BPX switch is equipped with redundant BCCs, an EIA/TIA-232 Y-cable must be used on each of these connections. If the auxiliary port will be used, it must be appropriately configured.

External Clock Connections

If the BPX node is synchronized to external equipment or a local digital central office, one of the external clock connectors on the BCC back card can be used to provide a clock input.

The DB-15 connector labeled EXT CLK IN can be used to connect a balanced T1 or E1 signal (EIA/TIA-422, not DS-1), as shown in Figure 11-23, synchronized from some higher-level source to the BPX switch. In the event that an unbalanced 75-ohm E1 signal is available as the timing source, a BNC EXT CLK IN connector is also provided. The BPX switch senses an active signal at any of these inputs and automatically synchronizes to this source rather than the internal Stratum 3-clock source.

Figure 11-23 *Making External Clock Connections*

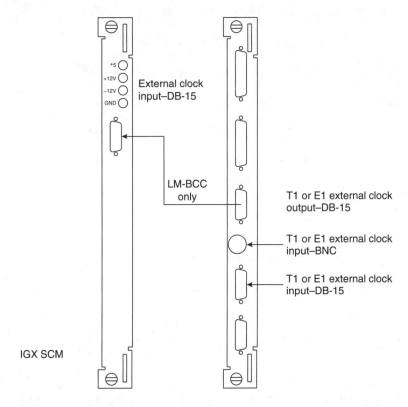

The BPX switch with the LM-BCC back card can provide a timing signal to synchronize the operation of an adjacent IGX node, which has an internal Stratum 4 clock source. A connector on the LM-BCC back card labeled EXT CLK OUT supplies a clock signal at either a T1 or an E1 rate. It can be connected to the IGX external clock connector on the SCM back card using a straight-through DB-15-to-DB-15 cable, male to male.

Alarm/Status Monitor

The Alarm/Status Monitor (ASM) is responsible for measuring local environmental conditions and reporting local and network alarms using LEDs and an external alarm relay, as shown in Figure 11-24. The ASM is always installed in card slot 15. The LEDs report local alarm conditions on the BPX node. The external alarm relay provides multiple dry-contact relay switch points that can be attached to audible and visual alarm notification devices to report local and remote network alarms.

Figure 11-24 *ASM LEDs and Interface*

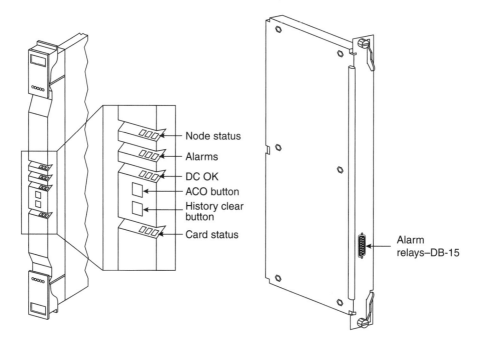

The ASM and LM-ASM cards are noncritical cards used for monitoring the operation of the node and are not directly involved in system operation. Therefore, there is no provision or requirement for card redundancy.

The ASM performs the following functions:

- **Measures cabinet temperature**—The ASM measures the BPX cabinet temperature and reports it to the software. If the temperature exceeds a configurable threshold, a minor alarm is declared on the node.

- **Monitors fans and power supplies**—The ASM monitors the fan RPMs and the power supply voltages to ensure that they are functioning correctly. If a fan drops below the configurable RPM threshold, or if a power supply is above or below the configurable voltage threshold, a minor alarm is declared.

- **Reports local and remote alarms with an external alarm connector**—The external alarm connector is a 15-pin interface that can be attached to audible or visual alarm notification devices, such as bells, sirens, or lights. The ASM either opens or closes relays when node or network alarms occur to set off the attached notification device.

- **Reports local alarms with LEDs**—Two LEDs, one for major alarms and one for minor alarms, are on the front of the ASM card. These LEDs are described in more detail on the following page.

Two LEDs, one for major alarms and one for minor alarms, report active local BPX node alarms. Table 11-2 summarizes the LEDs status.

Table 11-2   *BPX Node Alarm LEDs*

LED	Indicator
Minor alarm (yellow)	Indicates that a local minor alarm occurred.
Major alarm (red)	Indicates that a local major alarm occurred.
History LED	Indicates that an alarm occurred until the HIST CLR button was pressed.
Alarm Cut Off (ACO)	Indicates that the user pressed the ACO to silence the audible alarm.

Additionally, card status LEDs are provided as on the BCC front card.

The LM-ASM is the back card to the ASM card. It provides a 37-pin connector for interfacing to the customer alarm system. It is not required for system and ASM operation, but if present, it must be installed in back slot 15.

Broadband Network Interface

The Broadband Network Interface (BNI) card provides two or three network trunks between the BPX node and any of the following devices:

- Another BPX node with a BNI trunk card

- An MGX ATM concentrator with a T3, E3, or OC-3/STM-1 BNM trunk card

- An IGX node with a T3 or E3 BTM or ALM/B trunk card

- Four BNI models are supported in Release 9.2 system software:
  - BNI-T3
  - BNI-E3
  - BNI-155 with single-mode, single-mode long reach, or multimode fiber interface

— BNI-155E (enhanced) with single-mode, single-mode long reach, or multimode fiber interface

The BNI performs the following functions:

- **Transmits and receives Stratacom Trunk Interface cells**—The BNI card transmits and receives proprietary StrataCom Trunk Interface (STI) cells to and from the attached trunk.

- **Services egress queues**—Cells sent from other cards in the BPX node and through the crosspoint switch to the BNI are buffered before exiting on the trunk. Physical trunks queue cells by traffic type in OptiClass QBins. Virtual trunks queue cells per trunk. The BNI determines the cell sequence based on the defined queue service algorithm for each traffic type.

- **Checks header check sum on cells**—When cells arrive from the attached trunk, the BNI card calculates the header check sum (HCS) and compares it to the 8-bit cyclic redundancy check (CRC) in the cell header. If the HCS is incorrect, the cell is dropped.

- **Provides line and cell framing**—The BNI card generates line framing appropriate for the attached facility (T3, E3, OC-3c, or STM-1). Cell delineation and cell extraction also is done by the BNI card.

- **Extracts timing**—If the trunk is a configured clock source, or if the current network clock source is accessible across the trunk, the BNI card extracts the timing signal from the trunk and passes it to the BCC.

- **Monitors trunks for alarms and errors**—All physical-layer alarms, such as loss of signal (red alarm) or remote loss of signal (yellow alarm), are detected and reported by the BNI card.

In addition to the normal card status indicators, the BNI front card includes tricolor LEDs indicating the current status for each of the three ports, as shown in Figure 11-25. Port status is indicated as shown in Table 11-3.

Figure 11-25 *BNI-T3 and BNI-E3 LEDs and Interfaces*

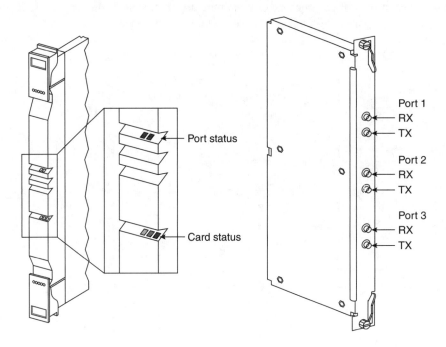

Port status

Card status

Port 1
RX
TX

Port 2
RX
TX

Port 3
RX
TX

Table 11-3 *TBNI Alarm LED Indicators*

LED	Indicator
Red	Local alarm
Yellow	Remote alarm
Green	Trunk is active
Off	Trunk is inactive

The BNI-T3 and BNI-E3 front cards appear identical except for the name on the front panel. The cards are functionally similar except for the two different electrical interfaces. The LM-3T3 back card is used with the BNI-T3, and the LM-3E3 back card is used with the BNI-3E3. The LM-3T3 back card provides three DS-3 interfaces on one card, while the LM-3E3 back card provides three E3 interface ports.

Port and card status indicators for the OC-3/STM-1 versions of the BNI are the same as the T3/E3 version, except that there are two port status LEDs instead of three.

The fiber optic interfaces for the BNI-155 are SC type for the multimode fiber version, or FC type for the single-mode version, as shown in Figure 11-26. Note that the connectors are angled downward for safety reasons—avoid looking directly into the open connector when the card is activated. Also avoid plugging in mismatched fiber modes; for example, do not plug a single-mode fiber into a multimode interface.

Figure 11-26 *BNI-155 LEDs and Interfaces*

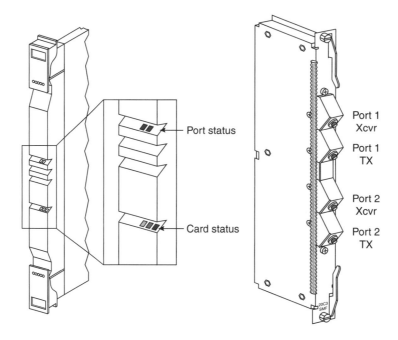

ATM Service Interface

The ATM Service Interface (ASI) card provides two ATM line interfaces to accept user traffic from an attached user device. The ASI line can terminate at any of the following devices:

- An ATM router, such as a Cisco 4500 or Cisco 7000

- An ATM switch, such as the Cisco LightStream 1010

- An ATM access device, such as the Cisco 3810

- Any device that transmits ATM User Network Interface (UNI) or Network-to-Network Interface (NNI) cells at T3, E3, or OC-3/STM-1 rates

The ASI card receives ATM cells, polices them, queues them (if necessary), and passes them to the crosspoint switch for transport across the network.

Four ASI models are supported in BPX Release 9.2 system software:

- ASI-T3
- ASI-E3
- ASI-155 with single-mode, single-mode long reach, or multimode fiber interface
- ASI-155E (enhanced) with single-mode, single-mode long reach, or multimode fiber interface

The ASI performs the following functions:

- **Transmits and receives standard UNI or NNI cells**—The ASI is responsible for interfacing with external ATM devices that are sending and receiving standard ATM cells. The ASI can, on a per-card basis, be defined to accept either UNI or NNI cells.

- **Performs the ForeSight algorithm**—A prestandard available bit rate (ABR) connection type using Cisco's ForeSight algorithm is available on the ASI-T3 and the ASI-E3. The ASI must assess network congestion and notify the remote ASI to adjust the service rate of each permanent virtual circuit (PVC).

- **Polices ingress traffic**—As traffic enters the BPX network, the ASI polices the traffic based on configured traffic requirements. If the user data exceeds the traffic requirements, the cells are either discarded or tagged with the cell loss priority (CLP) bit.

- **Services egress QBins**—After cells travel through the BPX network, and before they are sent out to the end-user equipment, they are queued in per-traffic-type QBins. The QBins are used to maintain the quality of service based on the traffic type.

- **Provides LMI or ILMI signaling protocols**—A signaling protocol between the BPX network and an attached device can be used to exchange PVC status information. The ASI supports both the Local Management Interface (LMI) and the Integrated Local Management Interface (ILMI) signaling protocols.

- **Provides the physical**—Like the BNI, the ASI performs physical-layer functions, such as checking the header error control (HEC) field, framing lines and cells, extracting timing, and detecting line alarms.

The ASI-1 T3 and E3 front cards have identical status indicators as the BNI-155, as shown in Figure 11-27.

Figure 11-27 *ASI-1 LEDs and Interfaces*

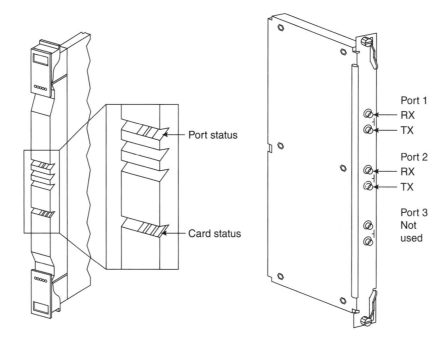

The ASI-1 uses the same back cards as the BNI T3/E3 versions, except that only the first two ports (lines) are available for use.

Status indicators for the ASI-155 are identical to the BNI-155, shown in Figure 11-28.

Figure 11-28 *ASI-155 LEDs and Interfaces*

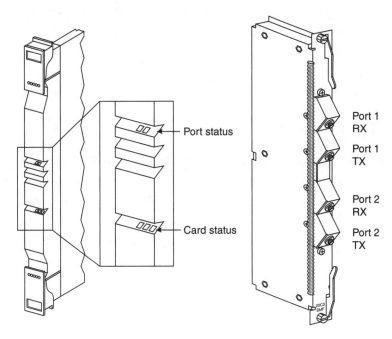

Two back cards are available for the ASI-155: the 2OC-3-SMF for single-mode fiber, and the 2OC-3-MMF for multimode fiber. These are the same back cards used with the BNI-155.

Broadband Switch Module

The Broadband Switch Module (BXM) card supports lines or trunks on a per-card basis. As a trunk card, the BXM can support broadband trunks to the following equipment:

- A BPX node with a BXM card
- An IGX node with a UXM or ALM/B card
- A MGX 8220 concentrator with a T3, E3, or OC-3/STM-1 BNM trunk card
- A MGX 8850 edge switch with a T3, E3, OC-3/STM-1, or OC-12/STM-4 Processor Switch Module (PXM) card

A line on a BXM card can terminate on any of the following devices:

- An IGX node with an ALM/A card
- An ATM router, such as a Cisco 4500 or Cisco 7000
- An ATM switch, such as the Cisco LightStream 1010

- An ATM access device, such as the Cisco 3810
- Any device that transmits ATM UNI or NNI cells at T3, E3, OC-3/STM-1, or OC-12/STM-4 rates

Four BXM T3/E3 models are supported in BPX Release 9.2 system software:

- BXM–T3-8
- BXM–T3-12
- BXM–E3-8
- BXM–E3-12

Four BXM models with fiber optic interfaces are supported in BPX Release 9.2 system software:

- BXM–155-4 with single-mode, single-mode long-reach, or multimode fiber interface
- BXM–155-8 with single-mode, single-mode long-reach, or multimode fiber interface
- BXM–622 with single-mode or single-mode long-reach interface
- BXM–622-2 with single-mode or single-mode long-reach interface

The BXM supports the following functions:

- **Acts as line or trunk card**—The BXM card can support either lines or trunks. With Release 9.1, if a line is activated after the BXM is installed in a BPX node, then the BXM is a line card. If a trunk is activated, then the BXM is a trunk card. If you want to change a BXM from a line card to a trunk card, then all connections, ports, and lines must be removed from the card. From Release 9.2, interfaces can activate as a trunk or a line on an individual basis.

- **Transmits and receives standard UNI or NNI cells**—The BXM card, in either line or trunk mode, transmits and receives standard ATM cells. The BXM uses STI cells toward the crosspoint switch to be compatible with the BNI and ASI cards.

- **Performs standard ABR and the ForeSight feature**—Like the ASI card, the BXM supports ForeSight ABR connections. The BXM also can terminate standard ABR connections as a virtual source/virtual destination (VS/VD).

- **Polices ingress traffic (line only)**—The BXM card, when in line mode, polices incoming user traffic as defined by ATM.

- **Services egress QBins**—Like the ASI and BNI cards, the BXM separates traffic types into egress OptiClass QBins.

- **Provides LMI or ILMI signaling protocols (line only)**—Like the ASI, when the BXM is in line mode, both the LMI and the ILMI signaling protocols are available.

- **Provides physical-layer functions**—Like the BNI and ASI, the BXM performs physical-layer functions, such as checking the HEC field, executing line and cell framing, extracting timing, and detecting line alarms.

The BXM front cards include card and port status indicators, which are identical in function to the BNI front cards. Figure 11-29 shows the LEDs and ports.

Figure 11-29 *BXM LEDs and Interfaces*

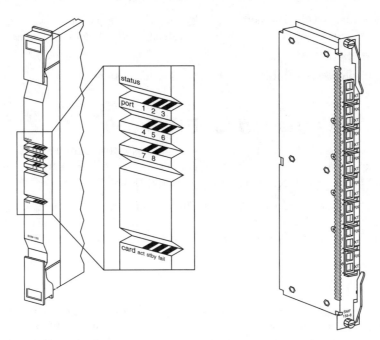

The number of port status LEDs varies from 2 to 12, depending on the type of card.

Broadband Multicast Engine

The Broadband Multicast Engine (BME) provides multicast services in the BPX switch with Release 9.1 and later. It is used with a two-port OC-12 back card. Multicasting point-to-multipoint services meets the demands of users requiring virtual circuit replication of data (Frame Relay and ATM) within the network, such as the following:

- Retail-point-of-sale updates
- Router topology updates
- Desktop multimedia
- Videoconferencing
- Video distribution (for example, IP multicast video networks to the desktop)
- Remote learning
- Medical imaging

The multicast service is implemented on an adapted version of the BXM front card, with a SMF-622-2 two port OC-12/STM-4 back card. The two ports on the back card are not connected to any user equipment; they are looped together. In addition, up to 1000 multicast groups with a total of 8064 connections are supported.

The BME functions in BPX nodes that have all BXM cards (with a BCC-4), or in nodes configured with legacy cards only (BCC-3, ASI, and BNI). (It does not function in systems with mixed cards.)

The BME supports CBR, UBR, VBR, and ATFR connections.

Additional Configuration for BPX 8650

This section describes the additional installation steps involved for the BPX 8650. This entails the physical installation and cabling of the Cisco 7200 or 7500 router, which provides the tag switch controller function in the BPX 8650 system.

The following procedure assumes that the BPX 8650 chassis has been rack-mounted as previously described. The remaining installation steps are for the physical installation of the Cisco 7200 or 7500 series router, and connection of the router to the BPX node.

7200/7500 Router Assembly

The steps in this procedure apply to a 7200 or 7500 Router Label Switch Controller assembly that is being installed in a Cisco cabinet as part of a BPX 8650 installation. A hardware kit, shown in Figure 11-30, is provided with the router and router enclosure that contains support brackets and other required hardware.

Complete the following steps to assemble the router into the router enclosure:

Step 1 Place the router into the router enclosure as shown, with the power connector side of the router toward the hinged front door of the router enclosure.

Step 2 Install the power cord along the top left side of the router and router enclosure.

Step 3 Mount the front hinged door to the router enclosure by spreading the sides of the router enclosure slightly so that the holes in each side of the cover engage the pins at the front of the router enclosure. To open the router enclosure door, use the tabs on the top of the door. If these are not accessible because another device is installed on top of the router, use a screwdriver in the access cutouts to gently pry open the door.

Figure 11-30 *Assembling the Router into the Enclosure*

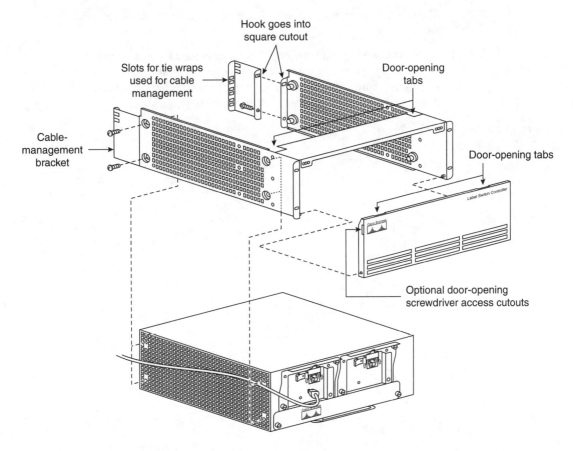

Hook goes into
square cutout

Slots for tie wraps
used for cable
management

Door-opening
tabs

Cable-
management
bracket

Door-opening tabs

Label Switch Controller

Optional door-opening
screwdriver access cutouts

Step 4 Secure the router to the router enclosure using four screws on each side.

Step 5 You can attach cable-management brackets now or later, as desired. The upper end of each bracket hooks into the square cutouts shown previously, and the bottom of each bracket is secured with screws.

Cisco 7200/7500 Router Installation into Cisco Cabinet

The following procedure applies to installation in a Cisco cabinet; installation in standard open racks (19- and 23-inch) is similar, except that midmount support brackets are used.

Complete the following steps:

Step 1 Slide the router enclosure assembly into the cabinet on top of the BPX shelf.

Step 2 Attach the two support brackets from the hardware kit, one to each vertical rail at the rear of the cabinet, as shown in Figure 11-31, using two screws to secure each bracket. The support brackets have a horizontal flange that supports the router enclosure assembly.

Figure 11-31 *Assembling the Router into the Cisco Rack*

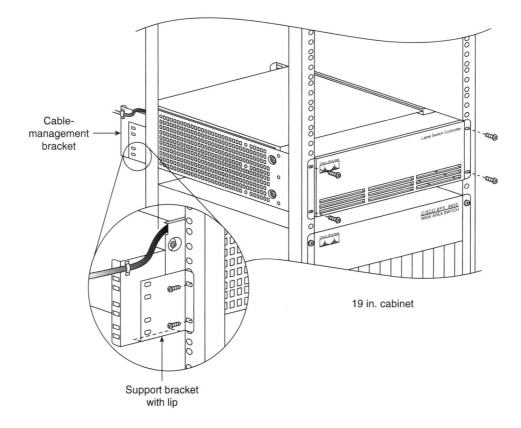

Step 3 Secure the front of the router assembly to the cabinet rails with two screws on each side.

Step 4 Secure the router enclosure assembly to the cabinet with mounting screws.

Step 5 Connect the power cord to the router connector receptacle at the front of the cabinet, and close the router enclosure assembly door.

Step 6 Use the tie wraps provided in the hardware kit to secure the power cord to a cable-management bracket.

Step 7 Using an appropriate cable, connect the ATM port adapter to a port on the BPX switch.

Summary

This chapter covered BPX installation as well as BPX components. Details on BPX card modules, functions, and services were covered, and installation considerations for particular cards were discussed.

Review Questions

The following questions test your retention of the material presented in this chapter. You can find the answers to the Review Questions in Appendix A, "Answers to Review Questions."

1 Which two of the following statements apply to the BPX 8620 node?

A. A separate fan cooling tray is required.

B. The AC power tray holds four power modules.

C. The system does not operate on 110 VAC power.

D. Redundant AC power supplies can have one or two AC feeds.

E. The optional AC power tray can be installed above or below the card chassis.

2 Mark the following statements as true or false

A. DC power supplies are optional equipment.

B. All BPX front cards have card status LEDs.

C. SONET APS is supported on single-mode fiber only.

D. A BPX system can be mounted only in a Cisco cabinet.

E. For a BPX 8620 with 15 cards, two AC power supplies are required.

3 Which three of the following elements are part of the BPX node?

A. Fan assembly

B. AC power shelf

C. Crosspoint switch

D. 32-card slot chassis

E. Multishelf bus cable

F. A standalone cabinet with front and back doors

4 Which card slots are reserved for the BCCs and the ASM?

A. 1, 2, and 3

B. 7, 8, and 1

C. 7, 8, and 15

D. 1, 2, and 15

5 Which card supports either lines or trunks?

A. ASM

B. BCC-4

C. BNI-E3

D. BXM-622

E. ASI-155E

6 How many ports are on an ASI-E3?

A. 2

B. 3

C. 8

D. 12

7 Match the card module in the table with its functions from the list that follows:

Card Module	Answer
BCC	
ASM	
BNI	
ASI	

A. Trunks with STI cells, egress queuing, and physical-layer processing

B. Central processor, crosspoint switch, software storage, and network management

C. Lines attached to end-user equipment, traffic policing, ForeSight feature, and egress queuing

D. Local alarm notification, temperature measurement, power supply monitor, and alarm relays

E. Lines or trunks, traffic policing, standard ABR and ForeSight feature, and physical-layer processing

8 Which two devices could you attach to a BPX node using an ASI card?

A. A Cisco 7000 router

B. A BPX node with a BXM trunk card

C. A Cisco LightStream 1010 ATM switch

D. An IGX node with a BTM or ALM/B trunk card

9 Which two devices could you attach to a BPX node using a BXM card in trunk mode?

A. A Cisco 7000 router

B. A BPX node with a BXM trunk card

C. A Cisco LightStream 1010 ATM switch

D. A MGX concentrator with a BNM trunk card

E. An IGX node with a BTM or ALM/B trunk card

CHAPTER 12

Establishing Initial Access to IGX and BPX Switches

Chapter 10, "Installing IGX 8400 Switches," and Chapter 11, "Installing BPX 8600 Switches," cover IGX and BPX installation. This chapter describes the steps you will follow in verifying that the physical installation process is complete and that the node is ready to be brought into service. The command line interface (CLI) and command structure are covered as well. Most commands discussed are used to display configuration information.

This chapter includes the following sections:

- Installation Checklist
- IGX Boot Process
- BPX Boot Process
- Console Information
- IGX and BPX Commands
- Summary
- Review Questions

Installation Checklist

Table 12-1 provides a checklist of the items you must check after completing installation of the BPX or IGX switch before proceeding with the fielding of the WAN switch.

It is particularly important to double-check that all circuit breakers in the power circuits are in the off position and that adequate arrangements have been made for grounding.

As a review, Figure 12-1 summarizes the physical connections for initial access to an IGX or BPX node. Your terminal or PC must be connected to either the control port or the auxiliary port using a straight-through EIA/TIA-232 cable. In the case of a switch that has not been reconfigured previously, you must ensure that your terminal is set for 9600 bps, with no parity, 8 data bits, 1 stop bit, and no flow control or XON/XOFF (software) flow control.

Table 12-1 *Installation Checklist*

Checked	Installation Checklist
	Ensure that all circuit breakers are off.
	Ensure proper grounding.
	Ensure proper AC/DC power connections.
	Ensure that fan cabling is connected.
	Ensure that card modules are seated properly.
	Attach necessary control terminal.
	Attach necessary peripherals.
	Ensure that trunk cabling is connected properly.
	Ensure that line/port cabling is connected properly.

Figure 12-1 *Physical Access Options*

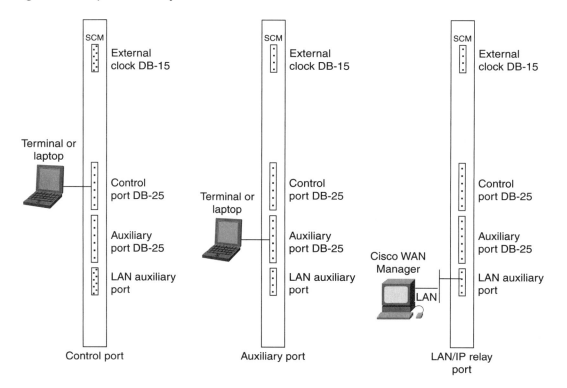

IGX Boot Process

After you complete the installation checklist, including connecting and configuring of your control terminal, you are ready to power up the unit and to observe the boot process. Example 12-1 shows the IGX boot process.

Example 12-1 *IGX Boot Process*

```
68000 clock test passed.
TDM memory test passed.
Muxbus Routing Table memory test passed.
TX FIFO Flag test passed.
RX FIFO Flag Test passed.
Dual-port SRAM memory test passed.
1024K of BRAM available.
512K BRAM test passed.
1024K BRAM test passed.
Dynamic RAM test from Hex Address 30000000 to Hex Address 31FFFFFF passed.
Tick Interrupt Test ... passed.
Clearing Dynamic RAM area.......................................................
...............................................................................
...............................................................................


                    Transition to Online in Progress


........................................
Clearing Dual-Port RAM area.

NPM Boot power up diagnostics complete.
*******************************************************************************

Starting code extraction ... PASSED
Validating compressed files ... PASSED
Decompressing code .............................................................
...............................................................................
.......................
Validating decompressed code ... PASSED
Transition to online in progress ..._

Copyright (c) Cisco Systems. 1986 - 1997



Last Command:



Enter User ID:
```

Follow these steps to determine whether the boot up is successful:

Step 1 At the back of your IGX node, move the power feed circuit breakers to the on position.

Step 2 If AC power supplies are installed, check that the AC and DC OK LEDs are lit immediately.

Step 3 Observe that, after the IGX node switches on, the cards go through a series of initial diagnostic self-tests.

Step 4 The red fail indicator should briefly flash on the front panel of the active NPM, after which the green Active indicator should light. The red indicator on the standby NPM should flash for several minutes while performing self-testing and configuration updating. If the process completes successfully, the active NPM should display green, and both indicators on the standby card should not be lit.

Step 5 Observe that the other cards will indicate a failure condition from several seconds to a minute or so, and then become active or standby.

Step 6 The NPM front panel might indicate a node alarm. You might see similar indications on the back card status indicators of the trunk or line cards. You will learn how to evaluate and resolve alarms in Chapter 18, "Network Alarms and Troubleshooting."

During the first 30 seconds of unit power-up, the results of the processor's power-up diagnostic will be displayed on the control terminal screen. It will be helpful to set your terminal program to Screen Capture if this feature is available.

The startup diagnostic indicates whether the NPM(s) has passed or failed. The screen displays the message, "Power-up diagnostics complete."

Boot Failure

If the boot process fails, complete the following steps:

Step 1 Remove the failed NPM from its slot.

Step 2 Install the NPM in the same slot again.

Step 3 Cycle the power on the switch.

Step 4 Wait for the power-up diagnostics to run.

Step 5 If the NPM fails the power-up diagnostics again, replace it with an NPM that is known to be good.

BPX Boot Process

The process for the BPX node is similar to that for the IGX node, with the following differences:

- Immediately after power-up, the BCC in slot 7 indicates an active status (green), the BCC in slot 8 indicates a standby status (yellow), and all other cards indicate a fail status (red).

- After 20 seconds or so, all service cards and the ASM in slot 15 start to flash red, indicating a download in progress.

- After several more seconds, the BCC in slot 8 indicates a fail status for a few seconds, and then flashes yellow for several minutes.

- When a BPX node is rebooted, the BCC in slot 7 is always the active controller.

- When the power-on diagnostics have completed, the initial logon screen is displayed.

Example 12-2 shows the BPX boot process.

Example 12-2 *BPX Boot Process*

```
**********************************************************************************

BCC FLASH Boot power up diagnostics starting.

Master BCC:
68040 Internal Registers Test   PASSED.
BRAM Stack Area Test   PASSED.
BRAM size: 2048K bytes.
DRAM size: 32 Meg bytes.
Reset Reason:   Power Low
BRAM Memory Test from 400 to 4FF PASSED.
Cachable DRAM Test from 30000000 to 31FFFFFF PASSED.
Non-CacPASSED.
UP DPRAM Test PASSED.
SAR DPRAM Test PASSED.
Address Validation Test   PASSED.
Interrupt Test PASSED.
CIO Interrupt Test PASSED.


Clearing Dynamic RAM area.......................................................
................................................................................
................................................................................
..........................................

BCC FLASH Boot power up diagnostics complete.
**********************************************************************************
Copyright (c) Cisco Systems. 1986 - 1997
                        StrataCom        Rev: H.C.M




                   Transition to Online in Progress
```

Console Information

Before you log in for the first time, the screen will provide the information (clockwise from the upper-left corner) shown in Example 12-3:

- **Node name**—The system default is NODENAME.

- **Access method**—Options are TRM-Control or auxiliary port direct access, or SV-StrataView Plus or StrataView Lite application.

- **User ID and privilege level**—The system default is No User.

- **Chassis and node type**—Options are BPX 15, IGX 8410, IGX 8420, or IGX 8430.

- **System software release**

- **System date and time and time zone**—The system default is to not set the date and the time.

- **Node alarm status**—Options are major, minor, or none.

Example 12-3 *Initial Logon Screen*

```
NODENAME        TRM      No User        IGX 8420  9.1.03     Date and Time Not Set



Last Command:



Enter User ID:
                                                                   MAJOR ALARM
```

IGX and BPX Commands

All commands are a single word made up of a combination of abbreviated verbs and nouns. Commands may be followed by a combination of required and optional parameters. Commands can have both types of parameters, only one type, or no parameters at all.

Required parameters are enclosed in angle brackets, and optional parameters are enclosed in square brackets. The brackets are used in the documentation to differentiate between the two types of parameters; the brackets need not be entered on the command line.

The **help** command provides the syntax and parameters, both required and optional, for the command. The **help** command is displayed in Example 12-4.

Example 12-4 *The **help** Command*

```
NODENAME      TRM    SuperUser        BPX 15    9.1.03    Date and Time Not Set

All commands fall into one (or more) of the following categories:

Control Terminal
Configuration
Lines
Network
Connections
Cards
Alarms and Failures
Diagnostics
Debug




This Command: help


Use cursor keys to select category and then hit <RETURN> key:
                                                              MAJOR ALARM
```

Use the arrow keys to highlight a command category. Press Return or Enter to select the category to list all the commands. You can then select a command in the same way.

You can enter a character string as an optional parameter with the **help** command to list commands that contain that character string, as shown in Example 12-5. You can use the character string to search for a specific command—very useful if you've forgotten how to spell the command.

Example 12-5 *The **help** Command String Screen*

```
NODENAME      TRM    SuperUser        BPX 15    9.1.03    Date and Time Not Set

Commands that contain the string "cd"

clrcderrs        - Clear Detailed Card Failure Information
clrcdstats       - Clear Card Statistics
cnfcdpparm       - Configure CDP Card Parameters
dncd             - Down Card
dspcd            - Display Card
dspcderrs        - Displays Detailed Card Failure Information
dspcds           - Display Cards
dspcdstats       - Display Card Statistics (Multisession Permitted)
prtcderrs        - Prints Detailed Card Failure Information
resetcd          - Reset Card
upcd             - Up Card


```

continues

Example 12-5 *The **help** Command String Screen (Continued)*

```
This Command: help cd


Use cursor keys to select command, then hit <RETURN> key for detailed help:

                                                                  MAJOR ALARM
```

If a character string is a complete command, the help screen for that command displays. The same screen also appears if you selected a command using the menu shown in the help screen. Table 12-2 summarizes the help system's contents.

Table 12-2 *help Command Summarization*

Item	Description
Command description	Gives the unabbreviated definition of the command
Availability in jobs	Identifies whether a command can be used in a predefined script (job)
Required parameters	Gives common required parameters
Optional parameters	Gives any optional parameters

Typically, commands begin with an abbreviated verb, followed by an abbreviated noun in the command. Some of the most commonly used verbs and nouns are shown in Table 12-3.

Table 12-3 *Commonly Used Command Verbs and Nouns*

Verb	Verb Abbreviation	Noun	Noun Abbreviation
Display	dsp	Trunk	trk
Up	up	Port	port
Add	add	Card	cd
Clear	clr	Line	ln
Configure	cnf	Connection	con
Down	dn	Statistics	stats

Most commands follow the conventions described in this chapter. However, there are always exceptions. The **help** command is very useful for finding the exact spelling of a command.

Command Entry

Commands can be entered at the CLI in several ways:

- **Menu driven**—The Esc key brings up a menu-driven command interface. You can highlight menu choices using the arrow keys and then make selections with the Return or Enter keys. When you select the command you want, it is issued. Then, prompts for the required parameters are provided.

- **Prompted**—By entering only the command (followed by pressing the Return or Enter key) on the command line, the system will prompt you for the next required parameter. The prompts continue until you have entered appropriate values for all required parameters. The system does not prompt you for optional parameters.

- **Direct entry**—The direct entry method is often used for commands with limited required parameters or when optional parameters are needed. Follow the command on the command line with each parameter value, in order, separated by spaces.

In all cases, you must enter appropriate values for all parameters. The system rejects any invalid parameters and does not complete the process until you provide an appropriate value. To abort a command, use the Delete key (or equivalent, such as Shift-Backspace).

Each command falls into a range of privilege levels that are made up of SuperUser, Service, StrataCom, and 1 through 6. When a user ID is created, it is assigned a privilege level and can issue only commands allowed by that level.

For example, the **cnfname** command can be issued by user level 1. If you were assigned a user ID of level 2, you cannot issue this command.

SuperUser, Service, and StrataCom levels rank above levels 1 through 6 (in order) and can issue all level 1 commands and below.

In some instances, it might be necessary to use commands at the service level, but those instances are not covered here.

Refer to the Release 9.2 command reference manuals on the Cisco Documentation CD-ROM for a complete listing of all commands at the SuperUser level and below. Table 12-4 lists some of the more common and useful commands, their descriptions, and the privilege level required to use the command.

Table 12-4   *Common IGX and BPX Commands*

Command	Description	Privilege
help	Displays command information and syntax	6
?	Displays command information and syntax	6
.	Displays the last 12 commands	6
adduser	Add user	5
	Defines a new user ID and an associated privilege level	

continues

316 Chapter 12: Establishing Initial Access to IGX and BPX Switches

Table 12-4 *Common IGX and BPX Commands (Continued)*

Command	Description	Privilege
cnfpwd	Configure password	6
	Changes the current user password to a new one	
dsppwd	Display password	6
	Displays the current user password or the password of a lower privilege level user ID	
dspcds	Display cards	6
	Displays summary information on all cards in the node	
dspcd	Display card	6
	Displays details on a particular card in the node	
dsppwr	Display power	6
	Displays environmental measurements for the node, including the power supply status and the cabinet temperature	
dspasm	Display Alarm/Status Monitor	6
	Displays environmental measurements for the node, including the power supply status, the fan speed, and the cabinet temperature	
cnfasm	Configure Alarm Service Monitor	1
	Configures the environmental alarm thresholds	
clrscrn	Clear screen	6
	Clears display information from the terminal	
redrscrn	Redraw screen	6
	Retransmits all current screen information to the terminal screen	
bye	Log out	6
	Logs out current user	

The **dspasm** and **cnfasm** commands are applicable only to the BPX node, not the IGX node.

The screen is divided into two sections. The top two-thirds of the screen contains display information. The bottom third is the command area and provides both a command prompt and any system responses associated with entering commands, such as error messages and appropriate parameter values.

After you log in, the screen shows the user ID and, if you are not using one of the three user IDs of SuperUser, Service, or StrataCom, displays the privilege that you have used. The number of categories displayed differs with the privilege level of the user. The Debug and the Diagnostics categories are not shown on the help screen for a user logged in at privilege level 1 or lower.

Required and optional parameters are listed in order following the command. For complex commands with many different possible required and optional parameters, only the common parameters are listed.

adduser

The **adduser** command, shown in Example 12-6, allows the definition of new network user IDs and associated passwords. A user may add new users with a lower privilege level than his or her own; a user at privilege level 6, therefore, may not add new users.

Example 12-6 *The adduser Command*

```
NODENAME        TRM    SuperUser      IGX 8420    9.1.03   Date and Time Not Set

SuperUser
Teacher         1




Last Command: adduser Teacher 1


Next Command:

                                                                    MAJOR ALARM
```

User IDs and passwords become shared network resources when nodes are joined into a single network. Therefore, usernames and passwords are global within the network.

Repeating Commands

Use the **.** (period) key to list the previous 12 commands. Repeat commands by entering the index number on the command line. The index number indicates which of the 12 commands will be repeated. For example, enter **1** for the last command, or type **4** for four commands back.

When you enter a command index number, the command and the parameters are placed on the command line. You can make changes to the command line before issuing the command. Table 12-5 lists some useful editing commands.

Table 12-5   *Editing Commands*

Key(s)	Action
Arrow keys	Moves the cursor left or right on the command without changing the existing text
Backspace key	Moves the cursor to the left and deletes the character just behind the cursor
Tab key (Ctrl-I)	Toggles between insert and overwrite modes

Changing Passwords

Passwords should be changed before placing systems in production. Passwords also should be changed on a regular basis. Two commands are useful for password management:

- **dsppwd**
- **cnfpwd**

The **dsppwd** command, shown in Example 12-7, displays the password of the current user and all users at any lower privilege level. The displayed password remains on the screen for 10 seconds.

Example 12-7 *The dsppwd Command*

```
NODENAME       TRM    Teacher:1      IGX 8420   9.1.03   Date and Time Not Set

The password for Teacher is newuser




Last Command: dsppwd Teacher

This screen will self-destruct in ten seconds
Next Command:
                                                             MAJOR ALARM
```

The **cnfpwd** command changes the password associated with a user ID. To change a password, you must log in to the node with the user ID whose password you want to change.

To change a password, complete the following steps:

Step 1   Enter the **cnfpwd** command. The system prompts for your current password.

Step 2   Enter your current password. The system prompts for a new password.

Step 3   Enter a new password. Passwords must have 6 to 15 characters and are case sensitive.

Step 4   Confirm the new password by entering it again.

dspcds

The **dspcds** command screen provides summary information on the status of all the cards in the node. Cards are automatically detected by the switch and are shown with **dspcds** without prior configuration of the cards. Example 12-8 shows the results of the **dspcds** command on an IGX switch, and Example 12-9 shows the results on a BPX switch.

Example 12-8 *The dspcds Command—IGX*

```
NODENAME        TRM    Teacher:1        IGX 8420    9.1.03    Date and Time Not Set

      FrontCard  BackCard                    FrontCard  BackCard
      Type  Rev  Type     Rev  Status        Type  Rev  Type     Rev  Status
   1  NPM   BWJ                 Active      9 UVM   ABC  E1-2     AA   Standby
   2  Empty reserved for NPM              10 UVM   ABC  E1-2     AA   Standby
   3  ALM   BDF  UAI-T3   AB   Standby    11 HDM   CFF  RS449    AT   Standby-F
   4  Empty universal backplane           12 UXM   AAB  T1-IMA   AA   Standby
   5  NTM   EKJ  T1       AL   Standby    13 UXM   AAB  T3       AA   Standby
   6  NTM   EKJ  T1       AJ   Standby-T  14 LDM   CKB  232-4    AL   Standby
   7  NTM   FDH  SR       AD   Standby    15 UFMU  ADB  X21      AA   Standby
   8  FTM   CH22 FRI-X21  AC   Standby    16 UFM   AEF  T1D      AB   Standby




Last Command: dspcds


Next Command:

                                                                  MAJOR ALARM
```

Example 12-9 *The dspcds Command—BPX*

```
NODENAME        TRM    Teacher:1        BPX 15     9.1.03    Date and Time Not Set

      FrontCard      BackCard                 FrontCard      BackCard
      Type     Rev  Type Rev  Status         Type     Rev  Type  Rev  Status
   1  BNI-T3   CBL  T3-3 BE   Standby      9  Empty
   2  BXM-T3   BDR  TE3-12BA  Standby     10  Empty
   3  Empty                               11  Empty
   4  BXM-155  BDR  SM-8 BA   Standby     12  Empty
   5  Empty                               13  BXM-155  BDR  SM-8  BA   Standby-T
   6  Empty                               14  ASI-T3   BFK  T3-2  FF   Standby
   7  Empty reserved for BCC3             15  ASM      ACC  LMASM AC   Standby
   8  BCC-3    CLM  LM-2 AC   Active




Last Command: dspcds


Next Command:

                                                                  MAJOR ALARM
```

(The IGX 8430 node contains two card shelves for a total of 32 slots. You can access the lower shelf directly by using the **dspcd l** command, where **l** stands for lower.)

The **dspcds** command provides the following information:

- **Card type**—This indicates the type of interface card, as discussed in Chapter 10, "Installing IGX 8400 Switches" and Chapter 11, "Installing BPX 8600 Switches."

- **Card revision**—The card revision is made up of three characters that indicate the model, the hardware revision, and the firmware revision. The model identifies the feature set for the card. The model is associated with the firmware on the card and can be changed only by Cisco or its partners with the firmware revision.

- **Back card type**—The back card type indicates the type of card, such as a T1 or E1 inserted in the back slot.

- **Back card revision**—The back card revision describes the model, the firmware, and the hardware version. Unlike the front cards, the version is stored permanently and cannot be changed with the firmware upgrade from Cisco.

- **Status**—This reports the conditions of the cards. Table 12-6 lists the possible card status.

Table 12-6 *Card Status*

Status	Description
Active	The card is in use, with no failures.
Active-T	The card in use, with the background test in progress.
Active-F	The card in use, and the background test failed.
Standby	The card is idle, with no failures.
Standby-T	The card is idle, with the background test in progress.
Standby-F-T	The card is idle, the background test failed, and another background test is in progress.
Failed	The card failed.
Down	The card was downed by the user.
Down-T	The card is down, and the background test is in progress.
Down-F	The card is down, and the background test failed.
Down-F-T	The card is down, the background test failed, and another background test is in progress.
Mismatch	A mismatch occurred between the front card and the back card. A mismatch also occurs if an active card is removed and an unlike card is used to replace it.
Update	The standby processor card is being updated by the active processor.
Locked	Old software is being maintained as a recovery method in case the new version of software does not function properly.
Update	The standby processor card is being updated by the active processor card.
Dnldr	Downloading software and configuration is taking place from the active processor card.

dspcd

The **dspcd** command provides detailed information on a card module. Use this command to see additional information about a card, including failure information.

Examples 12-10 through 12-12 show the output of the **dspcd** command for a UVM card on an IGX node, a BCC card on a BPX node, and a BXM card on a BPX node, respectively.

Example 12-10 *The dspcd Command—UVM*

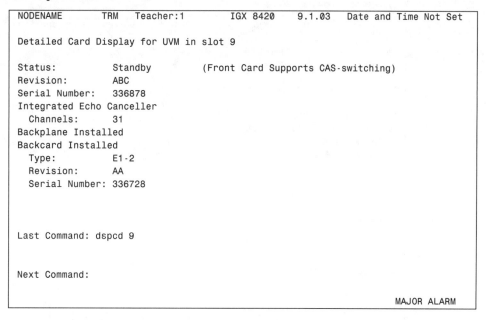

```
NODENAME        TRM    Teacher:1         IGX 8420    9.1.03    Date and Time Not Set

Detailed Card Display for UVM in slot 9

Status:          Standby          (Front Card Supports CAS-switching)
Revision:        ABC
Serial Number:   336878
Integrated Echo Canceller
  Channels:      31
Backplane Installed
Backcard Installed
  Type:          E1-2
  Revision:      AA
  Serial Number: 336728




Last Command: dspcd 9


Next Command:

                                                                MAJOR ALARM
```

Example 12-11 *The dspcd Command—BCC-3*

```
NODENAME        TRM    Teacher:1         BPX 15    9.1.03    Date and Time Not Set

Detailed Card Display for BCC-3 in slot 8

Status:          Active            Backcard Installed
Revision:        CLM               Type:          LM-2
Serial Number:   612953            Revision:      AC
Hardware Etch:   B                 Serial Number: 468858
Fab Number:      217702-00
RAM Id:          9.1.03
ROM Id:          9.1.03
BOOT Id:         H.B.J
BRAM Id:         9.1.03
RAM Size:        32 Meg
Flash EEPROMs:   Standard - 4 Meg
Sar Revision:    CJP
Up Revision:     CJ13
```

continues

Example 12-11 *The **dspcd** Command—BCC-3 (Continued)*

```
Last Command: dspcd 8



Next Command:
                                                              MAJOR ALARM
```

Example 12-12 *The **dspcd** Command—BXM*

```
NODENAME        TRM   Teacher:1       BPX 15    9.1.03   Date and Time Not Set

Detailed Card Display for BXM-T3 in slot 2
Status:          Standby
Revision:        BDR
Serial Number:   649753
Fab Number:      28-2218-02
Queue Size:      131000
Support:         FST, 8 Pts,T3
Chnls:16320,PG[1]:14128
PG[1]:1,2,3,4,5,6,7,8,
Backcard Installed
  Type:          LM-BXM
  Revision:      BA
  Serial Number: 693197
  Supports: 12 Pts, T3/E3




Last Command: dspcd 11



Next Command:
                                                              MAJOR ALARM
```

The information provided (in addition to what is shown in the **dspcds** command screen)
depends on the card type but typically includes the following:

- Front and back card serial numbers
- Card failure type
- Card features
- Number of ports supported
- Features supported, such as ForeSight
- Number of connections supported
- Buffer size
- Memory size
- Software revision

dsppwr

The **dsppwr** command provides information about environmental measurements made by the node. This command results in a slightly different display for the IGX and the BPX, as shown in Examples 12-13 and 12-14.

Example 12-13 *The dsppwr Command—IGX*

```
NODENAME    TRM    Teacher:1      IGX 8420    9.1.03    Date and Time Not Set

Power Supply Status                                Cabinet Temperature

Monitor Rev AK, Ser # 241813  -  Status: Active          23          73

     AC Supply    Status                       C  60  ¦   ¦   140   F
A   1  Present    OK                           e      ¦   ¦         a
B   1  Present    OK                           n  50  ¦--¦   122   h
C   1  Empty                                   t      ¦   ¦         r
D   2  Present    OK                           i  40  ¦   ¦   104   e
E   2  Present    OK                           g      ¦   ¦         n
F   2  Empty                                   r  30  ¦   ¦    86   h
                                               a      ¦   ¦         e
                                               d  20  ¦   ¦    68   i
                                               e      `--'         t


Last Command: dsppwr


Next Command:

                                                         MAJOR ALARM
```

Example 12-14 *The dsppwr Command—BPX*

```
NODENAME        TRM    Teacher:1      BPX 15    9.1.03   Date and Time Not Set

        Power Status                             Cabinet Temperature

ASM Status: Active                                      28          82

Power voltage A/B:      48 / 0 V               C  60  ¦   ¦   140   F
                                              e      ¦   ¦         a
PSU  Ins Type Rev SerNum Failure              n  50  ¦--¦   122   h
 A    Y   240V  0D  H27463  None              t      ¦   ¦         r
 B    Y   240V  0D  H27481  None              i  40  ¦   ¦   104   e
                                              g      ¦   ¦         n
                                              r  30  ¦   ¦    86   h
        Fan Status                            a      ¦   ¦         e
                                              d  20  ¦   ¦    68   i
     FAN   1    2    3                         e      `--'         t
          3300 3360 3360 RPM
```

continues

Example 12-14 *The **dsppwr** Command—BPX (Continued)*

```
Last Command: dsppwr


Next Command:


                                                              MAJOR ALARM
```

The information provided by the **dsppwr** command for the IGX includes the following:

- Monitor status, revision, and serial number
- Power supply type and status
- Actual cabinet temperature, in Celsius and Fahrenheit
- Temperatures alarm threshold, which is represented with the line across the thermometer in Example 12.14

For the BPX node, the output differs as follows:

- The current status of the ASM card is shown.
- AC power supply type and status fields are displayed only if AC supplies are installed.
- Fan speeds are displayed.

dspasm

The **dspasm** command, shown in Example 12-15, provides similar information to that provided by the **dsppwr** command, with additional output of statistics and statistics timeouts. The ASM card periodically polls environmental conditions and updates the statistics count. Unsuccessful polls are reported in the statistics timeouts.

Example 12-15 *The **dspasm** Command*

```
NODENAME         TRM    Teacher:1      BPX 15    9.1.03   Date and Time Not Set

ASM Status:              Active        ASM Alarms
Statistics count:        23565         Power supply B
Statistics timeouts:     0
Cabinet temperature:     28 C
Power voltage A/B:       48 / 0 V

PSU  Ins Type Rev SerNum Failure
 A    Y   240V  0D H27463  None
 B    Y   240V  0D H27481  None

FAN    1    2    3
      3300 3360 3360 RPM




```

Example 12-15 *The **dspasm** Command (Continued)*

```
Last Command: dspasm


Next Command:


                                                    MAJOR ALARM
```

cnfasm

Use the **cnfasm** command, shown in Example 12-16, to set ASM alarm thresholds and to enable or disable alarm notification on your BPX node.

Example 12-16 *The **cnfasm** Command*

```
NODENAME       TRM    Teacher:1       BPX 15     9.1.03    Date and Time Not Set


[1] Cabinet temp threshold:      50 C  [4] Polling interval (msec):     10000
[2] Power A deviation:      6 V (47.4) [5] Fan threshold (RPM):         2000
[3] Power B deviation:      6 V ( 0.0)



                      ALM                                    ALM
[6]   ACO button      -                 [14] BPX card slot    -
[7]   History button  -                 [15] PSU A failure    Y
[8]   Cabinet temp    Y                 [16] PSU A removed    Y
[9]   Power A volt    Y                 [17] PSU B failure    Y
[10] Power B volt    N                 [18] PSU B removed    Y
[11] Fan 1 RPM       Y
[12] Fan 2 RPM       Y
[13] Fan 3 RPM       Y



Last Command: cnfasm 10 n


Next Command:


                                                    MAJOR ALARM
```

The configurable parameters for the **cnfasm** command are shown in Table 12-7.

Table 12-7 *Configurable Parameters for the **cnfasm** Command*

Parameter	Description
Cabinet temperature threshold	Alarm notification threshold in degrees Centigrade (Celsius). This threshold determines the temperature that will generate an alarm on the BPX node.
Powers A and B deviation	Number of volts above or below -48 to declare an alarm.
Polling interval	Frequency of ASM measurements.
Fan threshold	Minimum fan RPM before declaring alarm.
Cabinet temperature	Enable or disable cabinet temperature alarms. If you disable the temperature alarm, the ASM will measure the temperature but will not declare an alarm when it exceeds the configured threshold.
Powers A and B voltage	Enable or disable power supply voltage alarms.
Fans 1, 2, and 3 RPM	Enable or disable fan RPM alarms.
Power supply units A and B failure	Enable or disable power supply failure alarms (failure latch).
Power supply units A and B removal	Enable or disable power supply removal alarms. (Configuring the temperature alarm threshold for an IGX node requires the SuperUser command **cnfnodeparm**.)

Summary

This chapter covered the tasks required to ensure correct switch installation, initial node access, and successful login procedure to the system. In addition, it covered various commands for system administration. Administration tasks, including changing passwords, adding users, displaying cards, and examining the alarm status, were also discussed.

Review Questions

The following questions test your retention of the material presented in this chapter. You can find the answers to the Review Questions in Appendix A, "Answers to Review Questions."

1 Which one of the following is not a valid choice of access method for a first-time installation?

A. StrataView Lite

B. Cisco WAN Manager

C. PC with terminal emulation

D. VT-100-compatible terminal

E. UNIX workstation with serial interface

2 Mark the following statements as true or false.

A. When an abnormal boot sequence occurs, the power should be turned off.

B. After a successful initial boot, the active BCC in a BPX node is always in slot 7.

C. Any trunk or line alarms must be cleared before the system can boot normally.

D. When an abnormal boot sequence occurs, the active BCC/NPM should be removed and reseated.

E. When an abnormal boot sequence occurs, the power should be turned off, and the active BCC/NPM should be removed and reseated.

3 Which two of the following statements are true?

A. The Esc key aborts a command.

B. All commands have required and optional parameters.

C. Most commands comprise abbreviated verbs and nouns.

D. A command is complete when all required parameters have been defined with appropriate values.

E. The node prompts you for all required and optional parameters when you use the prompted entry mode.

4 What is the purpose of the **help** command?

A. To teach you how to configure a node

B. To identify the definition and syntax of a command

C. To define the value range of the required parameters for a connection

D. To provide you with a detailed description of the use of each command

5 Match each command in the table with its following primary function.

A. Ends your CLI session

B. Modifies your password

C. Lists all cards in the node

D. Modifies the temperature alarm threshold on a BPX node

E. Shows the current IGX cabinet temperature

F. Shows the status and serial number of a card

G. Shows the status of the BPX power supplies and fans

6 Mark each of the following statements as true or false.

Command	Answer
bye	
dspcd	
dspcds	
dsppwr	
cnfasm	
dspasm	
cnfpwd	

A. The Delete key can be used to abort a command.

B. The abbreviation DIS means "display" on the CLI.

C. Cards can be in active and fail condition at the same time.

D. All cards provide the same information when you use the **dspcd** command.

E. A user ID with a privilege level of 4 can perform all the commands available to a user ID with a privilege level of 5.

7   A card is reporting QRS as the revision when you use the **dspcds** or **dspcd** command. Match each letter in the table with the information it provides.

A. The hardware revision

B. The firmware revision, which is a variation on the model

C. The model, which determines the feature set available on the card

Revision Report	Answer
Q	
R	
S	

CHAPTER 13

Initial Configuration of IGX and BPX Switches

This chapter covers the necessary configuration information to integrate WAN switch nodes into the network. Configuration parameters include the local characteristics of the node, such as the node name and the time zone, as well as management features, such as control, auxiliary and LAN port configurations, and printing mode. All the commands described in this chapter are identical for IGX and BPX, with some minor differences, which are explained.

This chapter includes the following sections:

- Auxiliary Port
- LAN Interface
- Print Modes
- Time Zone, Date, and Time
- Commands
- Summary
- Review Questions

Figure 13-1 shows an example network with IGX and BPX nodes connected by network trunks. The configuration examples covered are based upon this example network.

Each node in the network is identified with a node number and a name. Before introducing a node into a network, keep the following in mind:

- Node numbers must be unique within the network. (For structured networks, the node number must be unique within the domain.)
- All nodes default to 1 prior to installation and configuration, but they can be negotiated automatically when a single node is introduced into an existing network.
- Node names must be unique within the network. (For structured networks, the node name must be unique within the domain.)
- Node names must be one to eight characters in length and are case sensitive.
- Node names must start with a letter and can include hyphens, underscores, or periods.

Figure 13-1 *Network Topology Example*

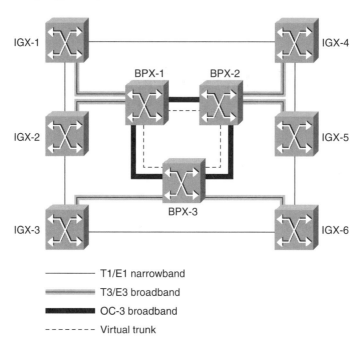

Auxiliary Port

WAN switches require facilities to report network conditions and provide out-of-band management at the location of the switch because a network outage between the switch and the management system prohibits visibility to the switch. The auxiliary port provides these functions in addition others, as shown in Figure 13-2.

Figure 13-2 *Auxiliary Port Functions*

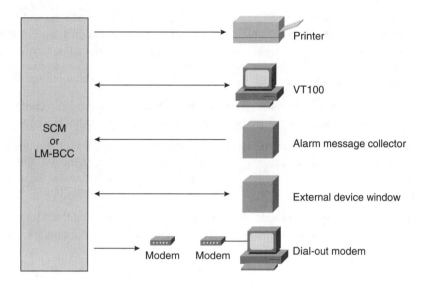

Table 13-1 summarizes the various auxiliary devices and their purposes, and shows the direction of communication.

Table 13-1   *Auxiliary Devices and Descriptions*

Auxiliary Device	Purpose	Direction of Communication
Printer	Print screens and information. Can also be used as a network event log.	Node sends data to printer.
VT100	Can be used as a management connection.	Bidirectional. Node prints information for the user, and the user can enter data.
Alarm message collector	Node receives messages from intelligent device that reports using ASCII.	Node receives data and time stamps messages. Messages are handled as local and network log entries.
External device window	Node initiates session with external device based upon user's request.	Bidirectional; however, the connection is initiated by the node.
Dial-out modem	Node initiates session based upon alarm status change.	Node sends alarm status with date, time, and network node name.

LAN Interface

The LAN interface on the SCM or BCC back card is used to attach the node to a LAN for management purposes. Both the Cisco WAN Manager workstation and other devices on the LAN can communicate with the nodes using, for example, Telnet, the Simple Management Protocol (SNMP), or TFTP. As with all IP hosts, each node attached to a LAN must have a unique IP address.

To enable communication with the Cisco WAN Manager, each node is configured with an IP address and an IP service port number. The service port number is 5120.

If the node is not connected to the same LAN segment as the network management system, a default gateway IP address must be configured. The default gateway is the address of a router interface to which the node directs all traffic to hosts not on the directly connected network.

It is not necessary for all nodes in the network to be attached to a LAN for network management access. An IP relay address can be used to allow the network-management system to manage the node through another node.

The IP relay address is also required by Cisco WAN Manager for node management and statistics collection. If Cisco WAN Manager is not implemented, the IP relay address does not need to be configured, although, as mentioned, it can be used to Telnet to a node inband through the network trunks to manage the node remotely.

The IP relay address, if configured, must be on a separate IP network or subnet than the LAN port IP address.

Print Modes

Although each node can support a printer on its auxiliary port, it is unlikely that a network will have a printer attached to every node. Therefore, it is possible to designate a remote printer for nodes that do not have a local printer. Figure 13-3 shows local and remote printing.

Figure 13-3 *Local and Remote Printing*

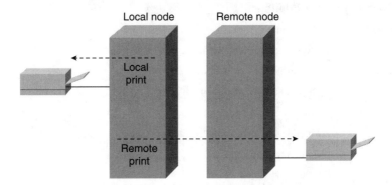

For remote printing, the remote node name must be configured. The print mode is modified using the **cnfprt** command. After it is configured, print commands (**prtscrn, prttrkerrs,** and so on) are sent to the node's defined printer, either local or remote.

Time Zone, Date, and Time

Each node shows the local date, time, and time zone in the upper-right corner of the CLI screen. The time zone for each node can be different, based on the physical location of the node. The date and time are consistent throughout the network but are displayed in the local time zone for each node. The local date and time are used in the node event and alarm log, and with statistics display screens. The **cnfdate** and **cnftime** commands change the network date and time, and should be used with caution within a production environment because the change has global affects on nodes and event and alarm logs.

Commands

The commands listed in Table 13-2 are necessary for initial configuration of a node. Informational commands are also available that report the same information that can be changed with the configuration command. These informational commands are also briefly discussed in this section when necessary.

Table 13-2 *Initial Configuration Commands and Privilege Level*

Command	Description	Privilege
clrcnf	Clear configuration.	0
	Clears configuration memory.	
dspnds	Display nodes.	6
	Displays all nodes in the network.	
cnfname	Configure node name.	1
	Modifies the node name for the node.	
cnftmzn	Configure time zone.	1
	Modifies the local time zone for the node.	
cnfdate	Configure date.	1
	Configures the date and time for the node.	
cnfterm	Configure terminal port.	6
	Configures the control and the auxiliary port interface configuration.	
cnftermfunc	Configure terminal functions.	0
	Modifies the function of the control and the auxiliary ports.	
cnfprt	Configure print mode.	6
	Modifies the current print mode.	
cnflan	Configure LAN port.	0
	Modifies the LAN IP address and the subnet mask for the node.	
cnfnwip	Configure network IP.	0
	Modifies the IP relay address of the node.	
window	Window to external devices.	4
	Provides an interface to an external EIA/TIA-232 device via the control or auxiliary ports.	

clrcnf

The **clrcnf** command in Example 13-1 clears the configuration memory of the node and resets the node. This command erases most network configuration data, including connections, trunks, circuit lines, and so on, for the local node. It may be required when updating a software release or when a node is physically moved to a different location and needs to be reconfigured. Before the command is performed, a warning is displayed and a confirmation is required.

Example 13-1 *The Clear Configuration Command—clrcnf*

```
far1igx1        TRM         SuperUser     IGX 8420  9.1.03    Date and Time Not Set




Last Command:clrcnf

*** Warning: ***
This command clears the configuration memory and resets the node.



Are you sure (y/n)? Y
```

The **clrcnf** command should be used only on a node that has not yet been placed in service, or when the network configuration has been previously saved so that it can be quickly reloaded.

For configuration backup, the current configuration can be saved as follows:

- **Cisco WAN Manager**—You can perform a save on a Cisco WAN Manager using the Save/Restore Configuration function.

- **Standby Controller**—If a redundant, standby controller is installed, remove the standby controller from its slot before entering the **clrcnf** command. The configuration data will be maintained in BRAM although the power was removed from the card.

An expanded command with a similar function as **clrcnf** is the **clrallcnf** command, which requires service-level access. In addition to deleting network trunks, lines, and so on, the **clrallcnf** command resets the node name, the number, all IP addresses, and many other system parameters to the factory system defaults.

dspnds

The **dspnds** command in Example 13-2 shows a list of all known nodes in the network. Initially, you should see only one node in the network (the local node). An optional parameter, +n, provides the node number.

Example 13-2 *The Display Nodes Command—dspnds*

```
far1igx1        TRM     SuperUser     IGX 8420  9.1.03    Date and Time Not Set


NodeName J/Num
far1igx1   /1



Last Command: dspnds +n
```

continues

Example 13-2 *The Display Nodes Command—dspnds (Continued)*

```
Next Command:
```

cnfname

The **cnfname** command in Example 13-3 specifies the name by which a node is known within the network. It may be changed at any time. The new node name is automatically distributed to the other nodes in the network. (Remember that node names are case sensitive and that duplicate names are not allowed in the same network.)

Example 13-3 *The Configure Name Command—cnfname*

```
test          TRM    SuperUser       IGX 8420   9.1.03     Date and Time Not Set


NodeName    Alarm               Packet Line
far1igx1    MAJOR




Last Command: cnfname test


Next Command:
```

As seen in the upper-left corner of Example 13-3, the name has been temporarily changed to "test."

cnftmzn

Use the **cnftmzn** command in Example 13-4 to set the local time zone for the node. Configuring the time zone for a node ensures that the node's time is correct for the local area, regardless of the node at which the network date and time are set. When configured, the time zone for the node is saved in nonvolatile memory. After a power failure, a node's date and time are restored if at least one other node in the network has the current time and date.

The time zone may be set using an abbreviation, such as **g** or **GMT** for Greenwich Mean Time, or **PST** for Pacific Standard Time; or by specifying an offset from GMT—for example, **g-8** for 8 hours behind GMT.

Example 13-4 *The Configure Time Zone Command—cnftmzn*

```
far1igx1        TRM    SuperUser       IGX 8420  9.1.03    Date and Time Not Set



This Command: cnftmzn pst
```

cnfdate

When the local time zone has been set for all nodes, the **cnfdate** command in Example 13-5 is used to set the date and time. As mentioned, this command has network-wide implications: setting a new date or time on one node will cause all the other nodes to reset their clocks. The time is set using the 24-hour clock (military time).

As shown by the warning indicated in Example 13-5, setting the time also affects the time stamp that is used by the Cisco WAN Manager management station for statistics.

Example 13-5 *The Configure Date Command—cnfdate*

```
far1igx1        TRM    SuperUser       IGX 8420  9.1.03    Date and Time Not Set




This Command: cnfdate 1999 05 24 18 03 00

Warning: Changing time affects Cisco StrataView Plus statistics timestamps
Hit RETURN to change clock, DEL to abort
```

cnfterm

The **cnfterm** command in Example 13-6 shows the configuration of the control and the auxiliary ports. The configuration parameters define the transmission characteristics of the interfaces.

Example 13-6 *The Configure Terminal Command—cnfterm*

```
far1igx1        TRM    SuperUser       IGX 8420  9.1.03    May  24 1999 18:04 PST


Control port                            Auxiliary port

Baud Rate:            19200             Baud Rate:            9600

Parity:              None              Parity:              None
Number of Data Bits: 8                 Number of Data Bits: 8
Number of Stop Bits: 1                 Number of Stop Bits: 1
```

continues

Example 13-6 *The Configure Terminal Command—*cnfterm *(Continued)*

```
Output flow control: XON/XOFF          Output flow control: XON/XOFF
Input flow control:  XON/XOFF          Input flow control:  XON/XOFF
CTS flow control:    No                CTS flow control:    Yes
Use DTR signal:      Yes               Use DTR signal:      No




Last Command: cnfterm c 19200 none 8 1 x x no yes


Next Command:
```

Table 13-3 lists the control and the auxiliary parameters and their definitions for the **cnfterm** command.

Table 13-3 *Control and Auxiliary Port Parameters for the* cnfterm *Command*

Parameter	Description
Baud rate	The bit rate of the data between the port and the attached devices. Rates supported are 1200, 2400, 4800, 9600, 19200, and 38400.
Parity	The parity of the asynchronous characters sent between the port and the attached device. Choices are O (odd), E (even), and N (none).
Number of data bits	The number of stop bits in the asynchronous characters sent between the port and the attached device. Choices are 1 and none.
Output flow control	The flow-control mechanism used by the port in the output direction. Choices are X for XON/XOFF and N for none.
Input flow control	The flow-control mechanism used by the port in the input direction. Choices are X for XON/XOFF and N for no flow control.
CTS flow control	The method by which to enable or disable CTS flow control. For terminals and modems, CTS flow control is usually disabled. Printers often use CTS flow control. An X specifies XON/XOFF, and an N specifies no flow control.
Use DTR signal	The method by which to enable or disable DTR detection to determine whether a session should be terminated. If DTR is disabled, a CLI session will remain active even if communication between the node and the attached terminal is broken. Choices are N (no) and Y (yes).

cnftermfunc

The **cnftermfunc** command in Example 13-7 is used to modify the current function of the control or the auxiliary port. (**dsptermfunc** can be used to display the information prior to changing it with the **cnftermfunc** command.)

Example 13-7 *The Configure Terminal Function Command—cnftermfunc*

```
far1igx1        TRM    SuperUser        IGX 8420  9.1.03     May   24 1999 18:05 PST


Control port                            Auxiliary port

1. VT100/Cisco StrataView               1. Okidata 182 Printer
2. VT100                                2. Okidata 182 Printer with LOG
3. External Device Window               3. VT100
                                        4. Alarm Message Collector
                                        5. External Device Window   $$$
                                        6. Autodial Modem




Last Command: cnftermfunc a 5 $$$

Warning: local printing is now disabled
Next Command:
```

cnfprt

The **cnfprt** command configures the printing function. As shown in Example 13-8, if remote printing is selected, the node name where the remote printer is located also appears.

Example 13-8 *The Configure Print Mode Command—cnfprt*

```
far1igx1        TRM    SuperUser        IGX 8420  9.1.03     May   24 1999 18:08 PST


Printing Mode

Remote Printing at far1bpx1
Local Printing
No Printing




Last Command: cnfprt r far1bpx1


Next Command:
```

The remote mode field indicates that the destination for any output resulting from a print command (such as **prtrts** or **prttrkerrs**) will be printed at the listed remote node.

Local mode indicates that any print commands issued on this node print on the local printer. Finally, no printing mode indicates that the log for the node does not print.

As a reference, use the **cnfterm** and the (superuser) **cnftermfunc** commands to configure the baud rate and the printer type—regular or log—on the port.

If the auxiliary port is configured for a printer with log, then the attached printer prints messages from the network log, which is an expanded version of the system log kept on each node. Each log printer configured in the network prints out a record of the same network log entries.

The **cnfprt** and **cnftermfunc** commands affect each other. If the auxiliary port on the node is configured for anything other than a printer (with or without the network log), the local printing configuration automatically changes to "no printing" because printing is not possible when the auxiliary port is being used for another purpose.

If the current settings do not need to be changed, then the **dspprtcnf** command can be used to display printing configuration for the node.

cnflan

The **cnflan** command shown in Example 13-9 is used to configure the LAN IP address information. The maximum LAN transmit unit and the Ethernet address cannot be modified. The active the IP address, the IP subnet mask, the IP service port, and the default gateway IP address should all be configured. The service port address should be set to 5120 for WAN Manager, but the rest of the fields should be configured to integrate with the LAN.

Example 13-9 *The Configure LAN Port Command—cnflan*

```
far1igx1        TRM     SuperUser       IGX 8420  9.1.03    May  24 1999 18:09 PST

Active IP Address:                      172.30.241.11
IP Subnet Mask:                         255.255.255.128
IP Service Port:                        5120
Default Gateway IP Address:             172.30.241.1
Maximum LAN Transmit Unit:              1500
Ethernet Address:                       00.C0.43.00.90.66

Type       State
LAN        READY
TCP        UNAVAIL
UDP        READY
Telnet     READY
TFTP       READY
TimeHdlr   READY
SNMP       READY
```

Example 13-9 *The Configure LAN Port Command—cnflan (Continued)*

```
Last Command: cnflan 172.30.241.11 255.255.255.128 5120 172.30.241.1


Next Command:
```

Additionally, the **dsplancnf** command displays the LAN port information that has been configured. Use **dsplancnfg** to learn the IP address of the node.

cnfnwip

The **cnfnwip** command shown in Example 13-10 is used to configure the IP relay address. As covered, the IP relay address can be used to Telnet to a node through the WAN switch network. In addition, the relay address is used by the Cisco WAN Manager for node management and statistics collection for the network.

Example 13-10 *The Configure Network IP Command—cnfnwip*

```
far1igx1          TRM    SuperUser      IGX 8420  9.1.03    May  24 1999 18:10 PST

Active Network IP Address:              10.10.4.11
Active Network IP Subnet Mask:          255.255.255.0




Last Command: cnfnwip 10.10.4.11 255.255.255.0

Changing current Network IP configuration
Next Command:
```

The **dspnwip** command displays the current IP relay address of all nodes in the network.

Any feeder device (MGX or IPX/IGX feeder nodes) IP relay addresses are also shown with the **dspnwip** command. All feeder devices are listed under the associated routing node. The IP relay address must be on a separate network (subnet) than the LAN.

window

The **window** command provides an interface to an external device connected to the node. Prior to establishing a session with an external device, use the **cnftermfunc** command to designate the port to serve as the external device window.

To begin the session, enter the **window** command and specify the port. The control terminal screen subsequently clears, after which characters entered at the control terminal go to the external device, and vice versa.

Example 13-11 shows a command session with a Cisco router attached to the auxiliary port. To return to the switch CLI, you must enter the window escape sequence, which is **$$$** in Example 13-11 and was created with the **cnftermfunc** command in Example 13-7.

Example 13-11 *The Window Command—window*

```
Next Command: window



far1rtr1#ping
Protocol [ip]:
Target IP address: 172.30.241.17
Repeat count [5]: 20
Datagram size [100]:
Timeout in seconds [2]:
Extended commands [n]:
Sweep range of sizes [n]:
Type escape sequence to abort.
Sending 20, 100-byte ICMP Echos to 172.30.241.17, timeout is 2 seconds:
!!!!!!!!!!!!!!!!!!!!!
Success rate is 100 percent (20/20), round-trip min/avg/max = 1/3/4 ms
far1rtr1#
far1rtr1#$$$
```

The **window** command also can be executed over a virtual terminal connection, which makes it possible to control all external devices from a single point in the network. The virtual terminal (vt) connection is discussed in the next chapter.

Summary

This chapter provided the information necessary to initially configure IGX and BPX systems. An introduction to the auxiliary port, the LAN interface and the IP relay network configuration, and configuration commands were covered. The LAN interface provides local access to the node, whereas the IP relay network provides an in-band management network for node management. Print modes and date and time issues were also covered in this chapter.

Review Questions

The following questions test your retention of the material presented in this chapter. You can find the answers to the Review Questions in Appendix A, "Answers to Review Questions."

1 Which three of the following statements are true?

A. Node names must be unique.

B. Node names are case sensitive.

C. Node names must start with a letter.

D. A node name can contain up to 10 characters.

E. Any keyboard character can be used in a node name.

2 Which one of the following devices cannot be attached to the auxiliary port?

A. Serial printer

B. Dumb terminal

C. Dial-out modem

D. Router console port

E. Cisco WAN Manager LAN interface

F. PC running VT100 terminal emulation

3 Which two of the following statements are true?

A. All nodes must be in the same time zone.

B. You can Telnet to the LAN or IP relay address.

C. The **cnfdate** command changes the date and the time on all nodes in the network.

D. A printer attached to a node's auxiliary port and configured to log events prints only the events for the local node.

4 Match the command in the table with its correct function from the following list:

A. Modifies the IP relay address

B. Configures the print mode

C. Modifies the control and the auxiliary port application

D. Shows the IP address and the subnet mask of the LAN port

E. Shows the node numbers of the nodes in the network

F. Communicates with an external device on the control or the auxiliary port

G. Shows the baud rate and the flow-control settings on the control and the auxiliary ports

Command	Function
dspnds	
window	
cnfnwip	
dsplancnf	
cnfprt	
dsptermcnf	
cnftermfunc	

CHAPTER 14

Network Configuration of IGX and BPX Switches

This chapter introduces the concept of trunking in a network. Also covered in this chapter is the process of configuring and activating trunks, which are used to connect IGX and BPX nodes to form a single network. Trunks are also used to connect feeder shelves to the network node, as covered in Chapter 15, "Installing MGX 8220 and MGX 8850 Nodes."

This chapter includes the following sections:

- Trunk
- Cell Types
- ATM Circuit Identification
- UNI and NNI Review
- ATM Trunk Addressing
- Trunk Redundancy
- Virtual Trunks
- Inverse Multiplexing over ATM
- Trunk Management
- Trunk Commands
- Summary
- Review Questions

Trunk

A *trunk* is a high-speed digital transport facility that carries information in FastPacket (FP) or ATM cells between any two Cisco WAN switches. Trunks can differ in technology and format.

A trunk must terminate on the same type of physical interface at each end node—for example, a T1. Trunks may directly connect nodes, perhaps in a campus network or a public wide-area network, in which case the carrier equipment will provide a termination point at each end. Trunks may be physical or virtual.

The actual network topology (trunk layout) usually represents a balance between redundancy and cost. A network could be implemented using a fully meshed design in which every node is physically connected via a trunk to every other node. In most cases, however, this would be prohibitively expensive, so a partial-mesh approach typically is used. A recommended minimum practice is that every node should be connected to the network by at least two trunks, each of which should terminate on a different node.

Many different trunk types are supported in the network. In general, narrowband trunks (less than 2 Mbps) are supported between IGX nodes carrying FastPackets. ATM trunks using StrataCom Trunk Interfaces (STIs) or standard ATM cells are supported at rates above 2 Mbps.

Figure 14-1 summarizes the trunk card module groups for BPX and IGX nodes, as covered in Chapter 10, "Installing IGX 8400 Switches," and Chapter 11, "Installing BPX 8600 Switches."

Figure 14-1 *Trunk Card Groups*

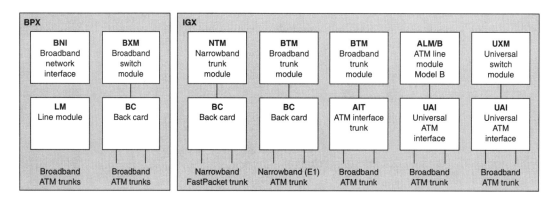

The card module groups are classified into narrowband and broadband trunks:

- **Narrowband trunks**—Narrowband trunks are implemented only on the IGX node and provide support for T1, E1, Y1, and subrate interfaces.

- **Broadband trunks**—Broadband trunks are supported on both IGX and BPX nodes. Broadband interface types supported on the IGX node are E2, High-Speed Serial Interface (HSSI), T3, E3, and OC-3/STM-1. T3, E3, OC-3/STM-1, and OC-12/STM-4 are supported on the BPX. The trunk types and interfaces are summarized in Table 14-1.

Subrate Trunks

A subrate trunk provides a serial interface (V.35, X.21, or EIA/TIA-449) and requires a separate clocking source, such as CSU/DSU. The transmit and receive clock signals are carried on defined leads on the serial interface. On the IGX node, the subrate data rate is configured as a multiple of 64 kbps, up to the maximum configurable rate of 1920 kbps.

Cell Types

As summarized in Table 14-1, the trunk type is defined by the cell type supported by the card. Subrate trunks use Cisco FastPackets, whereas the other narrowband cards and broadband cards can use STI or the standards-based User-Network Interface (UNI) cell. This means that all broadband trunks are made up of 53-byte ATM cells, as is traffic on T1 or E1 trunks, which terminates on IGX UXM trunk cards.

Table 14-1 *Trunk Types and Interfaces Supported*

Card Type	Narrowband				Broadband						Cell Type		
	T1	E1	Y1	SR	HSSI	E2	E3	T3	OC-3	OC-12	FP	STI	UNI/NNI
NTM	X	X	X	X							X		
BTM		X			X	X	X	X				X	X[1]
ALM/B						X	X					X	X[1]
UXM	X	X				X	X	X					X
BNI						X	X	X				X	
BXM						X	X	X					X

1. UNI cells supported on IGX to IGX trunks

All three cell types—FastPacket, STI, and UNI—have the same general format: a header and a payload section. The STI and UNI cells have a 5-byte header followed by a 48-byte payload section, for a total of 53 bytes per cell. The FastPacket cell has a 3-byte header and a 21-byte payload. The UNI cell format is covered in detail in Chapter 7, "Asynchronous Transfer Mode."

Figure 14-2 shows the UNI cell format. Compare this to the STI cell shown in Figure 14-3 and the FastPacket cell shown in Figure 14-4.

Figure 14-2 *ATM UNI Cell Format*

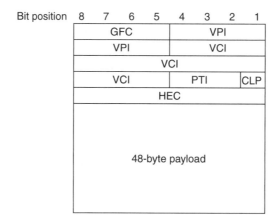

Figure 14-3 *STI Cell Format*

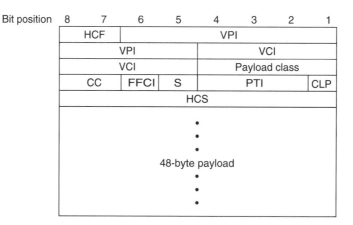

Figure 14-4 *FastPacket Cell Format*

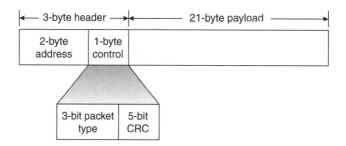

The STI cell header is used on broadband trunks between any two IGX nodes, and on BNI trunks connecting BPX nodes or connecting BPX nodes to IGX nodes.

The STI cell header differences are shown in Table 14-2.

Table 14-2 *STI Cell Header Specifics*

Field	STI Specification
Header control field (HF)	Always is set to 01
Virtual path identifier (VI)	Has the same function as UNI/NNI VPI, but uses different bits
Virtual channel identifier (VI)	Has the same function as UNI/NNI, but uses different bits
Payload class	Supports OptiClass, which segregates different traffic types to fairly allocate bandwidth resources in the network
Congestion control (CC)	Uses ForeSight congestion messages to determine rate adjustments set by the destination interface
ForeSight forward congestion indication (FFI)	Gives a congestion indication set on network trunks based upon configurable queue thresholds
Supervisory (S)	Is a supervisory cell used by the ForeSight algorithm to pass congestion control information if user data cells are not present that normally would be tagged with congestion control information
Payload type indicator (PI)	Has the same function as UNI/NNI, but uses different bits
Cell Loss Priority (CP)	Has the same function as UNI/NNI, but uses different bits
Header Check Sequence (HS)	Provides an 8-bit CRC on the cell header only

ATM Circuit Identification

When a cell arrives in the ATM network, the VPI and VCI are used to identify which permanent virtual circuit (PVC) the cell is transported across. VPIs and VCIs have local significance only to each interface. These fields might change as the cell moves through the network, depending on the routing and addressing needs of the network.

Multiple virtual channels can be combined into a single virtual path when necessary, to simplify routing and switching of cells with the same endpoints. Virtual paths also can be switched as single entities.

Figure 14-5 shows an ATM UNI with three terminating connections. Two of the connections are identified by both a VPI and a VCI (in the form VPI/VCI—here, 1/50 and 1/51). These are termed virtual channel connections (VCCs). The third connection is identified by a VPI only and can carry multiple channels transparently through the network. This is a *virtual path connection (VPC)*.

Figure 14-5 *ATM Circuit Identification*

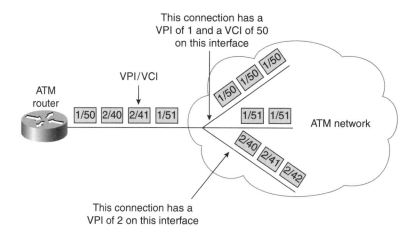

A VPC is a service that is a collection of virtual channels that share the same VPI. Sometimes this type of connection is referred to as a *virtual path (VP)* tunnel because it provides a tunnel for multiple channels in a network. VPCs often are used to carry traffic between two ATM switches through a public ATM cloud. The left portion of Figure 14-6 shows how VP switching passes data through a switch. Although the VPI might change, the VCI is unchanged throughout the process.

In most instances, VCCs identify end-to-end ATM connections. A VCC is a connection that depends on both the VPI and the VCI to determine a cell's path through the network. *Virtual channel (VC)* switching is the term used to describe this process, and this is illustrated in Figure 14-6.

The VPCs might change both the VPI and the VCI as they pass through the switch. Note that in many switches, both VP and VC switching are supported.

Figure 14-6 *ATM VC and VP Switching*

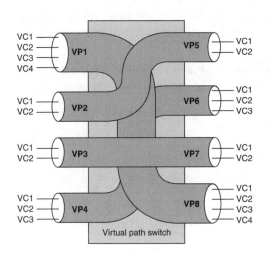
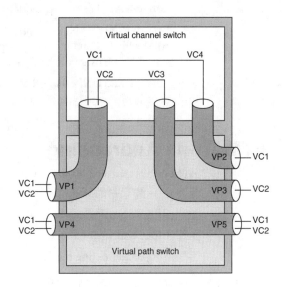

UNI and NNI Review

As covered in Chapter 7, "Asynchronous Transfer Mode", the User-Network Interface (UNI) and the Network-to-Network Interface (NNI) are identified as public or private. Refer to Figure 14-7 during the discussion of public and private UNI and NNI.

Figure 14-7 *UNI and NNI Definition*

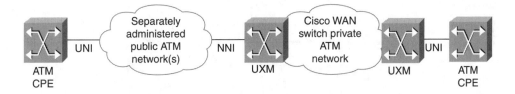

Read over the following definitions:

- **Public UNI**—A public UNI typically is used to interconnect an ATM user, such as the ATM customer premises equipment (CPE) shown in Figure 14-7, with an ATM switch deployed in a public service provider's network.

- **Private UNI**—A private UNI is used to interconnect an ATM user with an ATM switch managed as part of the same private enterprise network, as illustrated with the right CPE in Figure 14-7.

- **Public NNI**—A public NNI specifies the connection between switches from two different ATM service providers.

- **Private NNI (PNNI)**—A private NNI specifies the connection between two private ATM switches and includes a signaling protocol for automatic call setup, quality of service (QoS) support, and dynamic routing.

Public and private UNIs share the same cell header format and signaling. The only difference is often the type of facilities used to carry the cells.

ATM Trunk Addressing

ATM trunks that terminate on ALM/B or BTM cards on the IGX node support STI and UNI/NNI and have three types of addressing available, as shown in Figure 14-8:

- BPX addressing mode
- Cloud addressing mode
- Simple addressing mode

Figure 14-8 *IGX ATM Trunk Addressing Modes*

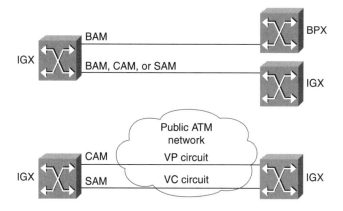

BAM

BPX addressing mode uses STI cells between the IGX and either a BPX or an IGX node. The addressing is done automatically by the network, and no additional configuration is necessary. *BAM* is the default for IGX ATM trunks using ALM/B or BTM cards.

CAM

Cloud addressing mode (CAM) uses UNI cells between two IGX nodes. Cells can route directly to the attached node or through a public ATM network utilizing a VPC. A VPI must be configured for a CAM trunk.

Simple Addressing Mode

As with CAM, *simple addressing mode (SAM)* uses UNI cells between two IGX nodes. Cells are sent either directly to the attached node or via a public network, utilizing a VCC. A VPI and a VCI must be configured for a SAM trunk.

These addressing modes are not applicable to UXM trunk cards because the UXM card supports only the UNI/NNI cell type.

Trunk Redundancy

Trunk redundancy can refer to one of the following three features:

- 1:1 redundancy with Y-cabling and a single trunk
- 1:1 redundancy with dual trunks (for certain ATM trunk cards)
- SONET automatic protection switching (APS) for BXM trunk cards from Release 9.2

Trunk Redundancy with Y-cables

Y-cable redundancy is achieved by installing two identical front and back card sets, connecting them with a Y-cable on each paired port, and then specifying redundancy with the **addyred** command. The installation of Y-cables is covered for the appropriate cards in Chapter 10, "Installing IGX 8400 Switches" and Chapter 11, "Installing BPX 8600 Switches."

Y-cable redundancy applies to the entire card and is not port- or line-specific. During normal operation, the primary set is active and carrying traffic, and the secondary set is in standby mode. The configuration of the primary set is the same configuration for both the primary and redundant set. If the primary card is reset or the primary card becomes inactive for any reason, the secondary card set also becomes active.

All service cards on the IGX and BPX nodes support Y-cable redundancy. The commands that apply to Y-cable redundancy are shown in Table 14-3.

Table 14-3 *Y-Cable Trunk Redundancy Commands*

Command	Description
addyred	Enables card redundancy for IGX and BPX cards. The **addyred** command specifies the slots of the primary and secondary (standby) cards that form the redundant pair.
delyred	Disables the Y-cable redundancy for the card set in the specified primary slot number.
dspyred	Displays information for Y-cable pairings.

ATM Trunk Redundancy

ATM trunk redundancy is the T3 and E3 trunk redundancy supported by the ALM/B and BTM cards on the IGX node. Trunk redundancy can exist between an IGX node and a BNI trunk card on a BPX node, but trunk redundancy between two IGX nodes is not supported. Trunk redundancy uses the standard trunk cables rather than a Y-cable.

The ATM trunk redundancy scheme requires two sets of ATM trunk cards on the IGX, two BNI ports on a BPX node, and two standard T3 or E3 cables (not Y-cables).

The commands used to configure trunk redundancy are shown in Table 14-4.

Table 14-4 *ATM Trunk Redundancy Commands*

Command	Description
addtrkred	Sets up redundancy for a pair of BTM or ALM/B cards.
deltrkred	Removes the redundant ATM trunk on the specified slot.
dsptrkred	Displays all redundant backup and primary ATM trunk pairs.

APS Redundancy

With Release 9.2, APS line redundancy is supported. APS line redundancy is available only on BXM SONET trunks and is compatible with virtual trunks. The trunk port supporting virtual trunks might have APS line redundancy configured in the same way that it would be configured for a physical trunk.

The commands shown in Table 14-5 are used to configure APS redundancy.

Table 14-5   *APS Redundancy Commands*

Command	Description
cnfcdaps	Sets the APS options on the card.
addapsln	Adds an APS redundant pair.
delapsln	Deletes an APS pair.
dspapsln	Displays the status of APS line pairs.
switchapsln	Controls the APS user-switching interface.
cnfapsln	Configures the APS parameters on a line.
addcdred	Adds redundancy across two cards. (Operates like the **addyred** command.)
dpscdred	Displays redundant cards. (Operates like the **dspyred** command.)
delcdred	Deletes redundancy configuration for cards. (Operates like the **delyred** command.)
switchcdred	Switches active and redundant cards. (Operates like the **switchyred** command.)

Virtual Trunks

A *virtual trunk* is an ATM trunk that is defined over a public ATM network in the form of a VPC. Multiple virtual trunks can terminate on a single physical trunk interface. Each virtual trunk corresponds to a single VPC and is identified by a unique VPI provided by the ATM service provider.

In Figure 14-9, six virtual trunks, indicated by the dashed lines, are configured in the network. Notice that multiple virtual trunks terminate on each physical interface. Physical trunks also terminate on the nodes, such as the lower two in Figure 14-9.

Virtual trunks can be implemented on IGX and BPX nodes. Virtual trunks are supported between BNI trunk cards on BPX notes and, with Release 9.2 of the system software, between any combination of BXM (BPX) and UXM (IGX) cards.

Virtual trunks based on BNI modules use a modified STI header that appears to the public network as an ATM UNI cell. BXM and UXM virtual trunks use standard UNI or NNI cells, as required by the service provider.

Figure 14-9 *Virtual Trunks*

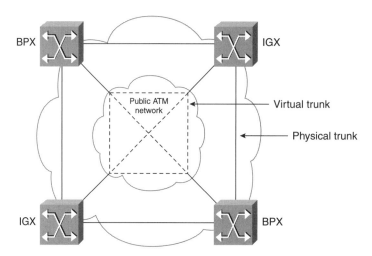

The range of VPI values supported differs by card, as shown in Table 14-6.

Table 14-6 *VPI Values for BXM and BNI Cards*

Card(s)	VPI Values
BXM/UXM (UNI)	1 to 255
BXM/UXM (NNI)	1 to 4095
BNI T3/E3	1 to 255
BNI OC3	1 to 63

Each virtual trunk is configured as a constant bit rate (CBR), variable bit rate (VBR), or available bit rate (ABR) trunk.

Each card has a limited number of virtual trunks per card. In addition, each node also is limited to the number of trunks supported. The BPX node with 32 MB of memory supports up to 50 virtual or physical trunks. With 64 MB, the BPX supports up to 64 trunks. The IGX supports up to 32 virtual or physical trunks. The card limitations are shown in Table 14-7.

Table 14-7 *Maximum Number of Trunks for BNI, BXM, and UXM*

Card	Number of Virtual Trunks
BNI T3/E3	32
BNI-155	11
BXM	31
UXM	15

Inverse Multiplexing over ATM

Inverse multiplexing over ATM (IMA) supported on UXM cards is shown in Figure 14-10. IMA enables you to group physical T1 or E1 lines to form a logical trunk. A logical trunk consisting of more than one T1 or E1 line can support user connections with data rates that are much higher than the T1 or E1 rate.

Figure 14-10 *Inverse Multiplexing over ATM*

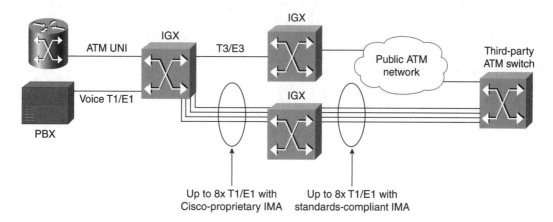

System software enables you to specify IMA so that one or more physical lines within the logical trunk can serve as a backup if a line fails. IMA is an attractive solution in applications in which ATM trunks are required but in which broadband facilities, such as E3 or T3, are either unavailable or not feasible.

Release 9.1 and later of the system software supports a Cisco-proprietary IMA protocol on UXM trunks that interoperates only with Cisco products, such as other UXMs or the IMATM module on the MGX 8220 edge concentrator.

With Release 9.2, a subset of the ATM Forum-compliant IMA protocol was added, which allows UXM trunks to interoperate with equipment from other vendors. This IMA protocol is supported only on UXM trunks. (The IMA protocol feature requires an upgrade to UXM firmware Model B.)

Trunk Management

Trunk management includes activating (upping) the hardware, configuring the trunk, and adding the trunk to the network.

The process of activating trunk hardware is referred to as *upping a trunk*. This process includes activating the hardware and the physical characteristics that support the trunk, as well as setting the correct frame format and a signal.

Virtual trunks are upped the same way as physical trunks. To activate the trunks, you must understand the naming convention for trunks. The next sections cover this in more detail.

Physical Trunk Names

Physical trunks are named after the card and slot number on the BPX node and IGX UXM trunk cards (except for older IGX cards, in which the trunk is only the slot number). For example, trunk 3.2 would be a BNI trunk in slot 3 using port 2 on the card. A trunk on an IGX NTM card in slot 4 would be called trunk 4.

Virtual Trunk Names

Virtual trunks are named after the card slot number, the port number, and the virtual trunk number. You assign the virtual trunk number when you up the virtual trunk. As an example, virtual trunk 3.2.4. would be the name for a BNI trunk in slot 3 using port 2 with virtual trunk number 4.

Trunk Commands

Trunks require several steps to enable and introduce them into the network, and these steps must be performed in a specific order to successfully complete the process. Specific commands are necessary to integrate trunks into the network. The first command, **uptrk**, is shown in Figure 14-11.

Figure 14-11 *Trunk Activation*

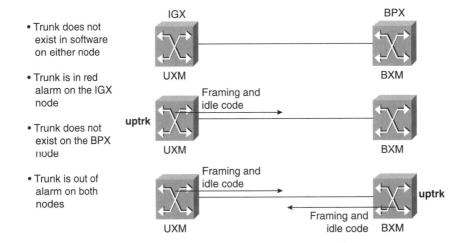

Table 14-8 gives a summary of the commands used to activate a trunk and provides additional commands necessary to configure network trunks. The remainder of this chapter covers these commands in detail.

Table 14-8   *Useful Trunk Commands*

Command	Description	Privilege
uptrk	Up trunk	2
	Activates trunk hardware and physical-layer characteristics	
cnftrk	Configure trunk	1
	Modifies trunk configuration parameters	
addtrk	Add trunk	1
	Introduces a trunk as a network resource; begins intelligent communication between nodes	
dsptrks	Display trunks	6
	Displays summary information of all trunks on the node	
dsptrkcnf	Display trunk configuration	6
	Displays configuration parameters for a particular trunk	
deltrk	Delete trunk	1
	Removes a trunk from the network	
dntrk	Down trunk	2
	Deactivates trunk hardware	
dspnw	Display network	6
	Displays all nodes in the network	
dspnds	Display nodes	6
	Displays all nodes in the network	
vt	Virtual terminal	6
	Creates a virtual link to another node in the network to access a remote user interface	
bye	Exit session	6
	Ends a VT or terminal session	

uptrk

The **uptrk** command must be issued from both sides of the trunk as part of the trunk activation. If the trunk is in alarm after it has been upped, this could be due to a physical failure or a configuration mismatch. Typically, many other devices exist on a trunk between two nodes, and all must be compatible. For example, an NTM card can support D4 and

Extended Superframe (ESF) framing on a T1 trunk; the card must be configured using the **cnftrk** command to match the framing method actually being used.

The nodes initially exchange their node name, node number, and trunk number when the **addtrk** command is issued. For **addtrk** to be successful, the two nodes must have unique node names and numbers. A database exchange occurs afterward that includes the network topology, user IDs and passwords, network clock sources, and trunk loading information.

After a trunk is added, some configuration parameters cannot be changed. If a change must be made to such a parameter, you must delete the trunk using the **deltrk** command before modifying the configuration.

Adding a trunk requires introducing the trunk as a bandwidth resource in the network. When a trunk is added, intelligent communication in the form of FastPackets or ATM cells begins between the two nodes.

Example 14-1 shows the effect of issuing the **uptrk** command at a node at which the other end of the trunk has not yet been activated. Immediately after performing **uptrk**, the trunk appears to be clear, but after several seconds, it goes into major alarm, as shown.

Example 14-1 *uptrk Command—with Major Alarm*

```
far3igx1        TRM    SuperUser        IGX 8420   9.1.03     May  29 1999 13:19 PDT

TRK       Type    Current Line Alarm Status              Other End
13.1      T3/636 Major - Loss of Sig (RED)               -




Last Command: uptrk 13.1

Warning: Bus bandwidth is undersubscribed.  Use cnfbusbw to reconfigure UBU.
Next Command:

                                                                   MAJOR ALARM
```

A trunk cannot be upped if the required cards are not available. Furthermore, if a card is executing a background self-test, a "card in test" message might appear onscreen. If this message appears, wait a moment and enter the **uptrk** command again.

The command syntax for different trunk types is shown in Table 14-9.

Table 14-9 *Trunk Command Syntax*

Trunk Type	Applicable Parameters
Physical trunk	**uptrk** slot or **uptrk** slot.port
Virtual trunk	**uptrk** slot.port.**vtrk**
IMA trunk	**uptrk** slot.start port–end port

For example, for an IMA trunk, you could enter **uptrk 8.1-4**. Subsequently, in later commands, such as **cnftrk**, you would refer to this logical trunk by using only the slot number and the first port number—8.1, in this example.

cnftrk

After it is activated with the **uptrk** command, a trunk has a default configuration that can be modified using the **cnftrk** command, shown in Example 14-2. With a limited number of exceptions, the same parameter values must be configured at each end of the trunk.

As seen in Example 14-2, the trunk has been reconfigured to increase the statistical reserve from the default of 1000 cps to 2000 cps. All other parameters remain at the default values for this type of trunk, a T3 UXM trunk on an IGX node.

Example 14-2 *cnftrk Command*

```
far3igx1          TRM    SuperUser      IGX 8420  9.1.03    May  29 1999 13:25 PDT


TRK 13.1 Config        T3/636  [96000 cps] UXM slot: 13
Transmit Trunk Rate:   96000  cps        Payload Scramble:     No
Rcv Trunk Rate:        96000  cps        Connection Channels:  256
Pass sync:             Yes               Gateway Channels:     200
Loop clock:            No                Valid Traffic Classes:
Statistical Reserve:   2000   cps              V,TS,NTS,FR,FST,CBR,VBR,ABR
Header Type:           NNT               Deroute delay time:   0 seconds
VPI Address:           1
Routing Cost:          10
Idle code:             7F hex
Restrict PCC traffic:  No
Link type:             Terrestrial
Line framing:          PLCP
Line cable length:     0-225 ft.
HCS Masking:           Yes


Last Command: cnftrk 13.1 96000 96000 Y N 2000 NNI 1 10 7F N TERRESTRIAL PLCP 1
Y N 256 200 V,TS,NTS,FR,FST,CBR,VBR,ABR 0

Next Command:
```

Detailed information on the configurable trunk parameters for each type of trunk is included with the **dsptrkcnf** command descriptions later in this chapter.

addtrk

Example 14-3 shows the trunk that was activated and configured in Examples 14-1 and 14-2, added using the **addtrk** command.

Example 14-3 *addtrk Command*

```
far3igx1        TRM    SuperUser        IGX 8420  9.1.03    May  29 1999 13:25 PDT

TRK      Type   Current Line Alarm Status            Other End
13.1     T3/636 Clear · OK                           far3bpx1/2.6




Last Command: addtrk 13.1


Next Command:
```

The **addtrk** command must be entered only at one end of the trunk, but the trunk must be free of major alarms before it can be added. If the **addtrk** command is used to join two previously separate networks, the local node verifies that all node names in both networks are unique before the trunk is added.

The **addtrk** command cannot be executed in the following circumstances:

- When another node is simultaneously attempting to change the network topology by adding or deleting a trunk
- When another node is notifying all nodes that it has been renamed
- When another node is adding or deleting a connection in the network with the **addcon** or **delcon** command
- When there is an unreachable node in the network
- When two networks are to be joined, and the node names are not unique across both networks

To delete a trunk, use the **deltrk** command. Because deleting a trunk removes the communication path between two nodes, using the **deltrk** command might split a network into two separate networks. If the **deltrk** command execution splits the network, it deletes any connections using the deleted trunk. After deletion, the trunk still carries framing signals and can generate alarms for counting, but no traffic can move across it. To remove the trunk completely, use the **dntrk** command after the **deltrk** command.

dsptrks

The **dsptrks** command, shown in Example 14-4, provides summary information on the status of all active trunks that terminate on this node. Trunks appear when the **uptrk** command is issued. Use the **dsptrks** command when you want to see which trunks are active, view their current state, and obtain the name and trunk number of the remote node.

Example 14-4 *dsptrks Command*

```
far3igx1        TRM    SuperUser      IGX 8420  9.1.03   May  29 1999 13:26 PDT


TRK       Type   Current Line Alarm Status              Other End
 5        T1/24  Clear - OK                             far1igx1/6
 6        E1/32  Clear - OK                             far5igx1/6
13.1      T3/636 Clear - OK                             far3bpx1/2.6




Last Command: dsptrks


Next Command:
```

Possible trunk states are not upped, upped, and added:

- **Not upped**—When the states is not upped, the trunk does not appear on the **dsptrks** screen.

- **Upped**—An upped trunk will have a "Current Line Alarm Status" reported, but no "Other End" information.

- **Added**—In an added state, the trunk is monitored for physical-layer status as well as other possible errors and alarms (such as dropped packets or cells) associated with FastPacket or cell transmission. An added trunk reports a destination node name and trunk number at the "Other End."

The **dsptrks** command screen also is displayed if any of the following commands are issued: **uptrk**, **dntrk**, **addtrk**, or **deltrk**.

dsptrkcnf and Parameters

The **dsptrkcnf** command, shown in Example 14-5, provides detailed configuration information about a particular trunk. The output screen is for a T1 NTM trunk on an IGX node. (The **dsptrkcnf** command screen also appears as the result of either **dsptrkcnf** or **cnftrk** commands.)

Example 14-5 *dsptrkcnf Command—T1*

```
far3igx1        TRM    SuperUser      IGX 8420  9.1.03   May  29 1999 13:49 PDT


TRK  5 Config            T1/24    [8000  pps] NTM slot: 5
Line DS-0 map:           0-23                 Deroute delay time:   0 seconds
Pass sync:               Yes
Loop clock:              No
Statistical Reserve:     600     pps
Routing Cost:            10
Idle code:               7F hex
```

continues

Example 14-5 *dsptrkcnf Command—T1 (Continued)*

```
Restrict PCC traffic: No
Link type:            Terrestrial
Line framing:         D4
Line coding:          B8ZS
Line cable type:      ABAM
Line cable length:    0-133 ft.
Valid Traffic Classes:
        V,TS,NTS,FR,FST

Last Command: dsptrkcnf 5


Next Command:
```

The **dsptrkcnf** command shows several parameters that should be addressed more closely. Parameters can fall into several categories:

- Does not apply to this trunk type (identified with "—" as the value)

- Cannot be modified; informational only

- Can be modified by SuperUser only

- Can be modified only when the trunk is upped but not added

- Can always be modified

Table 14-10 lists configuration parameters that are relevant for narrowband trunks: T1, E1, Y1, and subrate. In addition, this table shows usage and modification limitations of software prior to Release 9.2.

Table 14-10 *Configuration Parameters and Descriptions*

Parameter	Description	Usage and Modification Limitations Prior to Release 9.2
Subrate interface	Is X21, V.35, or MIL-188 (EIA/TIA-449). Default is X.21.	Cannot be changed after **addtrk**.
Subrate data rate	Gives the data rate for the subrate trunk. Range is 64 to 1920 kbps in 64 kbps increments; default is 1920 kbps.	Cannot be changed after **addtrk**.
Line DS-0 map	Shows allocated time slots for the trunk (which might be a fractional T1/E1). For E1 trunks, 0 and 16 are not allocated because time slot 0 is used for framing and 16 is used for signaling. Time slots are 0–23 for T1 and 0–31 for E1.	Cannot be changed after **addtrk**. Alternating time slot numbers are defined as start slot–end slot.

Table 14-10 *Configuration Parameters and Descriptions (Continued)*

Parameter	Description	Usage and Modification Limitations Prior to Release 9.2
Pass synchronization	Defines whether this trunk is allowed to pass synchronization signals from a clock source to another node. Default is yes.	None.
Loop clock	Loops the receive clock to the transmit clock. Default is no.	None.
Statistical reserve	Shows bandwidth reserved for statistical variations. Connections routing over the trunk cannot be allocated to the statistical reserve, although the bandwidth is available for traffic to use as needed. Range is 0 to 10,666 packets per second.	The configured value is applied to the transmit direction only. Increasing the statistical reserve after the trunk is added causes all connections to reroute.
Routing cost	Shows the user-defined cost of a trunk when cost-based routing is configured. Range is 1 to 50. Default is 10.	None.
Idle code	Places the hex character in unused time slots during idle periods. Range is 0 to FF. Default is 7F for T1, and 54 for E1.	Cannot be changed after **addtrk**.
Restrict PCC traffic	Limits control/management traffic on this trunk. Default is no.	Used by SuperUser only.
Link type	Is used to restrict certain connections from routing across the trunk. Choices are satellite or terrestrial. Default is terrestrial.	Cannot be changed after **addtrk**.
Line framing	Specifies D4 or ESF framing. Default is d$.	For T1, this cannot be changed after **addtrk**.
Line coding	Offers choice of coding: for T1, is ZCS/AMI/B8ZS; for E1, is AMI/HDB3. Default is B8ZS for T1, and HDB3 for E1.	Cannot be changed after **addtrk**.
CRC	Provides optional CRC checking. Default is no.	For E1, this cannot be changed after **addtrk**.
Receive impedance	Provides the receive impedance. 75-ohm with ground, 75-ohm no ground, 120-ohm. Default is 75-ohm with ground.	For E1, this cannot be changed after **addtrk**.
Cable type	Gives the type and length of cable used for line build-out purposes.	For T1, this cannot be changed after **addtrk**.

continues

Table 14-10 *Configuration Parameters and Descriptions (Continued)*

Parameter	Description	Usage and Modification Limitations Prior to Release 9.2
Length	Gives the length of cable, as specified with the cable type.	None.
Valid traffic classes	Indicates the traffic types valid for this trunk type.	None.
Deroute delay time	Gives the amount of time, in seconds, that connections will wait before derouting when trunk fails. This parameter prevents connections from derouting (and therefore failing) when a trunk experiences a brief outage. Range is 0 to 600 seconds. Default is 0.	None.

Example 14-6 shows the **dsptrkcnf** command display for an IGX E1 trunk.

Example 14-6 *dsptrkcnf Command—E1*

```
far3igx1        TRM    SuperUser       IGX 8420   9.1.03    May  29 1999 13:50 PDT

TRK  6 Config        E1/32   [10666 pps] NTM slot: 6
Line DS-0 map:       0-31
Pass sync:           Yes
Loop clock:          No
Statistical Reserve: 600     pps
Routing Cost:        10
Idle code:           54 hex
Restrict PCC traffic: No
Link type:           Terrestrial
Line coding:         HDB3
Line CRC:            No
Line recv impedance: 75 ohm + gnd
Valid Traffic Classes:
        V,TS,NTS,FR,FST
Deroute delay time:  0 seconds

Last Command: dsptrkcnf 6


Next Command:
```

Example 14-7 shows the **dsptrkcnf** command screen for a T3 trunk on an IGX node with a BTM card. Several of the trunk parameters for the BTM and ALM/B cards differ from those for the UXM card, described later in this section.

Example 14-7 *dsptrkcnf Command—BTM or ALM/B (T3)*

```
far1igx1        TN    SuperUser       IGX 8420  9.1.03    May  30 1999 16:16 PST


TRK  3 Config          T3/576  [192000pps] ALM slot: 3
Transmit Trunk Rate:  96000   cps        HCS Masking:           Yes
Rcv Trunk Rate:       192000  pps        Payload Scramble:      No
Pass sync:            Yes                Valid Traffic Classes:
Loop clock:           No                       V,TS,NTS,FR,FST
Statistical Reserve:  1000    pps        Deroute delay time:   0 seconds
Header Type:          STI
Gateway Type:         BAM
VPI Address:          0
VCI Address:          0
Routing Cost:         10
Idle code:            7F hex
Restrict PCC traffic: No
Link type:            Terrestrial
Line cable length:    0-225 ft.


Last Command: dsptrkcnf 3


Next Command:
```

Table 14-11 lists configuration parameters appropriate for IGX BTM and ALM/B.

Table 14-11 *Configuration Parameters for IGX BTM and ALM/B*

Parameter	Description	Usage and Modification Limitations
Transmit rate	Gives the maximum rate that data packets or cells can be sent out on the trunk. Usually is modified to accommodate external cell converters, virtual trunks, or IGX broadband trunks.	Cannot be changed after **addtrk**.
Receive rate	Specifies that the BTM card can support up to only 80,000 pps. The default receive rate is set at 1000 pps to avoid newly added trunks from taking too much cellbus bandwidth. The receive rate should be set to the actual rate using **cnftrk**.	Cannot be changed after **addtrk**. For BTM, is 0 to 80,0000 pps. For ALM/B, is 1 to 192,000 pps.
Pass synchronization	Determines whether this trunk is allowed to pass synchronization signals from a clock source to another node. Default is yes.	None.

continues

Table 14-11 *Configuration Parameters for IGX BTM and ALM/B (Continued)*

Parameter	Description	Usage and Modification Limitations
Look clock	Loops the receive clock to the transmit clock. Default is no.	None.
Statistical reserve	Shows bandwidth reserved for statistical variations. Connections routing over the trunk cannot be allocated to the statistical reserve, although the bandwidth is available for use as needed. Default is 1000 cells per second.	The configured value is applied to the transmit direction only. Increasing the statistical reserve after the trunk is added causes all connections to reroute.
Header type	Defines ATM header: UNI or STI. Default is STI.	Cannot be changed after **addtrk**.
Gateway type	Shows BAM (default), CAM, or SAM addressing mode.	Cannot be changed after **addtrk**.
VPI address	Shows the VPI address for ATM trunks using CAM or SAM. Range is 0 to 255. Default is 0.	Cannot be changed after **addtrk**.
VCI address	Gives the VCI address for ATM trunks using SAM. Range is 0 to 65535. Default is 0.	Cannot be changed after **addtrk**.
Routing cost	Gives the user-defined cost of a trunk when cost-based routing is configured. Range is 1 to 50. Default is 10.	None.
Idle code	Places the hex character into unused time slots during idle periods. Range is 0 to FF. Default is 7F.	Cannot be changed after addtrk.
Restrict PCC traffic	Limits control/management traffic on this trunk. Default is no.	Used by SuperUser only.
Link type	Restricts certain connections from routing across the trunk; does not affect traffic processing. Choices are satellite or terrestrial. Default is terrestrial.	Cannot be changed after **addtrk**.
Length	Specifies the length of cable used for line build-out purposes. Entered as a number (0 or 1). Default is 0, representing 0 to 255 feet.	Cannot be changed after **addtrk**.

Table 14-11 *Configuration Parameters for IGX BTM and ALM/B (Continued)*

Parameter	Description	Usage and Modification Limitations
HCS (header check sequence) masking	Specifies HCS masking (add 55 hex to all HCS fields) to facilitate cell delineation. Must be the same on both ends of the trunk; otherwise, the **addtrk** command fails. Default is yes.	Cannot be changed after **addtrk**.
Payload scramble	Indicates whether ATM standard payload scramble is used. Must be the same on both ends. Default is no.	Cannot be changed after **addtrk**.
Valid traffic classes	Indicates the traffic types valid for this trunk type. Informational only—cannot be modified.	Cannot modify.
Deroute delay time	Gives the amount of time, in seconds, that connections will wait before derouting when the trunk fails. Prevents connections from derouting (and therefore failing) when a trunk has a brief outage. Range is 0 to 600 seconds. Default is 0.	None.

Example 14-8 shows the **dsptrkcnf** command screen for a T3 UXM trunk on an IGX node.

Example 14-8 *dsptrkcnf Command—IGX UXM (T3)*

```
far3igx1         TRM     SuperUser      IGX 8420  9.1.03    May  29 1999 13:50 PDT


TRK 13.1 Config       T3/636  [96000 cps] UXM slot: 13
Transmit Trunk Rate:  96000   cps         Payload Scramble:      No
Rcv Trunk Rate:       96000   cps         Connection Channels:   256
Pass sync:            Yes                 Gateway Channels:      200
Loop clock:           No                  Valid Traffic Classes:
Statistical Reserve:  1000    cps               V,TS,NTS,FR,FST,CBR,VBR,ABR
Header Type:          NNI                 Deroute delay time:  0 seconds
VPI Address:          1
Routing Cost:         10
Idle code:            7F hex
Restrict PCC traffic: No
Link type:            Terrestrial
Line framing:         PLCP
Line cable length:    0-225 ft.
HCS Masking:          Yes

Last Command: dsptrkcnf 13.1


Next Command:
```

Table 14-12 lists configuration parameters for IGX UXM broadband and IMA trunks.

Table 14-12 *Configuration Parameters for IGX UXM*

Parameter	Description	Usage and Modification Limitations
Transmit rate	Gives the maximum rate that data packets or cells can be sent out on the trunk. Usually is modified to accommodate external cell converters (converts physical transport from one format to another, such as T3 to T1) or virtual trunks.	Cannot be changed after **addtrk**.
Pass synchronization	Determines whether this trunk is allowed to pass synchronization signals from a clock source to another node. Default setting is yes. The pass synchronization should be set to no for virtual trunks, trunks using ATM inverse multiplexing, or cell converters.	None.
Loop clock	Loops the receive clock to the transmit clock. Default is no.	None.
Statistical reserve	Shows bandwidth reserved for statistical variations. Connections routing over the trunk cannot be allocated to the statistical reserve, although the bandwidth is available for traffic to use as needed. Default is 1000 cells per second. The configured value is applied to the transmit direction only. Increasing the statistical reserve after the trunk is added causes all connections to reroute.	None.
Header type	Specifies ATM cell header type. Choices are UNI or NNI. Default is NNI.	None.
VPI address	Gives the virtual path address in an ATM cell.	Used for virtual trunks only.
Routing cost	Gives the user-defined cost of a trunk when cost-based routing is configured. Range is 1 to 50. Default is 10.	None.
Idle code	Places the hexadecimal character in the trunk during idle periods. Range is 0 to FF. Default is 7F.	None.
Restrict PCC traffic	Limits control/management traffic on this trunk. Default is no.	Used by SuperUser only.
Link type	Is used to restrict certain connections from routing across the trunk; does not affect traffic processing. Choices are satellite or terrestrial. Default is terrestrial.	Cannot be changed after **addtrk**.

Table 14-12 *Configuration Parameters for IGX UXM (Continued)*

Parameter	Description	Usage and Modification Limitations
Line framing	Specifies HEC for E3, HEC or PLCP for T3, and STS-3c or STM-1 for OC-3/STM-1. Default depends on back card.	Cannot be changed after **addtrk**.
Length	Gives the length of cable used for line build-out purposes. Entered as a number (0 or 1). Default is 0, representing 0 to 255 feet.	For T3, cannot be changed after **addtrk**.
HCS (header check sequence) masking	Uses HCS masking (add 55 hex to all HCS fields) to facilitate cell delineation. Be sure to configure this parameter the same on both ends of the trunk; otherwise, **addtrk** fails. Default is yes.	Cannot be changed after **addtrk**.
Payload scramble	Indicates whether ATM standard payload scramble is used. Be sure this parameter is the same on both ends; otherwise, the trunk fails. Default is yes for BNI-E3; otherwise, is no.	Cannot be changed after **addtrk**.
Frame scramble	Standard frame scramble for OC-3c. Be sure this parameter is the same on both ends; otherwise; the trunk fails. Default is yes.	For OC-3 only. Cannot be changed after **addtrk**.
Connection channels	Gives The number of channels permitted on this trunk. The UXM supports up to 8000 per card; 270 connections are reserved for management traffic for each trunk. The maximum number that can be allocated to a trunk is 8000 minus (270 × the number of active trunks). Default is 256.	For virtual trunks only.
Gateway channels	Specifies connections used for FastPacket traffic that either terminates on a FastPacket card or is carried across a FastPacket trunk at some stage. The number of gateway connections cannot exceed the number of connection channels, and cannot be greater than 4000. Default is 200.	None.
Valid traffic classes	Gives the connection types permitted to route across this trunk. The default setting includes all the standard IGX connection types (voice, time stamped, non-time stamped, Frame Relay, and Frame Relay with ForeSight), as well as CBR, VBR, and ABR.	None.

continues

Table 14-12 *Configuration Parameters for IGX UXM (Continued)*

Parameter	Description	Usage and Modification Limitations
Virtual trunk type	Specifies CBR, VBR, or ABR. Type of service provided by the public ATM network for this trunk. Default is CBR.	For virtual trunks from Release 9.2 only. Cannot be changed after **addtrk**.
Virtual trunk VPI	Gives the VPI address used for the virtual trunk. This parameter must be nonzero and must match the VPI used on the public network. Range is 1 to 255 for UNI, and 1 to 4095 for NNI.	For virtual trunks from Release 9.2 only. Cannot be changed after **addtrk**.

Example 14-9 shows the configuration for a UXM card configured as an IMA trunk with **dsptrkcnf**. Four E1 lines are included in the IMA group.

Example 14-9 *dsptrkcnf Command—IGX UXM (IMA)*

```
far4igx1         VT      SuperUser        IGX 8420   9.1.03    May  30 1999 21:12 GMT

TRK 15.1-4 Config      E1/119  [17962 cps] UXM slot: 15
Line DS-0 map:         1-15,17-31         HCS Masking:        Yes
Transmit Trunk Rate:   17962   cps        Payload Scramble:   Yes
Rcv Trunk Rate:        17962   cps        Connection Channels: 256
Pass sync:             Yes                Gateway Channels:   200
Loop clock:            No                 Valid Traffic Classes:
Statistical Reserve:   600     cps                V,TS,NTS,FR,FST,CBR,VBR,ABR
Header Type:           NNI                Retained links:     1
VPI Address:           1                  IMA link auto disable:Enable
Routing Cost:          10                   Window size:      1   (x10 secs)
Idle code:             54 hex               Max transition cnts:10
Restrict PCC traffic:  No                   Link reenable time: 6   (x10 mins)
Link type:             Terrestrial        Deroute delay time:  0 seconds
Line coding:           HDB3
Line recv impedance:   120 ohm


Last Command: dsptrkcnf 15.1



Next Command.
```

For each active port, the UXM reserves 270 gateway connections for management traffic, regardless of the interface type. Therefore, with a fully utilized 8-E1 or 8-T1 back card, the UXM reserves up to 2160 connections. Because this can represent a very significant reduction in the number of gateway connections for user data, switch software enables you to specify a maximum number of active ports on the back card. The most applicable interfaces for this capability are the T1 and E1 ports, especially with IMA.

You can specify the maximum number of logical trunks that can be active on a card using the **cnftrkport** command. For example, if you intend an eight-port card to have two IMA trunks, you can use **cnftrkport** to specify a maximum number of two trunks. Therefore, software would reserve 540 connections for network messages, rather than the 2160 connections reserved if you did not specify a maximum.

With the prestandard Automatic Link Disable option, you can specify a failure transition rate that causes a physical port within the logical trunk to acquire a failed status. If a specified number of failures occur within a specified time window, the physical line becomes inactive. After a user-specified wait period passes, the node attempts to reactivate the line and start another window for monitoring error transitions. This option is available only if the number of retained links is less than the number of physical lines in the logical trunk, as shown in Example 14-9.

Table 14-13 lists parameters that are applicable for IMA trunks. In addition to those parameters listed in Table 14-13, IMA trunks also use narrowband parameters specific to T1, such as DS-0 mapping, line coding, and so on. (Refer to Figure 14-10.)

Table 14-13 *IMA dsptrkcnf Parameters*

Parameter	Description	Usage and Modification Limitations
Retained links	Gives the number of IMA lines retained in standby for the IMA logical trunk.	Cannot be greater than the number of physical links in the IMA trunk.
IMA link auto disable	Enables the Automatic Link Disable option. Default is disabled. If enabled, the following additional parameters become available: **Window size**—The time window during which the number of failures is counted. Is a multiple of 10 seconds; range is from 1 to 255. **Maximum transition counts**—Number of failures in the window period. Range is 1 to 255. Default is 10. **Link reenable time**—Time period following a failure that the node will wait to reactivate the link. Is a multiple of 10 minutes, ranging from 1 to 255. Default is 6.	For Release 9.1 only; not used with Release 9.2.
IMA group member	Displays and allows modification of the physical lines, which are members of this IMA group.	For Release 9.2 only.

continues

Table 14-13 *IMA dsptrkcnf Parameters (Continued)*

Parameter	Description	Usage and Modification Limitations
IMA protocol option	Enables or disables the IMA protocol.	For Release 9.2 only.
IMA max. diff. delay	Gives the maximum amount of time between consecutive cells arriving on adjacent narrowband lines. Range is 0 to 200 ms. Default is 200 ms.	For Release 9.2 only.
IMA clock mode	Defines the clocking mode for the IMA trunk. Choices are Common Transmit Clock (CTC) or Independent Transmit Clock (ITC). CTC is the default.	For Release 9.2 only.

Example 14-10 shows the **dsptrkcnf** command screen for an OC-3 BXM trunk on a BPX node.

Example 14-10 *dsptrkcnf Command—BPX (OC-3)*

```
far3bpx1         VT      SuperUser       BPX 8600   9.1.03    May  29 1999 11:59 PDT

TRK  4.1 Config    OC3     [353207cps]    BXM slot:     4
Transmit Rate:         353208            Line framing:          STS-3C
Subrate data rate:     --                    coding:            --
Line DS-0 map:         --                    CRC:               --
Statistical Reserve:  1000     cps          recv impedance:    --
Idle code:             7F hex           cable type:        --
Max Channels/Port:     256                      length:        --
Connection Channels:   256            Pass sync:             Yes
Traffic:    V,TS,NTS,FR,FST,CBR,VBR,ABR  Loop clock:            No
SVC Vpi Min:           0               HCS Masking:           Yes
SVC Channels:          0               Payload Scramble:      Yes
SVC Bandwidth:         0       cps     Frame Scramble:        Yes
Restrict CC traffic:   No              Virtual Trunk Type:    --
Link type:             Terrestrial     Virtual Trunk VPI:     --
Routing Cost:          10              Deroute delay time:    0 seconds

Last Command: dsptrkcnf 4.1



Next Command:

Virtual Terminal
```

Screen displays for all BPX trunk types use the same screen template, as shown in Example 14-10. Parameters that are not configurable for the particular trunk type are indicated by "—" in the value field. Parameter descriptions are shown in Table 14-14.

Table 14-14 *BPX dsptrkcnf Parameters*

Parameter	Description	Usage and Modification Limitations
Transmit rate	Gives the maximum rate that data packets or cells can be sent out on the trunk. Usually is modified to accommodate external cell converters (converts physical transport from one format to another, such as T3 to T2), virtual trunks, or IGX broadband trunks.	Cannot be changed after **addtrk**.
Statistical reserve	Shows bandwidth reserved for statistical variations. Connections routing over the trunk cannot be allocated to the statistical reserve, although the bandwidth is available for traffic to use as needed. Default is 1000 cells per second. The configured value is applied to the transmit direction only. Increasing the statistical reserve after the trunk is added causes all connections to reroute.	None.
Idle code	Places the hexadecimal character in the trunk during idle periods. Range is 0 to FF. Default is 7F.	None.
Max channels/port	Shows the maximum number of connections supported on the trunk.	For BXM only.
Connection channels	Shows the number of channels permitted on this trunk. The total number of channels on a port (the sum of all virtual trunks) cannot exceed 1771 on the BNI-T3/E3 or 15,867 on the BNI-155. For the BXM, the number cannot exceed the number of channels supported on the card.	For virtual trunks only.
Valid traffic classes	Gives the connection types permitted to route across this trunk. The default setting includes all the standard IGX connection types (voice, time stamped, non-time stamped, Frame Relay, and Frame Relay with ForeSight), as well as CBR, VBR, and ABR.	None.
SVC channels	Gives the number of channels reserved for SVCs. Range is 0 to 1771 for T3 and E3, and 0 to 16199 for OC-3c. Default is 0.	None.
SVC bandwidth	Gives the amount of bandwidth reserved for SVCs. Range is 0 to 96000 cells per second for T3, 0 to 80000 for E3, and 0 to 353208 for OC-3c. Default is 0 in all cases.	None.

continues

Table 14-14 *BPX dsptrkcnf Parameters (Continued)*

Parameter	Description	Usage and Modification Limitations
Restrict CC traffic	Limits control/management traffic on this trunk. Default is no.	Used by SuperUser only.
Link type	Is used to restrict certain connections from routing across the trunk; does not affect traffic processing. Choices are satellite or terrestrial. Default is terrestrial.	Cannot be changed after **addtrk**.
Routing cost	Gives the user-defined cost of a trunk when cost-based routing is configured. Range is 1 to 50. Default is 10.	None.
Line framing	Specifies HEC for E3, HEC or PLCP for T3, STS-3c or STM-1 for OC-3/STM-1, and STS-12c or STM-4 for OC-12/STM-4. Default depends on back card.	Cannot be changed after **addtrk**.
Length	Gives the length of cable used for line build-out purposes. Entered as a number (0 or 1). Default is 0, representing 0 to 255 feet. Used for E3/T3.	Cannot be changed after **addtrk**.
Pass synchronization	Determines whether this trunk is allowed to pass synchronization signals from a clock source to another node. Default setting is yes. The pass synchronization should be set to no for virtual trunks, trunks using ATM inverse multiplexing, or cell converters.	None.
Loop clock	Loops the receive clock to the transmit clock. Default is no.	None.
HCS masking	Uses HCS masking (adds 55 hex to all HCS fields) to facilitate cell delineation. Be sure to configure this parameter the same on both ends of the trunk; otherwise, the **addtrk** command fails. Default is yes.	Cannot be changed after **addtrk**.
Payload scramble	Indicates whether ATM standard payload scramble is used. Be sure that this parameter is the same on both ends; otherwise, the trunk fails. Default is yes for BNI-E3; otherwise, is no.	Cannot be changed after **addtrk**.
Frame scramble	Indicates whether standard frame scramble for OC-3c is used. Be sure that this parameter is the same on both ends; otherwise, the trunk fails. Default is yes. Used for OC-3 only.	Cannot be changed after **addtrk**.
Virtual trunk type	Specifies CBR, VBR, or ABR. Gives the type of service provided by the public ATM network for this trunk. Default is CBR.	For virtual trunks only. Cannot be changed after **addtrk**.

Table 14-14 *BPX dsptrkcnf Parameters (Continued)*

Parameter	Description	Usage and Modification Limitations
Virtual trunk VPI	Gives the VPI address used for the virtual trunk. This parameter must be a nonzero number and must match the VPI used on the public network. Range is 1 to 255 for T3 and E3, and 1 to 63 for OC-3c.	Virtual trunks only. Cannot be changed after **addtrk**.
Deroute delay time	Specifies the amount of time, in seconds, that connections will wait before derouting when the trunk fails. This parameter prevents connections from derouting (and therefore failing) when a trunk experiences a brief outage. Range is 0 to 600 seconds. Default is 0.	None.

dspnw

The **dspnw** command, shown in Example 14-11, provides summary information about all nodes and trunks in the network. Use this command when you want to see the network topology and status.

Example 14-11 *dspnw Command*

```
far3igx1           TRM    StrataCom       IGX 8420  9.1.03    May  29 1999 12:38 PDT


NodeName     Alarm              Packet Line
far1igx1
     5-5/far2igx1               6-5/far3igx1              13.1-2.3/far1bpx1
     13.2-13.2/far3igx1         13.3-13.2/far2igx1
far1bpx1
     2.1-2.1/far3bpx1           2.2-2.1/far2bpx1          2.3-13.1/far1igx1
     4.1-4.2/far5bpx1           4.2-4.2/far4bpx1
far2igx1
     5-5/far1igx1               6-6/far4igx1              13.1-2.3/far2bpx1
     13.2-13.3/far1igx1         13.3-16.2/far4igx1
far2bpx1
     2.2-2.2/far4bpx1           2.1-2.2/far1bpx1          2.3-13.1/far2igx1
     4.1-4.1/far3bpx1           4.2-4.1/far5bpx1




This Command: dspnw


Continue?

          SW CD
```

Each node is listed followed by the trunk number, the remote node name, and the remote trunk number of every trunk terminating on the node.

The alarm status for each node is reported to the right of the node name. Table 14-15 lists the alarm and description.

Table 14-15 *dspnw Alarms and Descriptions*

Alarm	Description
Unrch	The node is unreachable from this node. An unreachable node is no longer in communication with other nodes in the network. A failure of all trunks to the node, a loss of power, or a severe processor failure without an available redundant processor can cause this state.
Major	There is a major alarm at this node. Further investigation is needed.
Minor	There is a minor alarm at this node. Further investigation is needed.

If the network has more nodes and trunk connections than can be displayed on a single screen, a "Continue?" prompt appears asking whether you want the remaining network topology to be displayed. If yes, press Return. If no, enter **n** and press Return.

dspnds

The **dspnds** command, shown in Example 14-12, provides a summary list of all nodes in the network and their current alarm status.

Example 14-12 *dspnds Command*

```
far3igx1         TRM     StrataCom      IGX 8420  9.1.03    May  29 1999 12:38 PDT

NodeName Alarm
far1igx1
far1bpx1
far2igx1
far2bpx1
far3igx1
far3bpx1
far4igx1
far4bpx1
far5igx1
far5bpx1




Last Command: dspnds


Next Command:

              SW  CD
```

For large networks, you might prefer the **dspnds** command to the **dspnw** command because it provides a list (in columns) of all nodes on a single screen. The alarm status fields are the same as those described in Table 14-15 for the **dspnw** command.

Optional parameters can be used to provide supplemental information for each node:

- **+n** to display node numbers
- **–p** to display the processor type (BCC, NPM)
- **–d** to display the node type (IGX, BPX)

vt

A *virtual terminal (VT)* session enables you to access a remote node inband through the network trunks.

To access a remote node using the **vt** command, both nodes must be in the network, although not necessarily connected by a direct trunk. Because user IDs and passwords are network-wide, you need not log in again when a VT session is established to another node.

By default, only one VT session can be active on a node at a time. However, with additional licenses, up to six concurrent VT sessions can be supported. Example 14-13 shows an example of the **vt** command.

Example 14-13 *vt Command*

```
far3bpx1        VT      StrataCom      BPX 8600   9.1.03    May  29 1999 12:40 PDT

TRK       Type       Current Line Alarm Status        Other End
 2.1      T3         Clear - OK                        far1bpx1/2.1
 2.2      T3         Clear - OK                        far5bpx1/2.1
 2.6      T3         Clear - OK                        far3igx1/13.1
 4.1      OC3        Clear - OK                        far2bpx1/4.1
 4.2      OC3        Clear - OK                        far4bpx1/4.1




Last Command: dsptrks


Next Command:

Virtual Terminal    SW
```

VT sessions cannot be chained. If you establish a VT session to one node, you cannot add a second VT session to a second node. To end a VT session, issue the **bye** command. **vt** cannot be used to access an MGX node.

Summary

This chapter covered the necessary steps and commands to configure network trunks. Network trunks are added using the **uptrk**, **cnftrk**, and **addtrk** commands. In addition to these commands, the chapter also covered the **dsptrkcnf** command, which provides detailed configuration information.

Review Questions

The following questions test your retention of the material presented in this chapter. You can find the answers to the Review Questions in Appendix A, "Answers to Review Questions."

1 Which of the following card modules can terminate a trunk on an IGX node? (More than one answer could be correct.)

A. CVM

B. NPM

C. NTM

D. ALM/B

E. UXM

F. UFM/C

2 Which two of the following card modules can terminate a trunk from an IGX on a BPX node?

A. BCC-4

B. BNI-T3

C. ASI-T3

D. BXM-E3

E. ASI-155E

F. BXM-622

3 Which three types of equipment can be attached to a node on a trunk?

A. A BPX node

B. An IGX node

C. A Cisco 7500 router

D. An MGX concentrator

E. A Cisco LightStream 1010

F. Another vendor's Frame Relay switch

4 What is the default size of the statistical reserve for a T3 trunk?

A. 600 cps

B. 992 cps

C. 1000 cps

D. 600 cps

E. 992 cps

5 How many virtual trunks can you terminate on a single port on a BXM-155 card?

A. 4

B. 11

C. 31

D. 32

E. 64

6 What is a virtual trunk?

A. A way to remotely log in to another node

B. An ATM connection that carries traffic for another switch network

C. A trunk that attaches a node to another vendor's ATM switch

D. A type of trunk that utilizes a public ATM service to trunk cell traffic to one or more IGX and/or BPX nodes

7 Which three of the following statements are true?

A. Some trunk parameters do not apply to all trunk types.

B. Cell scrambling affects the alarm condition of an upped trunk.

C. The **addtrk** command must be issued before the **uptrk** command.

D. Configuration parameters are configurable when a trunk is added.

E. When deactivating a trunk, you must delete a trunk first before it can be downed.

8   What information can you get using the **dspnw** command?

   A. Node name

   B. Node status

   C. Node number

   D. Number of connections

   E. Available trunk bandwidth

   F. Trunks terminating on the node

9   Match each trunk configuration parameter in the table with its function that follows.

Trunk Configuration Parameter	Answer
Loop clock	
Statistical reserve	
Frame scrambling	
Transmit trunk rate	
Connection channels	
Receive impedance	

   A. The number of connections allowed on a virtual trunk

   B. A way to use the receive clock in the transmit direction

   C. A portion of the bandwidth that cannot be allocated to connections

   D. Associated with E1 trunks

   E. A standards-based method for rearranging the frame on a trunk

   F. The maximum number of data cells permitted on a trunk per second

10   What information can you get using the **dspnds** command?

   A. Node name

   B. Node status

   C. Node number

   D. Number of connections

   E. Available trunk bandwidth

   F. Trunks terminating on the node

CHAPTER 15

Installing MGX 8220 and MGX 8850 Nodes

This chapter provides detailed information on the physical, mechanical, and electrical installation of the MGX 8220 edge concentrator and the MGX 8850 switch. A functional description is provided for each of the card module sets supported with Processor Switch Module (PXM) Release 1.1 and MGX Firmware Release 5.0.

This chapter includes the following sections:

- MGX 8850 Hardware Overview
- MGX 8220 Hardware Overview
- MGX 8850 Installation
- MGX 8220 Concentrator Installation
- Card Module Functions and Features
- Service Modules
- Summary
- Review Questions

MGX 8850 Hardware Overview

The MGX 8850 edge switch is a two-bay (shelf), rack-mounted chassis with 32 card slots. The upper and lower bays can be reconfigured to accommodate double-height card modules. The chassis includes a backplane with connectors on the front and the back to attach the front and back card modules. Because the backplane is located between the front and back card modules, it is also referred to as a midplane. The backplane provides multiple bus systems to allow the service cards to communicate with each other and the common core cards.

Cooling is required to keep the backplane and the card modules within operating temperatures. The cooling assembly for the MGX 8850 switch includes a fan module with intake and exhaust plenums. The fan module is mounted above the card shelf and draws in air through the front of the chassis and up through the card cage.

An AC or DC power source provides the MGX 8850 switch power. One or more power supplies can be used to power a single chassis, depending on redundancy needs. DC power supplies are connected directly into the chassis, whereas an AC powered unit requires a separate power distribution shelf that is mounted below the chassis.

A front card and one or more back cards create a card group. As with the IGX and the BPX, a single-height card supports one back card, and a double-height card supports up to two back cards. Each card group performs a specific function on the MGX 8850 switch. In general, the front card has the intelligence to run the software or firmware and to perform the features and functions for the card group. The back card interfaces with the attached equipment using a variety of connectors. In most cases, the back card has little, if any, intelligence and is responsible for only physical-layer functions. On each card, LEDs are used to report card status and line/port conditions (active, standby, failed, major or minor alarm, and so on).

Card Slot Numbering Conventions

Card slots are numbered from 1 to 16 on the upper bay and from 17 to 32 on the lower bay, as shown in Figure 15-1. If a double-height card is installed, the card is identified by the upper-bay card slot number.

Figure 15-1   *MGX 8850 Chassis Configuration*

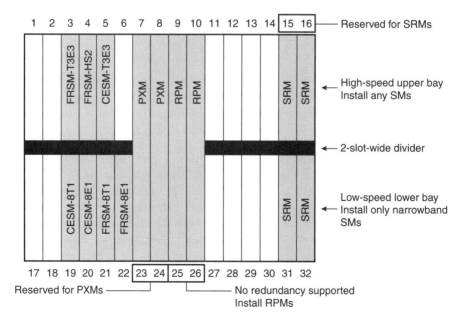

Reserved Card Slots

Of the 32 card slots, 8 are reserved for common core cards. These card slots are keyed and cannot accept any cards other than those defined. These are the eight reserved slots:

- Slots 7 and 8 (and 23 and 24) are reserved for double-height Processor Switch Modules (PXMs).

- Slots 15 and 16 are reserved for single-height Service Resource Modules (SRMs) that support bit error rate tester (BERT) and card redundancy for the upper bay.

- Slots 31 and 32 are reserved for SRMs that support the lower bay.

Although slots 15, 16, 31, and 32 are reserved for SRMs, they are not required unless BERT (covered in the "BERT Bus" section, later in this chapter), service module redundancy, or T3 line distribution is needed.

MGX 8850 Backplane

The MGX backplane supports eight different bus structures and connects front and back cards in the chassis.

Eight Cellbuses

Eight separate 155-Mbps buses carry cells to and from the card modules and the shared-memory switch on the PXM. There are six buses on the upper bay and two buses on the lower bay. The cellbuses are shown in Figure 15-2.

Figure 15-2 *MGX 8850 Cellbuses*

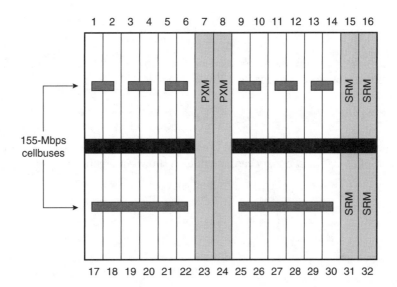

Although each bus runs at the same speed, the number of card slots supported by a bus determines the maximum bus bandwidth available for each card module. For this reason, high-speed cards should be installed in the upper bay, and low-speed cards should be installed in the lower bay.

High-speed cards supported by the MGX 8850 include the following:

- FRSM-2CT3
- FRSM-T3E3
- FRSM-HS2

Low-speed cards include the following:

- FRSM-8T1
- FRSM-8E1
- FRSM-HS1
- CESM-8T1
- CESM-8E1
- AUSM-8T1
- AUSM-8E1

Polling Bus

The *polling bus* is a serial bus used to poll service modules for cell transmission. The PXM polls the service modules in the shelf—if a cell is ready, it is sent across the cellbus to the PXM switch.

Local Bus

The *local bus* carries traffic between the common core cards to create one logical card. The common core cards include the PXM and the SRM.

Redundancy Bus

The *redundancy bus* carries traffic from the back card of a failed service module to the front card of an active secondary card module, as shown in Figure 15-3.

Figure 15-3 *MGX 8850 Redundancy Bus*

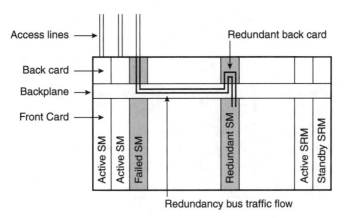

A special redundancy back card is installed to redirect line traffic from the failed service module front card to the standby redundant service module. The active and standby service modules form a redundancy group. All members of a redundancy bus must be of the same service module type and must have identical back cards.

T1 Distribution Bus

The MGX uses the T1 distribution bus, shown in Figure 15-4, to distribute demultiplexed T3 access lines between the SRM-3T3 and the destination service modules. The T1 distribution bus is used to pass traffic from the demultiplexed T3 on the SRM-3T3 to the destination service modules. Up to 80 T1 lines can be distributed across the MGX 8850 backplane.

This feature can assist customers in consolidating many access lines onto a few broadband lines, and in reducing cabling complexity at the termination points. No equivalent E1/E3 feature exists.

Figure 15-4 *MGX 8850 T1 Distribution Bus*

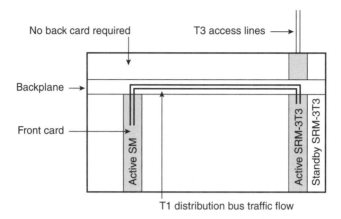

BERT Bus

The *BERT bus* carries bit patterns from the SRM to the service modules for line and port testing.

Timing Bus

The *timing bus* provides synchronization for the card modules. The PXM is responsible for switch timing and propagates synchronization signals across the timing bus.

Power Bus

The MGX *power bus* provides –48 VDC to the card modules.

MGX 8850 Card Modules

As mentioned, all MGX card groups consist of a front card and a back card. In most cases, the front card runs the necessary firmware to process traffic and to perform other functions. Back cards interface with any attached facilities and perform such tasks as line framing and line alarm detection. This section covers the MGX 8850 card modules, which are shown in Figure 15-5.

Figure 15-5 *MGX 8850 Card Modules*

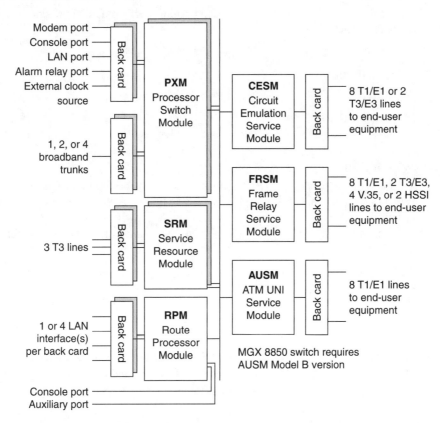

Processor Switch Module

The *Processor Switch Module (PXM)* is the central processor for the MGX 8850 node, and it stores system software and all configuration information. The PXM also communicates with network management platforms and enables connection of an external clock source to the node. The PXM includes a set of relays that can be used to signal a node or network alarm condition to external equipment.

A separate Broadband Network Module (BNM) back card provides two T3 or E3 trunks, four OC-3/STM-1 trunks, or one OC-12/STM-4 broadband trunk for connection to a BPX routing node or (in future releases) to other MGX or IGX nodes.

Service Resource Module

The *Service Resource Module (SRM)* is an optional card group that provides several functions for the node:

- Multiple 1:N redundancy groups for T1/E1 service modules
- T1 bulk distribution
- BERT
- Line loopbacks

Route Processor Module

The *Route Processor Module (RPM)* introduces the capabilities of the Cisco IOS operating system into the MGX 8850 node. The RPM provides an ATM interface into the MGX cellbus for LAN-attached devices. In future releases, it will support IP + ATM integration, including virtual private networks (VPNs) through Multiprotocol Label Switching (MPLS).

The RPM back cards provide four Ethernet, one Fast Ethernet, or one FDDI interface for user equipment.

Circuit Emulation Service Module

The *Circuit Emulation Service Module (CESM)* supports standards-based circuit emulation services for up to eight T1 or E1 lines, or two T3 or E3 lines.

Frame Relay Service Module

The *Frame Relay Service Module (FRSM)* supports channelized or unchannelized Frame Relay services for up to eight T1 or E1 lines, two T3 or E3 lines, four V.35 lines, or two High-Speed Serial Interface (HSSI) lines.

ATM UNI Service Module, Model B

The *ATM User-Network Interface Service Module, Model B (AUSM/B)* supports constant bit rate (CBR), variable bit rate (VBR), available bit rate (ABR) with ForeSight, and unspecified bit rate (UBR) ATM services for up to eight T1 or E1 lines.

MGX 8220 Hardware Overview

The MGX 8220 concentrator is a 16-card slot, rack-mounted chassis. It has a backplane with connectors on the front and back to attach the front and back card modules. A multiple bus structure on the backplane allows the cards to communicate with each other and the common core card.

The cooling assembly for the MGX 8220 concentrator includes a fan module and a plenum chamber or spacer unit and provides cooling necessary to the MGX 8220 within operating temperatures.

The fan module is mounted beneath the card shelf and contains fans that draw in air through the front of the chassis and up through the card cage.

Like the MGX 8850 switch, the MGX 8220 concentrator can be powered with either an AC or a DC source. The AC power shelf can support up to six power supplies and can be used to distribute power to up to four MGX 8220 concentrators in a multiunit installation.

All card modules in the MGX 8220 concentrator are single-height cards. Each card group consists of a front and a back card. As in the MGX 8850 switch, front cards house the intelligence for traffic processing; back cards support interface functions.

Card Slot Numbering Conventions

Card slots are numbered from 1 to 16 on the MGX 8220 concentrator. Figure 15-6 maps the card slots for the MGX 8220. Of the 16 card slots, 6 are reserved for common core cards. These card slots are keyed and cannot accept any cards other than those defined.

Figure 15-6 *MGX 8220 Chassis Configuration*

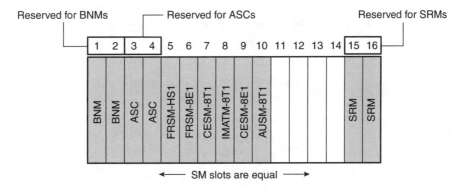

Reserved card slots are as follows:

- **Slots 1 and 2**—Reserved for Broadband Network Modules (BNMs)
- **Slots 3 and 4**—Reserved for AXIS (MGX) Shelf Controllers (ASCs)
- **Slots 15 and 16**—Reserved for SRMs

Although slots 15 and 16 are reserved for SRMs, these cards are not required unless BERT, service module redundancy, or T1 line distribution is needed.

The MGX 8220 backplane has eight separate bus structures, five of which have similar functions to those supported on the MGX 8850 switch. Highlights of the MGX 8220 differences are as follows:

- **Cellbus**—The cellbus is a 320-Mbps bus that carries cells to and from the card modules. All ATM cells from the service modules are sent across the cellbus to the active BNM.

- **Polling bus**—The polling bus is a serial bus used to poll service modules for cell transmission. The BNM polls the service modules in the shelf. If a cell is ready, it is sent across the cellbus to the BNM, not the PXM as in the MGX 8850.

- **Local bus**—The local bus carries traffic between the common core cards to create one logical card. The common core cards include the ASC, the BNM, and the SRM. (The MGX 8850's local bus is made up of the PXM and the SRM.)

MGX 8220 Card Modules

All MGX card groups, shown in Figure 15-7, consist of a front card and a back card. In most cases, the front card runs the necessary firmware to process traffic and perform other functions. Back cards interface with any attached facilities and perform such tasks as line framing and line alarm detection.

Several service modules are common to the MGX 8220 and 8850; a reference table (Table 15-1) is included later in this chapter to define which modules are common to both MGX platforms and which are unique.

Figure 15-7 *MGX 8220 Card Modules*

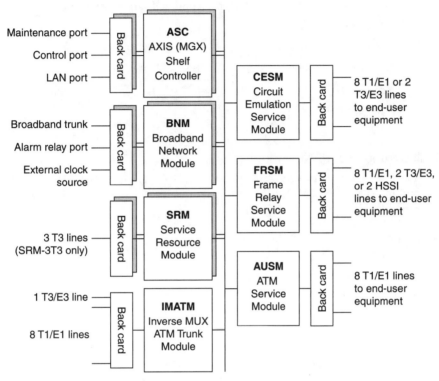

AXIS (MGX) Switch Controller

The *AXIS Switch Controller (ASC)* is the central processor for the MGX 8220 concentrator. It stores system software and all configuration information, and communicates with network management platforms.

Broadband Network Module

The *Broadband Network Module (BNM)* provides a single broadband connection to a BPX routing node; the trunk can be T3, E3, or OC-3/STM-1. The BNM also enables connection of an external clock source to the node, and includes an interface that can be used to signal a shelf alarm condition to external equipment.

Service Resource Module

The *Service Resource Module (SRM)* is an optional card group that provides several functions for the node:

- Multiple 1:N redundancy groups for T1/E1 service modules
- T1 bulk distribution
- BERT
- Line loopbacks

Inverse Multiplexing over ATM Module

The *Inverse Multiplexing over ATM Module (IMATM)* supports prestandard inverse multiplexing over ATM (IMA) trunk facilities between MGX 8220 devices using IMA groups of up to eight T1 or E1 lines.

Circuit Emulation Service Module

The *Circuit Emulation Service Module (CESM)* supports standards-based circuit emulation services for up to eight T1 or E1 lines, or two T3 or E3 lines.

Frame Relay Service Module

The *Frame Relay Service Module (FRSM)* supports channelized and unchannelized Frame Relay services for up to eight T1 or E1 lines, two T3 or E3 lines, four V.35 lines, or two High-Speed Serial Interface lines.

ATM UNI Service Module

The *ATM UNI Service Module (AUSM)* supports CBR, VBR, ABR with ForeSight, and UBR ATM services for up to eight T1 or E1 lines.

MGX 8850 Installation

The MGX 8850 switch ships either preinstalled in a Cisco closed rack, or in separate pieces for installation in an open rack. Most of the instructions in this chapter apply to an open-rack installation.

Installation Considerations for the MGX 8850

This section covers areas of particular interest for installation of the MGX 8850:

- **Space**—The MGX 8850 node requires a floor area either 19.9 inches (51 cm) wide or 23 inches (59 cm) wide. Sufficient clearance must exist around the cabinet for access to the front and back of the cabinet while the door is open. Suggested clearance is 30 inches (76 cm) at the front and back, and at least 12 inches (30 cm) on each side. The DC-powered version occupies 28 inches (71 cm) of vertical space in a rack. The AC-powered version occupies 33.25 inches (85 cm) of vertical space. The maximum number of MGX 8850 nodes you can fit in a rack is two.

- **Power**—For AC power use, an AC power source must be available within 6 feet (1.8 m) of the node. For systems using a DC source, Cisco does not supply the DC power cord, so the user or installer must determine the wire length and the distance to the DC source. The wire should be 6 AWG (10 square millimeters).

- **Heat dissipation**—A fully loaded, AC-powered MGX 8850 node dissipates up to 9560 British thermal units (BTUs) (1 kWh [kilowatt per hour]). A DC-powered MGX 8850 node dissipates up to 8200 BTUs.

- **Weight**—A fully loaded, DC-powered system can weigh up to 190 lb (87 kg). A fully loaded AC-powered system can weigh up to 250 lb (113 kg).

- **Seismic considerations**—Refer to Chapter 11, "Installing BPX 8600 Switches," for details on installing the stability plate with a Cisco rack.

- **Power requirements**—In general, consult Chapter 11, "Installing BP 8600 Switches", for power specifics. The following specifics apply to the MGX 8850:
  - **AC power circuit breakers**—MGX 8850 nodes use a 20A, two-pole circuit breaker for each AC input.
  - **DC power circuit breakers**—DC-powered nodes use a 70A, one-pole circuit breaker with a short trip delay on each –48V input.
  - **Electrical power for AC units**—The MGX 8850 AC power requirement is 220 VAC, with a worst-case range of 180 to 240 VAC.
  - **Electrical power for DC units**—Conductors must be suitable for 70A. Wiring that is 6 AWG (10 square millimeters) is adequate.

- **Bonding and grounding**—To maintain the full EMI and EMC integrity of this equipment, the rack must be bonded to an integrated ground plane or an isolated ground plane network. Except for the AC power supply module, every module in a rack-mounted system uses the rack for grounding. Therefore, the rack must connect to protective earth ground. Again, refer to Chapter 11, "Installing BPX 8600 Switches," for further details on bonding and grounding requirements.

MGX 8850 Components

When you receive the MGX switch packed in separate boxes, the card cage arrives with the cards installed and tested according to its planned configuration. If the unit includes an AC power assembly, the power supplies reside in the appropriate slots in the AC power tray. For a DC-powered system, the DC Power Entry Modules (PEMs) are mounted in the air intake chamber. For ease of installation, you should remove the cards and power supplies before rack-mounting the chassis. These operations are detailed later in this chapter.

The MGX 8850 rack-mounted system is mounted in a standard 19- or 23-inch rack, such as the Cisco-supplied Stratm cabinet. This installation uses standard EIA rail spacing.

Components included in an MGX 8850 system are shown in Figure 15-8. The components shown have specific space requirements—vertical dimensions of each are given in standard rack-mounted units (RMU = 1.75 inches, or 45 mm):

- Optional AC power tray (3 RMU), with up to six AC power modules

- Air intake plenum (3 RMU)

- Optional fan spacer (1 RMU), recommended as a placeholder for a booster fan tray, which is required if the higher-wattage version of the PXM card will be installed later

- 32-slot card cage (10 RMU), including the system backplane into which front cards, back cards, and DC-PEMs plug

- Main (upper) fan tray with nine fans (1 RMU)

- Exhaust plenum (2 RMU)

Figure 15-8 *MGX 8850 Components*

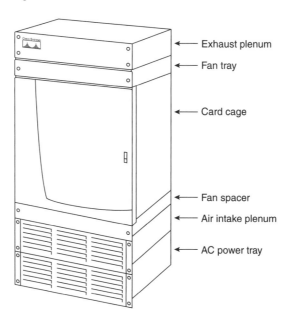

MGX 8850 Power Redundancy

MGX systems can be powered from an AC or a DC source.

An AC-powered system can include up to six internal power supplies, each with a 1200W rating. The MGX power supplies convert the incoming AC voltage to –48 VDC, which is distributed inside the switch on the system power bus.

AC power redundancy is provided through either power supply redundancy or dual AC sources.

Power Supply Redundancy

With power supply redundancy, additional 1200W power supply modules are provided as backup in case one unit fails. (A fully loaded MGX 8850 can draw more than 2 kilowatts [kW], so at least two supplies are needed. Refer to the section "Systems Specifications," in the Cisco MGX 8850 Installation and Configuration publication, for current information on power requirements for individual card modules.)

Dual AC Sources

Dual AC sources, on the other hand, provide redundant independent AC power sources, with each source connected to a different 400W power supply module.

DC Power Systems

For DC-powered systems, power redundancy is limited to dual DC sources. No DC equivalent of the AC power supply module exists in the switch.

Figure 15-9 shows the main components of the AC power supply system—in this case, a system with dual AC inputs.

The AC power supply tray is located horizontally beneath the air intake plenum between the card cage and the side wall of the node. Up to six 1200W power supplies can be installed. The AC system provides the system with –48 VDC from 180- to 240-VAC input.

One or two AC sources can be connected at the International Electrotechnical Commission (IEC) power receptacles, which have associated circuit breakers. Adjacent to the power receptacles is the frame bonding connection, used when a non–Cisco-supplied cabinet is used.

Figure 15-9 *AC Power Supply*

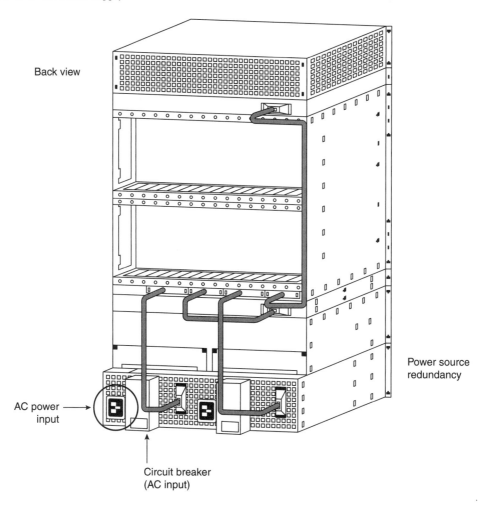

Figure 15-10 shows the slot designations for the maximum number of six AC power modules that can be installed in an MGX 8850 switch.

AC-powered systems include the following components:

- Power supplies (up to six)
- Power supply tray
- Mounting brackets
- Air inlet bezel

Figure 15-10 *Power Supply Slot Designations*

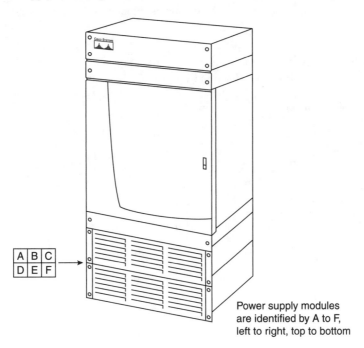

Power supply modules
are identified by A to F,
left to right, top to bottom

The actual number of power supplies required, as well as their physical placement in the power tray, depends on the number of AC power inputs and the number of cards in the system.

Removing an AC Power Supply

Removing AC power supplies makes the AC power tray installation much easier. For a mid-mount installation, however, you must remove the power units to avoid damaging the cabinet sides with the attachment screws. Complete the following steps to remove an AC power supply:

Step 1   Remove the air intake grill by inserting a flat-blade screwdriver into the access hole at the top, and then rotating the screw until the spring latch opens.

Step 2   Tilt the air inlet grill down to approximately a 45° angle, and then lift out the grill and set it aside. This action exposes the hinged door that serves as the power supply retainer bracket.

Step 3   With a flat-blade screwdriver, unscrew the captive retainer screw in the center of the hinged door, and tilt the door down.

Step 4 Loosen the captive screw at the front and bottom of the power supply you want to remove. Grip the handle, and then remove the supply.

Installing AC Power Supplies

The AC power module is shown in Figure 15-11.

Figure 15-11 *AC Power Module*

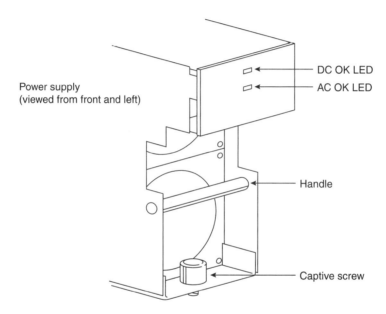

Complete the following steps to reinstall power supplies:

Step 1 Push each power supply into the tray. When it almost reaches the end of the slot in the tray, you feel a slight resistance. Push the power supply slightly further in to achieve the final position and full connector mating.

Step 2 At the front of each power supply, secure it to the tray by tightening the captive screw at the bottom and the front of the supply. For slots without a power supply, the hinged door on the tray should have a removable blank panel.

Step 3 Close the hinged door, and secure it with the screw at the top center of the door.

With the various system modules in place in the rack, you can move on to installing the system and the fan cables provided with the installation kit. Figure 15-12 shows the MGX 8850 AC power and fan cabling.

Figure 15-12 *MGX 8850 AC Power and Fan Cabling*

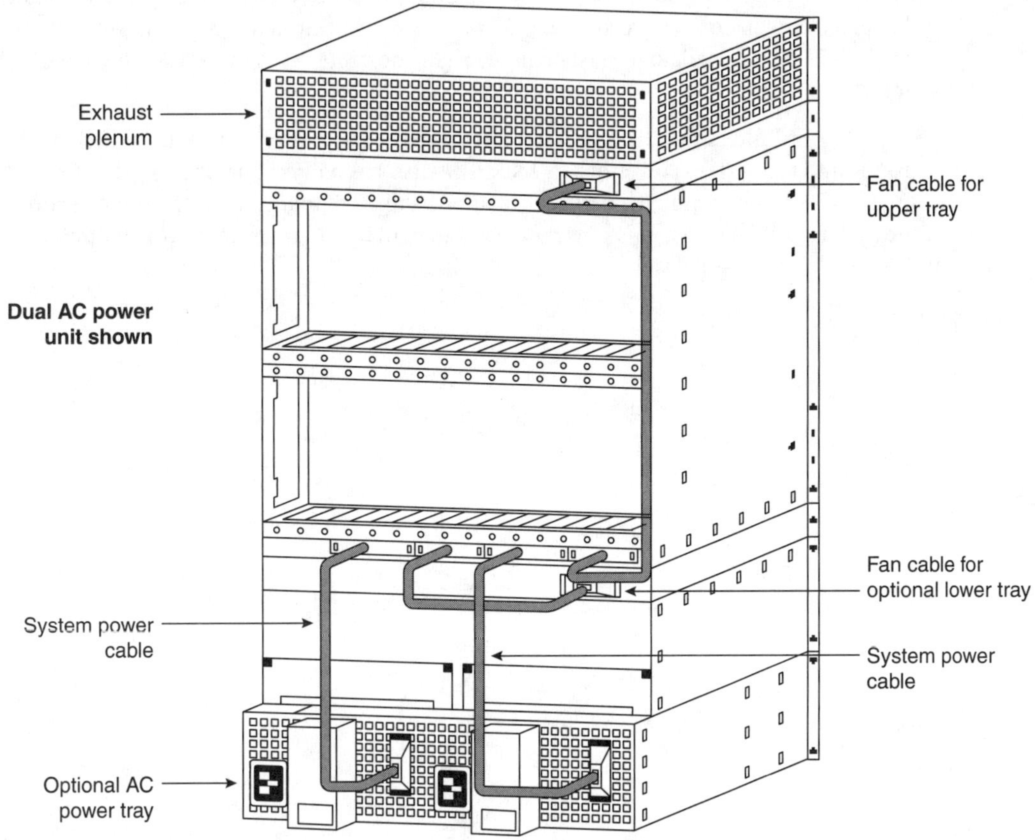

At the lower rear of the card cage are four apertures, which house the following, viewed left to right from the rear of the unit:

- System power in from input 2
- DC fan power out for optional lower fan tray
- System power in from input 1
- DC fan power out for main (upper) fan tray

Recheck that the AC power input is disconnected and that the system circuit breakers are off. Then connect the system power and fan cables as appropriate.

DC Power Entry Module

On the DC-powered system, the DC-Power Entry Module (DC-PEM) is a small module that plugs into one of the two slots at the lower rear of the air intake plenum. Note that only one DC-PEM is installed; it must be in the right-most slot, as viewed from the rear of the unit.

The DC-PEM filters the DC power directly from the DC power source in the building and passes it to the system power bus. A DC-PEM also has a circuit breaker, shown in Figure 15-13, for turning the power on and off, and an output connector for connection to the system bus. The system's power cable(s) then plug into the same rear aperture(s) described for the AC power tray.

Figure 15-13 *DC Power Entry Module*

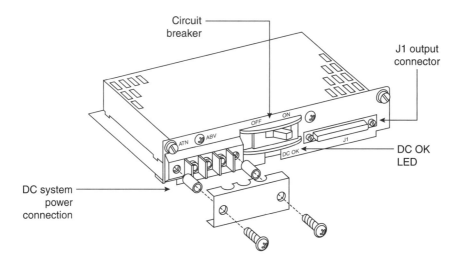

Customer-supplied DC power is connected into the terminal block on the DC-PEM. Ensure that the building circuit breaker for the DC branch circuit is off before connecting the power to the MGX switch. Redundancy of DC sources and DC-PEMs allows continued system operation if one of the two independent DC branch circuits fails.

Removing and Installing Cards

When removing and reinstalling card modules, keep the following guidelines in mind.

Service modules can go in any slot except reserved slots 7, 8, 15, 16, 23, 24, 31, and 32. The double-height and single-height PXMs and SRMs occupy these reserved slots. Additionally, upper slots 9 and 10, and lower slots 25 and 26 do not support 1:N service module redundancy or the T1 bulk distribution feature. For this reason, Cisco recommends that if the switch contains RPMs, the first two RPMs go in slots 9 and 10. Figure 15-14 provides the card mapping.

Figure 15-14 *Removing and Installing Cards into the Correct Slots*

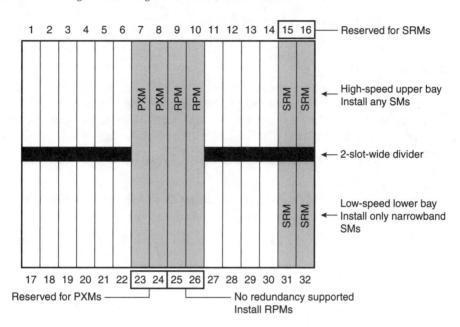

To prevent damage to the cards from static electricity, put on a wrist strap and connect the strap to any convenient metal contact on the switch before you touch any cards.

Handle the PXM front card very carefully to preserve the alignment of the attached disk drive. Do not drop or bump the PXM.

Inserting the cards in the correct slot is important for all cards, but especially for the back cards because of potential electrical damage. If you insert a service module back card into a PXM back card slot (7, 8, 23, or 24), you can damage the card and backplane.

Refer to the section "Converting Single-Height Slots to Double-Height Slots," later in this chapter, if you need to convert a single-height slot to a double-height slot, or vice versa.

Removing a Front Card

Each single-height front card has a latch to secure it when the card connects to the backplane. Each double-height card has a latch at the top and the bottom. Complete the following steps to remove a front card:

Step 1   Press the tip of a small, flat-blade screwdriver into the slot in the insertion/extractor lever until the latch springs open by approximately 10°. For double-height cards, repeat this action at the bottom latch.

Step 2   Lift the lever to dislodge the card from the connector.

Step 3   Gently pull the card out of the card cage.

Removing a Back Card

A screw at the top and the bottom of the faceplate of each back card (or line module or port adapter) secures the card in its backplane connector. Use the extraction levers to pull the card from the backplane connector after you loosen the screws. Complete the following steps to remove a back card:

Step 1   Use a flat-blade screwdriver to loosen the two retaining screws in the faceplate.

Step 2   Simultaneously pull out both extractor levers to pull the card from the backplane connector after you loosen the screws.

Step 3   Gently pull the card out of the card cage and store it in a safe location.

Installing a Front Card

Verify the accuracy of the intended slot for each card before you begin installing the cards. Complete the following steps to install a front card:

Step 1   Position the rear card guides over the appropriate slot at the top and bottom of the card cage.

Step 2   Gently slide the card all the way into the slot. The card should slide in and out with only slight friction on the adjacent board's EMI gaskets. Do not use force. Investigate any binding.

Step 3   Press the insertion/extractor lever until it snaps into the vertical position.

Installing a Back Card

Verify the accuracy of the intended slot for each card before you begin installing the cards. Complete the following steps to install a back card:

Step 1   Make sure that the two extractor levers are in the "in" position. As you move the card, the levers should be flush with the vertical edge of the back card.

Step 2   Gently slide the card all the way into the slot.

Step 3   Push the card into the connector.

Step 4   Tighten the two captive screws on the card faceplate just enough to secure the card.

Center Guides and Support Brackets

Center guides are required to support single-height modules in the upper bay. The center guides are secured in the shelf either by a bulkhead and an L-shaped support bracket (on the left in Figure 15-15), or by a one-piece vertical support bracket (on the right in Figure 15-15).

Figure 15-15 *Converting Card Slot Height*

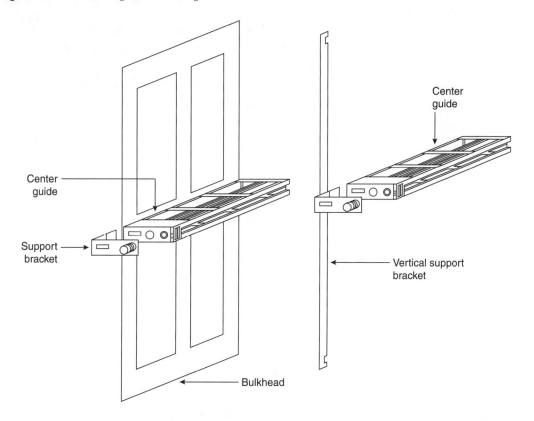

A factory-installed Cisco MGX 8850 node arrives with the single-height and double-height cards already installed in the preassigned locations. A factory-installed system has three bulkheads installed, to the right of slots 6, 8, and 14. Support brackets and center guides are installed in slots 9/10 and 15/16. No center guide is present in slots 7 and 8, where the PXMs normally reside.

A vertical support bracket and center guide is installed to the right of slots 2, 4, 10, and 12. The center guide for slots 1 and 2 is secured to the left enclosure wall with a support bracket.

Converting Single-Height Slots to Double-Height Slots

The wiring on the Cisco MGX 8850 backplane requires you to consider the conversion sequence and other details when you convert single-height slots to double-height slots.

One-slot conversion means that you convert four single-height slots to two double-height slots.

Slot conversions begin on the left (as you face the front of the switch) and progress to the right. The starting point can be either slots 1 and 2 or slots 9 and 10. The exceptions are reserved slots 15 and 16 for the SRMs. You can convert SRM slots out of sequence, but slot conversions take place in the following pairs: 1 and 2, 3 and 4, 5 and 6, 9 and 10, 11 and 12, and 13 and 14.

For conversions that involve either the left wall of the card cage or a bulkhead to the left of the slot, you must unscrew a track from the wall.

After conversion, the new double-height slots take the number of the upper slot. For example, after you convert slots 1 and 2, slot numbers 17 and 18 become meaningless.

Slots 7, 8, 15, 16, 31, and 32 are the reserved slots. The PXM cards (in a redundant configuration) reserve slots 7 and 8. If your system has one or more SRMs, the primary pair must reside in slots 15 and 31. The redundant pair resides in slots 16 and 32.

Do not attempt slot conversion unless the system power is off.

Complete the following steps to convert four single-height slots to two double-height slots in an operational system:

Step 1   Remove the cabling from the back card, unless it is the correct back card for the double-height card.

Step 2   Remove the back card.

Step 3   Remove the front card.

Step 4   Repeat Steps 2 and 3 for every other single-height module you need to remove.

Step 5   Rotate the screw that holds in the center guide. Where either the left wall of the card cage or a bulkhead exists on the left of the single-height card slots, an L-shaped support bracket holds in the center guide.

Step 6   If the center guide module has either type of wall to the left, unscrew the track attached to that wall. You might have to remove cards to remove it.

Step 7   Remove the vertical support bracket by moving it up and down until you can take it out. A hole becomes visible in the center guide module.

Step 8   Insert a screwdriver into the hole, and loosen the long screw that holds in the center guide module.

Step 9   Remove the center guide module.

Step 10 Install the double-height front card and back cards as needed.

A simpler situation exists when you install a new MGX 8850 switch in a non-Cisco rack or an existing Cisco cabinet. With the power off, unscrew the center guide module and remove it. Install a blank faceplate where you do not fill a double-height slot with a double-height card, unless the enclosure has the optional front door.

MGX 8220 Concentrator Installation

This section focuses on the physical installation of the MGX 8220 concentrator. The general arrangement of the modules in an MGX 8220 shelf is quite similar to that of the MGX 8850 node, except that the cooling unit fits under rather than above the card cage, as shown in Figure 15-16.

Figure 15-16 *MGX 8220 Components*

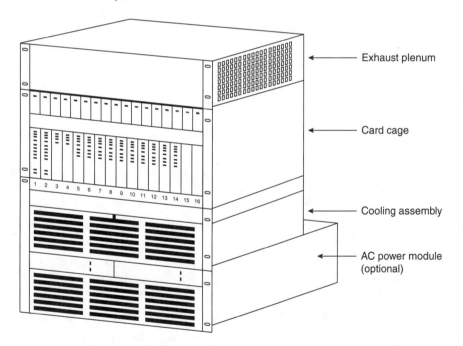

Components in a MGX 8220 system include the optional AC power tray, the main cooling module, the 16-slot card cage, and the exhaust conduit. These are the measurement requirements for the components (RMU = 1.75 inches, or 45 mm):

- Optional AC power tray (3 RMU), with up to four AC power modules
- Main cooling module (3 RMU)

- 16-slot card cage (10 RMU), including the system backplane into which front cards and back cards are plugged
- Exhaust plenum (2 RMU), or spacer unit (1 RMU), or booster cooling module (2 RMU)

A cooling assembly containing the MGX 8220 cooling fans consists of a rack-mounted fan unit below the main MGX 8220 shelf, and either a plenum or a spacer unit mounted above the shelves. The cooling assembly can cool two MGX 8220 shelves in the same rack. In racks that contain more than two shelves, a booster-cooling unit is used to provide additional cooling for up to two additional shelves. The cooling assembly is powered from the main MGX 8220 shelf.

MGX 8220 Installation Considerations

As with the MGX 8850 node, it is a good idea for you to review Chapter 11, "Installing BPX 8600 Switches." In addition, you should review the Cisco MGX 8220 Installation and Configuration document on the Documentation CD-ROM that is shipped with the MGX for any recent changes. Particular items to pay attention to for the MGX 8220 installation are as follows:

- **Space**—The MGX 8220 rack location should provide at least 3 feet (90 cm) clearance at the front, and 2 feet (60 cm) clearance at the rear to allow for card replacement. The DC-powered version requires 17.5 inches (10-RMU, 45 cm) of vertical space in a rack. The AC-powered version occupies 22.75 inches (13-RMU, 58 cm) of vertical space.
- **Weight**—A fully loaded, DC-powered system can weigh up to 190 lb (87 kg). A fully loaded AC-powered system can weigh up to 250 lb (113 kg). Care must be taken when mounting or moving any of the equipment.
- **Seismic considerations**—See Chapter 11, "Installing BPX 8600 Switches," for details on installing the stability plate with a Cisco rack.
- **Power requirements**—In general, see Chapter 11, "Installing BPX 8600 Switches," for power considerations and practices, noting the following specifics for the MGX 8220 switch:
  - The MGX 8220 nodes use a 20A, two-pole circuit breaker for each AC input.
  - DC-powered nodes use a 15A, one-pole circuit breaker with a short trip delay on each –48V input.
  - MGX 8220 AC power requirement is 220 VAC and can operate with the 180 to 240 VAC.
  - DC conductors must be suitable for 20A. Wiring that is 12 AWG is adequate.
- **Bonding and grounding**—To maintain the full EMI and EMC integrity of this equipment, the rack must be bonded to an integrated ground plane or an isolated ground plane network.

If the rack installation includes a BPX 8600 series switch, the BPX 8600 must reside at the bottom of the rack.

The MGX 8220 card cage arrives with the cards installed and tested according to its planned configuration. If the unit includes an AC power assembly, the power supplies reside in the appropriate slots in the AC power tray. For a DC-powered system, the DC-PEMs are mounted in the air intake chamber. However, for ease of installation, you should remove the cards and power supplies before rack-mounting the chassis.

MGX 8220 Unit Placement

MGX 8220 modules are designed to be mounted to two vertical rack-mounting rails in a standard 19-inch rack. A front-mounting rail is used as one mounting point, using the flanges provided at the front of each MGX 8220 module. A second rail, either at the rear of the rack or at an intermediate position, is used for the second mounting point (mounting brackets are provided for attaching the module to the second rail).

The MGX 8220 units are mounted in a specific order from the bottom to the top, as covered earlier and as shown in Figure 15-17.

Figure 15-17 *MGX 8220—Single and Two Shelves*

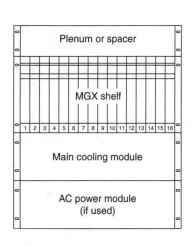
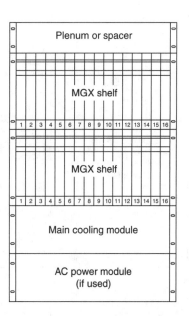

If a third or fourth shelf is installed, a booster cooling assembly must be mounted immediately above the second shelf and immediately below the third and fourth shelves. The plenum or spacer unit is mounted last above the highest shelf. If a cable management kit is used in a two- or four-shelf rack, the top unit must be a plenum because cable management hardware is not supported by the spacer unit.

When each module is installed, there should be approximately 1/16 inch (2 mm) of vertical space left between adjacent modules. This spacing can be achieved by ensuring that each module is installed at the center of each standard rack increment. This space is important because it allows card, fan, and power entry modules to be removed without interference.

MGX 8220 and BPX 8600 series units can be collocated in the same rack or cabinet. However, the positioning of MGX 8220 shelf power, cooling, booster, plenum, and spacer modules relative to the MGX 8220 shelf must be the same in this configuration as when an MGX 8220 shelf is used in a dedicated rack.

In multiple unit racks, as shown in Figure 15-18, the BPX 8600 series node, if included, should be mounted at the bottom. The MGX 8220 shelves—including the power, cooling, booster, plenum, and spacer modules—should be mounted in the proper order at the top to allow for growth.

Figure 15-18 *Multiple Unit Racking*

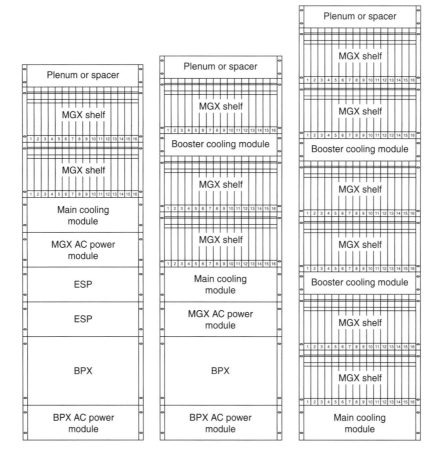

Start by mounting the lowest module first, and work upward. In an AC system, the lowest module is the AC power module; in DC systems, it is the main cooling module. Refer to Figure 15-19 to complete the six steps to rack mount a module:

Step 1   Determine the vertical position in the rack where the shelf or shelves are to be installed. Then determine the vertical position of the lowest module.

Figure 15-19 *Rack-Mounting a Module*

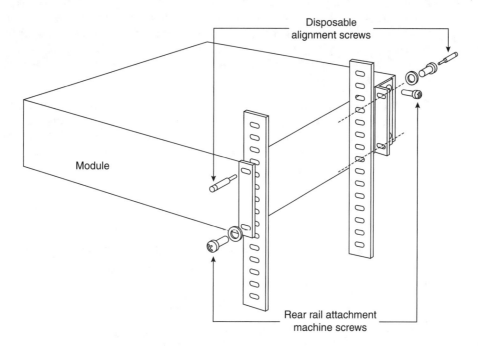

Step 2   Install disposable alignment screws in the upper mounting hole in the rack.

Step 3   Have one person lift the first module into its position and fasten the lower front-mounting screws. Attach the angle brackets (supplied with the module), one on each side of the mounted module.

Step 4   Position the brackets so that they can be used to secure the module to the rear rail of the rack. Holes are provided in the side of the module to accommodate various distances of the rear rail from the front rail. The angle bracket is attached to the side of the module using the provided self-tapping screws. Use the disposable alignment screws on the rear positioning and the front to ensure accurate positioning of the first unit.

Step 5   Attach the angle bracket to the rear rail in the rack using four #10-32 machine screws and flat washers (supplied with the module).

Step 6   Repeat Steps 2 through 5 for the remaining modules.

AC Input Power

The AC power assembly can be configured with either a single primary input AC source or optional primary and secondary (redundant) input AC sources. The AC power assembly holds up to six independent 875W power supplies, each of which supplies power to a common output bus. The number of power supplies in the assembly depends upon the number of MGX 8220 shelves that must be supported. A single AC power assembly can support four MGX 8220 shelves.

In a fully loaded configuration, each MGX 8220 shelf requires 500W. Therefore, a power assembly equipped with three power supplies, totaling 2625W, can supply enough power for a four-shelf rack. A power assembly equipped with four power supplies, totaling 3500W, provides enough power for a four-shelf rack, even in case of a single power supply failure. Installing additional power supplies provides even more protection in case of multiple power supply failures.

In addition to supplying power, each power supply provides a signal that indicates the status of the power supply.

In AC-powered systems, a separate AC power assembly is mounted under the cooling assembly in the rack. In a single AC source version, only the right-most input connector is provided.

The rear panel has seven connectors, as shown in Figure 15-20.

The connectors have the following functions:

- Connectors 1A, 2A, and 3A supply a primary –48 VDC feed from power supply modules A, B, and C, respectively, to three different shelves. Each of these connectors also includes sense leads to facilitate monitoring of the power supply status.

- Connector 4A provides –48 VDC from power module D for a fourth shelf. There is no status monitoring for module D within this connector, but connectors 1B, 2B, and 3B provide monitoring signals from power modules D, E, and F, respectively.

Figure 15-20 *AC Power Supply and Connectors*

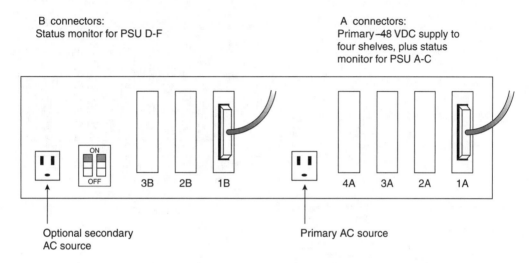

B connectors:
Status monitor for PSU D-F

A connectors:
Primary –48 VDC supply to
four shelves, plus status
monitor for PSU A-C

Optional secondary
AC source

Primary AC source

DC Input Power

DC power using customer-supplied wiring is connected to the MGX 8220 using DC-PEMs situated at the lower rear of the card cage. Two DC-PEMs are available for separate, redundant DC feeds.

In DC-powered systems, the MGX 8220 shelf contains two PEMs, each of which can be connected to an independent –48 VDC supply. The PEMs are installed horizontally, side by side in the bottom rear of the shelf, as shown in Figure 15-21. The two modules provide power supply redundancy. Each PEM can supply enough power for a fully loaded MGX 8220 shelf.

Each –48 VDC power source is made up of three wires: positive ground, –48 VDC, and safety ground. The –48 VDC cable is connected to the PEM through a three-position EURO block connector, which is a plug to the back of the PEM.

The PEM units should be installed and secured in the MGX 8220 shelf before you connect cables to the EURO block DC connector, as shown in Figure 15-21. The EURO block can be unplugged from the PEM even after the DC power cables have been inserted and secured.

Each PEM contains its own circuit breaker that also acts as an on/off switch. Pressing in the large black button until it latches in the closed position closes the circuit breaker. Pressing the smaller red button opens the circuit breaker. The DC-PEM also includes a bracket attached to the PEM to provide cable strain relief.

Figure 15-21 *DC Power Connection*

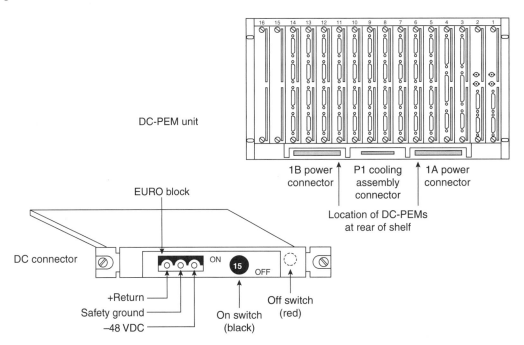

Before making power connections, make sure that the shelf power is off. Complete the following steps to connect DC power to the MGX 8220 shelf:

Step 1   Press the red button on each PEM so that the black buttons are in the out position. Now the circuit breakers in the PEMs are open and do not allow current to flow.

Each PEM has an EURO block three-pin male power receptacle for connecting the –48 VDC power sources, as shown in Figure 15-21. The mating female connector is supplied by Cisco with the PEM.

Step 2   Attach the two supplied female EURO connectors to the two cables supplying DC power to the PEMs. The cables should have three insulated #12 AWG wires (solid or stranded) with the insulation stripped back 0.25 inches (6 mm) on each wire.

Step 3   Test which way the female connector attaches to the male connector. For each cable, insert each of the wires into its correct hole in the connector. Secure each wire by tightening the screws in the connector.

Step 4   Connect a cable to each of the PEM connectors. The connectors are polarized so that they cannot be inserted the wrong way.

Step 5   Use the PEM cable clamp, shown in Figure 15-22, to secure the power cable. Place the cable clamp over the connector so that the small hole is positioned over the boss on the PEM, and secure it by attaching the clamp to the PEM with the captive screw. The cable clamp can be dressed to the left or the right and then secured to the clamp using a tie wrap.

Figure 15-22 *DC Power Receptacle and PEM Cable Clamp*

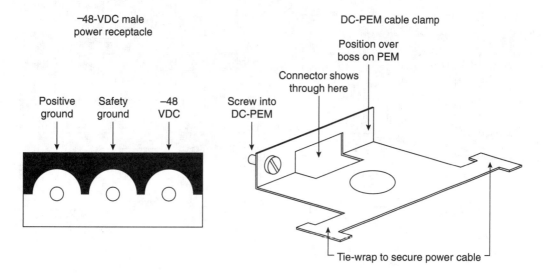

Step 6   If the redundant PEM is not used, the cover PEM (PN# 217076-00) must be installed in the empty position to ensure proper cooling of the rear cards.

DC System Power Distribution

Figure 15-23 illustrates the cable installation for distributing –48 VDC power to a single-shelf and two-shelf MGX 8220.

Figure 15-23 *DC System Power Distribution*

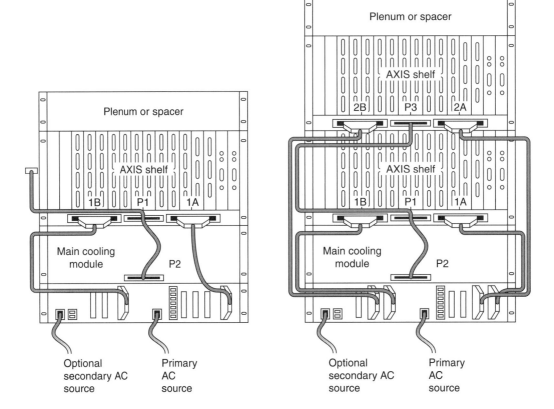

Power cables are used to feed power and power monitoring information from the AC power assembly to the MGX 8220 shelf. Four connectors—1A through 4A—on the right (viewed from the rear) of the power assembly rear panel supply –48 VDC power to up to four shelves. The left three connectors—1B, 2B, and 3B—provide a power status monitoring. Complete the following steps to make power connections:

Step 1 Before making power connections, make sure that the shelf power is off.

Step 2 Use the two special cables for each shelf that are supplied with the power assembly. Each shelf should be cabled from one of the right connectors at (1A) and from one the left connectors at (1B).

Step 3 Insert each of the two cables into one of the power entry apertures on the shelf, and secure them with the provided screws.

Step 4 Repeat Steps 1 and 2 for any other shelves in the rack being powered from the same power assembly.

Step 5 The AC power source is connected to the IEC receptacle(s) on the back of the power module. The ground (green) wire of the AC power cord is connected to the MGX 8220 system for safety ground. Make sure that the building AC receptacle is properly grounded.

Step 6 If the left-side power connector on an MGX 8220 shelf is not used, the Cover Power Entry (PN# 217076-00) must be installed in the empty position to ensure proper cooling of the rear cards.

DC Power Fan Assembly Connection

Figure 15-24 shows the DC power fan assembly for a single-shelf and a two-shelf MGX 8220 that can be referred to during the DC power fan assembly connection.

Figure 15-24 *DC Power Fan Assembly Connection*

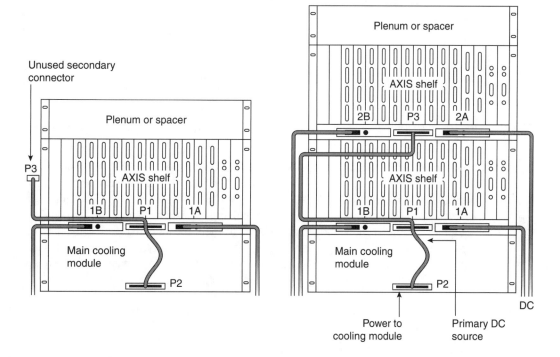

A cable is provided with the main and booster cooling assemblies for delivering DC power from the shelf to the fan cooling assembly. The cable provides redundancy, and the cooling unit can be powered from two independent shelves. Complete the following steps to make fan power connections:

Step 1 Connect the cable to the connector on the rear of the shelf located between the DC-PEMs (P1 for primary and P3 for redundant).

When fully inserted, the cable latches into place, preventing accidental removal. To unlatch the connector, use a small screwdriver to slide the catch lever (located inside the slot on the connector) to the right.

Step 2 Connect the other end of the cable to the receptacle on the rear of the fan cooling assembly, P2. If the redundant portion of the cable is not used, it should be secured to the side rack using a cable tie or a cable management tray.

Cooling Assembly in Multishelf Installations

In multishelf installations, the MGX 8220 cooling assembly consists of multiple rack-mounted units:

- Main cooling assembly
- Booster cooling assembly
- Plenum exhaust chamber
- Spacer unit

The booster cooling assembly is used in racks with three or four MGX 8220 shelves and is mounted above the first two shelves and below the remaining shelves, as shown in Figure 15-25. The booster cooling assembly consists of fans that draw air from the shelves below and exhaust air upward through the shelf or shelves above. The cooling assemblies rely on their contact with the rack for grounding, so the rack must be properly grounded to earth.

Either the plenum chamber or the spacer unit (not both) should be mounted immediately above the uppermost shelf. The decision of which one to use depends on the configuration of equipment in the rack and how the air is expelled. The plenum delivers air to the rear of the rack and is used in normal UL-compliant installations where the top of the unit must be covered. The spacer can be used for noncompliant installations that might have other equipment mounted above the upper MGX 8220 shelf assembly that acts as the necessary top cover. Furthermore, the plenum supports the attachment of a cable management kit, whereas the spacer does not. This is an important factor if cable management is to be used for the upper shelf in two- and four-shelf configurations.

Figure 15-25 *Cooling Assembly in Multishelf Installation*

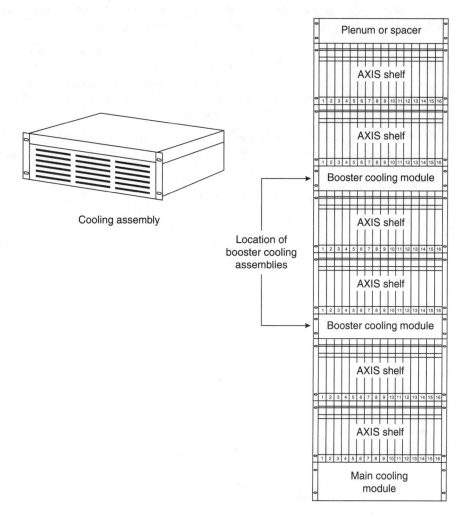

Installing and Removing MGX 8220 Card Modules

Card module installation and removal for the MGX 8220 are the same as for the MGX 8850.

Card Module Functions and Features

The remainder of this chapter provides a description of each card module set supported in MGX systems. The components comprising each card module—usually a front card and a back card set—are listed. The physical interfaces on each back card, as well as the status indicators located on both front and back cards, also are described. A brief functional description of each card module, including the user services supported, is included as well.

Table 15-1 lists the MGX card modules and the platform support for each. Many of the service modules are supported in both the MGX 8850 switch and the MGX 8220 concentrator. A service module of a specific type runs the same firmware release, regardless of the chassis type. For example, an FRSM-8T1 loaded with Release 5.0.0 firmware can be installed in either an MGX 8850 switch or an MGX 8220 concentrator.

Table 15-1 is current as of PXM Release 1.1 and AXIS firmware Release 5.0.0. New service modules and additional cross-platform compatibility are planned for future releases.

Table 15-1 *MGX 8850 and MGX 8220 Card Module Compatibility*

Card Module	MGX 8850	MGX 8220
PXM	X	
ASC		X
BNM		X
SRM-3T3	X	X
SRM-T1E1		X
RPM	X	
FRSM-8T/E1	X	X
FRSM-HS1		X
FRSM-HS2	X	X
FRSM-2CT3	X	
FRSM-T3E3	X	
CESM-8T1/E1	X	X
CESM-T3E3	X	X
AUSM-8T1/E1	X[1]	X
IMATM-8T1/E1		X

1. Model B Only

MGX 8850 Common Core Cards

The common core cards on the MGX 8850 switch are responsible for shelf management and control.

The two common core cards—the PXM and the SRM—form a single logical card using the local bus on the backplane for connectivity. The odd-numbered cards (7, 15, and 31) are linked to each other, as are the even-numbered cards (8, 16, and 32).

The first release of the MGX 8850 PXM (Release 1.0 firmware) did not support redundancy. Therefore, the PXM card must be in either slot 7 or slot 8, and the SRMs must be in the appropriate odd- or even-numbered card slots with version 1.0. Release 1.1 does support PXM redundancy.

PXM

The PXM double-height card module, shown in Figure 15-26, is the central processor of the MGX 8850 switch and is responsible for switching cells and storing configuration and firmware images for the other card modules in the shelf. The PXM also is responsible for network management, including the command line interface and communicating with the Cisco WAN Manager station.

Figure 15-26 *Processor Switch Module*

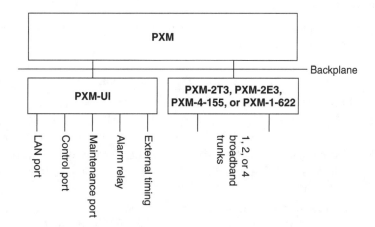

The PXM card module consists of a front card and a broadband line back card.

The front card can be one of the following:

- PXM with daughter card for two-port T3/E3 back card (PXM1-2T3E3)
- PXM with daughter card for four-port OC-3/STM-1 back card (PXM1-4-155)
- PXM with daughter card for one-port OC-12/STM-4 back card (PXM1-622)
- A user interface back card (PXM1-UI)

The broadband line back card can be one of the following:

* Two-port E3 back card with grounded BNC interfaces (BNC-2E3)

* Two-port E3 back card with ungrounded BNC interfaces (BNC-2E3A)

* Two-port T3 back card with BNC interfaces (BNC-2T3)

* Four-port OC-3/STM-1 back card with multimode fiber SC interfaces (MMF-4-155)

* Four-port OC-3/STM-1 back card with single-mode fiber SC interfaces—intermediate range (SMFIR-4-155) or long range (SMFLR-4-155)

* One-port OC-12/STM-4 back card with single-mode fiber SC interfaces, intermediate range (SMFIR-1-622), or long range (SMFLR-1-622)

PXM Functions

The PXM performs shelf management, cell switching, bus mastering, SRM management, network management, module and firmware storage, shelf timing (clocking), environmental alarm measurements, and local alarm notification. A discussion of each function follows:

* **Shelf management**—The PXM is responsible for monitoring and controlling the card modules in the MGX 8850 switch.

* **Cell switching**—The PXM houses the shared-memory switch that sends ATM cells to and receives ATM cells from the network trunk and the service modules.

* **Bus mastering**—All ATM cells created by the service modules are sent to the PXM card to be switched to other service modules or the attached ATM network. The PXM is responsible for managing the flow of cells on the cellbus for the MGX 8850 switch.

* **SRM management**—As mentioned, the PXM and SRM(s) form a single logical card on the MGX 8850 switch. All SRM firmware and configuration is managed by the PXM card.

* **Network management**—Network-management devices—such as a Cisco WAN Manager workstation, a PC, or a dumb terminal—communicate directly with the PXM. When you log in to an MGX 8850 switch to access the command line interface (CLI), you are communicating with the PXM.

* **Module and firmware stores**—The PXM stores service module configuration and firmware images. A copy of the configuration database and firmware image for each service module installed in the MGX 8850 switch is stored on the PXM on a Personal Computer Memory Card International Association (PCMCIA) disk drive. If a service module is replaced, the configuration and firmware are downloaded from the PXM. The RPM configuration is not automatically saved on the PXM, but it can be manually saved onto the disk.

- **Shelf timing**—The PXM is responsible for extracting a clock signal from either an external clock source or the trunk to the ATM network. The PXM propagates the timing signals across the switch's timing bus.

- **Environmental alarm measurement**—Chassis temperature, fan, and power supply status are monitored by the PXM. Environmental alarms can be displayed from the PXM with the **dspshelfalm** command.

- **Local alarm notification**—Local major and minor alarms are reported by the PXM via front card LEDs or dry contact relays on the PXM-UI back card.

PXM Front Card

The PXM front card, shown in Figure 15-27, contain a front panel status indicator and controls that are made up of a port and alarm status LED, alarm pushbuttons, and a system status LED.

Figure 15-27 *PXM Front Card*

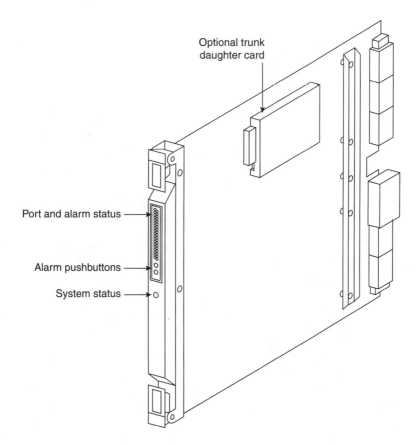

A discussion of the port status, alarm status, pushbuttons, and other LEDs shown in Figure 15-27 follows:

- **Port status**—The port status LED is a tri-state LED for each broadband line on the back card (up to four). Table 15-2 summarizes the alarms and status.

Table 15-2   *PXM Front Card Port Status LEDs*

Alarm	Status
Green	Port is active. No alarm.
Yellow	Remote alarm.
Red	Local alarm.

- **Node alarm**—Separate LEDs indicate minor and major alarms for the node. Table 15-3 summarizes the node alarms and their status.

Table 15-3   *PXM Node Alarm Status LEDs*

Alarm	Status
All off	No alarm
Minor alarm (yellow)	Minor alarm
Major alarm (red)	Major alarm

- **Alarm cutoff**—The Alarm Cutoff (ACO) indicates that a user has pressed the ACO button.
- **History**—The History (HIST) LED indicates that a major or minor alarm might be present, or has been present at this node. This LED is on if either the MAJOR or MINOR LED is on. It remains on until the major or minor alarm condition clears and the HIST CLR button is pressed.
- **ACO pushbutton**—The ACO pushbutton cuts off an alarm or silences an audible alarm.
- **History clear pushbutton**—The HIST pushbutton enables the user to turn off (clear) the HIST LED.
- **LAN activity**—The LAN LED flashes green to indicate an active LAN port.
- **System status**—This LED indicates PXM status, as shown in Table 15-4.

Table 15-4   *PXM System Status Alarms*

Alarm	Status
Green	The PXM is active.
Yellow	The PXM is in standby mode.
Yellow flashing	The PXM is updating in standby mode.
Red	The PXM has failed.

PXM Back Cards

The interfaces for the PXM back cards are shown in Figure 15-28.

Figure 15-28 *PXM Back Cards*

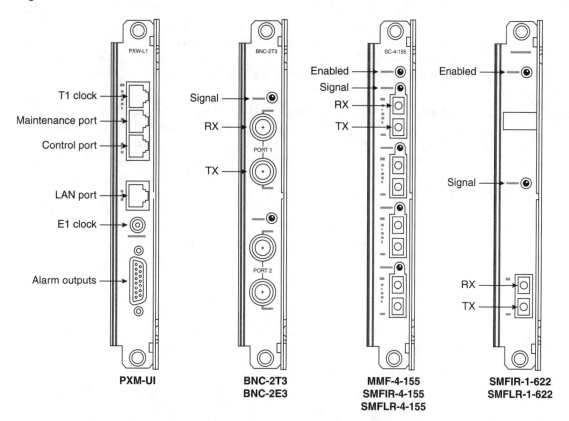

As shown in Figure 15-28, the PXM back cards are these:

- PXM-U1
- BNC-2T3/BNC-2E3
- MMF-4-155/SMFIR-4-155/SMFL4-4-155
- SMFIR-1-622/SMFLR-1-622

A brief summarization of each back card's interfaces follows.

The PXM-U1 has a T1 clock port, a maintenance port, a control port, a LAN port, an E1 clock port, and an alarm output port:

- **T1 clock port**—The T1 clock port is a RJ-45 connector for attachment of an external T1 synchronization source.

- **Maintenance port**—The maintenance port is a RJ-45 data terminal equipment (DTE) port that supports the Serial Line Internet Protocol (SLIP) for command-line access. If redundant PXMs are installed in the switch, you should Y-cable the two maintenance ports together. This is analogous to the control port on the MGX 8220 concentrator.

- **Control port**—The control port is a RJ-45 DTE port that is used to attach a VT100 terminal or a PC running terminal emulation for CLI access. The control port is similar in function to the MGX 8220 maintenance port, except that it is not configurable. Communication parameters are fixed at 9600 baud, with 1 start bit, 1 stop bit, and no parity. If redundant PXMs are installed in the switch, you should Y-cable the two control ports together.

- **LAN port**—The LAN port is a RJ-45 802.3 LAN 10BaseT port that provides Cisco WAN Manager station access for network management, and Telnet access for other LAN devices to the CLI. If redundant PXMs are installed in the switch, you should not Y-cable the two LAN ports together—each LAN port should be attached to the network.

- **E1 clock port**—The E1 clock port is a BNC coaxial connector for attachment of an external E1 synchronization source.

- **Alarm output port**—The alarm output port is a DB-15 connector for connection of external equipment that can receive alarm indications from the PXM.

The BNC-2T3/BNC2E3 (T3/E3) back card has the following LEDs and interfaces:

- **Signal status**—This LED indicates green if the line is active; otherwise, it is off.

- **T3/E3 interfaces**—Two T3 or E3 interfaces with 75-ohm coaxial connectors are provided by the T3/E3 back card. The E3 can be grounded or ungrounded.

The MMF-4-155/SMFIR-4-155/SMFL4-4-155 (OC3/STM-1) back card has the following LEDs and interfaces:

- **Enabled LED**—The enabled LED indicates that the card is recognized by the system.

- **Signal status LED**—The signal status LED indicates green if the line is active; otherwise, it is off.

- **Fiber**—The OC3/STM-1 back card has four multimode or single-mode interfaces with SC connectors.

The SMFIR-1-622/SMFLR-1-622 (OC12/STM-4) back card has an enabled LED, a signal status LED (green if the line is active; otherwise, is off), and one single-mode interface with SC connectors.

Service Resource Module

The SRM-3T3 manages 1-to-N service module redundancy and can perform BERTs on service module lines. The SRM-3T3 also can manage T3 to T1 line distribution on the shelf.

Like the PXM, one SRM is active, and a second one can be installed as a hot standby. Unlike the PXM, the SRM is not required for an MGX device to function.

On the MGX 8850 switch, a pair of SRMs can be installed in both the upper and lower bays of the chassis. If any SRM functions are needed on one of the bays, SRMs must be installed in that bay.

The SRM-3T3 card module, shown in Figure 15-29, consists of an SRM front card (SRM-3T3/B) and a back card with three T3 interfaces with BNC connectors (BNC-3T3-M).

Figure 15-29 *Service Resource Module*

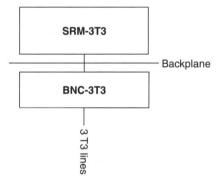

SRM-3T3 Functions

The SRM-3T3 performs service module redundancy, BERT, and T1 line distribution:

- **Service module redundancy**—The SRM manages the optional 1-to-N redundancy for T1/E1 service modules on the MGX device. A single service module can be installed as a backup card for a number of like cards in the concentrator. The SRM reroutes the incoming traffic to the backup card in the event of a failure.

- **BERT**—The SRM can perform service module line and port BERT functions to isolate transmission errors between MGX service modules and the attached equipment. The SRM BERT function also includes local, remote, and far-end loopback activation.

- **T1 line distribution**—The SRM-3T3 can accept up to three T3 lines that comprise multiplexed T1 lines. The SRM demultiplexes the T3 lines into T1 lines (up to 80) and forwards the traffic on the T1 lines to specified service module interfaces. T1 bulk distribution also is called *bulk distribution*. For operation in bulk distribution mode with the SRM-3T3, the service modules do not require back cards.

SRM Front and Back Cards

The SRM front card provides the three card status LEDs, as shown in Table 15-5.

Table 15-5 *Card Status Alarm*

Alarm	Status
Green	Active, no alarm
Yellow	Standby
Red	Failure

The redundancy LED lights green if the 1:N redundancy feature is active, and the BERT LED lights green if active and yellow if failed. A separate LED for each T3 line indicates green if the line is active.

The SRM T3 back card includes three pairs of BNC connectors for the three T3 lines. The SRM front and back cards are shown in Figure 15-30.

Figure 15-30 *SRM-3T3 and BNC-3T3*

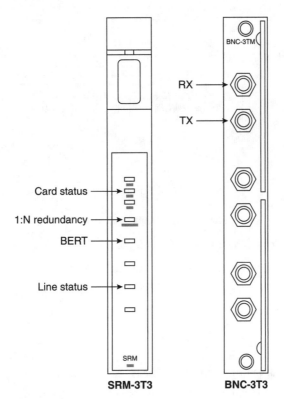

SRM-3T3   BNC-3T3

Router Processor Module

The Router Processor Module (RPM), shown in Figure 15-31, is a Cisco 7200 series router redesigned to the MGX 8850 double-height card form factor. The RPM can support Ethernet, Fast Ethernet, or FDDI LAN interfaces. The RPM runs Cisco IOS software and is configurable from the MGX command line using Cisco IOS commands. Traffic from the RPM LAN interfaces can be routed to any of the trunk or line ports on the MGX 8850 switch.

Figure 15-31 *Router Processor Module*

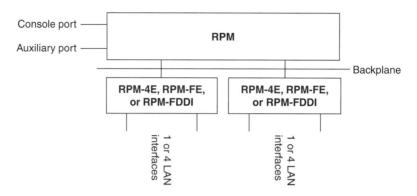

A RPM card module consists of a front card and a back card.

The front card can be either of the following:

- RPM with 64 MB DRAM (RPM-64M)
- RPM with 128 MB DRAM (RPM-128M)

The back card can consist of one or two of the following:

- Four-port Ethernet back card with 10BaseT RJ-45 interfaces (RJ45-4E)
- One-port Fast Ethernet back card with either a FE-TX RJ-45 interface (RJ45-FE) or a FE-FX multimode fiber interface (MMF-FE)
- One-port FDDI back card with either a multimode fiber interface (MMF-FDDI) or a single-mode fiber interface (SMF-FDDI)
- One-port full-duplex FDDI back card with either a multimode fiber interface (MMF-FDDI/FD) or a single-mode fiber interface (SMF-FDDI/FD)

RPM Features

The RPM supports the following features:

- **Cisco 7200 series router**—The RPM is a Cisco 7200 series router that runs a customized version of Cisco IOS Release 12.0 software. The RPM has a 150-MHz R4700 processor with 512 KB of Layer-2 cache, 64 or 128 MB of DRAM, and 4 MB of SRAM.
- **ATM interface to MGX cellbus**—The RPM communicates with the other MGX card modules via a 155-Mbps ATM cellbus interface.

- **Ethernet, Fast Ethernet, and FDDI interfaces**—Up to two LAN interface cards can be installed on the RPM. Each interface card has four Ethernet ports, one Fast Ethernet port, or one FDDI port on it. Connections can be made from any of these LAN interfaces through an ATM cellbus interface to interfaces on other MGX 8850 service modules, such as the FRSM.

Software and configuration can be stored on the PXM hard drive. The Cisco IOS software is stored on the PCMCIA disk on the PXM and is downloaded to the RPM as part of the boot process. By default, the RPM configuration is stored on the RPM but can be uploaded to the PXM disk drive.

The RPM front and back card LEDs are shown in Figure 15-32.

Figure 15-32 *RPM LEDs and Interfaces*

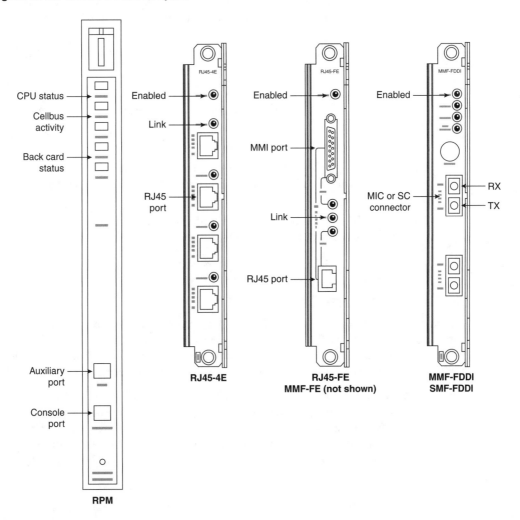

RPM Front Card LEDs and Interfaces

The RPM provides the following status indicators and interfaces:

- **CPU status**—The CPU OK LED turns green when the CPU is running.

- **Cellbus activity**—Two LEDs flash green if cells are being transmitted to (CB TX), or received from (CB RX), the cellbus.

- **Back card status**—Two LEDs turn green if the upper back card (LM1 OK) and the lower back card (LM2 OK) are installed and active, respectively. If either is not present, the LED is off.

- **Auxiliary port**—The auxiliary port usually is configured to provide remote access to the RPM using a modem. (Straight-through cable is required.)

- **Console port**—The console port provides terminal access to the RPM CLI. A crossover cable is required to connect a terminal or PC to the RPM.

RPM Back Card

Status indicators on the back cards (refer to Figure 15-32) are listed here:

- **Enabled**—This LED indicates that the back card has been correctly initialized and is receiving power.

- **Link**—This LED flashes to indicate presence of a carrier signal.

- **RJ-45 or MMI**—For the RJ-45-FE back card only, one of these LEDs is lit when the RJ-45 or the multimode fiber MMI transceiver interface has been selected as the active port.

- **Fiber or MMI**—For the MMF-FE back card only, one of these LEDs is lit when the SC single-mode fiber or the multimode fiber MMI transceiver interface has been selected as the active port.

MGX 8220 Common Core Cards

The common core cards on the MGX 8220 concentrator are responsible for shelf management and control. The three common core cards—ASC, BNM, and SRM—form a single logical card using the local bus on the backplane for connectivity. The odd-numbered cards (1, 3, and 15) are linked to each other, as are the even-numbered cards (2, 4, and 16).

In most MGX 8220 concentrators, two of each card are installed for redundancy. If a switchover is required, all three cards (ASC, BNM, and SRM) switch over together. For this reason, if you want redundancy, all six cards must be installed. If no redundancy is needed, then install the common core cards in either the odd-numbered card slots or the even-numbered card slots.

AXIS (MGX) Shelf Controller

The Axis (MGX) Shelf Controller (ASC) card module is the central processor of the MGX 8220 concentrator, and it stores configuration and firmware images for the card modules in the shelf. The ASC also is responsible for communicating with the Cisco WAN Manager station for network management purposes.

Most MGX 8220 concentrators have redundant ASC cards installed in card slots 3 and 4. One ASC (and its associated BNM and SRM) is always active; the other is a hot standby. All information—including configurations, statistics, and event logs—is passed between the two ASCs so that they are both up to date.

The ASC card module, as shown in Figure 15-33, consists of an ASC front card and a LM-ASC back card.

Figure 15-33 *AXIS Shelf Controller*

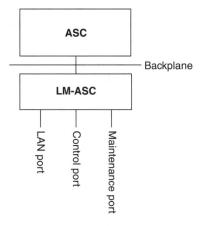

The ASC is responsible for shelf management, BNM and SRM management, network management, configuration, and firmware image storage:

- **Shelf management**—The ASC is responsible for monitoring and controlling the card modules in the MGX 8220 concentrator.

- **BNM and SRM management**—The ASC, the BNM, and SRM form a single logical card on the MGX 8220 concentrator. The ASC card manages all BNM and SRM configuration and firmware.

- **Network management**—Network management devices—such as a Cisco WAN Manager workstation, a PC, or a terminal—communicate directly with the ASC. When you log in to an MGX 8220 concentrator to access the CLI, you are communicating with the ASC.

- **Configuration and firmware storage**—The ASC stores service module configuration and firmware images. A copy of the configuration database and firmware image for each service module installed in the MGX 8220 concentrator is stored on the ASC on a PCMCIA disk drive. If a service module is replaced, the configuration and firmware are downloaded from the ASC.

The ASC front card has the following LEDs and physical ports:

- **Card status**—The three top LEDs indicate card or system status, as shown in Table 15-6.

Table 15-6 *ASC Card Status LEDs*

Alarm	Status
ACT LED (green)	The card is active.
STBY LED (slow-blinking yellow) and green ACT LED	The card is booting.
STBY LED (fast-blinking yellow) and green ACT LED	Software is being downloaded to this ASC or to another ASC.
STBY LED (steady yellow)	The card is in standby mode.
FAIL LED (steady red), and ACT and STBY LEDs off	The card is in reset condition or has failed, or the card set is not complete.
FAIL LED (steady red) and green ACT LED	The card was active but has failed.
FAIL LED (steady red) and STBY LED (yellow)	The card was in standby but has failed.
FAIL LED (blinking red)	The card is booting.
LAN LED (flashing green)	LAN traffic was seen on the interface.

- **Maintenance port**—The maintenance port provides terminal access to the MGX CLI. Unlike the PXM control port, the ASC maintenance port is configurable.

- **Control port**—The control port provides serial line IP (SLIP) connectivity for Telnet access.

- **LAN port**—The LAN port is identical functionally to the PXM LAN port and provides LAN access to the node.

The ASC LEDs and ports are shown in Figure 15-34.

Figure 15-34 *ASC LEDs and Ports*

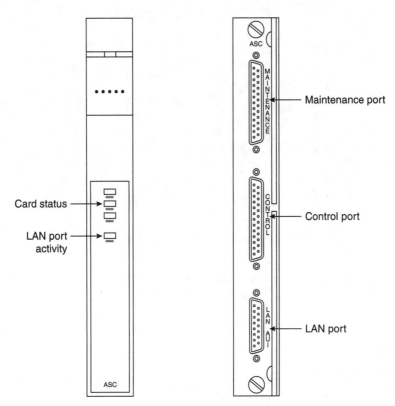

Card status

LAN port activity

Maintenance port

Control port

LAN port

Broadband Network Module

The Broadband Network Module (BNM), shown in Figure 15-35, maintains the trunk between the MGX 8220 concentrator and an ATM network (typically a BPX network). In addition, the BNM is responsible for shelf synchronization and alarm reporting. The ASC and the BNM on the MGX 8220 concentrator together perform the same functions as the PXM on the MGX 8850 switch.

Figure 15-35 *Broadband Network Module*

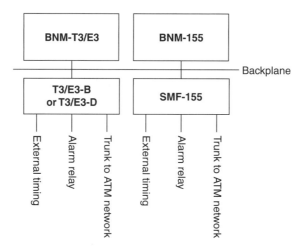

Most MGX 8220 concentrators have redundant BNM cards installed in card slots 1 and 2. One BNM (and the associated ASC and SRM) is always active, and the other acts as a hot standby.

Two BNM models are supported on an MGX 8220 concentrator running Release 5.0 firmware:

* BNM T3/E3

* BNM OC3/STM-1

The BNM T3/E3 consists of a BNM T3/E3 front card and either a T3/E3-B back card with a BNC connector for an E1 clock input, or a T3/E3-D back card with a DB-15 external timing connector for a T1 or E1 clock input.

The BNM OC3/STM-1 consists of a BNM-155 front card and an SMF-155 back card with a single-mode fiber (SMF) trunk interface.

BNM Functions

The BNM performs the following functions:

* **Cell transport to ATM network**—The BNM transmits and receives UNI or StrataCom Trunk Interface (STI) cells from the attached ATM network. The BNM must create the appropriate header (UNI, NNI, or STI) on the cells before passing them to the ATM backbone. All necessary framing, cell delineation, and error checking is done by the BNM.

- **Cellbus master**—All ATM cells created by the service modules are sent to the BNM card to be forwarded to the attached ATM network. The BNM manages the flow of cells on the cellbus on the MGX 8220 concentrator.

- **Shelf timing**—The BNM extracts a clock signal from either an external clock source or the trunk to the ATM network. The BNM propagates the timing signals across the concentrator's timing bus.

- **Environmental alarms**—The BNM monitors chassis temperature, fan, and power supply status, and reports this information to the ASC.

- **Local alarm notification**—The BNM reports local major and minor alarms via front card LEDs or dry contact relays on the back card.

BNM LEDs and Ports

The front card and back card LEDs and ports are shown in Figure 15-36.

Figure 15-36 *BNM LEDs and Interfaces*

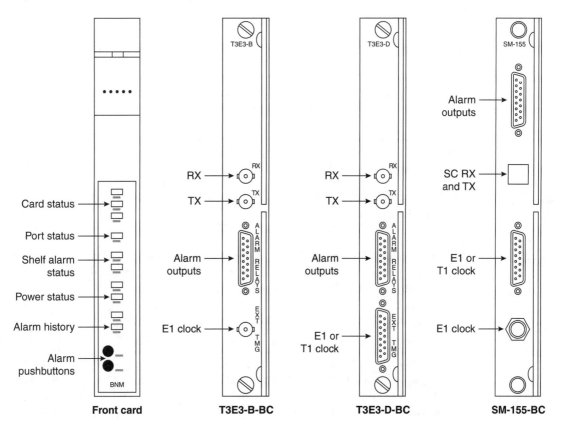

The BNM front card provides the following front panel LEDs and controls:

- **Card status**—The BNM card status is indicated by the top three LEDs on the front card. The alarms and status are shown in Table 15-7.

Table 15-7 *Card Status Alarms*

Alarm	Status
ACT LED (green)	The card is active.
STBY (yellow)	The card is in standby mode.
FAIL (red)	The card has failed, or the back card is missing.

- **Port status**—A tri-state LED reports the broadband line status of the back card. Table 15-8 summarizes the port status alarms.

Table 15-8 *Port Status Alarms*

Alarm	Status
Green	Port is active
Yellow	Remote alarm
Red	Local remote

- **Shelf (node) alarm**—Separate LEDs indicate minor and major alarms on the node. Table 15-9 lists the shelf alarms.

Table 15-9 *Shelf Alarms*

Alarm	Status
Off	No alarms
Minor alarm (yellow)	Minor alarm
Major alarm (red)	Major alarm

- **Power status**—The DC-A or DC-B is green when the A or B power module is present and operating correctly. The A module is connected to the right power connector, as viewed from the rear. An unlit power LED indicates that the module is missing or is at 0V output.

- **Alarm cutoff**—The Alarm cutoff (ACO) indicates that a user has pressed the ACO button.

- **History**—This History (HIST) LED indicates that a major or minor alarm might be present, or has been present at this node. This LED is on if either the MAJOR or MINOR LED is on. It remains on until the major or minor alarm condition clears and the HIST CLR button is pressed.

- **ACO pushbutton**—The ACO pushbutton is a user control to cut off or silence an audible alarm.
- **History clear pushbutton**—The HIST pushbutton is a user control to turn off the HIST LED.

Service Resource Module

The Service Resourc Module (SRM), shown in Figure 15-37, manages 1-to-N service module redundancy and can perform BERTs on service module lines.

Figure 15-37 *Service Resource Module*

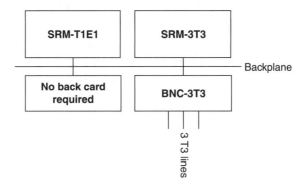

The SRM-3T3 also can manage T3 to T1 line distribution on the shelf.

As with the ASC and BNM, one SRM is active and a second one can be installed as a hot standby. Unlike the ASC and BNM, the SRM is not required for an MGX device to function.

The SRM-3T3 card module is covered in the previous section "MGX 8850 Common Core Cards," and is not repeated here.

The SRM T1/E1 card module, which is supported on the MGX 8220 concentrator only, consists of an SRM-T1E1 front card; no back card is required.

The SRM-T1E1 front card LED indicators are shown in Figure 15-38.

Figure 15-38 *SRM-T1E1 LEDs*

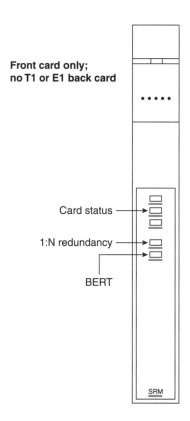

The LEDs include card status, redundancy, and BERT LEDs:

- **Card status**—Three LEDs indicate the card status and are shown in Table 15-10.

Table 15-10 *Card Status Alarms*

Alarm	Status
Active (green)	The card is active.
Standby (yellow)	The card is in standby mode.
Failure (red)	The card has failed.

- **Redundancy**—The redundancy LED turns green if the 1:N redundancy feature is active.
- **BERT**—An LED indicates green if BERT is active, or yellow if a failure is detected.

Service Modules

MGX service modules receive end-user traffic, perform segmentation and reassembly (SAR) functions, perform all necessary interface functions (policing, queuing, and congestion control), and pass the ATM cells to the cell bus. The service modules include these:

- Circuit Emulation Service Module
- Frame Relay Service Module
- ATM UNI Service Module
- Inverse Multiplexing over ATM Module

Standard Back Cards

Figure 15-39 shows the standard cards that are used for CESM, FRSM, and AUSM service modules. Certain FRSM service modules use different back cards with serial interfaces, which are described later in this chapter.

Figure 15-39 *Standard Back Cards*

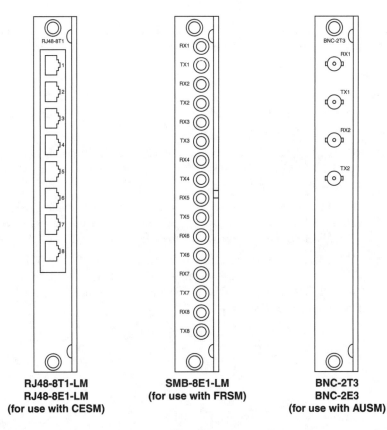

RJ48-8T1-LM
RJ48-8E1-LM
(for use with CESM)

SMB-8E1-LM
(for use with FRSM)

BNC-2T3
BNC-2E3
(for use with AUSM)

Circuit Emulation Service Module

The Circuit Emulation Service Module (CESM), shown in Figure 15-40, segments and reassembles up to eight channelized or unchannelized T1/E1 lines of user traffic, or one line of unchannelized T3/E3 traffic, using ATM adaptation layer 1 (AAL1).

Figure 15-40 *Circuit Emulation Service Module*

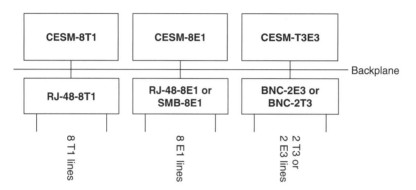

All incoming traffic, including signaling and framing bits, is segmented and transported through the network to a destination CESM.

CESM Modules

As shown in Figure 15-41, there are CESM T1 format, CESM E1 format, and CESM T3 or E3 format modules:

- **CESM T1**—The CESM T1 consists of a CESM-8T1 front card and a back card with eight RJ-48 T1 interfaces (RJ48-8T1), or a special back card to support 1:N redundancy (R-RJ48-8T1).

- **CESM E1**—The CESM E1 consists of a CESM-8E1 front card and a back card with eight RJ-48 E1 interfaces (RJ48-8E1), eight SMB E1 interfaces (SMB-8E1), or a special back card to support 1:N redundancy (R-RJ48-8E1 or R-SMB-8E1).

- **CESM T3 or E3**—The CESM T3 or E3 consists of a CESM-T3E3 front card and a back card with two BNC T3 interfaces (BNC-2T3) or two BNC E3 interfaces (BNC-2E3). Although the CESM-T3E3 has two physical interface lines, only the upper line can be used for user traffic.

CESM Functions

The CESM supports data transfer, multiplexing and demultiplexing, and segmentation and reassembly; monitors on- and off-hook states; provides clock recovery; and performs physical-layer functions:

- **Performs data transfer**—The CESM supports structured and unstructured data transfer. Structured data transfer identifies framing and signaling bits in the data stream; unstructured mode treats all bits as part of the data stream.

- **Performs multiplexing and demultiplexing**—If the optional channelized feature is available on a T1 or E1 CESM, the individual time slots are multiplexed and demultiplexed on the CESM. The T3/E3 version supports only unstructured (unchannelized) mode.

- **Handles segmentation and reassembly**—The CESM segments bit-stream traffic into ATM cells using AAL1. All traffic is forwarded to the ATM network and is transported on a CBR circuit to the destination MGX CESM.

- **Monitors on- and off-hook signaling states**—CESMs can monitor channel associated signaling (CAS) on channelized T1 or E1 lines. These signaling states are used to turn on and off the SAR process, eliminating the transmission of traffic during on-hook periods. This feature is available only on 64-kbps structured connections.

- **Provides clock recovery**—The T1 and E1 CESM can use one of two methods for clock recovery that enables end-to-end timing between the two circuit-terminating devices. Clock recovery is available only on full unstructured T1 or E1 connections.

- **Performs physical-layer functions**—The CESM performs all necessary physical-layer functions on the attached T1 or E1 access lines.

CESM Status LEDs

The CESM front card provides the status indicators shown in Figure 15-41.

Figure 15-41 *CESM Status LEDs*

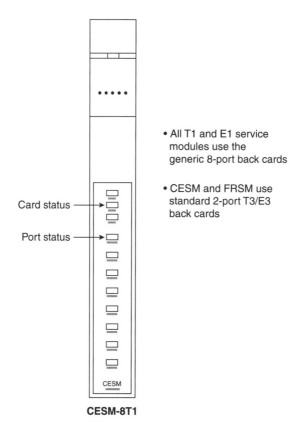

- All T1 and E1 service modules use the generic 8-port back cards

- CESM and FRSM use standard 2-port T3/E3 back cards

Card status →

Port status →

CESM

CESM-8T1

A summary of these status indicators follows:

- **Card status**—Three LEDs indicate card status, as shown in Table 15-11.

Table 15-11 *CESM Status LEDs*

Alarm	Status
ACT LED (green)	The card is active.
STBY LED (slow-blinking yellow) without active ACT LED	The card is in boot state.
STBY LED (fast-blinking yellow) with green/active ACT LED	Card software is being downloaded.
STBY LED (steady yellow)	The card is in standby mode.

Table 15-11 *CESM Status LEDs (Continued)*

FAILED (steady red) with ACT and STBY LEDs off	The card is resting or has failed, or there is no line module.
FAILED (steady red) with ACT LED on	The card was active prior to failing.
FAILED (steady red) with STBY LED on	The card was in standby prior to failing.
FAILED (blinking red)	The card is booting.

- **Line status**—When the PORT LED is green, the port is active; red indicates a local alarm on the port. When the PORT LED is off, the port has not been activated (upped).

Frame Relay Service Module

The Frame Relay Service (FRSM), shown in Figure 15-42, converts Frame Relay frames into ATM cells using AAL5. It also performs policing and congestion management functions on all incoming user traffic.

Figure 15-42 *Frame Relay Service Module*

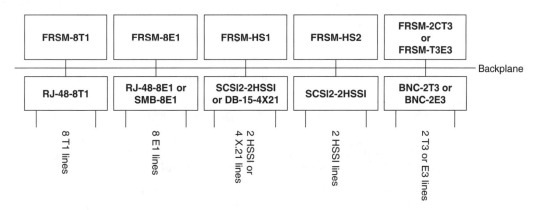

The lines on an FRSM card can terminate on any of the following devices:

- A Cisco Frame Relay router with a T3, E3, T1, E1, HSSI, or X.21 interface
- A time-division multiplexer (TDM) with a T1 or E1 interface that supports multiple Frame Relay devices with subrate interfaces
- Any device that transmits Frame Relay traffic with a T3, E3, T1, E1, HSSI, or X.21 interface
- Six FRSM models are supported on an MGX:
  - FRSM-8T1 with RJ-48 back card

— FRSM-8E1 with RJ-48 or SMB back card

— FRSM-HS1 with HSSI or X.21 back card (MGX 8220 concentrator only)

— FRSM-HS2 with HSSI/B back card

— FRSM-2CT3 with T3 back card (MGX 8850 switch only)

— FRSM-T3E3 with T3 or E3 back card (MGX 8850 switch only)

The collective name for the MGX-FRSM-2CT3, MGX-FRSM-2T3E3, and MGX-FRSM-HS2/B is FRSM-VHS (very high speed). When installing in a MGX 8850 switch, the FRSM-VHS cards should go in the upper bay of the card cage because the backplane provides higher bandwidth per slot on the upper half of the backplane.

FRSM Functions

The FRSM is responsible for the following functions:

- **Data transfer**—The T1 and E1 versions of the FRSM are available in channelized or unchannelized versions. However, the FRSM-2CT3 is available only in channelized form, and all other models support unchannelized user lines only.

- **Segmentation and reassembly**—The FRSM segments and reassembles Frame Relay frames using AAL5.

- **Signaling**—The FRSM supports all Frame Relay signaling protocols, including the Enhanced Local Management Interface (ELMI).

- **Policing**—The FRSM supports ingress policing based on configurable burst sizes and data rates.

- **ForeSight use**—The FRSM optionally can support congestion management using the ForeSight feature.

- **ATM-Frame Relay interworking**—ATM-Frame Relay service interworking, both transparent and translational, is supported on the FRSM.

- **Frame forwarding**—An FRSM port can support a frame-forwarding connection. Frame forwarding forwards frames (HDLC, SDLC, X.25, and so on) to the destination Frame Relay interface. A frame-forwarding port supports only a single connection.

- **Physical-layer functions**—Like the CESM, the FRSM performs all necessary physical-layer functions.

FRSM LEDs and Interfaces

FRSM front cards provide status indicators, which are the same as for the CESM. Note that the number of line status LEDs is two or eight, depending on the model. The cards are shown in Figure 15-43.

Figure 15-43 *FRSM LEDs and Interface*

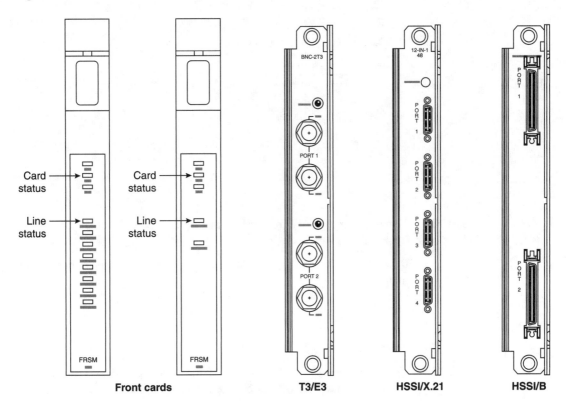

ATM UNI Service Module

The ATM UNI Service Module (AUSM), shown in Figure 15-44, provides narrowband (T1 or E1) ATM UNI services. The AUSM also supports ATM inverse multiplexed (AIM) services.

The lines on an AUSM card can terminate on any of the following devices:

* An ATM device with a T1 or E1 interface
* An ATM device with inverse multiplexed T1 or E1 interfaces

Two AUSM models are supported on the MGX 8220 concentrator:

* AUSM-8T1 with RJ-48 back card
* AUSM-8E1 with RJ-48 or SMB back card

Figure 15-44 *ATM UNI Service Module*

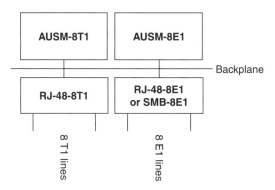

The AUSM card modules consist of a front card, either the AUSM-8T1 or the AUSM-8E1, and one of the standard T1 or E1 back cards.

The MGX 8850 switch supports only the AUSM Model B; the MGX concentrator supports both Model A and Model B.

AUSM Functions

The AUSM supports the following:

- **UNI or NNI cell format support**—The ATM ports on the AUSM card can be configured to accept either the UNI or NNI cell header formats.

- **CBR, VBR, ABR, and UBR services**—The AUSM supports CBR, VBR, ABR, and UBR types of ATM services. ABR services on the AUSM use the ForeSight feature; standard ABR is not supported.

- **Policing**—Single and dual leaky bucket models are used to police ingress ATM traffic on the AUSM. Policing is defined on a per-channel basis.

- **Virtual path or virtual channel connections**—The AUSM supports both virtual path (VP) and virtual channel (VC) connections.

- **ATM inverse multiplexed access lines**—Multiple T1 or E1 lines can form a single ATM port using AIM. This facility sometimes is called IMA UNI to distinguish it from IMA trunking, as implemented on the IMA trunk module.

  - Current AUSM support for IMA UNI includes a prestandard proprietary Cisco version and support for the standard ATM Forum IMA 1.0 on AUSM/A with firmware Release 5.0. Standard IMA will be supported on a latter release of the software for the AUSM/B on the MGX 8220. On the MGX 8850, the current AUSM also includes the standard IMA 1.0 with firmware 5.0 and PXM Release 1.1.

- **ILMI signaling protocol**—The ILMI signaling protocol can be configured on the AUSM on a per-port basis. ATM LMI is not supported.

- **Physical–layer functions**—Like the CESM and FRSM, all necessary physical-layer functions are performed by the AUSM.

Inverse Multiplexing over ATM Trunk Module

The Inverse Multi over ATM Trunk Module (IMATM), shown in Figure 15-45, supports one broadband line (T3 or E3), up to eight narrowband lines (T1 or E1), and performs AIM between the broadband and narrowband lines.

Figure 15-45 *Inverse Multiplexing over ATM Trunk Module*

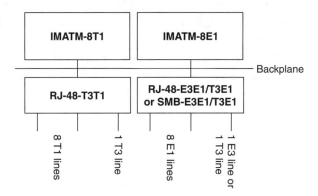

The broadband line on an IMATM card can terminate at any of the following devices:

- BPX BNI or BXM trunk card
- IGX BTM or ALM/B trunk card
- BPX ASI or BXM line card
- IGX ALM/A line card
- A Cisco 4000 or 7000 series router with a T3 or E3 ATM interface
- A Cisco LightStream 1010 switch T3 or E3 interface
- Any device that supports T3 or E3 ATM traffic that can limit its traffic to NxT1 or NxE1 rates (N is from 1 to 8)

Two IMATM models are supported on an MGX 8220:

- IMATM-8T1 with RJ-45 T1 interfaces, and a single T3 broadband interface.
- IMATM-8E1 with RJ-48 or SMB E1 connectors and a single E3 broadband interface. E1 back cards with a T3 broadband interface and eight RJ-48 or SMB E1 interfaces also are available.

The original IMATM Model A supports a Cisco prestandard AIM; the newer IMATM Model B supports the ATM Forum AIM.

IMATM Functions

The IMATM is responsible for the following functions:

- **ATM inverse multiplexing**—The IMATM extracts ATM cells from a broadband line and distributes the cells across multiple narrowband lines.

- **Narrowband line resiliency**—If a narrowband line fails, traffic can be configured to redistribute over the remaining narrowband lines.

- **Signaling**—Signaling that is required between the local and remote IMATM cards is maintained to establish synchronization between the two cards.

- **Timing**—IMATM synchronization can be referenced to any of the lines or the MGX 8220 concentrator.

- **Physical–layer functions**—All physical-layer functions for both the broadband and the narrowband lines are performed by the IMATM, including line and cell framing, alarm and error detection, and clocking.

IMATM LEDs and Interfaces

The IMATM card status indicators are the same as in the CESM.

In addition to the card status indicators, the card provides a PORT LED that shows green for an active T1/E1 line, yellow for a remote alarm, and red for a local alarm. The broadband trunk status (HSPORT LED) indicator indicates green for an active, alarm-free trunk, yellow for a remote alarm, and red for a local alarm. The IMATM LEDs and interfaces are shown in Figure 15-46.

Figure 15-46 *MATM LEDs and Interfaces*

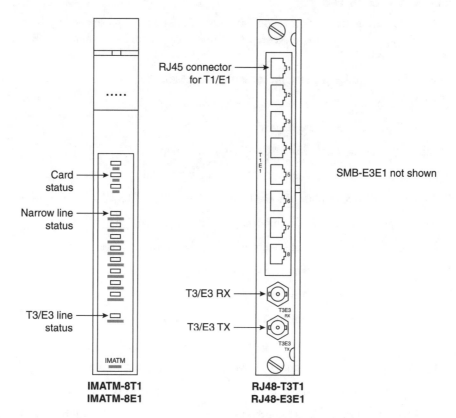

Summary

This chapter covered the components of MGX nodes, as well as the card groups and the steps necessary to install MGX nodes. The chapter also covered card group capabilities and features, and discussed issues related to redundancy and failover for each card that supports redundancy.

Installation steps included configuring the chassis, installing the rack, installing the power source, installing the cooling system, and removing and installing cards. The card groups covered were PXM, ASC, BNM, SRM-3T3, SRM-T1E1, RPM, FRSM-8T/E1, FRSM-HS1, FRSM-HS2, FRSM-2CT3, FRSM-T3E3, CESM-8T1/E1, CESM-T3E3, AUSM-8T1/E1, and IMATM-8T1/E1.

Review Questions

The following questions test your retention of the material presented in this chapter. You can find the answers to the Review Questions in Appendix A, "Answers to Review Questions."

1 Which two of the following statements apply to the MGX 8850 switch?

A. A booster fan unit is required.

B. Dual AC power sources are required.

C. The AC power shelf holds up to six 875W-power modules.

D. The AC power shelf holds up to six 1200W-power modules.

E. High-speed service modules should be located in the upper bay.

F. The backplane supports 1:N redundancy for all slots except 7 and 8.

2 Which one of the following statements applies to the MGX 8220 concentrator?

A. Service modules always require a matching back card.

B. LAN ports on redundant ASC modules should not be Y-cabled.

C. Power modules deliver regulated 220 VAC to the shelf power bus.

D. At least two AC power modules are required for a fully loaded shelf.

E. The AC power shelf can supply full redundant power to four shelves.

F. A booster fan is required if the number of shelves in a rack is two or more.

3 What is the total vertical space required in RMUs for an MGX 8850 switch with all optional modules?

A. 21

B. 19

C. 20

D. 16

4 Which card slots are reserved for the PXMs on the MGX 8850 switch?

A. 1 and 2

B. 1 and 3

C. 3 and 4

D. 7 and 8

E. 15 and 16

F. 31 and 32

5 Which card slots are reserved for the ASCs on the MGX 8220 concentrator?

A. 1 and 2

B. 1 and 3

C. 3 and 4

D. 7 and 8

E. 15 and 16

F. 31 and 32

6 Which card slots are reserved for the BNMs on the MGX 8220 concentrator?

A. 1 and 2

B. 1 and 3

C. 3 and 4

D. 7 and 8

E. 15 and 16

F. 31 and 32

7 Match the ASC and PXM back card port with its description.

A. LAN port

B. Control port

C. Maintenance port

Description	Answer
A VT100 interface on the MGX 8850 switch for CLI access	
An Ethernet interface for Telnet, TFTP, and SNMP access	
A VT100 interface on the MGX 8220 concentrator for CLI access	
A SLIP interface on the MGX 8850 switch for Telnet, TFTP, and SNMP access	
A SLIP interface on the MGX 8220 concentrator for Telnet, TFTP, and SNMP access	

8 How many E1 ports are on a CESM?

A. 2

B. 4

C. 8

D. 12

9 Match the card module in the table with its functions from the list that follows:

Card Module	Answer
PXM	
ASC	
BNM	
SRM	
RPM	
CESM	
FRSM	
AUSM	
IMATM	

A. Layer 3 traffic router

B. AAL5 for Frame Relay traffic

C. AAL1 for T1 and E1 formatted traffic

D. CBR, VBR, ABR, and UBR ATM services

E. ATM inverse multiplexing for T3 or E3 lines

F. Service module redundancy, BERT, and optional line distribution

G. Trunk to ATM backbone network, synchronization, and local alarm reporting

H. Storage for configuration, network management, and shelf management on the MGX 8850 switch

I. Storage for configuration, network management, and shelf management on the MGX 8220 concentrator

10 If you had an MGX 8220 concentrator with the following requirements, which card module set would meet your needs?

- — Redundant processors
- — OC-3 trunk to the ATM backbone network
- — BERT for access lines
- — T3 line distribution
- — Nine E1 circuit emulation lines
- — Five T1 Frame Relay lines
- — One HSSI Frame Relay line
- — Two T1 ATM lines

A. 2 ASC, 1 BNM, 1 SRM-3T3, 2 CESM-8E1, 1 FRSM-8T1, 1 FRSM-HS1, 1 AUSM-T1

B. 2 ASC, 2 BNM, 2 SRM-T1E1, 1 CESM-8E1, 1 FRSM-8T1, 1 FRSM-HS1, 1 AUSM-T1

C. 2 ASC, 2 BNM, 2 SRM-3T3, 2 CESM-8E1, 1 FRSM-8T1, 1 FRSM-HS1, 1 AUSM-T1

D. 2 ASC, 2 BNM, 2 SRM-3T3, 2 CESM-8E1, 1 FRSM-8T1, 1 FRSM-HS1, 1 IMATM-T3T1

11 If you had an MGX 8850 switch installed with full redundancy (core cards and service modules), two RPMs, two FRSM-2T3E3, and two FRSM-8T1 cards, which of the following card slot configurations would be recommended?

Option	Card Slots
PXM	
SRM	
RPM	
FRSM-2T3E3	
FRSM-8T1	

CHAPTER 16

Initial Configuration of MGX Nodes

This chapter is designed to introduce you to the MGX command-line interface (CLI). In addition, initial shelf configuration characteristics are examined to help you prepare the MGX 8850 or 8220 concentrator for introduction into a network.

This chapter includes the following sections:

- Command-Line Access Methods for the MGX 8220 and the MGX 8850
- CLI Syntax
- Enhanced CLI on the MGX 8850 Switch
- Node Names
- MGX Feed Date and Time
- MGX IP Addresses
- RPM Configuration
- MGX Commands
- Summary
- Review Questions

Command-Line Access Methods for the MGX 8220 and the MGX 8850

The four ways to access the MGX CLI are shown in Figure 16-1. The CLI is used to monitor and configure the MGX platform, including shelf, trunk, line, port, connection, and channel characteristics.

Figure 16-1 *MGX 8850 CLI Access*

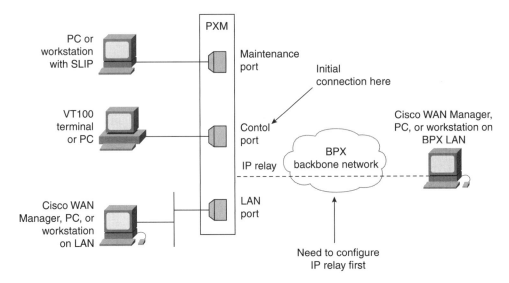

MGX 8850 Access Methods

The four methods to access the MGX 8850 are control port, maintenance port, LAN port, and IP relay.

- **Control port**—The control port is an EIA/TIA-232 DCE interface on the Processor Switch Module User Interface (PXM-UI) back card. Initially, the control port is the only method available to access the shelf. A terminal or a PC running a VT100 terminal emulation program can be used.

- **Maintenance port**—The maintenance port is an EIA/TIA-232 DCE Serial Line Internet Protocol (SLIP) interface on the PXM-UI back card. To use this port, an IP address must be configured, and a PC a or workstation running a SLIP application must be used.

- **LAN port**—The LAN port allows the switch to communicate with other devices (PCs, workstations, and so on) across a LAN. The LAN port is a 15-pin attachment unit interface (AUI) connector for use with an Ethernet LAN.

  When installing a new system, LAN access is not available until further configuration has been completed, so the control port must be used for initial configuration.

- **IP relay**—As covered in Chapter 13, "Initial Configuration of IGX and BPX Switches," IP relay is a method to propagate IP traffic (Telnet, Simple Network Management [SNMP], and TFTP) in-band through the network. The originating workstation communicates with one of the BPX switches in the network via a LAN port.

MGX 8220 Access Methods

Physical access methods for the CLI on the MGX 8220 concentrator, shown in Figure 16-2, are functionally the same as those for the MGX 8850 switch; however, the ports are named the opposite of the MGX 8850 ports, which can seem confusing.

- **Maintenance port**—Initially, the maintenance port is the only method available to access the shelf. It functions the same as the control port on the MGX 8850. The maintenance port is the top port of the three ports on the ASC back card. Like the control port on the MGX 8850, a VT 100 terminal (or terminal emulation) with a serial cable can be used to access and configure the shelf.

- **Control port**—The control port functions the same as the maintenance port on the MGX 8850. The control port and the IP address must be configured on the switch to use this port. In addition, the PC or the terminal being used must be configured to use SLIP to communicate with the switch.

Figure 16-2 *MGX 8220 CLI Access*

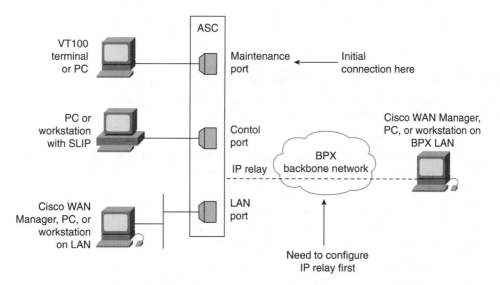

CLI Syntax

The command syntax for the MGX nodes, although similar to the command syntax for the IGX and BPX switches syntax, has some important differences. The most obvious difference is that the MGX commands are case sensitive. For example, when issuing the **Help** command, it must be entered exactly, including the capital H.

As with the IGX and BPX series, all commands on the MGX 8850 and 8220 devices consist of a single word made up of a combination of abbreviated verbs and nouns. Commands may be followed by a combination of required and optional parameters. Commands can have both types of parameters, only one type, or no parameters at all. Issuing a command without any parameters prompts the MGX device to return the correct syntax, including all required parameters.

As with the IGX and BPX nodes, MGX commands typically begin with an abbreviated verb, followed by abbreviated nouns. Many of the verbs and nouns will already be familiar, such as **dsp** and **add**. Others differ from their IGX and BPX counterparts—for example, **chan** is used in place of **ch** for channel, and **cnt** (counter) is used instead of **stat** for statistic.

Most commands follow the conventions described; however, there are exceptions. The **Help** (or **?**) command is very useful for finding the exact spelling of a command.

A second form of unique syntax for the MGX nodes involves the use of delineators, usually in the form of **–xx**, which must precede some parameters. In most cases, parameters preceded by a delineator are optional. Here is an example:

```
cnfln -sonet 1 -slt 2 -sps 2
```

Command privilege levels follow the same general scheme as for IGX and BPX nodes.

Enhanced CLI on the MGX 8850 Switch

The MGX 8850 supports a number of extra CLI features to help you manage the switch mode more easily. You can use the up and down arrows to move through the command history.

If you press the up arrow, the previous command-line entry is placed on the current command line. You can press the up arrow between 1 and 10 times to issue any of the 10 most recent command entries.

The left and right arrows move the cursor on the command line so that you can edit what you have entered. By default, the insert mode is active. You can change to the overwrite mode or back to the insert mode by using the Insert key.

The **history** command lists the last 10 command entries that you have made. You can use this command to review the steps that you have performed.

Node Names

Before introducing an MGX feeder into the network, ensure that the shelf names are unique on each BPX switch, as follows:

* Shelf names must be one to eight characters in length.
* Shelf names must start with a letter.
* Shelf names may include . or _.
* Shelf names are case sensitive.
* Shelf names can be modified using the **cnfname** command.

MGX Feed Date and Time

A MGX feeder attached to a BPX routing node with an active trunk usually derives its time and date setting from the core network. The **cnfdate** and **cnftime** commands are available if you need to modify these settings; as an exception to global time management, these commands affect the local shelf only.

The **cnftmzn** command allows the local time zone to be set to GMT or to one of the standard North American time zones (EDT, CDT, and so on). In other locations, use the **cnftmzngmt** command to set the local time zone to an offset, in hours, from GMT.

MGX IP Addresses

The LAN port, serial slip port, and IP relay can all be configured with IP addresses. If configured, the IP relay address must be on a separate network (subnet) than the LAN port IP address. (The IP relay network is a dedicated network to network management.)

RPM Configuration

Detailed configuration and setup of the RPM falls outside the scope of this book because detailed knowledge of the Cisco IOS is required. However, the RPM CLI can be accessed using any of the following three methods (shown in Figure 16-3):

* **RPM console port**—The RPM has a RJ-45 connector on the front of the card module. A PC or dumb terminal can be directly attached to this port with an EIA/TIA RS-232 to RJ-45 cable for CLI access. The console port is the only way to access the RPM CLI when the card module is first installed into an MGX 8850 chassis.

- **cc command from another MGX 8850 card**—You can access the RPM CLI by using the **cc** (change card) command from any of the other cards in the MGX 8850 switch. The ATM switch interface on the RPM must be enabled before you can use the **cc** command.

- **Telnet from a workstation, a PC, or another router**—The RPM CLI can be accessed from a PC or a workstation on any of the LANs attached to the RPM. Also, after the RPM is installed and has permanent virtual circuits (PVCs) to other RPMs or routers in the network, you can Telnet to the RPM CLI remotely from these other devices.

Figure 16-3 *RPM CLI Access*

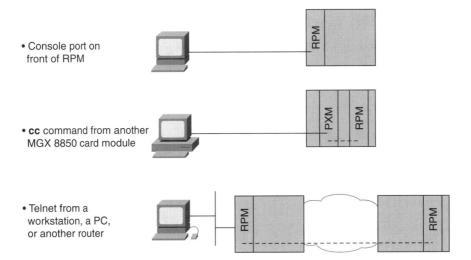

- Console port on front of RPM

- **cc** command from another MGX 8850 card module

- Telnet from a workstation, a PC, or another router

MGX Commands

The commands shown in Table 16-1 are covered in this chapter. A brief description of the command, the privilege levels necessary to issue the command, and the applicable card type are included in Table 16-1. Commands are listed in the order in which they are covered.

Table 16-1 *MGX Commands*

Command	Description	Privilege	Card
Help	Displays all commands associated with the card and the user privilege level.	6	All
?	Same as **Help**.	6	All
adduser	Add user. Defines a new user ID and associated privilege level.	5	PXM ASC

Table 16-1   *MGX Commands (Continued)*

Command	Description	Privilege	Card
passwd	Configure user password. Modifies the current user password.	6	PXM
cnfpwd	Configure user password. Modifies the current user password.	6	ASC
dsppwd	Display user password.	6	ASC
cnfname	Configure shelf name. Modifies the node name for the shelf.	1	PXM ASC
dspcds	Display cards. Displays the current or another, lower privileged user's password.	6	PXM ASC
dspcd	Display characteristics of card hardware. Displays the card's characteristics, including serial number and hardware and firmware revision levels. The command also gives the status of the card, which may indicate the reason for the last reset.	6	All
cc	Change card. Switches to another card in the shelf.	6	All
cnftime	Configure time. Configures the time for the shelf.	0	PXM ASC
cnftmzn	Configure time zone. Configures the local time zone for the shelf.	0	PXM ASC
cnftmznmgmt	Configure time zone offset. Configures the local time zone, in hours offset from GMT.	0	PXM
cnfdate	Configure date. Configures the date for the shelf.	0	PXM ASC
xdsplns	Display configuration parameters for all lines on card. The displayed parameters are specific to the card.	6	All
xdspln	Extend display line. Displays the configuration of the maintenance and control ports.	6	ASC
xcnfln	Extend configure line. Modifies the configuration of the maintenance and control ports.	1	ASC
dspifip	Display interface IP. Displays the IP addresses associated with the shelf, including the SLIP, LAN, and IP relay addresses.	6	PXM ASC
cnfifip	Configure IP interface. Modifies the IP addresses associated with the shelf, including the SLIP, LAN, and IP relay addresses.	1	ASC
dspshelfalm	Display shelf alarm. Displays the environmental conditions for the shelf, including the power supply status.	6	PXM ASC

continues

Table 16-1 *MGX Commands (Continued)*

Command	Description	Privilege	Card
history	History. Lists the last 10 command-line entries.	6	PXM
bye	Exit system. Logs out the current CLI session.	6	All

System Startup

Example 16-1 illustrates a powerup boot sequence for the MGX 8850 switch. Prior to configuration, the bootup sequence should be watched carefully to ensure the switch does not report any system errors and that all cards are recognized and reported present with an insertion message.

Example 16-1 *MGX 8850 Boot Process*

```
reset type: 0x00000002
pio input: 0x8c175770
Error EPC: 0x80000044
Status Reg: 0x40400104
Cause Reg: 0x00000200
CacheErr Reg: 0xa000c040

Reset L2 cache...
DRAM size: 0x08000000
Reset L1 cache...
Clear Edac...

Backup Boot Version: 1.0.00Eh
Verify Checksum... Valid


DRAM Size : 08000000
Testing DRAM up to: a8000000... Passed
jumping to romStart

absUncompress:a001d240
From:a001dc10
To:a1e00000
Len:0008f02f
uncompressing BACKUP_BOOT image..
Jumping to 0xa1e00000
rmPriMibDbRegister(): cardState = 3 slot = 11
rmPriMibDbRegister(): cardState = 3 slot = 13
slot 1 (cardInx 2) is present, insertion msg from 7
slot 3 (cardInx 4) is present, insertion msg from 7
slot 9 (cardInx 8) is present, insertion msg from 7
slot 11 (cardInx 10) is present, insertion msg from 7
slot 13 (cardInx 12) is present, insertion msg from 7
slot 9 (cardInx 8) is present, insertion msg from 13
SM Feature Bit Map is = 0
SM Feature Bit Map is = 0
```

Example 16-1 *MGX 8850 Boot Process (Continued)*

```
switchmMgmtIpAddr(0x0a0a042d)
slot 9 (cardInx 8) is present, insertion msg from 7
slot 9 (cardInx 8) is present, insertion msg from 13
slot 3 (cardInx 4) is present, insertion msg from 7
slot 11 (cardInx 10) is present, insertion msg from 7
slot 13 (cardInx 12) is present, insertion msg from 7
slot 1 (cardInx 2) is present, insertion msg from 7
slot 3 (cardInx 4) is present, insertion msg from 7
slot 11 (cardInx 10) is present, insertion msg from 7
slot 13 (cardInx 12) is present, insertion msg from 7
slot 1 (cardInx 2) is present, insertion msg from 7
slot 9 (cardInx 8) is present, insertion msg from 7
slot 9 (cardInx 8) is present, insertion msg from 13
Login:
```

Example 16-2 shows the boot sequence on the MGX 8220. Because of the amount of output during powerup, several sections of the system output are not shown.

Example 16-2 *MGX 8220 Boot Process*

```
AXISNAME.1.4.ASC.a >
LR33310 CPU O.K.
DRAM O.K.
Reset Reason PIO = 6
***************  Power Reset    ***************
sys hw init
store checksum = 152 calculated checksum = 152

Loading ASC2 xilinx image

  Load BSC chain  GRAM -> SHAR -> CBS
Done bit went high
Ready to start vxWorks

Starting usrRoot

Ready to start TTY

Symbol initialized
Exc initialized
ENV initialized
initialize File System
pcMcia: perform dosFsDevInit........
pcMcia: Create dev routine........
initPCMCIA: initialize PCMCIA for ATA mode.......
pcMcia ident: ID: 3
              Cylinders = 1008
.
.
.
          .........
```

continues

Example 16-2 *MGX 8220 Boot Process (Continued)*

```
Reading CONFIG.SYS
No config parameter specified to set 0,30,0,C:/FW/SM30.FW
.
.
.Reading BOOT file C:/fw/asc.fw
...............................................
Done Verify Boot Image Checksum.
Booting
sys hw init

Loading ASC2 xilinx image
.
.
.
Network initialized
initialized done              ***** Stratacom Inc. AXIS ASC Card *****2
Firmware Version       = 5.0.00
    Backup Boot version    = ASC_BT_1.0.00
    ASCFRSM Xilinx file    = asc025.h
    ASC2 Xilinx file       = ASC2_28.h
    ASCBNM Xilinx file     = A:bnm_a E:bnm_e
    ASCBNM Altera file     = bnm155_2
    SRM-T1E1 Xilinx file   = A:srm038.h, E:srmE038.h
    SRM-3T3 Xilinx file    = srm038.h
    SRM-3T3 Encoder file   = encoder42_004.ttf
    SRM-3T3 Encoder-2 file = encoder80_001.ttf
    SRM-3T3 Decoder file   = decoder42_004.ttf
    SRM-3T3 Clock file     = clkctrl_40.ttf
    SRM-3T3 I-Cube file    = ic320.h
 CPU: STRATACOM.  Processor #0.
                             Memory Size: 0x1000000.
.
.
.
sarSb0Size = 8980
sarSb1Size = 24
login:
```

After communications are established between the MGX device and terminal and bootup, the MGX CLI prompts you for your user ID and password (see Example 16-3 and Example 16-4). Following a correct password entry, the MGX CLI prompts you for a card number. On the MGX 8850 switch, the active PXM is the default card number (shown in brackets); pressing Return logs you in to the active PXM. On the MGX 8220, enter either **3** or **4** for the active ASC.

Example 16-3 *MGX 8850 Initial Login Screen*

```
Login: SuperUser
password:
card number [7]:

NODENAME.1.7.PXM.a >
```

Example 16-4 *MGX 8220 Initial Login Screen*

```
Login: SuperUser
password:
card number :4

AXISNAME.1.4.ASC.a >
```

The MGX command prompt concatenates the following fields:

- Shelf name
- Shelf number (always 1)
- Card number
- Card type
- Card status ("a" for active, "s" for standby)

Help

The MGX CLI provides a list of available commands with the **Help** command. These are shown in Example 16-5. The command list is dependent on the card type (PXM, ASC, FRSM, and so on) and your user privilege level.

Example 16-5 *Help Command*

```
AXISNAME.1.4.ASC.a > Help

Command                 Logging  State   Priority
--------------------    -------  ------  -------------------------
?                       No       Any     Any User
Help                    No       Any     Any User
addlink                 No       Active  Any User
addln                   No       Active  Any User
addrasdsk               Yes      Active  Group 1
addred                  No       Active  Any User
adduser                 Yes      Active  Group 5
clralm                  No       Any     Group 5
clralmcnt               No       Any     Group 5
clralmcnts              No       Any     Group 5
clrbnmcnf               No       Any     Any User
clrbnmcnt               No       Any     Group 5
clrlmistats             No       Active  Any User
```

continues

Example 16-5 *Help Command (Continued)*

```
clrlog             Yes      Any      Group 1
clrmsgcnt          No       Any      Group 5
clrsarcnt          No       Any      Group 5
clrsarcnts         No       Any      Group 5
clrscrn            No       Any      Group 5
clrslftst          No       Any      Any User
clrsrmcnf          Yes      Any      Any User

Type <CR> to continue, Q<CR> to stop: q
```

The **Help** command display includes the following information:

- Command

- Logging

- Whether the command is logged on the local MGX alarm and the event log

- State

- What state the card must be in to issue the command (either Active or Any)

- Priority

- The user privilege level required to issue the command

To determine the parameters associated with a command, enter the command (without any parameters), and then press Return or Enter. The MGX CLI responds with an error message and the correct syntax required for the command.

Example 16-6 shows the MGX system response for the **cnfifip** command.

Example 16-6 *Checking Command Syntax*

```
AXISNAME.1.4.ASC.a > cnfifip

cnfifip "-ip <ip addr> -if <Interface> -msk <NetMask> -bc <Brocast addr>"
  -ip <IP addr> where IP addr = nnn.nnn.nnn.nnn
  -if <Interface> where Interface = 26,28,37, 26: Ethernet, 28: Slip 37: ATM
  -msk <NetMask> where NetMask = nnn.nnn.nnn.nnn
  -bc <BrocastAddr> where BrocastAddr = nnnnnnnn,  n is hexdecimal, ethernet only
```

adduser

The **adduser** command in Example 16-7 allows the definition of new shelf user IDs and associated passwords. A user may add new users with a lower privilege level than his or her own; a user at privilege level 6 may therefore not add new users.

Example 16-7 *adduser Command*

```
AXISNAME.1.4.ASC.a > adduser Teacher 1

AXISNAME.1.4.ASC.a > dspusers

        User Id       level
      SuperUser       0
        Teacher       1
```

Password Maintenance

Password maintenance for the MGX 8850 and the MGX 8220 is covered in this section.

MGX 8850 Password Maintenance

The **passwd** command changes passwords on the MGX 8850 switch. Unlike most MGX commands, the **passwd** command provides prompting. The following example changes the current user's password to Ciliebd:

```
passwd Ciliebd Ciliebd
```

Passwords can contain any keyboard characters (but no control characters) and must be 6 to 15 characters in length.

MGX 8220 Password Maintenance

The **cnfpwd** command is used to modify your user password on the MGX 8220 concentrator. All new user IDs are automatically assigned the password newuser when they are added to the MGX 8220 concentrator. During the first login, the MGX 8220 concentrator prompts you to change the password from the default to a new, secure password. The **cnfpwd** command, like the MGX 8850 **passwd** command, provides prompting. Neither the old password nor the new password is displayed onscreen. To display your password or the password of a user with a lower privilege level, use the **dsppwd** command.

The command syntax is **cnfpwd** old-password new-password new-password.

For example, the following command changes the password from newuser to cimild:

```
cnfpwd newuser cimild cimild
```

MGX 8220 passwords can contain any keyboard characters (but no control characters) and must be 6 to 15 characters in length. The password can be displayed using the **dsppwd** command, as shown in Example 16-8.

Example 16-8 *dsppwd* *Command*

```
AXISNAME.1.4.ASC.a > dsppwd Teacher

The password for Teacher is newuser


This screen will self-destruct in ten seconds .........
```

cnfname

The **cnfname** command, shown in Example 16-9, specifies the name by which a feeder
node is known by the routing node to which it is attached. Node names are case sensitive.
Duplicate shelf names are not allowed on the same routing node.

Example 16-9 *cnfname* *Command*

```
AXISNAME.1.4.ASC.a > cnfname
cnfname "<node name>"
  Name = up to 8 chars

AXISNAME.1.4.ASC.a > cnfname far5mgx1

far5mgx1.1.4.ASC.a >
```

dspcds

The **dspcds** command, shown in Example 16-10, provides summary information on the
status of all the cards installed in the MGX platform. The command is very useful to learn
what kinds of cards are installed in your shelf and to determine their status.

Example 16-10 *dspcds* *Command*

```
far5pop1.1.7.PXM.a > dspcds

    Slot  CardState    CardType    CardAlarm  Redundancy
    ----  -----------  --------    ---------  -----------
    1.1   Active       CESM-8T1    Clear
    1.2   Empty                    Clear
    1.3   Active       AUSMB-8T1   Clear
    1.4   Empty                    Clear
    1.5   Empty                    Clear
    1.6   Empty                    Clear
    1.7   Active       PXM1-T3E3   Clear
    1.8   Empty                    Clear
    1.9   Active       RPM         Clear
    1.10  Empty                    Clear
    1.11  Standby      FRSM-8T1    Clear
    1.12  Empty                    Clear
    1.13  Active       FRSM-8T1    Clear
    1.14  Empty                    Clear
    1.15  Active       SRM-3T3     Clear
```

Example 16-10 *dspcds Command (Continued)*

```
    1.16  Empty                     Clear
    1.17  Empty                     Clear
    1.18  Empty                     Clear
    1.19  Empty                     Clear

Type <CR> to continue, Q<CR> to stop:
Slot  CardState   CardType      CardAlarm  Redundancy
----  ----------  --------      ---------  ----------
    1.20  Empty                     Clear
    1.21  Empty                     Clear
    1.22  Empty                     Clear
    1.25  Empty                     Clear
    1.26  Empty                     Clear
    1.27  Empty                     Clear
    1.28  Empty                     Clear
    1.29  Empty                     Clear
    1.30  Empty                     Clear
    1.31  Empty                     Clear
    1.32  Empty                     Clear

    NumOfValidEntries:     32
    NodeName:              far5pop1
    Date:                  07/04/1999
    Time:                  18:01:59
    TimeZone:              GMT
    TimeZoneGMTOff:        0
    StatsMasterIpAddress: 0.0.0.0

Type <CR> to continue, Q<CR> to stop:

    shelfIntegratedAlarm: Clear
    BkplnSerialNum:        12345
    BkplnType:             2
    BkplnFabNumber:        28-1234-01
    BkplnHwRev:            80

far5pop1.1.7.PXM.a >
```

The **dspcds** command screen provides the following information:

- Card number
- Card status (active, failed, or standby, or a mismatch between front and back cards)
- Card type
- Card alarm status (minor or major)
- Redundancy status

The second part of the **dspcds** command screen provides information on higher-numbered card slots (MGX 8850) and the following shelf-level information:

- Node name
- Date
- Time
- Time zone
- Time zone GMT offset
- Statistics master IP address
- The statistics manager IP address of the StrataView Plus Statistics Master, which is the station that is responsible for enabling statistics collection on the shelf

The third part of the **dspcds** command screen includes the following information:

- Shelf integrated alarm.
- Highest level of alarm currently on the shelf. The alarm status is reported to the attached BPX switch and the WAN Manager station.
- Backplane-specific information, such as serial and fabrication numbers.

dspcd

The **dspcd** command provides detailed information on a particular card module. PXM (shown in Example 16-11) and SRM cards are displayed from the appropriate PXM on the MGX 8850 switch. ASC (shown in Example 16-12), BNM (shown in Example 16-13), and SRM cards are displayed from the appropriate ASC on the MGX 8220 concentrator. All other cards can be displayed only when logged in to that card. (Use the **cc** command to move from one card to another.) The **dspcd** output from the **dspcd** command for the FRSM is shown in Example 16-14.

The card information provided depends on the card type and may include the following:

- Slot number
- State (active, standby, failed, or mismatch).
- Type
- Serial number
- Hardware revision
- Firmware revision
- Reset reason (last reset cause)
- LM type (line module type)
- LM state (line module state)
- Fabrication number

Example 16-11 *dspcd Command—PXM*

```
far5pop1.1.7.PXM.a > dspcd

    ModuleSlotNumber:         7
    FunctionModuleState:      Active
    FunctionModuleType:       PXM1-T3E3
    FunctionModuleSerialNum:  SBK0307001U
    FunctionModuleHWRev:      17
    FunctionModuleFWRev:      1.1.01
    FunctionModuleResetReason: Reset From Shell
    LineModuleType:           PXM-UI
    LineModuleState:          Present
    SecondaryLineModuleType:  LM-BNC-2T3
    SecondaryLineModuleState: Present
    mibVersionNumber:         0.0.00
    configChangeTypeBitMap:   No changes
    cardIntegratedAlarm:      Clear
    cardMajorAlarmBitMap:     Clear
    cardMinorAlarmBitMap:     Clear

far5pop1.1.7.PXM.a >
```

Example 16-12 *dspcd Command—ASC*

```
far5mgx1.1.4.ASC.a > dspcd


    ModuleSlotNumber:         4
    FunctionModuleState:      Active
    FunctionModuleType:       ASC
    FunctionModuleSerialNum:  835137
    FunctionModuleHWRev:      bd
    FunctionModuleFWRev:      5.0.00
    FunctionModuleResetReason: Power reset
    LineModuleType:           LM-ASC
    LineModuleState:          Present
    mibVersionNumber:         7
    configChangeTypeBitMap:   No changes
    cardIntegratedAlarm:      Clear
    fab number:               28-2217-01   ASC2

far5mgx1.1.4.ASC.a >
```

Example 16-13 *dspcd Command—BNM*

```
far5mgx1.1.4.ASC.a > dspcd 2

    ModuleSlotNumber:         2
    FunctionModuleState:      Active
    FunctionModuleType:       BNM-T3
    FunctionModuleSerialNum:  207737
    FunctionModuleHWRev:      ak
```

continues

Example 16-13 *dspcd Command—BNM (Continued)*

```
    FunctionModuleFWRev:       5.0.00
    FunctionModuleResetReason: Power reset
    LineModuleType:            LM-BNM-T3E3-B
    LineModuleState:           Present
    mibVersionNumber:          0
    configChangeTypeBitMap:    No changes
    cardIntegratedAlarm:       Major
    cardMajorAlarmBitMap:      Line Alarm
    cardMinorAlarmBitMap:      ASM Physical Alarm
                               Line Statistical Alarm
    fab number:                214682-0

far5mgx1.1.4.ASC.a >
```

Example 16-14 *dspcd Command—FRSM*

```
far2pop1.1.4.VHS2T3.a > dspcd


    ModuleSlotNumber:          4
    FunctionModuleState:       Active
    FunctionModuleType:        FRSM-2T3
    FunctionModuleSerialNum:   SBK0321000Z
    FunctionModuleHWRev:       ex
    FunctionModuleFWRev:       10.0.02
    FunctionModuleResetReason: Reset by ASC from PIO
    LineModuleType:            LM-BNC-2T3
    LineModuleState:           Present
    mibVersionNumber:          21
    configChangeTypeBitMap:    CardCnfChng, LineCnfChng

Type <CR> to continue, Q<CR> to stop:

Front Card Info

    pcb part no-(800 level):   800-02911-03
    pcb part no-(73 level):    73-02665-03
    pcb revision (800 level):  A0
    fab par no-(28 level):     28-02325-03
    pcb serial no:             SBK0321000Z
    clei code:                 BAI9BD0AAA
    manufacturing eng:         0x306D
    rma test history1:         0x0
    rma test history2:         0x0
    rma history:               0x0
    platform features:         0x0
    self test result:          0x0

Type <CR> to continue, Q<CR> to stop:

Back Card Info
```

Example 16-14 *dspcd Command—FRSM (Continued)*

```
pcb part no-(800 level):     800-04057-02
pcb part no-(73 level):      73-03340-02
pcb revision (800 level):    A0
fab par no-(28 level):       28-02678-02
pcb serial no:               SBK03210067
clei code:                   BAI9A6NAAA
manufacturing eng:           0x10A4
rma test history1:           ??
rma test history2:           ??
rma history:                 ??

far2pop1.1.4.VHS2T3.a >
```

cnftime and cnfdate

Example 16-15 shows the **cnftime** and **cnfdate** commands. Notice that the time is entered in 24-hour clock format (military time), and the date is entered in the U.S. month-first format.

Example 16-15 *cnftime and cnfdate Commands*

```
far5mgx1.1.4.ASC.a > cnftime
cnftime "hh:mm:ss"
  Time = hh:mm:ss

far5mgx1.1.4.ASC.a > cnftime 11:32:00

far5mgx1.1.4.ASC.a > cnfdate
cnfdate "mm/dd/yyyy"
  Date = mm/dd/yyyy

far5mgx1.1.4.ASC.a > cnfdate 07/04/99
```

xdsplns and xdspln

The **xdsplns** command, shown in Example 16-16, shows the configuration of the maintenance and control ports on the MGX 8220 concentrator. The control port is port number 1, and the maintenance port is port number 2.

Example 16-16 *xdsplns and xdspln Commands*

```
far5mgx1.1.4.ASC.a > xdsplns -rs232
  Port            Type           Enable    Baudrate
  ----    --------------------   --------  --------
  4.1     Control RS232 Port     Enabled   19200
  4.2     Maintenance RS232 Port Enabled   9600

SerialPortNumOfValidEntries: 2
```

continues

Example 16-16 *xdsplns and xdspln Commands (Continued)*

```
far5mgx1.1.4.ASC.a > xdspln -rs232 1
  Port              Type          Enable    Baudrate
  ----  ----------------------    --------  --------
  4.1   Control RS232 Port        Enabled    19200

 SerialPortNumOfValidEntries: 2

far5mgx1.1.4.ASC.a > xdspln -rs232 2

  Port              Type          Enable    Baudrate
  ----  ----------------------    --------  --------
  4.2   Maintenance RS232 Port    Enabled     9600

 SerialPortNumOfValidEntries: 2
```

The separate **xdspln** command (also shown in Example 16-16) can be used to display the configuration of the BNM and SRM broadband lines.

One of the four required delineators in Table 16-2 must be used with the **xdspln** command. Table 16-2 lists the extended line display delineators and all required parameters.

Table 16-2 *xdspln Delineators*

xdspln delineator	Description
–rs232	Displays the control or maintenance ports
–ds3	Displays the BNM DS-3 (T3 or E3 lines) line characteristics
–plcp	Displays the BNM physical-layer convergence procedure (PLCP) line characteristics
–srmds3	Displays the SRE DS-3 line characteristics

In addition to the delineator, the line number should be entered as the last parameter for the **xdspln** command:

- **1**—control port
- **2**—maintenance port

xcnfln

The **xcnfln** command can be used to modify the rate of the maintenance and control ports on the MGX 8220 concentrator. The command syntax for the **xcnfln** command is:

```
xcnfln -rs232 port-number -e enabled -b rate
```

The parameters for **xcnfln** are shown in Table 16-3.

Table 16-3   *xcnfln Parameters*

Parameter	Description
–rs232	Used to modify the control or maintenance ports on the MGX 8220. The –rs232 must then be followed by the port number.
port-number	The serial port number. (1 = control port, 2 = maintenance port.)
–e	Following by one of the enabled parameters.
enabled	1 = disable, 2 = enable.
–b	Used to identify the baud rate, which follows the **–b**.
rate	The port baud rate is 2400, 9600, or 19200.

dspifip

The **dspifip** command, shown in Example 16-17, provides the following IP configuration information for the three IP interfaces available on the MGX platform:

- Ethernet
- Control port (SLIP)
- Control port on the PXM-UI and LM-ASC
- ATM (inband access from the BPX network)

Example 16-17 *dspifip Command*

```
far5mgx1.1.4.ASC.a > dspifip

    IPAddress      Interface      NetMask           BroadcastAddress
 ---------------   ---------    ---------------    ----------------
  172.30.241.44    Ethernet     255.255.255.128    090.255.255.255
     10.10.4.44    ATM          255.255.255.0           N/A

far5mgx1.1.4.ASC.a >
```

If an interface has not been configured, it will not be displayed on the **dspifip** screen.

cnfifip

The **cnfifip** command is used to modify the IP configuration for MGX nodes. The **cnfifip** parameters are shown in Table 16-4.

Table 16-4 *cnfifip Parameters*

Parameter	Description
–if	This delineator is used to identify the interface that is modified. 26 = Ethernet, 28 = SLIP, 37 = ATM.
–ip	The IP address.
–msk	The netmask.
–bc	The broadcast address.

dspshelfalm

The **dspshelfalm** command, shown in Example 16-18, displays the environmental shelf alarms for the MGX node. Alarms are provided for cabinet temperature, AC and DC power voltages, and cooling fan speed.

Example 16-18 *dspshelfalm Command*

```
far5mgx1.1.4.ASC.a > dspshelfalm

 Alarm     Type     Unit Thresh Severity Measurable Val  State
 -----  -----------  ---- ------ -------- ---------- ---  -----
    1   Temperature   1   50     Minor     Yes        25  Normal
    2   Power Supply  1   0      Minor     No         0   Normal
    3   Power Supply  2   0      Minor     No         0   Failed Power Supply due
                                                          to AC Power Failure
    4   DC Level      1   42-54  Minor     Yes        48  Normal
    5   DC Level      2   42-54  Minor     Yes        0   Below normal
    6   Fan Unit      1   2000   Minor     Yes        3099 Normal
    7   Fan Unit      2   2000   Minor     Yes        3041 Normal
    8   Fan Unit      3   2000   Minor     Yes        3068 Normal
    9   Fan Unit      4   2000   Minor     Yes        3084 Normal
   10   Fan Unit      5   2000   Minor     Yes        3133 Normal
   11   Fan Unit      6   2000   Minor     Yes        3065 Normal

 ASMNumOfValidEntries: 11
 ASMShelfAlarmState:    2

far5mgx1.1.4.ASC.a >
```

Information displayed by the **dspshelfalm** command includes the following:

- **Alarm number**—The index number corresponding to a physical component.
- **Type**—The indication of whether the alarm relates to cabinet temperature, AC voltage status, DC voltage status, or fan performance.
- **Threshold**—The system default threshold beyond which an alarm will be generated.
- **Severity**—The level of alarm that will be reported to the ASC or PXM; this is always Minor for environmental alarms.

- **Measurable**—An indication of whether the physical element can be sensed by the PXM or BNM.

- **Value**—The current measured value; in this example, the cabinet temperature is 40° Celsius.

- **State**—An indication of whether the alarm has been asserted. Normal means that no alarm has been asserted. If an alarm exists, State shows "Above Normal" or "Below Normal." The word "Missing" in the State column means that the input is missing or ignored.

Summary

This chapter covered the necessary commands for initial configuration of MGX nodes using the command-line interface. CLI syntax, logging in, and configuring the system date and time were covered. The commands **dspcd** and **dspcds** were introduced to display information on the MGX cards. In addition, several other MGX commands were covered.

Review Questions

The following questions test your retention of the material presented in this chapter. You can find the answers to the Review Questions in Appendix A, "Answers to Review Questions."

1   Match the command-line access method in the table with its definition from the list that follows.

Command-Line Access Method	Definition
IP relay	
LAN port	
MGX 8850 control port	
MGX 8220 control port	

A. A SLIP port for Telnet access

B. A 15-pin AUI port connected to an Ethernet

C. The default CLI access using a VT100 terminal

D. A way to Telnet to a device inband through the BPX/IGX network

2 Which two of the following statements are true?

A. The Esc key aborts a command.

B. All commands have required and optional parameters.

C. Many commands comprise abbreviated verbs and nouns.

D. The MGX CLI prompts you for all required and optional parameters.

E. A command is complete when all required parameters have been defined with the appropriate values.

3 What is the purpose of the **Help** command?

A. To teach you how to configure an MGX device

B. To identify the definition and the syntax of a command

C. To list all commands supported by a card type and a user privilege level

D. To provide you with a detailed description of the use of each command

4 Match the command in the table with its primary function from the list that follows.

Command	Primary Function
cc	
bye	
dspcd	
dspcds	
dspifip	
cnfpwd	

A. Modifies your password on MGX 8220 and MGX 8850

B. Lists all cards on the shelf

C. Ends your CLI (and Telnet) session

D. Logs in to another card on the concentrator

E. Shows the status and the serial number of a card

F. Shows the IP addresses configured for the shelf

5 Mark each of the following statements as true or false.

   A. The **dspshelfalm** command shows trunk and line alarms.

   B. The abbreviation "DIS" means "display" on the MGX CLI.

   C. You can check the shelf date and the time by issuing the **cnfdate** and **cnftime** commands at the active ASC or PXM.

   D. A user ID with a privilege level of 4 can perform all the commands available to a user ID with a privilege level of 5.

CHAPTER 17

Adding MGX Nodes to the Network

This chapter introduces the procedure for creating an MGX network. It does so by presenting the MGX 8850 or 8220 concentrator as a feeder into an existing BPX network or in a standalone configuration.

This chapter includes the following sections:

- Integrated Tiered and Standalone Networks
- Adding a MGX Feeder
- Standalone Configuration
- Commands
- Summary
- Review Questions

Integrated Tiered and Standalone Networks

A MGX network comprises geographically dispersed MGX devices attached to an ATM backbone network with broadband ATM trunks. Most installations use the BPX wide-area switch for the backbone network, although many networks also include IGX switches in the backbone network. MGX 8220 concentrators and MGX 8850 switches cannot be directly connected to an IGX switch. In future releases, it will be possible to use the MGX 8850 node as a feeder to an IGX routing hub. Figure 17-1 shows a MGX network supported by BPX switches and a single Cisco WAN Manager station.

Figure 17-1 *Integrated Tiered Network*

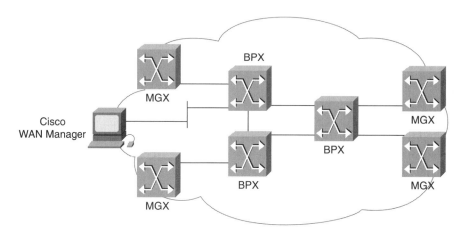

Figure 17-2 shows an MGX network supported by an independent public or private ATM
backbone network. An MGX concentrator installed in this type of network topology is
called a *standalone MGX concentrator.* Standalone concentrators require an ATM
backbone to transport cells between them.

Figure 17-2 *Standalone MGX Concentrator*

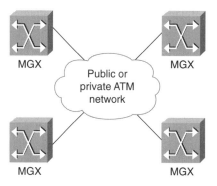

Because Cisco WAN Manager is available only in a tiered BPX/MGX topology, the only
network management for the network in Figure 17-2 would be the CLI accessed using the
control, maintenance, or LAN ports on the MGX concentrator. Integrated network
management, which involves the use of the Cisco WAN Manager, is available only in a
tiered BPX/MGX topology.

As covered in Chapter 15, "Installing MGX 8220 and MGX 8850 Nodes," the interface
between the MGX 8850 switch and the ATM backbone network is maintained by the

Processor Switch Module (PXM) card. The PXM interface type is defined by the daughter card installed on the PXM front card and the back card in use. The PXM supports T3, E3, OC-3/STM-1, or OC-12/STM-4 trunk interfaces.

When the MGX 8850 switch is configured as a feeder node (concentrator), only one of the trunks can be used. Additional PXM broadband interfaces can be used as an ATM User-Network Interface (UNI).

The interface between the MGX 8220 concentrator and the ATM backbone network is provided by a Broadband Network Module (BNM). The following three BNM card variations are available:

- T3
- E3
- OC-3/STM-1

A BPX network supports the MGX 8850 and 8220 concentrators in an integrated tiered network. In this case, the MGX device attaches to the BPX network via a trunk. A Broadband Switch Module (BXM) or a Broadband Network Interface (BNI) supports the trunk on the BPX switch. The BNI can be used only with the MGX 8220 concentrator.

The MGX platform can also be implemented as a generic ATM access device using an ATM backbone network, which could consist of BPX switches. When used only as an ATM access switch (feeder node) the MGX concentrator is not visible from the ATM network (BPX switches or otherwise) and behaves like any other ATM customer premises equipment (CPE) that is not managed or maintained with the ATM network. A BXM or an ATM Service Interface (ASI) supports the line on the BPX switch, which connects to the MGX feeder node.

Table 17-1 lists the different interfaces that can be used to attach the MGX device to an ATM backbone network.

Table 17-1 *ATM Network Interfaces*

Features	BPX BXM (Trunk)	BPX BNI	BPX BXM (Line)	BPX ASI	Other ATM Switch
MGX device supported	8850 or 8220 feeder	8220 feeder	8850	8850	8850
Line format	T3, E3, OC-3c, STM-1, OC-12c, STM-4	T3, E3	T3, E3, OC-3c, STM-1, OC-12c, STM-4	T3, E3, OC-3c, STM-1	T3, E3, OC-3c, STM-1, OC-12c, STM-4
Cell type	NNI	STI	UNI or NNI	UNI or NNI	UNI or NNI

During the configuration of the feeder, trunks verify that the cell header type is correctly configured for the type of feeder and the corresponding BPX trunk card.

The BPX BNI-155 does not support the UNI or NNI header and cannot be used to attach a MGX 8220 concentrator to the BPX network because the BNM-155 supports only the UNI and NNI cell header formats.

Both MGX platforms can be installed in a tiered network with BPX switches supporting the ATM backbone. The steps required to add a MGX feeder to a BPX network depend on the MGX type (8850 or 8220) that is used.

Adding a MGX Feeder

This chapter emphasizes the installation of the MGX nodes as feeder nodes for BPX switches. This section covers the necessary steps and commands to add both MGX 8850 and MGX 8220 feeders to the network.

Adding a MGX 8850 Feeder

The steps necessary to add and remove a feeder from the network are represented graphically in Figure 17-3. Although Figure 17-3 shows the removal process, the actual steps are beyond the scope of this book.

The steps to add a feeder follow:

Step 1   Attach the trunk interfaces at both ends. The appropriate cables and transmission equipment must be set up and attached to the trunk interfaces at both the MGX PXM trunk port and the BPX trunk port.

Step 2   Activate the line. The PXM line must be activated using the **addln** command.

Step 3   If needed, modify the PXM line. The PXM line can be changed using the **cnfatmln** (to change the ATM cell header type) and the **cnfln** commands.

Step 4   Create a logical port. A logical port must be created to support the trunk. PXM Release 1.1 firmware allows one port on each physical line; future releases allow multiple logical ports on each physical line (virtual trunking). Each logical port is limited to a percentage of the physical bandwidth and a range of virtual path identifier (VPI) values. A logical port is defined using the **addport** command.

Figure 17-3 *Adding an MGX 8850 Feeder*

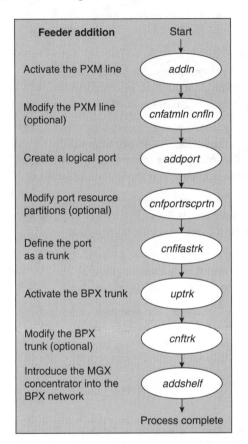
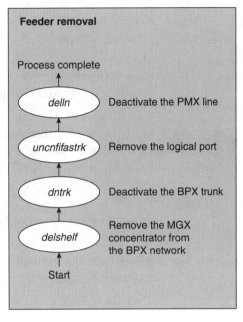

Step 5 Configure port resource partitions. A logical port's resources, such as bandwidth and addressing values, are divided among three routing controllers: Portable AutoRoute (PAR), Private Network-Network Interface (PNNI), and Multiprotocol Label Switching (MPLS).

These partitions determine how resources are allocated by the MGX switch as new connections are established.

Step 6 Define the port as a trunk. A PXM logical port can be used as a trunk or a line to end-user equipment (UNI). For network traffic to route over the port, it must be defined as a trunk. The **cnfifastrk** command is used to make a logical port a trunk. The MGX 8850 switch must be configured as a feeder node prior to installation, using the **cnfswfunc** command.

The next part of adding the feeder to the network entails logging into the BPX node.

Step 7 Activate the BPX trunk. The trunk on the BPX switch is activated using the **uptrk** command.

The **uptrk** command sends out the correct frame format and a signal, when configured properly. However, even after the **uptrk** command is issued, there are no intelligent communications between the two devices.

The **uptrk** command needs to be issued only from the BPX switch (BXM or BNI trunk card). The trunk on the MGX 8220 concentrator (BNM card) is already activated when the concentrator is powered up; the trunk on the MGX 8850 switch should be activated and configured as described previously in this section.

Step 8 Modify the BPX trunk. If necessary, the BPX trunk can be configured using the **cnftrk** command. In most cases, the default settings are used.

Step 9 Add the shelf. The MGX 8850 feeder node (shelf) is added to the BPX network with the **addshelf** command. At this time, intelligent communication is flowing between the BPX and MGX switches.

The trunk must be out of alarm before issuing the **addshelf** command, which can be issued only from the BPX switch. At this point, the BPX and MGX devices exchange node/shelf information, such as name, date, time, and alarm status.

Adding a MGX 8220 Feeder

The configuration of the MGX 8220 concentrator as a feeder is not required prior to activating the BPX trunk because the MGX 8220 concentrator is always a feeder node in a tiered network.

The addition and removal of an MGX 8220 feeder are represented graphically in Figure 17-4.

As shown in Figure 17-4, the steps necessary to add the MGX 8220 feeder are a subset of the MGX 8850. To add a shelf is to introduce it into the BPX network. When a shelf is added, intelligent communications, in the form of ATM Local Management Interface (LMI) messages encapsulated into cells, begin between the MGX concentrator and the attached BPX switch. MGX 8220 removal is also shown in Figure 17-4 for reference, but the process is not covered here.

Figure 17-4 *Adding MGX 8220 Feeder*

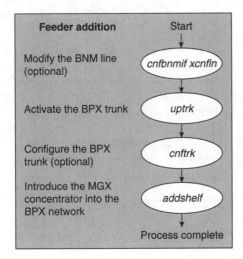
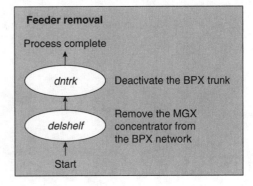

Standalone Configuration

Both MGX platforms can be installed as standalone devices using any type of switch (including the BPX switch) for the ATM backbone. The steps required to create a standalone MGX concentrator depend on the MGX type (8850 or 8220) that is used.

MGX 8850 Standalone Configuration

The steps listed to configure an MGX 8850 as a standalone unit are shown in Figure 17-5.

The MGX 8850 switch should be configured as a routing node prior to installation using the **cnfswfunc** command. The steps shown are a subset of those already covered for the MGX 8850 feeder configuration.

Figure 17-5 *MGX 8850 Standalone Configuration*

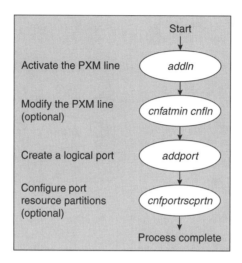

MGX 8220 Standalone Configuration

Figure 17-6 lists the steps necessary to configure the MGX 8220 for standalone configuration. The steps, like those of the MGX 8850 standalone, are a subset of those steps covered earlier for feeder configuration.

Figure 17-6 *MGX 8220 Standalone Configuration*

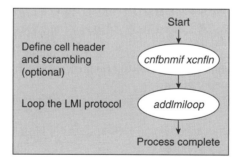

Commands

The commands shown in Table 17-2 are used for adding MGX nodes to the network. This section covers these commands.

Table 17-2 *MGX Network Configuration Commands*

Command	Description	Privilege	Card
dsplns	Display lines. Displays the summary information for the PXM or BNM line (trunk).	6	PXM AXM
dspln	Display line. Displays configuration information for the PXM or BNM line (trunk).	6	PXM AXM
addln	Add line. Activates a PXM line.	1	PXM
delln	Delete line. Deactivates a PXM line.	1	PXM
cnfln	Configure line. Modifies the PXM line characteristics.	1	ASC
xcnfln	Extended configuration line. Modifies the BNM line characteristics.	1	ASC
dspatmlncnf	Display ATM line configuration. Shows the ATM cell header in use on a line.	6	PXM
cnfatmin	Configure ATM line. Modifies the ATM cell header (UNI or NNI) on a line.	6	PXM
dspbnmif	Display BNM interface. Displays the cell header type on the BNM line (trunk): UNI, NNI, or STI.	6	ASC
cnfbnmif	Configure BNM interface. Modifies the cell header type on the BNM line (trunk).	6	ASC
dspports	Display port. Displays information for a specific logical port.	6	PXM
addport	Add port. Creates a logical port.	6	PXM
dspportrscprtn	Displays port resource partition.	6	PXM

continues

Table 17-2   *MGX Network Configuration Commands (Continued)*

Command	Description	Privilege	Card
dsptrks	Display trunks.	6	PXM
	Lists all the active network trunks.		
cnfswfunc	Configure software function.	1	PXM
	Defines whether the MGX 8850 node will operate as a routing or a feeder node.		
cnfifastrk	Configure interface as a trunk.	1	PXM
	Defines a logical port as a network trunk.		
uncnfifastrk	Unconfigure interface as trunk.	1	PXM
	Removes a logical port as a network trunk.		
addlmiloop	Add LMI loop.	0	ASC
	Creates a loop on the LMI protocol on an MGX 8220 concentrator so that it can be configured as a standalone device.		
dellmiloop	Delete LMI loop.	0	ASC
	Removes a loop on the LMI protocol.		

In addition to the commands covered in Table 17-2, the BPX network configuration commands shown in Figure 17-2 are used to configure the BPX node for connecting to a BPX. Table 17-3 summarizes these commands.

Table 17-3   *BPX Network Configuration Commands*

Command	Description	Privilege
dsptrks	Display trunks.	6
	Displays summary status information of all trunks on the BPX switch.	
dsptrkcnf	Display trunk configuration.	6
	Displays detailed BPX trunk configuration information.	
uptrk	Up trunk.	2
	Activates BPX trunk hardware and physical-layer characteristics.	
dntrk	Down trunk.	2
	Deactivates the PBX trunk hardware.	
cnftrk	Configure trunk.	1
	Modifies the BPX trunk configuration parameters.	

continues

Table 17-3   *BPX Network Configuration Commands (Continued)*

Command	Description	Privilege
addshelf	Add shelf.	2
	Introduces the MGX concentrator into the BPX network.	
delshelf	Delete shelf.	2
	Removes the MGX concentrator from the BPX network.	
dspnode	Display nodes.	6
	Displays summary status information of all feeder nodes (shelves) on the BPX switch.	

dsplns

The **dsplns** command provides summary configuration information on the BNM and PXM lines on an MGX feeder device. The information displayed on the **dsplns** command screen depends on the platform and the interface type used. Example 17-1 shows the two DS-3 (T3) lines on the PXM, which initially are both disabled.

Example 17-1 *dsplns Command*

```
far5pop1.1.7.PXM.a > dsplns ds3 7

 Line       Type        Status/Coding      Length       Criteria    AIScBitsCheck
 ----   --------------  ---------------  -------------  -----------  -------------
    1   dsx3CbitParity   Dis / dsx3B3ZS  lessThan225    fBits3Of8    Check C-bits
    2   dsx3CbitParity   Dis / dsx3B3ZS  lessThan225    fBits3Of8    Check C-bits
```

addln

Either of the two DS-3 lines may be activated as the feeder trunk using the **addln** command, shown in Example 17-2. The command syntax is **addln** *line-number,* where *line-number* is in the format *slot.port. slot* must always be 7, *port* is a value in the range 1–*n*, and *n* is the highest numbered port on the card.

Only one PXM line on the feeder implementation of an MGX 8850 node can be activated. With an OC-12/STM4 trunk, the only active port with any MGX 8850 switch implementation is port 1.

Example 17-2 *addln Command*

```
far5pop1.1.7.PXM.a > addln -ds3 7.1
```

dspln

The **dspln** command, shown in Example 17-3, provides configuration information on the BNM or PXM line on the MGX feeder device. The information on the **dspln** command output screen is very similar to the information shown with the **dsplns** command.

Example 17-3 *dspln Command*

```
far5pop1.1.7.PXM.a > dspln -ds3 7.1
  LineNum:               1
  LineType:              dsx3CbitParity
  LineCoding:            dsx3B3ZS
  LineLength:            lessThan225
  LineOOFCriteria:       fBits3Of8
  LineAIScBitsCheck:     Check C-bits
  LineLoopbackCommand:   NoLoop
  LineRcvFEACValidation: 4 out of 5 FEAC codes
  LineEnable:            Enabled
```

cnfln

The **cnfln** command is used to modify the characteristics of the lines on the MGX 8850 PXM card. Different characteristics can be set depending on the specified line type. On the MGX 8220 concentrator, the **xcnfln** command is used.

The **cnfln** command syntax for a DS-3 line is as follows:

```
cnfln -ds3 line number -lc line coding -len line length -oof line OOF criteria
     -cb line AIS C-bit check -lpb loop -rfeac FEAC validation
```

The following is a DS-3 line example:

```
cnfln -ds3 7.1 -cb 1
```

Table 17-4 summarizes the configuration parameters for the DS-3 lines.

Table 17-4 *cnfln Configuration Parameters—DS-3 Line*

Parameter	Description
line-number	The line number is the form *slot.port*. The PXM line is always on slot 7, regardless of the active PXM card slot number.
line-coding	This is the ones density enforcement used on the line. For a DS-3, the line coding is always 1, which indicates B3ZS.
line-length	This is the length of cable used for build-out purposes. 1 = less than 450 feet; 2 = more than 450 feet.

The **cnfln** command syntax for an E3 line is as follows:

```
cnfln -e3 line number -lc line coding -len line length -lpb loop
     -topt trail trace option -txtt transmit trail trace
     -txma transmit timing marker -rxma receive timing marker
     -txpt transmit payload type
```

The following is an E3 line example:

```
cnfln -e3 7.1 -len 2
```

Table 17-5 summarizes the configuration parameters for the E3 lines.

Table 17-5   *cnfln Configuration Parameters—E3 Line*

Parameter	Description
line-number	The line number is in the form *slot.port*. The PXM line is always on slot 7, regardless of the active PXM card number.
line-coding	This is the ones density enforcement used on the line. For an E3, the line coding is always 2, which indicates HDB3.
line-length	This is the length of cable used for line build-out purposes. 1 = less than 450 feet; 2 = more than 450 feet.
loop	This creates a loop on the line for testing purposes. 1 = no loop; 2 = remote loop; 3 = local loop; 4 = in-band local loop.

The **cnfln** command syntax for a SONET line is as follows:

```
cnfln -sonet line number -slt line type -lpb loop -smask HCS masking
    -sps payload scramble -sfs frame scramble
```

The following is a SONET line example:

```
cnfln -sonet -slt 3 -smask 2 -sfs 1
```

Table 17-6 summarizes the configuration parameters for the SONET lines.

Table 17-6   *cnfln Configuration Parameters—SONET Line*

Parameter	Description
line-number	The line number is in the form *slot.port*. The PXM line is always on slot 7, regardless of the active PXM card slot number.
line-type	This is the SONET line framing type. 1 = OC3c; 2 = STM-1; 3 = OC-12c; 4 = STM-4
loop	This creates a loop on the line for testing purposes. 1 = no loop; 2 = remote loop; 3 = local loop.
HCS-masking	HCS masking (add hexadecimal 55 to all HEC/HCS fields) facilitates cell delineation. Be sure to configure this parameter the same on both ends of the trunk; otherwise, the cell framing may fail. 1 = disable; 2 = enable.
payload-scramble	This enables or disables standard cell payload scrambling. Be sure to configure this parameter the same on both ends of the trunk; otherwise, the **addshelf** command will fail. 1 = disabled; 2 = enabled.
frame-scramble	This is the standard frame scramble for SONET. Be sure to configure this parameter the same on both ends of the trunk; otherwise, the trunk will fail. 1 = disabled; 2 = enabled.

dspatmlncnf

The **dspatmlncnf** command shows the cell header type used on a PXM line on the MGX 8850 switch. The cell header type can be changed using the **cnfatmln** command.

cnfatmln

The command **cnfatmln** is shown in Example 17-4. Cell header choices include UNI and NNI.

Example 17-4 *cnfatmln Command*

```
far5pop1.1.7.PXM.a > cnfatmln 1 3


far5pop1.1.7.PXM.a > dspatmlncnf 1

 lineNum    atmLineInterfaceFormat
--------------------------------
    1              NNI
```

The command syntax for **cnfatmln** is as follows:

```
cnfatmln line-number cell-type
```

line-number is 1–*n*, with *n* being the highest port on the PXM back card. *cell-type* is 2 (UNI) or 3 (NNI, the default).

dspports

The **dspports** command lists all logical ports on the MGX 8850 PXM card. The **dspport** command is used to display similar information on a single port. (These commands are used in many of the examples in this chapter.) Ports are added and removed with the **addport** and **delport** commands, respectively.

addport

The **addport** command, shown in Example 17-5, creates a new logical port on a physical line. When activating a trunk on the MGX 8850 switch, at least one logical port must be defined for each physical line. The port characteristics can be changed using the **cnfport** command.

Example 17-5 *addport Command*

```
far5pop1.1.7.PXM.a > addport 1 1 100 0 255

far5pop1.1.7.PXM.a > dspports
```

Example 17-5 *addport Command (Continued)*

```
Port  Status  Line  PctBw  minVpi  maxVpi
-----------------------------------------------------
   1    ON      1    100      0      255
```

The command syntax for the **addport** command is as follows:

```
addport port-number line-number percent-bandwidth minimum-VPI maximum-VPI
```

Table 17-7 describes parameter options for the addport command.

Table 17-7   *Parameter Options for the addport Command*

Parameter	Description
port-number	A unique number between 1 and 32 that identifies the logical port.
line-number	The physical line number that the logical port is associated with.
percent-bandwidth	The percentage of the physical line's bandwidth that the logical port can use.
minimum-VPI	The minimum value for the VPI on cells that use the port. If the line uses the UNI cell header, this value must be less than or equal to 255. If the line uses the NNI cell header, this value must be less than or equal to 4095.
maximum-VPI	The maximum value for the VPI on cells that use the port. This value must be greater than or equal to the minimum VPI.

cnfswfunc and cnfifastrk

Before configuring the interface as a feeder trunk, the option must be activated with the **cnfswfunc** command because the default configuration permits operation as a routing node or a standalone node.

The command syntax for **cnfswfunc** is as follows:

```
cnfswfunc [-vsvd yes|no] | [-ndtype fdr|routing]
```

–vsvd indicates that the virtual source/virtual destination (VSVD) for ATM ABR service is enabled or disabled. **–ndtype** defines whether the node is a routing or a feeder node. The defaults are VSVD disabled and routing, respectively. The command example in Example 17-6 shows the node type being modified to feeder operation.

Example 17-6 *cnfswfunc Command*

```
far5pop1.1.7.PXM.a > cnfswfunc -ndtype fdr
```

The **cnfifastrk** command allows specification of a logical interface on the PXM (created with the **addport** command) and operates as a feeder trunk.

The command syntax for **cnfifastrk** is as follows:

```
cnfifastrk slot.port iftype
```

slot.port is the slot and port number of the line to serve as the trunk. *iftype* is the type of trunk—**ftrk** for a feeder trunk, or **rtrk** for a routing trunk. The default is **rtrk**. Example 17-7 shows the **cnfifastrk** command.

Example 17-7 *cnfifastrk Command*

```
far5pop1.1.7.PXM.a > cnfifastrk 7.1 ftrk
```

dsplns

The **dsplns** command screen issued from the active ASC provides summary configuration information on the BNM line on an MGX feeder device. (The **dsplns** on the PXM is shown in Example 17-1.) The **dsplns** command from the active ASC is shown in Example 17-8.

The **dspln** command screen provides very similar information on the BNM line on the MGX feeder device, with some additional parameters displayed. The **dspln** command is also shown in Example 17-8.

Example 17-8 *dsplns and dspln Commands*

```
MGX1.1.3.ASC.a > dsplns


  Line        Type         Coding       Length         Criteria     AIScBitsCheck
  ----   -------------    --------    -------------   -----------   -------------
  1.1    dsx3CbitParity   dsx3B3ZS    LessThan450ft   3 out of 8    Check C-bits

MGX1.1.3.ASC.a > dspln 1
  LineNum:               1
  LineType:              dsx3CbitParity
  LineCoding:            dsx3B3ZS
  LineLength:            LessThan450ft
  LineOOFCriteria:       3 out of 8
  LineAIScBitsCheck:     Check C-bits
  LineLoopbackCommand:   NoLoop
  LineRcvFEACValidation: 4 out of 5 FEAC codes
```

xcnfln

The **xcnfln** command is used to modify the line characteristics of the trunk on the MGX 8220 BNM. The **xcnfln** command is most useful for turning payload scrambling on and off and for defining the line framing (OC-3c or STM-1) on a 155 Mbps SONET line. Different characteristics can be set depending on the specified line type.

The **xcnfln** command is identical to the **cnfln** command previously described for the MGX 8850 PXM line. All parameter options for the **cnfln** command listed in Tables 17-4 through 17-6 apply to the **xcnfln** command. The exception is the line number format, which for the **xcnfln** command is always 1 for the BNM line.

Although payload scrambling is configurable with the **xcnfln** command, payload scrambling is hard coded to be disabled on the BNM-T3 and BNM-E3. If the **xdspln** command is used, payload scrambling appears to be enabled.

Table 17-8 lists the physical-layer convergence procedure (PLCP) parameter options for the **xcnfln** command on the MGX 8220 concentrator.

Table 17-8   *xcnfln Parameters*

Parameter	Description
line-number	For the BNM, the line number is always 1.
PLCP-cell-framing	This is the type of cell framing used on the line. Ensure that the cell framing is the same on both ends; otherwise, the line will fail. 1 = PLCP; 2 = ATM (cell self-delineation using the HEC field).
PLCP-payload-scramble	This enables or disables standard cell payload scrambling. This parameter is not valid on BNM-T3 and BNM-E3 lines where scrambling is always disabled.

dspbnmif

The **dspbnmif** command, shown in Example 17-9, reports the cell header type in use on the BNM line (trunk). Use this command to learn the cell header type being transmitted on the trunk between the MGX concentrator and the attached ATM network.

To modify the cell header type to be STI, UNI, or NNI, use the **cnfbnmif** command (also shown in Example 17-9). Remember that the BNM-155 does not support the STI cell header format.

As shown in Example 17-9, changing the cell header on the BNM card causes the MGX 8220 switch to reset and disrupts all user services.

Example 17-9 *cnfbnmif and dspbnmif Commands*

```
far5mgx1.1.4.ASC.a > cnfbnmif
cnfbnmif "-if <interfaceFormat>"
  <interfaceFormat> where interfaceFormat = 1-3, 1: STI, 2: UNI, 3: NNI

far5mgx1.1.4.ASC.a > cnfbnmif -if 1
changing format to 1
LR33310 CPU O.K.
Reset Reason PIO = 4
**************  Power Reset    **************
 .
 .
 .

Far5mgx1.1.4.ASC.a > dspbnmif


  bnmLineInterfaceFormat:  bnmSti
```

uptrk

Example 17-10 shows the effect of issuing the **uptrk** command at a BPX node for the
feeder trunk terminating at slot 2, line 6.

Example 17-10 *uptrk Command*

```
 far5bpx1         TRM    Teacher:0        BPX 8600  9.1.03    July 4 1999  12:36 PST


 TRK      Type      Current Line Alarm Status           Other End
  2.1     T3        Clear - OK                           far3bpx1/2.2
  2.2     T3        Clear - OK                           far4bpx1/2.1
  2.6     T3        Clear - OK                           -
  4.1     OC3       Clear - OK                           far2bpx1/4.2




 Last Command: uptrk 2.6



 Next Command:

                                                                   MAJOR ALARM
```

The **dsptrks** command screen is also displayed if the **uptrk** or the **dntrk**, **addshelf**, or
delshelf commands are issued.

The possible trunk states are these:

- Not upped
- Upped
- Added

If the status is not upped, the trunk does not appear on the **dsptrks** command screen. An
upped status means that the trunk is monitored for physical-layer status but has no traffic
on the trunk. An upped trunk has a "Current Line Alarm Status" reported but no "Other
End" information.

If the trunk is added, the trunk is monitored for physical-layer status as well as other
possible errors and alarms (for example, dropped cells) that are associated with cell
transmission. An added trunk reports a destination switch name and trunk number at the
"Other End."

After being activated with the **uptrk** command, a trunk has a default configuration, which
may be modified using the **cnftrk** command.

dsptrnkcnf

The **dsptrkcnf** command, shown in Example 17-11, provides detailed configuration information about a trunk. Use this command to examine the current configuration of a trunk on either a BNI or a BXM card module.

The **dsptrkcnf** command screen is a template for any type of trunk in a Cisco WAN switched network (IPX, IGX, and BPX switches). Some of the parameters might not apply to all the trunks.

Example 17-11 *dsptrkcnf Command*

```
far5bpx1         TRM    Teacher:0      BPX 8600  9.1.03    July 4 1999  12:40 PST


TRK  2.6 Config    T3     [96000 cps]     BXM slot:      2
Transmit Rate:        96000             Line framing:        PLCP
Subrate data rate:    - -                 coding:           - -
Line DS-0 map:        - -               CRC:                - -
Statistical Reserve:  1000    cps         recv impedance:   - -
Idle code:            7F hex            cable type:         - -
Max Channels/Port:    256                       length:     0-225 ft.
Connection Channels:  256               Pass sync:          Yes
Traffic:    V,TS,NTS,FR,FST,CBR,VBR,ABR  Loop clock:        No
SVC Vpi Min:          0                 HCS Masking:        Yes
SVC Channels:         0                 Payload Scramble:   No
SVC Bandwidth:        0       cps       Frame Scramble:     - -
Restrict CC traffic:  No                Virtual Trunk Type: - -
Link type:            Terrestrial       Virtual Trunk VPI:  - -
Routing Cost:         10                Deroute delay time: 0 seconds


Last Command: dsptrkcnf 2.6


Next Command:
```

addshelf

The **addshelf** command, shown in Example 17-12, is issued on the BPX switch to add the ATM trunk link to the attached feeder node. The trunk must be free of major alarms at both ends before the **addshelf** command is issued.

Example 17-12 *addshelf Command*

```
far5bpx1        TRM    Teacher:0        BPX 8600  9.1.03    July 4 1999  12:45 PST


BPX 8600 Interface Shelf Information

Trunk     Name      Type         Part ICtrl Id    Alarm
 2.6      far5pop1  PAR            -    -          OK




Last Command: addshelf 2.6 x

Shelf has been added
Next Command:


                                                              MAJOR ALARM
```

The command syntax for **addshelf** is as follows:

addshelf *slot.port shelf-type*

shelf-type is the type of feeder node: i for IGX/AF, a for MGX 8220, or x for MGX 8850.

The **addshelf** command screen provides the following information:

- Trunk number
- Shelf name
- Shelf type, such as PAR (MGX 8850), AXIS (MGX 8220), or IPX (IGX) feeder node
- Alarm (the highest alarm on the MGX concentrator: clear, minor, major, unreachable, or OK)

dspnode

The **dspnode** command, shown in Example 17-13, provides the same information as the **addshelf** command, but for all feeder shelves added to the BPX switch. In this case, an MGX 8220 shelf (AXIS) was added previously to trunk 2.4 on this BPX node.

Example 17-13 *dspnode Command*

```
far5bpx1        TRM    Teacher:0        BPX 8600  9.1.03    July 4 1999  12:45 PST


BPX 8600 Interface Shelf Information

Trunk     Name      Type         Part ICtrl Id    Alarm
 2.4      far5mgx1  AXIS           -    -          MIN
 2.6      far5pop1  PAR            -    -          OK

```

Example 17-13 *dspnode Command (Continued)*

```
Last Command: dspnode


Next Command:

                                                              MAJOR ALARM
```

Summary

This chapter covered the necessary steps and commands to add MGX nodes into both tiered and standalone MGX networks. In addition to the commands, the parameters and common examples were given to show the configuration of MGX nodes.

Review Questions

The following questions test your retention of the material presented in this chapter. You can find the answers to the Review Questions in Appendix A, "Answers to Review Questions."

1 Which one of the following line formats cannot be used on the MGX 8850 PXM trunk?

A. T1

B. T3

C. E3

D. OC-3c

E. STM-1

F. STM-4

G. OC-12c

2 Which four of the following line formats can be used on the MGX 8220 BNM trunk?

A. T1

B. T3

C. E3

D. OC-3c

E. STM-1

F. STM-4

G. OC-12c

3 What is an MGX standalone concentrator?

A. A homogeneous MGX 8850 switch network

B. An MGX 8220 or 8850 device that is not attached to any other switch

C. An MGX 8850 switch that is a feeder in an MGX/BPX tiered network

D. An MGX 8220 or 8850 device used as a UNI feeder to any ATM backbone network

E. An MGX 8220 concentrator that is attached directly to another MGX 8220 concentrator

4 Which two of the following BPX trunk cards can you attach to an MGX 8220 concentrator and have integrated network management using the WAN Manager station?

A. BNI-T3

B. BNI-155

C. ASI-155

D. BXM-E3 in line mode

E. BXM-622 in trunk mode

F. BXM-155 in trunk mode

5 Which two of the following BPX trunk cards can you attach to an MGX 8850 concentrator and have integrated network management using the WAN Manager station?

A. BNI-T3

B. BNI-155

C. ASI-155

D. BXM-E3 in line mode

E. BXM-622 in trunk mode

F. BXM-155 in trunk mode

6 What type of cell formats can you use between the following card modules (STI, UNI, NNI, or none)?

Card Module	Cell Format
PXM-T3 to ASI-T3	
BNM-T3 to BNI-T3	
BNM-E3 to ASI-E3	
BNM-155 to BNI-155	
PXM-155 to BXM-155 in line mode	
BNM-155 to BXM-155 in trunk mode	

7 Which two of the following statements are true?

A. You must delete the shelf before downing the trunk on the BPX switch.

B. A mismatch in the payload scrambling configuration will cause the **addshelf** command to fail.

C. A mismatch in the payload scrambling configuration will cause the trunk to fail and report an LOS alarm.

D. The WAN Manager station can manage the MGX concentrator and any ATM backbone network to which it is attached.

8 Which four line characteristics can you modify with the **cnfln** command on the MGX 8850 switch?

A. Line loopbacks

B. Frame scrambling

C. Payload scrambling

D. The SONET framing

E. The ATM cell header type

F. The ones density enforcement method

9 Which line characteristic can you modify with the **cnfbnmif** command on the MGX 8220 concentrator?

A. Line loopbacks

B. Frame scrambling

C. Payload scrambling

D. The SONET framing

E. The ATM cell header type

F. The ones density enforcement method

CHAPTER 18

Network Alarms and Troubleshooting

This chapter covers troubleshooting steps needed to isolate and identify installation-related hardware problems and network-level alarms.

This chapter includes the following sections:

- Hardware Failures
- Alarms
- Network Alarm and Troubleshooting Commands
- Summary
- Review Questions

Alarms can be caused by either hardware failures or alarm conditions, such as a loss of signal on a line. Hardware failures are usually indicated by an alarm LED on the card.

Alarm conditions are notifications received on the network management station (NMS) console. Most hardware failures also cause an alarm notification on the NMS.

Hardware Failures

Hardware failures are reported for these major components:

- Power supplies or fans
- Front cards
- Back cards
- Backplanes

Backplanes fail very rarely. If a backplane fails, first indications suggest that there is a card failure. Upon troubleshooting, the problem can be isolated to the backplane by ensuring that all other components are functioning correctly.

Power Supply or Fan Failures

Figure 18-1 shows the flow chart for troubleshooting power supply or fan failures.

Figure 18-1 *Power Supply or Fan Failures*

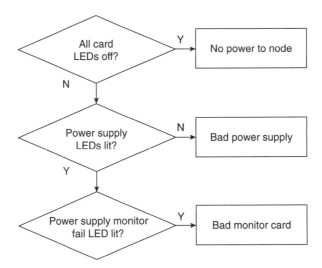

Complete the following steps to troubleshoot a possible fan or power supply failure:

Step 1 Check whether any card LEDs are lit. If there are no lit LEDs in the entire node, there is probably no power to the unit. Try the following solutions:

— Switch on the power switch.

— Check whether the breaker has been tripped.

— Verify that the power cord is plugged into the power receptacle and that the power receptacle is offering current.

— Replace the power supplies.

Step 2 Check whether the power supply Fail LED is lit.

If the Fail LED is lit, either a power supply or the power supply monitor card has failed. Replace each component as needed, and verify operation.

Step 3 Check whether the power supply monitor Fail LED is lit.

If the Fail LED is lit, try these solutions:

— Verify that all fans are rotating. If they are not, check the plugs for the fan assemblies. If the fans still do not rotate, replace the fan assemblies.

— Verify that the temperature sensor is working. Reconnect the wires if they have come loose. Replace the sensor, if necessary.

— If the fan assemblies and sensor are working, replace the power monitor card.

Front or Back Card Failures

Figure 18-2 shows the flow chart for troubleshooting front or back card failures.

Figure 18-2 *Front or Back Card Failures*

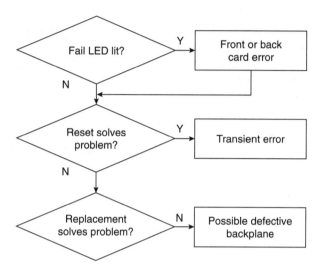

Complete the following steps to troubleshoot a possible front or back card failure:

Step 1   Use the **resetcd** *slot* **h** command to reset the card.

Step 2   If the **resetcd** command does not solve the problem, remove the card and carefully reinsert it.

Step 3   If the card cannot be successfully reset, replace the card.

Step 4   If the replacement card does not operate correctly, check for backplane failure.

More information can be determined about the nature of the card fault by using commands discussed later in this chapter.

Alarms

After login, the network alarm status is always displayed in the lower-right corner of the screen. The network alarm status reports the most severe alarm in the network. If one node is in major alarm and all others are in minor alarm, the network alarm status reports a major alarm. The **dspnw** and **dspnds** commands can be used to determine which nodes are in alarm.

The network alarm status reports whether the network is clear of alarms, whether there is a major or minor alarm, or whether a node in the network is unreachable. If a minor alarm is reported, then there are no major alarms in the network because the major alarm alert would override the minor report.

Major alarms always affect traffic, primarily because they often result in failed user connections. It is important to remember that a failed connection is frequently the result of another major alarm, such as a failed trunk, line, or card.

Major Alarms

When a network trunk experiences a condition that prevents traffic from being carried over that trunk, the trunk is declared failed and all connections routing over the trunk are rerouted, if possible. The **dsptrks** command reports the status of all trunks on a node. Examples of trunk failures include loss of signal (LOS), out of frame (OOF), or a communications failure. A communications failure occurs when a node does not receive acknowledgments to trunk keepalive messages from the neighbor node.

A line might also experience LOS or OOF conditions that cause it to fail. No capability exists to reroute connections that enter the network on a failed line, so all connections on the line fail and do not recover until the line failure is resolved. The **dsplns** command reports the states of the lines on the node.

A severe card failure on an active card causes a missing card alarm. A missing card is one that supports services (such as a BNI card with active trunks on it) that can no longer perform their functions. Most often, hardware failures cause cards to be in a missing state. Not all card failures cause a card to be declared missing; some self-test failures, failures on active cards with Y-cable redundancy, or failures on standby cards do not generate major alarms.

The **dspcds** or **dspcd** command shows the status of a card module.

If a connection fails for any reason, it generates a major alarm. The major alarm is declared at both terminating ends of the connection, but not on any intermediate nodes. The **dspcons** command lists all the connections on the node and the status of each connection. To list only the failed connections, the **dspcons** command with the **–fail** option should be used. The **dspcon** command can be used to determine the cause of a connection failure.

Unreachable Node

An unreachable node occurs as a result of a complete failure of control communications between a node or nodes and the rest of the network. This results in a partitioned network. An unreachable condition is a serious event and requires immediate action to remedy the situation. If the node is unreachable because of a local hardware or software failure, then efforts should be made to rectify the problem as soon as possible, usually with the assistance of the Cisco Terminal Access Controller (TAC). If the problem cannot be fixed quickly, the recommended short-term remedy is to delete the trunk(s) connecting the unreachable node(s) to the main network.

An unreachable node condition generally has a severe impact on the network because many operations that affect the network topology could have network-wide implications. In addition to the direct outages caused by the node failure, the failure might prohibit management and topology configuration, including adding or deleting trunks, modifying connection classes, and managing other nodes that might be managed using an IP relay through the failed node.

Minor Alarms

Minor alarms do not result in failed connections and do not necessarily affect traffic. However, a degraded trunk or line can create problems on a connection (usually from the end user's perspective), such as retransmissions or low throughput.

A port signaling failure occurs when the configured signaling protocol (LMI or ILMI) breaks down. Each protocol has configurable error threshold parameters that determine whether the protocol is communicating correctly. In general, the signaling protocol fails if responses are not received from the attached customer premises equipment (CPE) within specified time periods.

A degraded trunk or line can generate an alarm in the network. Statistical alarm thresholds determine the error rate for determining both major and minor alarms.

To see the errors on a trunk or line, use the **dsptrkerrs** or **dsplnerrs** commands, respectively. Connections are never rerouted due to a statistical alarm, even if it is a major alarm. However, often a high error rate on a trunk causes the communications to break down between the two nodes, which generates a communication failure.

On the BPX node, the interface between a card module and the backplane is monitored for slot errors. Like trunk and line errors, slot errors can generate major or minor alarms based on configured alarm thresholds. Use the **dspslotalms** command to see the alarm status of each card slot. The **dspsloterrs** command shows the error counters for each slot.

On the IGX node, environmental measurements are made by the System Clock Module (SCM) card module and can be displayed using the **dsppwr** command. Cabinet temperature is compared to the configured threshold to determine a minor alarm condition.

On the BPX node, environmental measurements are made by the Alarm/Status Monitor (ASM) card module and can be displayed using the **dspasm** command. Cabinet temperature, power supply voltages, and fan RPMs are all compared to configured thresholds to determine a minor alarm condition.

Environmental measurements on MGX nodes are made by the Processor Switch Module (PXM) or the Broadband Network Module (BNM) and can be displayed using the **dspshelfalm** command. Cabinet temperature, power supply voltages, and fan speeds are all compared to configured thresholds to determine a minor alarm condition.

IGX and BPX Alarms

IGX and BPX alarm types are shown in Figure 18-3.

Figure 18-3 *IGX and BPX Node Alarm Types*

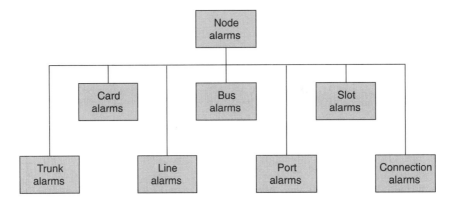

This chapter focuses on node, card, bus, slot (BPX), and trunk troubleshooting. The line, port, and connection troubleshooting issues and strategies are outside the scope of this book.

The easiest way to identify the cause of an alarm is to start at the network level and begin to isolate the problem by narrowing the elements until the problem is determined. Table 18-1 lists the commands to use when troubleshooting particular alarms on IGX and BPX nodes.

Table 18-1 *Useful Commands for Alarm Troubleshooting of IGX and BPX Nodes*

Step	Command	Function
Determine level and location of alarm	**dspnds**	Lists node alarm status.
	vt	Logs in to node with alarm.
Determine alarm type	**dspalms**	Lists alarm summary information.
	dsplog	Displays log.
Use for bus alarms	**dspbuses**	Displays buses.
	cnfbus t	Toggles between the active and standby busses.
	diagbus	Runs a bus diagnostic.

Table 18-1   *Useful Commands for Alarm Troubleshooting of IGX and BPX Nodes (Continued)*

Step	Command	Function
Use for slot alarms	**dspslotalms**	Determines which slot is in alarm.
	dspsloterrs	Lists slot errors.
Use for card failure	**dspcds**	Determines which card has failed.
	dspcd	Determines what type of failure occurred.
	dspcderrs	Displays card errors.
	clrcderrs	Clears card errors.
	resetcd f	Clears the card that has failed the test.
	resetcd h	Clears the card. Clears the card completely, if possible.
Use for trunk alarms	**dsptrks**	Determines which trunk is reporting an alarm.
	dsptrkerrs	Lists trunk errors.

MGX Alarms

MGX alarm types are shown in Figure 18-4.

Figure 18-4   *MGX Node Alarm Types*

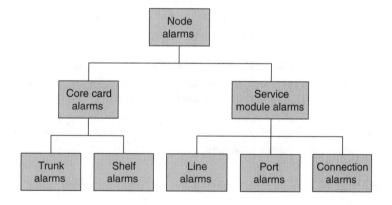

This chapter focuses on node and core card alarms. Service module alarms are outside the scope of this book.

Table 18-2 lists the steps to follow to determine the cause of an alarm on a MGX 8850 switch or a MGX 8220 concentrator.

Table 18-2 *Useful Commands for Alarm Troubleshooting of MGX Nodes*

Step	Command	Function
Determine level and location of alarm	**dspnds**	Lists node alarm status.
	vt	Logs in to node with alarm.
Determine alarm types	**dspalms**	Lists alarm summary information.
	dsplog	Displays log.
Use for bus alarms	**dspbuses**	Displays buses.
	cnfbus t	Toggles bus.
	diagbus	Runs bus diagnostic.
Use for slot alarms	**dspslotalms**	Determines which slot is in alarm.
	dspsloterrs	Lists slot errors.
Use for card failures	**dspcds**	Determines which card has failed.
	dspcd	Determines what type of failure occurred.
	dspcderrs	Displays card errors.
	clrcderrs	Clears card errors.
	resetcd f	Clears card alarm.
Use for trunk alarms	**dsptrks**	Determines which trunk is in alarm.
	dsptrkerrs	Lists trunk errors.

Automated Card Testing and Monitoring

The IGX and BPX cards are automatically tested periodically via background tests and self-tests to verify proper operation, as shown in Figure 18-5. A card might fail a test because it is too busy to process the test pattern, which is a low processing priority. Also, the node processor might be too busy to deal with the card's response to a background test or self-test command; this causes a spurious failure condition.

Figure 18-5 *Card Tests*

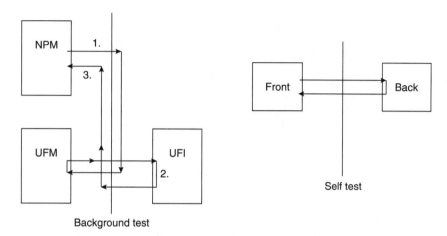

These tests can be enabled and disabled, and the frequency with which each is run can be managed with the **cnftstparm** command.

Background Tests

The node controller (NPM or BCC) initiates and executes background tests.

The background test sends a test pattern to the card being tested, and then waits for the test pattern to be echoed back by the card. If the packet or cell is not returned within a (configurable) time period, the card is marked as failed.

Self-Tests

Self-tests are also initiated by the controller but are executed by the card module front card. Self-tests are available for all IGX and BPX card modules.

When a card receives a self-test request, the card sends a test packet or cell to its back card. If the packet or cell is not returned, a failure is reported.

Alarm Reports

IGX and MGX nodes report alarms to other nodes in the network and to the Cisco WAN Manager station, as shown in Figure 18-6. Each switch posts the highest level of alarm (major, minor, clear, or unreachable) for every routing node in the network. Each node also reports the highest level of alarm from each of its active feeder shelves, although shelf alarms are not visible to other routing nodes.

Figure 18-6 *Reporting Alarms*

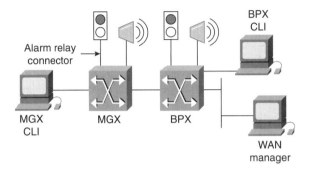

MGX devices report their alarm status to both the BPX backbone network and the Cisco WAN Manager station. The MGX alarm status identifies the most severe alarm on the shelf (major, minor, or clear). If you have access only to the MGX command line interface (CLI), then the MGX alarm status is shown on the last page of the **dspcds** command screen as the "shelf integrated alarm."

The **dspcds** command also reports the alarm status of each card installed in the shelf. Knowing which card is reporting an alarm is the first step in alarm isolation and identification.

Network Alarm and Troubleshooting Commands

Table 18-3 lists common IGX and BPX commands used to troubleshoot network problems. The table includes descriptions and the necessary user level to execute the command. Table 18-4 lists the MGX equivalents as well as the cards that support the command.

Table 18-3 *IGX and BPX Network Alarms and Troubleshooting Commands*

Command	Description	Privilege
dspalms	Display alarms	6
	Displays an alarm summary for the node	
dsplog	Display log	6
	Displays an alarm and an event log for the node	
clrlog	Clear log	5
	Clears entries from the alarm and event logs	
dspbuses	Display bus status	0
	Displays control bus status and, for the IGX, the cell bus utilization	

Table 18-3   *IGX and BPX Network Alarms and Troubleshooting Commands (Continued)*

Command	Description	Privilege
cnfbus	Configure control bus	0
	Selects the active control bus on the IGX	
diagbus	Diagnose bus	0
	Runs a diagnostic test of the control bus	
dspslotalms	Display slot alarm	6
	Displays the alarm summary for all card slots in the node	
dspsloterrs	Display slot errors	6
	Displays errors on all card slots on the node or for a particular card slot	
clrsloterrs	Clear slot errors	5
	Displays errors on all card slots on the node or for a particular card slot	
clrslotalm	Clear slot alarm	5
cnftrkalm	Configure trunk alarm	1
	Enables or disables alarm reporting on a trunk	
resetcd	Reset card	3
	Performs either a failure or a hardware reset on a card to clear a failure condition or to switch from an active to a standby card with Y-cable redundancy	
switchcc	Switch control card	3
	Switches from the active processor to the standby processor	

Table 18-4   *MGX Network Alarms and Troubleshooting Commands*

Command	Description	Privilege	Card
dspalms	Display line alarm	6	PXM, ASC, IMATM, CESM, FRSM, AUSM
	Displays summary alarm status on all lines		
dspalm	Display line alarm	6	PXM, ASC, IMATM, CESM, FRSM, AUSM
	Displays line alarm for details on a particular line		
clralm	Clear line alarm	5	PXM, ASC, IMATM, CESM, FRSM, AUSM
	Clears statistical alarms from a line		
dspalmcnt	Display line alarm count	6	PXM, ASC, IMATM, CESM, FRSM, AUSM
	Displays historical statistical line errors		

continues

Table 18-4 *MGX Network Alarms and Troubleshooting Commands (Continued)*

Command	Description	Privilege	Card
clralmcnt	Clear line alarm count	6	PXM, ASC
	Clears historical statistical line errors		
dsplog	Display log	6	PXM, ASC
	Displays alarm and event log for the shelf		
clrlog	Clear log	1	PXM, ASC
	Clears all events from the event log		

dspnds

The **dspnds** command, shown in Example 18-1, lists the current alarm status of all nodes in the network. For large networks, the **dspnds** command might be preferred over the **dspnw** command because it provides a list (in columns) of all nodes on a single screen.

Example 18-1 *dspnds Command*

```
far5bpx1        TN     Teacher:0      BPX 8600  9.1.03    July 16 1999 10:05 PST

NodeName Alarm
far1igx1
far1bpx1
far2igx1
far2bpx1 MAJOR
far3igx1 MAJOR
far3bpx1 MAJOR
far4igx1 MAJOR
far4bpx1 MAJOR
far5igx1 MAJOR
far5bpx1 MAJOR




Last Command: dspnds


Next Command:

                                                              MAJOR ALARM
```

Optional parameters can be used to provide supplemental information for each node:

- **+n** to display node numbers
- **–p** to display processor type (BCC, NPM)
- **–d** to display node type (IGX, BPX)

dspalms

The **dspalms** command, shown in Example 18-2, provides summary information on all alarms on the node. Use this command when you want to know the number and the type of alarms on a node. To learn which nodes are in alarm, use the **dspnw** or **dspnds** command.

Example 18-2 *dspalms Command*

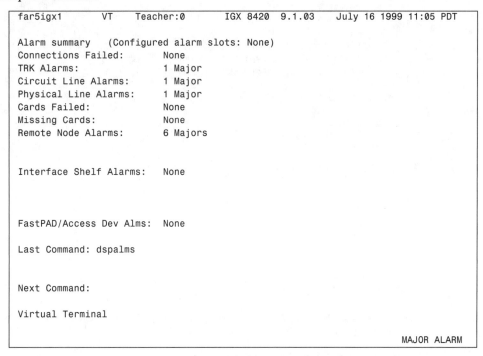

```
far5igx1       VT      Teacher:0        IGX 8420  9.1.03    July 16 1999 11:05 PDT

Alarm summary    (Configured alarm slots: None)
Connections Failed:        None
TRK Alarms:                1 Major
Circuit Line Alarms:       1 Major
Physical Line Alarms:      1 Major
Cards Failed:              None
Missing Cards:             None
Remote Node Alarms:        6 Majors


Interface Shelf Alarms:    None



FastPAD/Access Dev Alms:   None

Last Command: dspalms


Next Command:

Virtual Terminal

                                                              MAJOR ALARM
```

Alarms are listed by category. Additional categories that are not shown in Example 18-2 are the following:

- **Slots Alarmed**—Indicates slot alarms on the BPX node
- **Bus Failed**—Indicates a control bus failure
- **Bus Needs Diagnostics**—Indicates a control bus problem that is not severe enough to cause a bus failure

dsplog

The **dsplog** command, displayed in Example 18-3, provides a node event and an alarm log for the node. The log can hold up to 500 messages before overwriting the oldest events.

Example 18-3 *dsplog Command*

```
far2bpx1         TN    Teacher:0         BPX 8600  9.1.03    July 16 1999 11:24 PDT

Most recent log entries (most recent at top)
Class  Description                                         Date       Time
Info    T3-3 1 Inserted                                    07/16/99 11:21:00
Info    BNI-T3 1 Inserted                                  07/16/99 11:21:00
Info    T3-3 1 Removed                                     07/16/99 11:20:46
Info    BNI-T3 1 Removed                                   07/16/99 11:20:46
Info    User Teacher:0 logged in (Local)                   07/16/99 11:20:40
Info    Invalid Login Attempt via LAN Port (Local)         07/16/99 11:20:22
Info    User Teacher:0 logged out (Local)                  07/16/99 11:20:00
Info    T3-3 1 Inserted                                    07/16/99 11:19:30
Info    BNI-T3 1 Inserted                                  07/16/99 11:19:30
Info    T3-3 1 Removed                                     07/16/99 11:19:20
Info    BNI-T3 1 Removed                                   07/16/99 11:19:20
Info    T3-3 1 Inserted                                    07/16/99 11:19:20
Info    BNI-T3 1 Inserted                                  07/16/99 11:19:20

This Command: dsplog


Continue?

                                                               MAJOR ALARM
```

Use the **clrlog** command to clear the events in the event log.

Connection event logging, such as failures and reroutes, can be enabled or disabled with the **cnffunc** command. If connection events are not being reported, check that logging is enabled. In large networks, connection event logging can fill the event log very quickly.

Information reported in every event log includes:

- Event class—major, minor, info, clear
- Event description
- Date
- Time

dspbuses

On the IGX node, use the **dspbuses** command, shown in Example 18-4, to verify the active control bus (A or B) and to check the bandwidth utilization on the cell bus. The display does not dynamically receive updates and, therefore, is a snapshot.

On the BPX node, the **dspbuses** command indicates which BCC is the active processor.

Example 18-4 *dspbuses Command*

```
far2igx1          VT       Teacher:0        IGX 8420   9.1.03     July 16 1999 18:26 GMT

                                    Bus Info

Bus Bandwidth usage in Fastpackets/second      (Snapshot)

    Allocated = 82000        ( 8%)

    Available = 1086000      (92%)



-----------
Bus A: Active - OK
Bus B: Standby - OK


Last Command: dspbuses


Next Command:

Virtual Terminal

                                                                    MAJOR ALARM
```

cnfbus

The **cnfbus** command, shown in Example 18-5, is implemented only for the IGX node and is used to select the active system bus and to toggle between an active cell bus lane and the redundant standby lane. Use this command only when you suspect a problem with the active system bus.

Example 18-5 *cnfbus Command*

```
far2igx1          VT       Teacher:0        IGX 8420   9.1.03     July 16 1999 18:28 GMT

                                    Bus Info

Bus Bandwidth usage in Fastpackets/second      (Snapshot)

    Allocated = 80000        ( 7%)

    Available = 1088000      (93%)



-----------
Bus A: Standby - OK
Bus B: Active - OK
```

continues

Example 18-5 *cnfbus* *Command (Continued)*

```
Last Command: cnfbus b


Next Command:

Virtual Terminal

                                                              MAJOR ALARM
```

Command syntax for the **cnfbus** command is as follows:

```
cnfbus [a | b | t | l ]
```

The following are explanations of the parameters of this command:

- **a** makes bus A the active bus
- **b** makes bus B the active bus
- **t** toggles the current active and standby buses
- **l** toggles between the active cell bus lane and the redundant standby lane

diagbus

The **diagbus** command, shown in Example 18-6, runs detailed diagnostics to isolate bus problems to a failed card or bus. It is used when a minor alarm is indicated and the **dspalms** command screen indicates the message "Bus failed" or "Bus needs diagnostics." This command can be run only locally with a terminal connected directly to the control port, or remotely from a modem connection. It cannot be executed through a **vt** command or from a LAN or Telnet session.

Example 18-6 *diagbus* *Command*

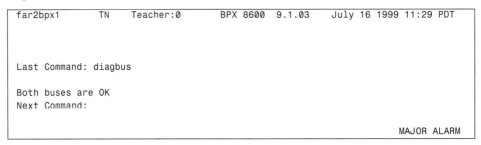

```
far2bpx1        TN      Teacher:0        BPX 8600  9.1.03    July 16 1999 11:29 PDT



Last Command: diagbus

Both buses are OK
Next Command:

                                                              MAJOR ALARM
```

This test can cause major disruption in the operation of the node, so it should not be performed except as a last resort. To fully isolate the failure might require manual removal of cards, including controller cards and so on.

If the test is successful and no problems are found, the system displays the message "Both buses are OK." Otherwise, the system displays various messages to the operator for additional steps to perform in isolating the problem. These messages depend on the results of the diagnostics testing.

Bus Failure Identification

If the test reports a bus failure, complete the following steps to identify the cause of a bus failure:

Step 1   Use the **dspbuses** command to locate the failed bus.

Step 2   Use the **diagbus** command to clear the failure.

Step 3   Use the **cnfbus t** command to toggle between the A and B buses and to ensure integrity.

Step 4   If the failure does not clear, use the **switchcc** command to determine whether the failure follows the NPM slot. Repeat Steps 2 and 3. If the bus failure does not follow the NPM slot, power down the node and replace the SCM. If the failure does follow the NPM slot, replace the SCM and NPM cards.

Step 5   Use the **switchcc** and **cnfbus t** commands to verify operation of the bus on the replacement cards.

The commands for configuring slot alarms and for displaying and clearing slot alarms and errors are applicable only to the BPX node.

dspslotalms

The **dspslotalms** command, shown in Example 18-7, shows the current alarm state (most severe) for each card slot. Use this command when the node is reporting a slot alarm to determine the slot number and alarm type.

Example 18-7 *dspslotalms Command*

```
far2bpx1          TN     SuperUser        BPX 8600   9.1.03     July 16 1999 11:19 PDT


Slot   Type       Current Slot Alarm Status
    1 BNI-T3      Clear - Slot OK
    2 BXM         Clear - Slot OK
    4 BXM         Clear - Slot OK
    8 BCC3        Clear - Slot OK
   14 ASI-T3      Clear - Slot OK
```

continues

Example 18-7 *dspslotalms Command (Continued)*

```
Last Command: dspslotalms


Next Command:
```

In general, slot alarms indicate one of the conditions shown in Table 18-5.

Table 18-5   *Slot Alarm Conditions Shown with* **dspslotalms**

Condition	Description
Bad card	Card cannot communicate with the processor or pass data across the backplane
Bad backplane	Backplane cannot pass data
Firmware/hardware/software mismatch	Incompatibility exists within the BPX among the various versions of firmware, hardware, or software

dsploterrs

The **dspsloterrs** command, shown in Example 18-8, on the BPX node provides a summary of historical statistical errors that have occurred on all card slots on the node.

Example 18-8 *dspsloterrs Command*

```
far2bpx1        TN     Teacher:0        BPX 8600  9.1.03    July 16 1999 11:21 PDT

                       Summary of Slot Errors

              Invld Poll  Poll              Tx    Rx          B-    Rx
       Stdby  Rx    A Bus B Bus Bad   BIP-  BIP-  SIU    Frame FIFO  Poll  CK-
       PRBS   Port  Par   Par   Grant 16    16    Phase  Par   Sync  Clk   192
  Slot Errs   Errs  Errs  Errs  Errs  Errs  Errs  Errs   Errs  Errs  Errs  Errs
  1    0      0     0     0     0     0     0     0      0     0     0     0
  2    0      0     0     0     0     0     0     0      1504  0     0     0
  4    0      0     0     0     0     0     0     0      1524  0     0     0
  8    0      0     0     0     0     0     0     0      0     0     0     0
  14   0      0     0     0     0     0     0     0      0     0     0     0



Last Command: dspsloterrs


Next Command:

                                                               MAJOR ALARM
```

These errors are related to card interface functions such as bus and BFrame transmit and receive errors. Use this command to see the number of errors of each type reported by the card slots. Possible errors reported by the **dsploterrs** command are shown in Table 18-6.

Table 18-6 *dsploterrs Errors*

Error	Description
Standby PRBS errors	Errors running a pseudorandom bit sequence test on the standby bus.
A bus parity errors	A bus parity errors.
B bus parity errors	Parity errors on the B polling bus (BCC in slot 8).
Bad grant errors	Arbiter did not issue a grant to send a cell to the crosspoint switch within a set time period.
Transmit BIP-16 errors	Transmit (to crosspoint switch) BFrame had a BIP 16 error on the cell header or payload.
Receive BIP-16 errors	Receive (from crosspoint switch) BFrame had a BIP 16 error on the cell header or payload.
SIU phase errors	Serial interface unit (SIU) on card could not synch up on the BFrame from the crosspoint switch.
BFrame parity errors	Error in the parity bits of the BFrame header.
Receive FIFO synchronization errors	Receive buffer could not synchronize to the Bframe.
Polling clock errors	Arbiter polling clock was not present.
CK-192 errors	Synchronization clock from BCC was not present.

The **dsploterrs** command, when used with an optional slot number parameter, provides detailed error statistics for a particular card slot and can be used to determine the frequency of slot errors, as shown in Example 18-9. Error counters are arranged in a similar fashion to those provided on the **dsptrkerrs** command screens.

Example 18-9 *dsploterrs slot Command*

```
far2bpx1       TN    Teacher:0       BPX 8600  9.1.03    July 16 1999 11:22 PDT

BXM 2          Status: Clear - Slot OK            Clrd: Date/Time Not Set
Type             Count ETS   Status    Type         Count ETS    Status
Stby PRBS Errs       0     0
Rx Invld Prt Errs    0     0
Poll Bus A Parity    0     0
Poll Bus B Parity    0     0
Bad Grant Errs       0     0
Tx BIP-16 Errs       0     0
Rx BIP-16 Errs       0     0
SIU Phase Errs       0     0
Bfrm. Par. Errs   1504  1345
```

continues

Example 18-9 *dspsloterrs slot Command (Continued)*

```
Rx FIFO Sync Errs      0      0
Poll Clk Errs          0      0
CK 192 Errs            0      0
BXM Errs               0      0


Last Command: dspsloterrs 2


Next Command:


                                              MAJOR ALARM
```

dspcds

The **dspcds** command, shown in Example 18-10, provides information on the status of each card in the IGX node.

Example 18-10 *dspcds Command*

```
far5igx1          VT      Teacher:0      IGX 8420   9.1.03     July 16 1999 11:05 PDT



      FrontCard  BackCard                    FrontCard  BackCard
      Type  Rev  Type      Rev  Status       Type  Rev  Type     Rev  Status
1     NPM   BWP                 Active     9  UVM   ABC  E1-2     AA   Standby
2     NPM   BTJ                 Standby   10  UVM   ABC  E1-2     AA   Standby
3     Empty universal backplane           11  HDM   CFF  RS449    AT   Standby
4     Empty                               12  LDM   CKB  232-8    AH   Standby-T
5     NTM   FDH  T1        P07  Active    13  UFMU  ADA  Empty         Standby
6     NTM   FDH  E1        BD   Active    14  UFM   AEF  E1D      AB   Standby
7     NTM   EKJ  SR        P11  Standby   15  UXM   AAD  E1-IMA   AA   Active
8     FTM   CH22 FRI-X21   AC   Mismatch  16  UXM   AAD  T3       AA   Active



Last Command: dspcds


Next Command:

Virtual Terminal

                                                            MAJOR ALARM
```

Possible card status reports are shown in Table 18-7.

Table 18-7   *Card Status Reports*

Status	Description
Active	Card in use. No failure.
Active-T	Card in use, with background test in progress.
Active-F	Card in use, but background test failed. This card generates a minor alarm. Use **resetcd slot f** command to clear the alarm.
Active-F-T	Card in use, with minor failures detected and background test in progress. This card generates a minor alarm. Use the **resetcd slot f** command to clear the alarm.
Standby	Card idle, with no failures.
Standby-T	Card idle, with self-test in progress.
Standby-F	Card idle, and self-test failure occurred. This card generates a minor alarm. Use the **resetcd slot f** command to clear the alarm.
Standby-F-T	Card idle, self-test failure occurred, and another self-test is in progress. This card generates a minor alarm. Use the **resetcd slot f** command to clear the alarm.
Failed	This card generates a major alarm if it was active, or a minor alarm if it was not active. Use the **resetcd slot h** command to attempt to clear the alarm. Often, the card needs to be replaced.
Down	Card was downed by the user.
Down-T	Card was downed, and background test is in progress.
Down-F	Card was downed, and background test failure occurred. This card generates a minor alarm. Use the **resetcd slot f** command to clear the alarm.
Down-F-T	Card was downed, background test failure occurred, and another background test is in progress. This card generates a minor alarm. Use the **resetcd slot f** command to clear the alarm.
Mismatch	Mismatch between front card and back card occurred.
Update	Processor card is being updated by active processor card.
Locked	Incompatible revision of old software is being maintained, if needed.
Dnlding	Downloading new system software from adjacent node or workstation.
Dnldr	Downloading software and configuration from active processor card.
Missing	An active card has been removed or has experienced a severe hardware failure. This card generates a major alarm. Use the **resetcd slot h** command to attempt to clear the alarm. Most likely, the card needs to be replaced.

resetcd

The **resetcd** command is used to clear an alarm or to reinitialize a card module in the node. Use this command when a card is failed or is missing to clear the alarm.

Command syntax for **resetcd** is as follows:

```
resetcd card-number [f | h]
```

The **f** is for failure reset, and the **h** is for hardware reset.

Use the **f**-required parameter to perform a failure reset that clears the alarm condition on a card that has experienced a self-test or a background test failure. For example, use this command on cards in the Active-F or Standby-F state. The failure reset does not disrupt service on the card.

Use the **h**-required parameter to perform a hardware reset on a card module. Use this option when a card is in a failed or missing state. This command briefly disrupts service on the card module. The hardware reset is also used to cause a switchover between a Y-cabled redundant pair of cards.

Keep in mind that using the **resetcd** command on the active NPM or BCC in a node resets the node, causing a complete node disruption during the time the node is resetting. To switch to the standby processor, use the **switchcc** command.

Complete the following steps to use the **resetcd** command to resolve a card failure:

Step 1 Use the **resetcd slot f** command to clear the failure report.

Step 2 If the failure happens again, use the **resetcd slot h** command to reset the card hardware.

Step 3 If the failure happens again, move the card set to another slot in the node.

Step 4 If the card fails again, the card is damaged. Replace it with an identical card.

dspcderrs

The **dspcderrs** command, shown in Example 18-11, displays a node-level summary or detailed card failure information resulting from diagnostics testing (background tests and self-tests).

If no card is specified, a summary is displayed indicating which slots have failures recorded. The command displays the results of the self-tests and background tests, as well as the total hardware errors.

Example 18-11 *dspcderrs Command*

```
far4igx1        VT      Teacher:0       IGX 8420  9.1.03    July 16 1999 18:15 GMT


  Slot    Failure     Slot    Failure
 Number   Records    Number   Records
 ------  --------    ------  --------
     0     None        12     None
     1     None        13       18
     2     None        14       21
     3     None        15        2
     4     None        16     None
     5     None
     6     None
     7     None
     8        1
     9     None
    10     None
    11     None


Last Command: dspcderrs


Next Command:

Virtual Terminal

                                                                  MAJOR ALARM
```

The **clrcderrs** command clears the history of all card failures on this node. After the command is entered, the system prompts to confirm clearing this data.

The **dspcderrs** [*slot*] command, shown in Example 18-12, provides a detailed history of all the test and hardware failures associated with this slot since the node was installed or since the last **clrcderrs** command. This display typically runs to multiple screens, with detailed information on each failure.

Example 18-12 *dspcderrs [slot] Command*

```
_far4igx1       VT      Teacher:0       IGX 8420  9.1.03    July 16 1999 18:17 GMT

UFM in Slot 14 : 482831 Rev AEE      Failures Cleared: Date/Time Not Set
----------------------------------- Records Cleared:  Date/Time Not Set
Self Test       Threshold Counter: 0         Threshold Limit: 300
Total Pass: 13384         Total Fail: 0            Total Abort: 0
First Pass: Date/Time Not Set        Last Pass: July 16 1999 18:11:14 GMT
First Fail:                          Last Fail:


Background Test    Threshold Counter: 0         Threshold Limit: 300
Total Pass: 13385         Total Fail: 21           Total Abort: 0
First Pass: Date/Time Not Set        Last Pass: July 16 1999 18:12:14 GMT
First Fail: May  25 1999 13:29:17 GMT  Last Fail: July 15 1999 08:03:13 GMT
```

continues

Example 18-12 *dspcderrs [slot] Command (Continued)*

```
        Hardware Error    Total Events: 0    Threshold Counter: 0
        First Event:                         Last Event:



        This Command: dspcderrs 14


        Continue?


        far4igx1        VT    Teacher:0      IGX 8420  9.1.03    July 16 1999 18:17 GMT

        UFM in Slot 14 : 482831 Rev AEE
        ---------------------------------
        Failure Type: FR Background Test
        Failure Time: July 15 1999 08:03:13 GMT

        Last Failure: Frame Received by UFM from NPM was Bad

        Last Test Frame Transmitted (DATA and CRC):
        60 61 62 63 64 65 66 67 68 69 6A 6B 6C 6D 6E 6F 70 9D E7

        Last Test Frame Received (DATA and CRC):
        60 61 62 63 64 65 66 67 68 69 6A 6B 6C 6D 6E 6F 70 6F 70



        This Command: dspcderrs 14


        Continue?

        Virtual Terminal

                                                              MAJOR ALARM
```

dsptrkerrs

The **dsptrkerrs** command, shown in Example 18-13, provides a summary of historical statistical errors that have occurred on all trunks on the node. Use this command when a trunk has a major or minor statistical alarm, or when you suspect that trunk errors are causing degraded service on a connection. Degraded service does not result in an alarm on the node, so you know about it only if an end user reports the problem. Displaying the trunk errors is not useful if the trunk is failed.

Example 18-13 *dsptrkerrs Command*

```
 far5igx1        VT      Teacher:0         IGX 8420   9.1.03     July 16 1999 11:09 PDT

 Total Statistical Errors
                                                            Tx Pkts
            Code    Rx Pkts Out of  Loss of Frame   CRC     /Cells  Packet  Packet
 PLN        Errors  Dropped Frames  Signal  BitErrs Errors  Dropped Errors  Oofs
   5          0       -       0       0       0       0        0       2       0
   6          -       -       0       0       0       0        0       4       3
  16.1        -       -       -       -       -       -        0       -       -
  16.2        -       -       -       -       -       -        0       -       -
  16.3        -       -       -       -       -       -        0       -       -




 Last Command: dsptrkerrs


 Next Command:

 Virtual Terminal


                                                                    MAJOR ALARM
```

The trunk counters can be cleared using the **clrtrkerrs** command.

Example 18-13 shows the screen display for an IGX node, which has a combination of narrowband and broadband trunks.

Table 18-8 shows IGX-specific trunk errors. Table 18-9 shows BPX-specific errors.

Table 18-8   *IGX Trunk Errors*

Error	Description
Code errors	Bipolar violations (BPVs) or coded mark inversion (CMI) line code violations (LCVs) occurred.
Rx packets dropped	Ingress packets were dropped due to queue overflow. ATM/ALM only.
Out of frames	Statistical out-of-frames occurred; short duration.
Loss of signal	A signal (digital or optical) is not being received.
Frame bit errors	Errors occurred in the framing bit.
CRC errors	Optional frame cyclic redundancy check (CRC) did not match the truck card's calculated CRD. Applicable to trunks with CRC checking enabled.
Tx packets dropped	Packets were dropped due to egress trunk queue overflow or packet expiration.

continues

Table 18-8 *IGX Trunk Errors (Continued)*

Error	Description
Packet errors	FastPacket header CRC did not match the trunk card's calculated CRC. Performed on receive packets only.
Packet out of frames	System was incapable of delineating packets on the trunk. Usually due to multiple packet errors.

Table 18-9 *BPX Trunk Errors*

Error	Description
Code errors	Bipolar or line-code violations occurred.
Rx cells dropped	Cells were received with errors dropped.
Out of frames	Statistical out-of-frames occurred. Short duration.
Loss of signal	Statistical loss of signal occurred. Short duration.
Frame bit errors	Errors occurred in the framing bit.
HCS errors	Cell header CRC did not match trunk card's calculated CRC. Performed on receive cells only.
Tx cell dropped	Cells were dropped due to egress trunk queue overflow or expiration. Cell errors occurred.
Cell OOFs	Out-of-frame occurred. The system was incapable of delineating cells on the trunk. Usually due to multiple packet errors.

The **dsptrkerrs** command, when used with an optional trunk number parameter, provides detailed error statistics for a trunk, as shown in Example 18-14.

Example 18-14 *dsptrkerrs [slot] Command*

```
far5igx1        VT      Teacher:0       IGX 8420  9.1.03    July 16 1999 11:09 PDT

TRK  6               Status:Clear - OK
                                                         Clrd: 05/11/99 00:04:28
Statistical Alarm Count ETS    Status   Integrated Alarm  Count ETS    Status
Out of Frms          0     0            Comm Fails            0     -
Loss of Sig          0     0            Loss of Sig (RED)     0     -
Frame BitErrs        0     0            AIS        (BLUE)     0     -
CRC Err              0     0            Out of Frms (RED)     0     -
Tx Voice Pkt Drp     0     0            Frm Err Rate(RED)     0     -
Tx TS Pkt Drp        0     0            Rmt OOF     (YEL)     0     -
Tx Non-TS Pkt Drp    0     0            Packet Oofs (RED)     0     -
Tx CC Pkt Drp        0     0            Rmt Alarms  (YEL)     1     -
Packet Err           4     4
Packet Oofs          3     3


                                        Last failure time: Date/Time Not Set


Last Command: dsptrkerrs 6
```

Example 18-14 *dsptrkerrs [slot] Command (Continued)*

```
Next Command:

Virtual Terminal

                                                        MAJOR ALARM
```

Example 18-14 shows a narrowband trunk on an IGX node. In the case of broadband trunks, there are two screens to this command, which might differ slightly depending on the type of trunk you are looking at. However, the overall structure of the display is the same for narrowband and broadband trunks.

The **dsptrkerrs** display screens are laid out in two sections. The left section or column lists statistical errors or errors that occur for a short duration. The right section or column lists physical errors, which result in trunk failure and occur for a longer period of time. The alarm time period is configurable per trunk using a SuperUser command.

Some types of errors, such as OOF and LOS, appear twice as statistical and physical errors.

Error counts and errored ten seconds (ETS) are provided for each type of statistical error. The ETS field indicates during how many 10-second periods the errors occurred, which helps you determine how the errors were distributed over time. For example, if 2000 HCS errors occurred in one 10-second period (ETS = 1), then it can be assumed that the errors were a single, short-lived event (a burst or hit on the trunk). However, if the 2000 HCS errors occurred in 500 different 10-second periods (ETS = 500), then you can assume that the errors were spread over a longer period of time (dribbling or ongoing) and probably need to be monitored.

Error counts that show an ETS might cause major or minor alarms if they exceed the configured alarm thresholds. Error counts that do not indicate an ETS are physical errors; in other words, the trunk experienced an error that caused the trunk to fail and traffic to be rerouted. These physical errors always generate major alarms.

clrtrkalm

The **clrtrkalm** command clears statistical alarms associated with either a physical or a virtual trunk. Because the statistical alarms associated with a trunk have associated integration times, they can keep a major or minor alarm active for some time after the cause has been rectified. The **clrtrkalm** command enables you to clear these alarms, allowing any new alarms to be quickly identified.

The **clrtrkalm** command can clear only alarms caused by the collection of statistical data. Alarms caused by a network failure cannot be cleared. For example, an alarm caused by a series of bipolar errors can be cleared, but an alarm caused by a card failure cannot.

cnftrkalm

The **cnftrkalm** command configures trunk alarm reporting. When trunks are upped and added to the network, alarm reporting automatically is enabled. The **cnftrkalm** command enables you to disable alarms on a trunk. Disabling alarms might be useful, for example, for trunks that are connected to the node but not yet in service, or if the node is experiencing occasional bursts of errors but is still operational.

dspnode

The **dspnode** command, shown in Example 18-15, lists the alarm status of all feeder nodes (shelves) attached to the BPX node.

Example 18-15 *dspnode Command*

```
far4bpx1         TN      Teacher:0       BPX 8600   9.1.03    July 16 1999 15:40 PST


                       BPX 8600 Interface Shelf Information

Trunk     Name       Type        Part ICtrl Id    Alarm
 2.4      far4mgx1   AXIS          -     -         MIN
 2.6      far4pop1   PAR           -     -         MAJ




Last Command: dspnode


Next Command:


                                                             MAJOR ALARM
```

The **dspnode** command screen provides the following information:

- **Trunk number**
- **Shelf name**
- **Shelf type**—PAR (MGX 8850), AXIS (MGX 8220), or IPX (IGX) feeder node
- **Alarm**—The highest alarm on the feeder node: clear, minor, major, or unreachable

dspcds

The **dspcds** command, shown in Example 18-16, shows the alarm status of each card module installed in the MGX 8850 switch or 8220 concentrator.

Example 18-16 *dspcds Command*

```
Slot  CardState   CardType     CardAlarm  Redundancy
----  ----------- --------     ---------- -----------
 1.1  Active      CESM-8T1     Major
 1.2  Empty                    Clear
 1.3  Active      AUSMB-8T1    Major
 1.4  Empty                    Clear
 1.5  Empty                    Clear
 1.6  Empty                    Clear
 1.7  Active      PXM1-T3E3    Clear
 1.8  Empty                    Clear
 1.9  Active      RPM          Clear
 1.10 Empty                    Clear
 1.11 Standby     FRSM-8T1     Clear
 1.12 Empty                    Clear
 1.13 Active      FRSM-8T1     Major
 1.14 Empty                    Clear
 1.15 Active      SRM-3T3      Major
 1.16 Empty                    Clear
 1.17 Empty                    Clear
 1.18 Empty                    Clear
 1.19 Empty                    Clear

Type <CR> to continue, Q<CR> to stop:
Type <CR> to continue, Q<CR> to stop:
 1.27 Empty                    Clear
 1.28 Empty                    Clear
 1.29 Empty                    Clear
 1.30 Empty                    Clear
 1.31 Empty                    Clear
 1.32 Empty                    Clear

     NumOfValidEntries:     32
     NodeName:              far4pop1
     Date:                  07/16/1999
     Time:                  15:43:46
     TimeZone:              PST
     TimeZoneGMTOff:        -8
     StatsMasterIpAddress:  0.0.0.0

Type <CR> to continue, Q<CR> to stop:

     shelfIntegratedAlarm: Major
     BkplnSerialNum:        12345
     BkplnType:             2
     BkplnFabNumber:        28-1234-01
     BkplnHwRev:            80

far4pop1.1.7.PXM.a >
```

The **dspcds** command also identifies the shelf-integrated alarm, which is sent to the BPX network and Cisco WAN Manager station as the MGX alarm status.

dspalmcnt

The **dspalmcnt** command lists statistical line alarm counters, as shown in Example 18-17.

Example 18-17 *dspalmcnt Command*

```
far4pop1.1.7.PXM.a > dsptrks
TRK        Current Alarm Status        Other End

7.1        CLEAR                       far4bpx1

far4pop1.1.7.PXM.a > dspalmcnt -ds3 7.1

  LineNum:              1
  LCVCurrent:           0
  ...
  SEFSLast24hrBucket:   0

Type <CR> to continue, Q<CR> to stop:
  AISSCurrent:          0
  AISSLast15minBucket:  0
  AISSLast24hrBucket:   0
  UASCurrent:           0
  UASLast15minBucket:   0
  UASLast24hrBucket:    0
  PercentEFS:           100
  RcvLOSCount:          2
  RcvOOFCount:          0
  RcvRAICount:          0
  ....

far4pop1.1.7.PXM.a >
```

Example 18-17 shows the alarm counters for a PXM T3 trunk interface. The counters listed using the **dspalmcnt** command fall into one of the following categories:

- **Current**—The current error count shows the number of errors since the previous 15-minute period ended.

- **Last 15-minute bucket**—The last 15-minute error count shows the number of errors for the previous 15-minute period.

- **Last 24-hour bucket**—The last 24-hour count shows the number of errors that occurred in the last 24 hours.

dspalm and dspalms

The **dspalm** command, shown in Example 18-18, shows the alarms on a specified line type and number. The **dspalms** command summarizes the alarm status of all lines on a card module.

Example 18-18 *dspalm Command*

```
far4pop1.1.7.PXM.a > dspalm -ds3 7.1
  LineNum:                  1
  LineAlarmState:           No Alarms
  LineStatisticalAlarmState: No Statistical Alarms
```

The **dspalmcnt** command can be used with the **dspalm** command to further isolate problems, as shown in Example 18-19. In Example 18-19, the alarm condition on the SRM-3T3 is caused by a loss of signal (LineAlarmState) and indicates that the condition has likely existed for at least 24 hours (UASLast24hrBucket).

Example 18-19 *dspalm and dspalmcnt Commands*

```
far4pop1.1.7.PXM.a > dspalm -ds3 15.1

  LineNum:                  1
  LineAlarmState:           XmtRAI,RcvLOS
  LineStatisticalAlarmState: UAS15minAlarm,UAS24hrAlarm

far4pop1.1.7.PXM.a > dspalmcnt -ds3 15.1
  LineNum:              1
  LCVCurrent:           0
  LCVLast15minBucket:   0

Type <CR> to continue, Q<CR> to stop:
  AISSCurrent:          0
  AISSLast15minBucket:  0
  AISSLast24hrBucket:   0
  UASCurrent:           196
  UASLast15minBucket:   900
  UASLast24hrBucket:    85500
  PercentEFS:           100
  RcvLOSCount:          1
  RcvOOFCount:          0
  RcvRAICount:          0
  RcvCCVCount:          0
  RcvFECount:           0
```

dspcds

In Example 18-20, the **dspcds** command on the ASC for this MGX 8220 indicates that there is a minor alarm associated with the active BNM-T3 in slot 3. (The **dspcds** output is very similar to the IGX **dspcds** output shown earlier.)

Example 18-20 *dspcds Command*

```
far4mgx1.1.3.ASC.a > dspcds

 Slot  CardState    CardType     CardAlarm  Redundancy
 ----  -----------  -----------  ---------  ------------------
 1.1   Active       BNM-T3       Minor
 1.2   Standby      BNM-T3
 1.3   Active       ASC
 1.4   Standby      ASC
 1.5   Standby      AUSM-8T1
 1.6   Active       CESM-8T1
 1.7   Standby      FRSM-8T1
 1.8   Standby      FRSM-8T1
 1.9   Empty
 1.10  Standby      IMA-8T1
 1.11  Empty
 1.12  Empty
 1.13  Empty
 1.14  Empty
 1.15  Active       SRM-3T3
 1.16  Standby      SRM-3T3

Type <CR> to continue, Q<CR> to stop:

NumOfValidEntries:     16
  NodeName:            far4mgx1
  Date:                07/16/1999
  Time:                15:59:03
  TimeZone:            PST
  TimeZoneGMTOff:      -8
  StatsMasterIpAddress: 0.0.0.0
  shelfIntegratedAlarm: Minor
  BkplnSerialNum:      763144
  BkplnType:           1
  BkplnFabNumber:      218412-00
  BkplnHwRev:          ba

Syntax : dspcds
```

At this point, to determine what alarm is on this BNM-T3, the **dspcd** *slot* and **dspalm** commands identify the source and type of alarm, as shown in Example 18-21.

Example 18-21 *dspcd slot and dspalm Commands*

```
far4mgx1.1.3.ASC.a > dspcd 1

  ModuleSlotNumber:          1
  FunctionModuleState:       Active
  FunctionModuleType:        BNM-T3
  FunctionModuleSerialNum:   768774
  FunctionModuleHWRev:       bd
  FunctionModuleFWRev:       5.0.00
```

Example 18-21 *dspcd slot and* **dspalm** *Commands (Continued)*

```
     FunctionModuleResetReason: Power reset
     LineModuleType:            LM-BNM-T3E3-D
     LineModuleState:           Present
     mibVersionNumber:          0
     configChangeTypeBitMap:    No changes
     cardIntegratedAlarm:       Minor
     cardMinorAlarmBitMap:      ASM Physical Alarm
                                Line Statistical Alarm
     fab number:                21791

far4mgx1.1.3.ASC.a > dspalm -ds3 1

     LineNum:                   1
     LineAlarmState:            No Alarms
     LineStatisticalAlarmState: Alarm(s) On --
                                    UAS24hrAlarm
```

dspalmcnt

The **dspalmcnt** command, shown in Example 18-22, lists statistical line alarm counters.
Example 18-22 shows the alarm counters for a BNM-T3 card module.

Example 18-22 *dspalmcnt Command*

```
far4mgx1.1.3.ASC.a > dspalmcnt -ds3 1

     LineNum:               1
     LCVCurrent:            0
     LCVLast15minBucket:    0


     ...
     UASCurrent:            0
     UASLast15minBucket:    0
     UASLast24hrBucket:     84435
     CCVCurrent:            0
     CCVLast15minBucket:    0
     CCVLast24hrBucket:     0
     CESCurrent:            0
     CESLast15minBucket:    0
     CESLast24hrBucket:     0
     CSESCurrent:           0
     CSESLast15minBucket:   0
     CSESLast24hrBucket:    0
     PercentEFS:            100
     RcvLOSCount:           2
     RcvOOFCount:           3
     RcvRAICount:           3
     RcvCCVCount:           0
```

The counters listed using the **dspalmcnt** command fall into one of the same three categories shown for the **dspalmcnt** for the PXM card:

- Current
- Last 15 minutes
- Last 24 hours

dspshelfalm

The **dspshelfalm** command, shown in Example 18-23, reports all the environmental alarms measured by the PXM or BNM card on the MGX.

Example 18-23 *dspshelfalm Command*

```
far4mgx1.1.3.ASC.a > dspshelfalm

Alarm      Type     Unit Thresh Severity Measurable Val State
----- ------------- ---- ------ -------- ---------- --- -----
   1   Temperature    1  50       Minor     Yes      27  Normal
   2   Power Supply   1  0        Minor     No       0   Normal
   3   Power Supply   2  0        Minor     No       0   missing
   4   DC Level       1  42-54    Minor     Yes      49  Normal
   5   DC Level       2  42-54    Minor     Yes      0   Below normal
   6   Fan Unit       1  2000     Minor     Yes      3441 Normal
   7   Fan Unit       2  2000     Minor     Yes      3487 Normal
   8   Fan Unit       3  2000     Minor     Yes      3472 Normal
   9   Fan Unit       4  2000     Minor     Yes      3547 Normal
  10   Fan Unit       5  2000     Minor     Yes      3510 Normal
  11   Fan Unit       6  2000     Minor     Yes      3571 Normal

ASMNumOfValidEntries: 11
ASMShelfAlarmState:    2

far4mgx1.1.3.ASC.a >
```

Use this command if the PXM or BNM card is reporting an "ASM physical alarm."

Table 18-10 shows the information provided by the **dspshelfalm** command

Table 18-10 *dspshlalm Alarm Types*

Information Field	Description
Alarm type	Temperature, power supply, or fan.
Unit number	If there is more than one unit (there are two power supplies and six fans), each unit is numbered.
Threshold	The alarm threshold. For the temperature, the threshold is in degrees Celsius. The power supply DC-level threshold is a VDC range. The fan thresholds are in RPMs.

Table 18-10 *dspshlalm Alarm Types (Continued)*

Severity	The severity of the alarm if the threshold is exceeded. All environmental alarms are minor.
Measurable	Whether the MGX device can make the appropriate measurement.
Value	The measure valued.
State	The current state of the measurement.

dsplog

The **dsplog** command, shown in Example 18-24, shows historical events and alarm logs on the MGX 8850 switch or MGX 8220 concentrator.

Example 18-24 *dsplog Command*

```
far4mgx1.1.3.ASC.a > dsplog

Searching ..done

07/16/1999-15:58:56 03 Teacher:0   ASC-7-0                     login
07/16/1999-15:28:58 03 aum         ASC-6-2097                  Line statistical
07/16/1999-15:26:25 03 lmi         ASC-6-1510                  Clear Alarm:LMI e
07/16/1999-16:24:28 08 cmm         FRSM-6-4002                 Message Rx Error
07/16/1999-16:24:28 07 cmm         FRSM-6-4002                 Message Rx Error
07/16/1999-16:24:28 05 cmm         AUSM-6-7002                 Message Rx Error
07/16/1999-16:24:28 03 aum         ASC-6-2096                  Line alarm
07/16/1999-16:13:13 03 aum         ASC-6-2097                  Line statistical
07/16/1999-16:11:01 03 aum         ASC-6-2097                  Line statistical
07/16/1999-15:56:43 03 aum         ASC-6-2097                  Line statistical
07/16/1999-15:54:31 03 aum         ASC-6-2097                  Line statistical

Type <CR> to continue, Q<CR> to stop:
```

If **dsplog** is entered without any parameters, then all events are listed. If the card number is given as a parameter to the **dsplog**, then only today's events that apply to that particular card will be displayed. By including the card number and the number of days as a parameter to the **dsplog**, the events for a particular card for the past number of days can be displayed.

The **clrlog** command is used to clear the MGX event log.

Summary

This chapter provided an overview of troubleshooting IGX, BPX, and MGX nodes. The common commands used to troubleshoot node, card, bus, slot, and trunk problems were covered. Additionally, statistical commands to view current and past errors also were covered.

Review Questions

The following questions test your retention of the material presented in this chapter. You can find the answers to the Review Questions in Appendix A, "Answers to Review Questions."

1 What is the meaning of a major alarm status on the lower-right corner of the node console screen?

A. The local node has a major alarm.

B. The network has at least one major alarm.

C. All nodes in the network have major alarms.

D. A major alarm has occurred in the last five minutes on a remote node.

2 Which two events will generate a major network alarm?

A. Card self-test failure

B. Loss of signal on a feeder trunk

C. Loss of signal on a network trunk

D. Missing processor in a redundant configuration

E. Cabinet temperature above the configured threshold

F. Loss of communication between an MGX feeder node and the WAN Manager station

3 Which one of the following statements is true?

A. Use the **resetcd slot f** command to clear a self-test failure alarm on a card.

B. Use the **resetcd slot h** command to clear a self-test failure alarm on a card.

C. Use the **resetcd slot h** command to switch from the active to the standby processor.

D. Use the **resetcd slot f** command to switch from an active to a standby Y-cabled card module.

4 Which two of the following statements are true?

A. The ASC reports environmental shelf alarms.

B. The **dspalms** command screen summarizes all alarms on a card module.

C. The **dspshelfalm** command screen summarizes all alarms in the MGX device.

D. The MGX alarm status is reported to the BPX wide-area switch in an integrated tiered network.

5 Match each command in the table with its function in the list that follows.

Command	Answer
dspcds	
dspnds	
resetcd	
dspnode	
clrcderrs	
dspshelfalm	

A. Verifies the alarm status of feeder shelves

B. Determines whether a fan has failed

C. Deletes card failure history without resetting card

D. Deletes card failure history and resets card

E. Determines which routing nodes have alarms

F. Determines which feeder service modules are in alarm

CHAPTER 19

Upgrading Software and Firmware

This chapter describes the process for upgrading software images in IGX and BPX nodes, and for updating firmware images in IGX, BPX, and MGX nodes. In addition, the chapter covers software and firmware images identification by release number and name, and tells how to obtain new or updated images from Cisco. Several alternative methods for downloading images to the nodes are described, followed by a detailed discussion on how to activate the new software release in a node.

This chapter includes the following sections:

- System Software and Firmware
- Overview of Software and Firmware Upgrade
- Activating the Upgrade
- Performing a Bootload
- IGX and BPX Switch Firmware Upgrade
- MGX 8850 Firmware Overview
- MGX 8220 Firmware Upgrade
- Summary
- Review Questions

System Software and Firmware

IGX and BPX nodes maintain the primary version of the network operating software in the RAM of the active controller card. If redundant controllers are installed, the standby controller maintains a secondary version, which may or may not be the same release level as the primary. The primary version of the operating software typically is the same release level on all nodes in the network, although this is no longer mandatory with the introduction of version interoperability in Release 9.1.

Systems with redundant controller cards can be upgraded without disrupting user services because the new software can be switched to without booting the primary controller card. Single controller card systems, however, require a reboot of the primary (only) controller card to activate the new software.

All IGX and BPX card modules also have card- and version-specific firmware, which is stored in Flash memory on the front card. If necessary, firmware upgrades are downloaded to the switch controller card, and then are distributed to the other cards within that switch. IGX and BPX nodes do not provide long-term storage of firmware images on the controller card.

MGX nodes do not use network-switching software as on IGX and BPX nodes—they use firmware, which controls shelf and card operation. However, the MGX 8850 currently uses Cisco IOS software on the RPM, and future releases of Processor Switching Module (PXM) will include a switching capability as well as other software-based controller functions, such as the Mutiprotocol Label Switching controller.

The controller cards in MGX nodes, whether AXIS Switch Controller (ASC) or PXM, maintain copies of firmware for all cards in the shelf. Firmware is loaded or reloaded whenever a service module or the shelf itself is reset.

Software and firmware images typically are stored on a network management system (NMS) for download to the network nodes as required. The NMS could be any of the following:

* Cisco WAN Manager
* UNIX workstation or PC with TFTP support
* PC with the StrataView Lite application

Cisco Software Resources

Cisco provides several corporate resources to enable customers, partners, and support personnel both to assess software and firmware requirements for their network and to download images.

A primary resource is the Software Release Notes (SRN) document, which is published for each release. The SRN details software and firmware dependencies for a particular release. Recent versions of the SRN for all current releases are included on the Cisco Documentation CD-ROM. Refer to the Cisco Connection Online (CCO) web site (http://www.cisco.com/) for the latest version.

Cisco maintains an Electronic Software Distribution (ESD) server that contains software files available either for unrestricted public distribution or with restricted access. Switch software and firmware upgrades are restricted, and a CCO login and password are required. In some cases, a valid Software Maintenance contract number is also required to download files. The ESD server is accessible via the File Transfer Protocol (FTP) at ftp://ftp.cisco.com/cisco/wan.

If you have a CCO login account and an Internet browser, you may also access the WAN Switching Upgrade Planner web page. This web page includes copies of other useful documents related to software and firmware upgrades, as well as copies of current and previously released images for download. The URL is http://www.cisco.com/kobayashi/sw-center/wan/wan-planner.shtml.

If you cannot download the files, Cisco can ship the upgrades in UNIX tape format or on CD-ROM.

Software Version File-Naming Conventions

Software versions are identified with a hierarchical numbering scheme, in which the number consists of three fields. For example, consider 9.1.11.

The first field (9) denotes a major release. The second field (.1) identifies a minor release, which typically introduces new features or support for new hardware. The third field (.11) identifies a subrelease or a maintenance release, which is usually restricted to a correction of software anomalies. Figure 19-1 shows the file-naming conventions for both software and firmware.

Figure 19-1 *File-Naming Conventions*

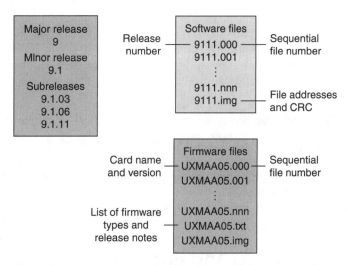

The complete version number identifies software upgrade files, with the following filename extensions:

- **.nnn**—This is the file number to distinguish the (many) files in a typical release.
- **.img**—This file associates the addresses of the numbered files and includes a cyclic redundancy check (CRC) to verify the integrity of those files.

Firmware Version File-Naming Conventions

Firmware version numbering differs depending on whether the card is an older type (prior to Release 8.2). Firmware version for older cards is identified by a three-letter code, such as HBF. In this scheme, H denotes the card type (a BCC), B is the model number, and F is the firmware revision.

Firmware for newer hardware is identified by the card type and a version identifier, as shown in Figure 19-1.

The firmware image file set includes a text file (.txt), which lists the firmware types and release notes.

Download Options

After the required image has been downloaded to the NMS, it must be unarchived because images are distributed in .tar (UNIX) or .zip (Windows) format.

The standard method of transferring an image to a network node is to use the Trivial File Transfer Protocol (TFTP). IGX and BPX switches require Release 8.4 or later for TFTP download.

If the NMS is a Cisco WAN Manager station, you can use the Image Download utility to initiate the download. This utility is accessible through the CWM Topology Map or through HP OpenView. Alternately, you can use any workstation or PC that has a TFTP server and a LAN connection.

Another PC application is the bootload program, which downloads software images to IGX or BPX nodes in boot mode. A switch enters boot mode when, for some reason, it does not have a valid operational software image available. The boot loader comes in two versions: serial and LAN.

The StrataView Lite application can download images using a proprietary protocol to IGX and BPX nodes only. StrataView Lite operates through the serial control port on the switch controller port.

Overview of Software and Firmware Upgrades

All IGX and BPX controller cards (NPM and BCC) incorporate Flash memory, which can be reprogrammed and still retain its contents when power is removed. This Flash memory permits upgrading both the system software and the firmware for individual cards.

Software downloading provides a quick and simple method of upgrading the node-operating software from one revision to another and does not require dedicated personnel at each site. If the node is equipped with redundant controllers, the upgrade can be accomplished with no disruption in node operation.

Updated software is supplied by Cisco for loading onto an NMS, usually the Cisco WAN Manager. From there, the software is downloaded directly to the local node over a LAN connection to the network. Software can also be loaded into a local node from a PC running the StrataView Lite application, or from any computer that supports TFTP.

For nodes equipped with redundant controller cards, the new release is loaded into the standby controller while the active controller continues to run the existing release. Nodes are designed to run properly with different software releases in active and standby controllers.

In a similar manner, each node in the network is loaded with the new software release. Software for nodes not directly connected to a Cisco WAN Manager NMS is transmitted over network trunks. As each node completes its download, the software can be automatically downloaded to the next adjacent node, subject to control of the network administrator.

Download Process with Cisco WAN Manager

Downloading the software with the Cisco WAN Manager (CWM) is simple, fast, and reliable, but it has the disadvantage that only a single node can be downloaded at a time. The following are the steps for downloading using CWM:

Step 1 After the image files have been uncompressed and transferred to the appropriate directory on the Cisco WAN Manager station, log in to the switch via the CLI. You must have SuperUser access to perform this activity.

Step 2 Enter the **cnffwswinit** command to identify for the switch the IP address of the Cisco WAN Manager station that will be initiating the download.

Step 3 If the switch to which the software is to be downloaded is not the gateway node, enter the **cnffunc** command to enable Download from Remote StrataView.

Step 4 On the Cisco WAN Manager station, access the Network Topology window, and select the node to which you want to download.

Step 5 Select Software Mgmnt and then SW/FW Images, and verify that the required image is listed in the window.

Step 6 Select the download image, and click the Download button.

Step 7 Return to the switch CLI, and monitor the download progress with the **dspdnld** command. A firmware image will take up to 2 minutes, while a software image may need between 5 and 10 minutes to completely download.

Step 8   You can enter the **dsprevs** or **dspfwrev** commands to verify the
download status for software and firmware images, respectively. In the
case of a software download, verify that the secondary image in the Flash
memory of the active processor has been upgraded to the downloaded
release version.

Download Process with TFTP

Downloading an image to a single switch can also be accomplished from any workstation
or PC with a TFTP client and a LAN connection to the network. This option enables
downloads in situations in which Cisco WAN Manager is not installed. The following are
the steps for downloading using TFTP:

Step 1   After the image files have been uncompressed and transferred to the
appropriate directory on the TFTP station, log in to the switch via the
CLI. You need SuperUser access to perform this activity.

Step 2   Verify that you have connectivity to the network node by using the **telnet**
or the **ping** commands.

Step 3   Enter the **cnffwswinit** command to identify for the switch the IP address
of the TFTP station that will be initiating the download.

Step 4   On the TFTP station, create (edit) a request file named dnld.sw to
download a software image with the following content:

    — **tftp_request**

    — **IP**—IP address of the TFTP station; from the cnffwswinit
      command

    — **PathName**—Full path to the directory where the image is stored

    — **RevNum**—Image filename without extensions

Step 5   If you are downloading a firmware image, create a request file dnld.fw,
as follows:

    — **tftp_request**

    — **IP**—IP address of the TFTP station; from the **cnffwswinit**
      command

    — **PathName**—Full path to the directory where the image is stored

    — **CardName**—For example, UXM

    — **RevNum**—Image filename without extensions

Step 6   Change to the directory where the image is stored, and initiate the TFTP
transfer. A command sequence similar to the following should be seen:

```
hostname#tftp 172.30.241.11
tftp>bin
tftp>put dnld.sw
Sent 1,322,611 bytes in 321.1 seconds
tftp>quit
```

The IP address in the first line is the LAN address of the switch.

Step 7 Return to the switch CLI, and monitor the download progress using the **dspdnld** and **dsprev** (or **dspfwrev**) commands.

Download Process from Switch CLI

Downloading with CWM and TFTP involves an image download initiated by an NMS. A download can also be initiated and managed from the switch CLI. This process is more flexible in that a single node or group of nodes, or the complete network, can be upgraded with new software with minimal user intervention. The following are the steps for downloading from the switch CLI:

Step 1 In this case, in which the image is to be transferred from an NMS using TFTP, verify that the required image is loaded on the NMS and in the correct directory.

Step 2 If the initiating switch is not the gateway node for the NMS, enter the **cnffunc** command to enable a download from a remote Cisco WAN Manager station.

Step 3 In the case of a software download, enter the **loadrev** command to specify the software revision and the node or nodes that are to be upgraded. With Release 9.1, the **upggrp** command is used to create, display, and modify groups of nodes for upgrade purposes. Note that upgrade groups apply to software downloads only, not firmware.

Step 4 To download firmware, enter the **getfwrev** command. This command enables you to download a specified firmware image to a single node or to all nodes in the network.

Step 5 As with CWM or TFTP, enter the **dspdnld** and **dsprevs** (or **dspfwrev**) commands to monitor download status and verify successful completion.

Download Process with StrataView Lite

The StrataView Lite application provides a convenient and simple means of downloading software and firmware images. It is particularly useful in situations in which a Cisco WAN Manager station is not installed, such as during the implementation phase of a new network, or in which LAN access is not readily available. StrataView Lite uses a proprietary download protocol and, therefore, cannot be used with the MGX family, which supports only TFTP.

In addition to the proprietary download protocol, StrataView Lite also provides DOS-based terminal emulation.

StrataView Lite is an MS-DOS application and does not operate from Windows or the MS-DOS prompt accessed from Windows. You must boot your computer in MS-DOS to use StrataView Lite.

When the program is active, you can use the PC function keys to control its operation. The program has two operating modes: VT100 terminal emulation and StrataView Lite mode. You can toggle between the two modes by using the F8 function key. The function key definitions are shown in Table 19-1.

Table 19-1 *StrataView Lite Function Key Assignments*

Function Key	Assignment
F1	Displays help text.
F4	Lists any files containing software or firmware images that have been placed in the c:\svlite directory.
F5	Prints the current screen.
F6	Dials out to a number specified in the StrataView Lite configuration (see the entry for F9). This requires a modem connected to COM1.
F7	Hangs up the modem.
F8	Toggles between StrataView Lite mode and terminal mode.
F9	Configures the serial port parameters, including an autodial number.
F10	Exits from the current screen or the application.

Complete the following steps to download an image with StrataView Lite:

Step 1 StrataView Lite must be connected to the control or auxiliary port on the node controller back card. Enter the **cnftermfunc** and **cnfterm** commands to configure the port function and communications parameters on the switch.

Step 2 Before the upgrading process can begin, the image files must be present in the c:\svlite directory of the StrataView Lite computer. Verify this by pressing F4 to list the available images.

Step 3 If necessary, press F8 to toggle StrataView Lite into terminal mode (TRM). Log into the target node using the CLI.

Step 4 Initiate the download using the **loadrev** or **loadfwrev** commands at the node CLI.

Step 5 Press F8 to toggle back to StrataView mode, and verify that the download commences by checking for loading message.

Step 6   When the download is under way, return to terminal mode and enter the
dspdnld and **dsprevs** (or **dspfwrev**) commands to monitor the status and
progress. Downloading a software image file at the maximum rate of 19.2
kbps takes 40 to 45 minutes.

Activating the Upgrade

After the image is downloaded, it must still be activated before the node can use the new
software.

This section shows how to activate the software with and without redundant controllers.
Performing a software upgrade in a production network is a complex and potentially risky
activity. Many network-specific factors are involved that are beyond the scope of this book.
A full-scale upgrade without consultation and assistance from Cisco TAC or similarly
qualified sources generally should be avoided.

Checking Current Software

Before you activate the software, you must check the node's current versions. Figure 19-2
shows redundant controllers with the same versions of software.

Figure 19-2   *Redundant Controllers Prior to Upgrade*

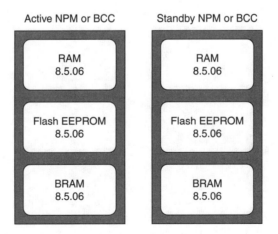

The **dsprevs** command is used to check the software versions, and the **dspcd** command can
be used to see the current version of the Flash memory and BRAM.

Before the upgrade, use the **cnfnodeparm** command to verify that each node with
redundant controllers has the redundancy feature turned on.

Download to Active

When a switch has redundant controllers, the upgrading process can be initiated and completed while the switch continues to operate normally. The first phase of upgrading a switch with redundant controllers, illustrated in Figure 19-3, occurs as follows:

Step 1 The initial download is initiated by the NMS or from the switch command line (**loadrev**). A typical upgrade scenario involves the initial upgrade of one of each type of node in the network. In this example, the network is being upgraded from 8.5.06 to 9.1.11.

Step 2 The contents of Flash EEPROM for the active controller are automatically erased.

Step 3 The software image files are copied from the NMS to the Flash EEPROM of the active controller module.

Step 4 The contents of RAM for the standby controller are erased.

Step 5 Files are then copied from the Flash EEPROM of the active switch to the RAM of the standby switch.

Step 6 The configuration database in the standby node is updated to reflect the new release version.

Figure 19-3 *Download to Active*

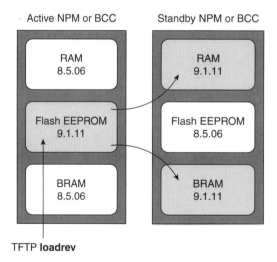

At this point, the **dspcd** command verifies the active and standby controllers.

Switch Controllers

Now the node is ready for the **runrev** command, which causes the processor modules to switch over. The active module switches to standby mode, and the standby module becomes active, as shown in Figure 19-4. The node immediately begins to run on the new software release. Because this happens almost instantaneously, there is minimal disruption of network service.

Figure 19-4 *Switch Controllers*

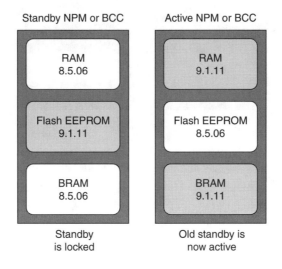

An additional advantage of upgrading using redundant cards is that you can operate the network for an indefinite period of time with the configuration. If any problem develops with the new software release, you can restore the network to its previous operating configuration. Restoring a network to the old software revision causes all nodes to rebuild, although redundant modules might exist.

At this point, the standby module is in locked mode. The original version of the software is maintained in RAM in case a fallback is necessary. Leave the modules in this state for a burn-in period to ensure that the node is operating correctly on the new release.

Download to Standby

The final action in upgrading this single node is to unlock the standby controller by issuing a second **loadrev** command. This might take up to 20 minutes to complete. Figure 19-5 shows a logical view of the **loadrev** command.

Figure 19-5 *Download to Standby*

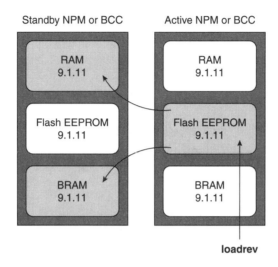

Use the **dsprevs** command and the **dspcd** *slot number* command for each controller to verify that the upgrade is complete.

Use the **switchcc** command to switch between the processors to verify that the download was successful on both modules. The software upgrade then is complete for this switch.

Nonredundant Controller Update

The procedure for the nonredundant update is the same, up to the **loadrev** command.

With a nonredundant controller update, following a TFTP **put** or **loadrev** command, the contents of the Flash memory are erased, and the new software image is written into the EEPROM and then to RAM. After upgrading the database, the card is reset. There will be a 15- to 20-minute outage during this process.

Upgrading a Complete Network

So far, the discussion has been confined to downloading and upgrading a single node in the network. When this is completed satisfactorily, it is possible to upgrade the entire network at once or, more likely in the case of larger networks, in several stages.

The general plan is to upgrade a single node of each type and to use those nodes to upgrade neighbor nodes across the network trunks, as shown in Figure 19-6. Each node downloads the software to any nodes to which it is directly connected. Those nodes then download the nodes to which they are connected, and so on.

Figure 19-6 *Upgrading a Network*

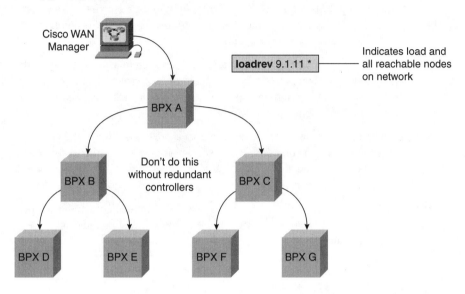

The following steps provide a brief outline of the upgrade process. These steps cannot replace a good plan—production network upgrades should be well planned and tested prior to implementation. Complete the following steps to upgrade a network:

Step 1   Upgrade a single node of each type of node in the network.

Step 2   Decide on a strategy for upgrading the rest of the network from the following options:

— Upgrade all nodes in the network as a single group

— Upgrade the network in stages by setting hop count limits

— Separate the network into upgrade groups

Step 3   If the first option is chosen, use the * parameter with the **loadrev** command to initiate a download of the new revision to the secondary controller of all nodes in the network.

Step 4   Each node in the network will then attempt to locate the new revision by first checking its own Flash memory, and it requests a download from its neighbor nodes. To limit the number of requests, and to perform the upgrade in manageable stages, use the **cnfdlparm** command to set the Request Hop Limit parameter on each node to a low number, such as 3 or less. By keeping this number small, you prevent a single node from trying to upgrade every other node on the network.

Step 5   With networks running Release 9.1 or later, use the **upggrp** command to create upgrade groups. Up to 20 upgrade groups can exist in a network. Each group is downloaded separately following successive **loadrev** *revision group-name* commands.

Step 6   When the software is downloaded to all required nodes, the group or the network can switch to the new revision in response to the **runrev** command. This command also takes group-name as an alternative parameter to node-name or *.

Step 7   The **runrev** command causes the processors to switch and the nodes to run the new revision as the active software version. Be sure to verify that all nodes have been correctly downloaded and are stable before issuing the **runrev** command.

Step 8   After a further settling period of at least 30 minutes, unlock the standby controllers by issuing one or a series of **loadrev** commands, as appropriate.

Performing a Bootload

If the operating software in a node becomes corrupted, a good copy of the software must be installed before the node will operate. Two versions of the utility program bootload will download operating software to a node in boot mode. One version runs on a PC and loads through the serial control or auxiliary port on the node controller. The second version runs on either a PC or a UNIX workstation and loads via the LAN. Complete the following steps for a bootload:

Step 1   Log in at either the SuperUser or the service level.

CAUTION   This procedure clears all configuration information and should be used only on switches in which the system has become corrupted.

Step 2   Enter the **clrallcnf** or **runrev** 0.0 command to clear the BRAM configuration.

Step 3   If you are using the serial version (bootld.exe), set the PC serial port (COM1) and enter the **cnfterm** command to set the control or auxiliary port to 19200 baud.

Step 4   If you are using the LAN version (lanbtld.exe), enter the **cnflan** command to set the IP address of the node LAN port. (The IP address configuration was erased in Step 2.)

Step 5   Enter the **btld** or **lanbtld** command to start the bootload process on the node.

Step 6   On the PC or workstation, start the boot load application by entering one of the following:

— **bootld** *revision*

— **lanbtld** *node ip address revision*

In both of these, revision is the software revision name, such as 9111g.

Step 7   After the software image is downloaded, log in to the node and enter the **setrev** *revision* **p** command to set the new software as the primary version.

IGX and BPX Switch Firmware Upgrade

The process for downloading and distributing firmware revisions to IGX and BPX nodes is similar to that for switch software. The important differences are listed here:

- Firmware images are downloaded into an image buffer in the DRAM of the active controller. Only one firmware image is stored at a time. The **dspfwrev** command is used to verify which image is currently loaded. If an unwanted image is currently loaded, the **getfwrev** *0.0* command clears the image from the buffer.

- Use the **getfwrev** command to download an image from a TFTP server or StrataView Lite. The image can be downloaded to a single node or to all nodes in the network, but upgrade groups are not supported for firmware upgrades.

- When the image has been successfully downloaded, the **burnfwrev** command writes the image into Flash memory on a single card, multiple cards, or all cards of the same type on a single node. After the burn operation, the card(s) reset and the configuration is reloaded from the controller.

- The **dspcd** command can be used to verify that the firmware burn has been successful with the **burnfwrev** command.

MGX 8850 Firmware Overview

The PWM controller on the MGX 8850 has a disk drive in which runtime firmware images for the controller and all service modules are stored. Firmware and Cisco IOS software upgrades are downloaded to the PXM and RPM, respectively, from an external TFTP server. Note that StrataView Lite does not support the MGX 8850 (or the MGX 8220).

PXM and MGX service module software is available from CCO or via FTP; IOS software is also available from CCO. PXM files have a different form of filenames depending on whether the file contains boot code or firmware:

* Boot code format is pxm_bkup_version.fw, where version defines the release version number, such as 1.0.00.

* Firmware code format is pxm_version.fw.

Filename conventions for the service modules are described later in this chapter.

MGX 8850 Upgrade

When upgrading MGX modules, it might be necessary to install new boot code as well as operating firmware. The following process assumes that this is the case, and the directions for installing boot code can be found in the next section, "MGX 8850 Boot Code Installation." Refer to the SRNs to determine whether new boot code is required for the firmware version you plan to install. Complete the following steps to upgrade the MGX 8850. (Remember that PXM redundancy is not supported in Release 1.0. Release 1.1 is required to support this feature.)

Step 1   From the workstation where the boot code is stored, enter and observe a command sequence similar to the following:

```
hostname#tftp 172.30.241.15
tftp>bin
tftp>put boot-file POPEYE@PXM.BT
.....Sent xxxxx bytes in nnn seconds
tftp>quit
```

Note that the IP address is the LAN port IP address configured using the **cnfifip** command.

The boot filename follows this format: pxm_bkup_version.fw

The last part of the TFTP **put** command defines the destination locator—that is, where the boot code is to be loaded. In the case of the PXM, valid locators are these:

— **POPEYE@PXM.BT**—Loads boot code into both active and standby PXMs

— **POPEYE@PXM_ACTIVE.BT**—Loads boot code into active PXM only

— **POPEYE@PXM_STANDBY.BT**—Loads boot code into standby PXM only

Step 2   After successful completion of the file transfer, the boot code is stored on the hard disk. Enter the **downloadflash** command to update the boot code in Flash memory using the newly downloaded version.

Step 3   Reboot the switch in preparation for downloading the operating firmware.

Step 4   Initiate a TFTP file transfer for the PXM firmware as discussed previously, except using a put statement similar to the following:

```
tftp>put firmware-file POPEYE@PXM.FW
```

The firmware filename (identified as *firmware-file* in this **put** command) follows this format PXM_*version*.fw.

Valid locators are PXM.FW (active and standby), PXM_ACTIVE.FW (active only), and PXM_STANDBY.FW (standby only).

Step 5   Initiate another TFTP file transfer for the ComMat.dat file, ensuring that the file is placed in the root directory of the active PXM:

```
tftp>cd c:/
tftp>put ComMat.dat
```

Step 6   The upgrade process for the PXM depends on whether redundant controllers are installed.

If only a single, nonredundant controller is installed, enter the **install** *version* command to reset the PXM, and to upgrade the primary and secondary images and the configuration database to the new version. Note that this action initiates a service-disruptive, nongraceful upgrade. Skip to Step 10.

If redundant controllers are installed, a graceful upgrade, which does not disrupt user service, can be done. The general process is quite similar to that used to upgrade IGX and BPX nodes, except that different commands are used instead of **loadrev** and **runrev**. Continue with Step 7.

Step 7   Enter the **install** *version* command, which puts the standby PXM into upgrade state and updates the standby connection database and the secondary image on both PXMs to the new version.

Step 8   Enter the **newrev** *version* command to switch controllers and update the old, active (now standby) PXM.

Step 9   If the switch remains stable in this configuration, enter the **commit** *version* command to update the standby database and release it from hold status. If you need to revert to the original configuration, which existed before the **install** command, use the **abort** command.

Step 10 At this point, the controller(s) are upgraded, and you can move to upgrade the service modules.

MGX 8850 Boot Code Installation

When upgrading MGX service modules, it might be necessary to install new boot code as well as operating firmware. Refer to the SRNs to determine whether new boot code is required for the firmware version you plan to install. Complete the following steps to update the MGX 8850 boot code:

Step 1 From the workstation where the boot code is stored, enter and observe a command sequence similar to the following:

```
hostname#tftp 172.30.241.15
tftp>bin
tftp>put boot-file POPEYE@SM_1_slot.BOOT
.....Sent xxxxx bytes in nnn seconds
tftp>quit
```

172.30.241.15 is the IP address of the MGX 8850 node.

Step 2 Note that the IP address is the boot-level LAN port address configured in Step 1.

The boot filename follows the format *card id* BT_*version*.fw, where *card id* is the card type, such as frsm_8t1e1, and *version* is the boot code version, such as 5.0.00.

The *slot* parameter defines a target service module for the boot upgrade. Note that the boot code is automatically burnt into Flash memory on the service module; the PXM does not store boot code for service modules.

Step 3 Initiate a TFTP file transfer for the service module firmware as described previously, except use a **put** statement similar to the following:

```
tftp>put firmware-file POPEYE@SM_1 slot.FW
```

The firmware filename (identified as firmware-file in the previous **put** command) follows the format *card id_version*.fw.

The *slot* parameter defines which service modules are to receive the new version. 0 specifies that the firmware is to be used for all cards of the same type in the switch.

Step 4 After the firmware has been transferred to the PXM disk, the file is renamed as shown in Table 19-2.

Table 19-2 *PXM Filenames*

Card Identifier	PXM Filename
ausm8t1e1	sm50
cesm8t1e1	sm90
cesmt3e3	sm140
frmsm2ct3	sm130
frsm8t1e1	sm35

This naming convention applies to the firmware. Because this convention does not specify the slot, a slot-specific prefix is identified with a suffix. For example, sm90_7 is the firmware image for the CESM card in slot 7.

Step 5 The upgrade process for a service module depends on whether it is part of a 1:n redundant group.

For a single, nonredundant card, enter the **resetcd** *slot* command to initiate the download from the PXM of the new firmware version. Note that this action initiates a service-disruptive, nongraceful upgrade.

For cards in a 1:n redundant group that are installed, a graceful upgrade can be done using the **install**, **newrev**, and **commit** commands. Note that the **abort** command is not applicable to service modules because the previous firmware version will have been overwritten.

MGX 8220 Firmware Upgrade

The download and upgrade procedure for the MGX 8220 concentrator is similar to that for the MGX 8850 switch. For a complete shelf upgrade, boot code and firmware are upgraded first on the ASC(s), and then the service modules are upgraded. Complete the following steps to upgrade the MGX 8220:

Step 1 Establish connection to the MGX shelf via the Ethernet port, the control port, or the in-band IP Relay.

Step 2 Initiate a TFTP file transfer for the boot code to the active ASC, using a **put** statement similar to this one:

```
tftp>put boot-file AXIS_ASC_BACKUP.FW
```

The boot filename is user-defined but typically has the format asc_BT_*version*.fw.

Step 3 Use the **chkflash** and **version** commands to verify the correct download of the boot code.

Step 4   If redundant ASCs are installed, use the **switchcc** command to switch controllers, and then load the boot code into the new active controller. Check completion using the **chkflash** and **version** commands.

Step 5   If there are redundant ASCs, enter the **donotupdatestandby** command to prevent the active ASC from modifying the reset standby (original active) controller.

Step 6   Initiate another TFTP file transfer to download runtime firmware to the standby ASC:

```
tftp>put firmware-file AXIS_ASC_STANDBY.FW
```

The firmware filename (*firmware-file* in the **put** command above) is user-defined but typically has the format asc_*version*.fw.

Step 7   Enter the **dspfwrevs** command to verify the successful download of the firmware to the ASC.

Step 8   Next, download the boot code to the service module(s), as follows:

```
tftp>put boot-file AXIS_SM_1_slot.BOOT
```

The boot filename (*boot-file* in this **put** command) is user-defined but typically has the format *card id*_BT_*version*.fw.

Step 9   Check completion using the **chkflash** and **version** commands.

Step 10   The final download transfers the runtime firmware for the service module(s):

```
tftp>put firmware-file AXIS_SM_1_[slot ¦ 0].FW
```

The firmware filename (*firmware-file* in the previous **put** command) is user-defined but typically has the format *card id_version*.fw.

The slot parameter defines the target service module, or 0 may be used to define a generic (non-slot-dependent) download.

Step 11   After using **dspfwrevs** to confirm the service module(s) firmware download, enter **resetcd** to reset the standby and active controllers in turn. This causes the new ASC boot and runtime firmware to become effective.

Step 12   Enter the **resetcd** *slot* command for each service module to invoke the new firmware version.

If the download process is disrupted for a timeout or similar errors, restart the TFTP download process without resetting the MGX shelf.

Summary

This chapter covered the very important tasks of upgrading system software and firmware on the IGX, BPX, and MGX switches. CWM, TFTP, and StrataView Lite can be used to upgrade IGX and BPX switches. The MGX supports only TFTP upgrades. In addition to individual nodes, portions of networks or complete networks can be upgraded. The chapter also discussed the necessary commands to perform the upgrades.

Review Questions

The following questions test your retention of the material presented in this chapter. The answers to the Review Questions can be found in Appendix A, "Answers to Review Questions."

1 Which of the following are not valid download options for new versions of software or firmware?

   A. StrataView Lite for firmware download to an IGX or BPX node

   B. StrataView Lite for firmware download to the MGX 8850 switch

   C. A TFTP server for software and firmware download to all IGX, BPX, and MGX nodes

   D. Cisco WAN Manager for software and firmware download to all IGX, BPX, and MGX nodes

   E. Using the CLI on an IGX or BPX node to initiate software download from either a TFTP server or StrataView Lite

2 Which of the following best defines version interoperability?

   A. Extension of the node-by-node upgrade feature to Release 9.1

   B. Capability of PXM controller to retain slot-specific and generic firmware

   C. Use of Cisco IOS to facilitate interoperation of RPM and PXM in the MGX 8850 node

   D. Capability of network operation over an extended period of time with nodes at different software release levels

   E. Capability of a node to operate with different software versions in its active and standby controller cards

3 Which of the three letters in the firmware release portion of the CCO filename identifies the release level?

4 Which two of the following statements are true?

A. TFTP is the only valid download protocol for MGX nodes.

B. New boot code is always downloaded into the standby ASC.

C. You need to reboot the switch to invoke new boot code on an MGX 8850.

D. The MGX 8850 retains a copy of service module boot code on the PXM hard drive.

E. The command sequence for a graceful firmware upgrade on an MGX 8850 is **install, newrev, commit, reboot**.

F. You cannot store both slot-specific and generic firmware files for a particular type of service module on the ASC hard drive.

5 Look at the following table containing output that would come from a **dspcd** command, and answer the questions that follow.

	Active	Updated
RAM ID	9.1	9.2
Flash EEPROM ID	9.2	9.1
BRAM ID	9.1	9.2

A. Which processor is in use by the node now?

B. How can you tell?

C. Which command was issued to get you to this point?

D. If the active module failed now, what version would be started by the standby module?

Look at the following table containing output for the same node that would come from a **dspcd** command, and answer the questions that follow.

	Locked	Active
RAM ID	9.1	9.2
Flash EEPROM ID	9.2	9.1
BRAM ID	9.1	9.2

E. Which processor is in use by the node now?

F. How can you tell?

G. Which command was issued to get you to this point?

H. If the active module failed now, what version would be started by the standby module?

Appendix

Answers to Review Questions

This appendix contains the answers to each chapter's review questions. The correct answers are in bold.

Chapter 2

1 How much overhead does asynchronous communication have per 8 bits?

   A. 4 bits
   B. 3 bits
   C. None
   D. 2 bits
   E. Depends on the protocol being used

2 What do the start and stop bits in asynchronous communications provide?

   A. Improved communications
   B. Identification of octets within the data stream to avoid 2 individual bits from being identified as one
   C. Priority synchronization
   D. Framing

3 What overhead does synchronous communication have?

   A. 2 bits and start and stop bits
   B. Start and stop bits and CRC
   C. Header and CRC
   D. Header, payload, and CRC

4 Is a terminal a DTE or a DCE?

   A DTE

5 Is a modem a DTE or a DCE?

   A DCE

6 What is the maximum signaling rate of HSSI?

   A. 1.54 Mbps
   B. 45 Mbps
   C. 52 Mbps
   D. 2.048 Mbps

7 Which normally provides clocking, the DTE or the DCE?

   The DCE

Chapter 3

1 Which of the following facilities are considered narrowband?

   A. T1, DS-3, E1, E3
   B. T1, E1, J1, Y1
   C. E3, D3
   D. OC-3, Ethernet, T1

2 How many time slots does T1 have?

   24 time slots

3 How many time slots does E1 have?

   32 time slots

4 True or false: T1 offers better performance than E1.

   False

5 What type of multiplexing is used in narrowband transmissions?

   A. Statistical multiplexing
   B. Time-division multiplexing
   C. Inverse multiplexing
   D. ATM inverse multiplexing

6 What is line coding?

   A. The number of bits that can be multiplexed per second
   B. The way logical bits are represented on the transmission facility
   C. The encoding used by the DCE to interpret the signal
   D. The decoding used by the DTE to interpret the signal

7 What type of line coding does T1 use?

   Alternate mark inversion

8 What two types of framing does T1 support?

A. B8ZS
B. ESF
C. AMI
D. D4

9 True or false: Unlike T1, E1 does not use AMI for line coding.

False

10 Which E1 time slot is used for signaling?

A. 0
B. 4
C. 8
D. 16

11 What types of signaling does E1 support?

A. Q.931
B. CAS
C. CCS
D. AMI

Chapter 4

1 What line coding does DS-3 use?

A. None
B. Raw AMI
C. Alternate mark inversion bipolar, return to zero
D. Alternate mark inversion bipolar, return to one

2 What represents a logical 0 in DS-3 line coding?

Zero voltage

3 How is 1s density enforced on DS-3?

A. HDB3
B. B8ZS
C. B3ZS

4 What line coding does E3 use?

A. Alternate mark inversion bipolar, return to zero
B. None
C. Raw AMI
D. Alternate mark inversion bipolar, return to one

5 How is 1s density enforced for E3?

   A. HDB3
   B. B8ZS
   C. B3ZS

6 Which two of the following are E3 framing methods?

   A. G.832
   B. H.323
   C. Q.931
   D. G.804

7 What cabling is typically used on customer premises for DS-3/E3?

   A. STP
   B. UTP
   C. CAT5 STP
   D. 75-ohm coaxial

8 SONET uses which medium for transport?

   A. STP
   B. Fiber
   C. UTP
   D. 75-ohm coaxial

9 Which is usually less expensive?

   A. Single-mode fiber
   B. Multimode fiber

Chapter 5

1 What does PBX stand for?

Private branch exchange

2 What performs analog-to-digital conversion in a private network?

   A. CODEC
   B. Modem
   C. a/d converter
   D. D/C modulator

3 What is the available bandwidth of DS-0?

   A. 56 kbps

   B. 63 kbps

   C. 64 kbps

   D. 1.54 Mbps

4 What two companding standards are discussed in this chapter?

   A. my-law

   B. mu-law

   C. a-law

   D. pi-law

   E. ILD-law

5 How does T1 support CAS signaling?

   A. Time slot 16.

   B. It does not support CAS.

   C. Robbed bit signaling.

   D. Time slot 0.

   E. Time slot 4.

6 What are the two most common dialing formats supported?

   A. Rotary dialing

   B. Pulse dialing

   C. Tone dialing

   D. DTMF

7 Which of the following does not add delay to voice communication?

   A. Compression

   B. Companding

   C. Network congestion

   D. Silence suppression

Chapter 6

1 True or false: Frame Relay is the digital version of X.25.

False

2 What is the major advantage of Frame Relay over point-to-point networks?

   A. Frame Relay uses digital facilities.

   B. One physical interface supports multiple virtual circuits.

   C. Compression ratios on Frame Relay are much higher than point-to-point.

   D. Frame Relay has no advantage over point-to-point networks.

3 How many bits in the Frame Relay frame are used by the DLCI?

A. 6

B. 8

C. 10

D. 12

4 True or false: The DLCI is globally unique within a Frame Relay network.

False

5 What is the Local Management Interface responsible for?

A. Management features, such as dial-on-demand and routing updates

B. Management features, such as dial backup and compression

C. Management features, such as reporting failed PVCs and providing keepalives

D. Management functions for the network layer

6 How does Frame Relay provide congestion notification?

A. Frame Relay does not provide congestion notification.

B. BECN and FECN

C. FECN

D. FECN and BFECN

Chapter 7

1 How many octets make up an ATM cell?

53

2 How large is the ATM header?

A. 5 cells.

B. 5 octets.

C. 8 bytes.

D. ATM has no headers.

3 What is the function of the UNI?

A. To connect legacy network hosts to ATM networks

B. To connect ATM switches with the ATM network

C. To connect ATM nodes (user nodes) to the ATM network

D. To translate between legacy networks and ATM

4 What is the purpose of the ATM adaptation layer (AAL)?

   A. To provide cell switching to the network

   B. To convert upper-layer protocols and larger service data units to ATM cells

   C. To translate synchronous services to ATM

   D. To provide network-management capability to the ATM network

5 What is the ATM layer responsible for?

   A. Converting upper-layer protocols and larger service data units to ATM cells.

   B. Converting the cells to a transmission understood by the physical media.

   C. Establishing connections and passing cells through the ATM network based upon the ATM header.

   D. There is no ATM layer.

6 What role does the physical layer provide?

   A. It controls transmission and receipt of bits on the physical medium.

   B. It converts cells to a format understood by the AAL.

   C. It functions as a TDM for the ATM network.

   D. The physical layer is not important for the functionality of ATM.

7 Which protocol provides ATM with management capabilities?

   A. Link Management Interface

   B. Integrated Local Management Interface

   C. Private Network-Network Interface

   D. B-ISDN AAL (I.362)

Chapter 8

1 How many bits are assigned to the network in a Class C network?

   A. 6

   B. 8

   C. 24

   D. 32

2 What Class A network is reserved for loopback?

   A. 10.0.0.0

   B. 127.0.0.0

   C. 1.0.0.0

   D. 192.168.1.0

3 How many classes does CIDR support?

A. 3
B. 4
C. None
D. 8

4 What does SNMP stand for?

A. Slow Node Management Protocol
B. Simple Node Management Protocol
C. Simple Network Management Protocol
D. Synchronous Network Management Protocol

5 Which SNMP operation allows objects to be configured?

A. Write
B. Read
C. SNMP Set
D. SNMP Write

6 What mechanism allows a node to report problems to the NMS?

A. Trap
B. Get
C. SNMP Set
D. Not supported with SNMP

Chapter 9

1 What are the two principal functions of the IGX node?

A. A multiservice concentrator
B. A time-division multiplexer
C. A Frame Relay access device
D. A wide-area node for backbone applications

2 What is a BPX node?

A. An ATM switch
B. An ATM access device
C. A multiprotocol access device
D. A multiprotocol packet switch

3   Which of the following best describes the MGX 8220 edge concentrator?

    A. A multiprotocol router

    B. An ATM-only access device

    C. A multiservice access device

    D. An ATM switch with ATM interfaces

    E. An ATM switch with multiservice interfaces

4   Which of the following best describes the MGX 8850 edge switch?

    A. A multiprotocol router

    B. An ATM-only access device

    C. A multiservice access device

    D. An ATM switch with ATM interfaces

    E. An ATM switch with multiservice interfaces

5   Which one of the following is not an IGX function?

    A. Supports analog voice

    B. Supports Frame Relay

    C. Can be a feeder node for a BPX node

    D. Can be a feeder node for another IGX node

    E. Supports CBR, VBR, and ABR ATM traffic

6   Which three of the following functions does the BPX node perform?

    A. Switches ATM cells

    B. Can be a feeder node in a tiered network

    C. Segments and reassembles Frame Relay frames

    D. Supports CBR, VBR, ABR, and UBR ATM traffic

    E. Communicates with a Cisco WAN Manager network-management station

7   Which two of the following functions do both MGX devices perform?

    A. Route ATM traffic

    B. Perform ADPCM voice compression

    C. Provide a feeder function to an IGX routing node

    D. Segment and reassemble Frame Relay traffic into ATM cells

    E. Communicate with a Cisco WAN Manager network management station

8   Match the service type in the table with its definition.

    A. ATM cells that carry Frame Relay traffic

    B. Traffic without a service guarantee

    C. Serial bit stream up to 1.344 Mbps

    D. Time-dependent, variable-rate, traffic-compressed voice, data, and video

    E. Variable-rate traffic with congestion avoidance-router LAN-WAN traffic

    F. Time-dependent, constant-rate, traffic-uncompressed voice, data, and video

Service Type	Definition
CBR	F
VBR-rt	D
ABR	E
UBR	B
ATM-Frame Relay	A
Synchronous data	C

9 Match the networking feature in the table with its definition.

   A. Routing and rerouting of network connections

   B. Per-PVC ingress queuing for Frame Relay and ABR connections

   C. A closed-loop congestion-avoidance mechanism used on Frame Relay and ABR connections

   D. Per-traffic type queuing to prevent unlike traffic types from competing for trunk bandwidth

Networking Feature	Definition
AutoRoute	A
OptiClass	D
ForeSight	C
FairShare	B

10 Match the network type in the table with its definition.

   A. A network of routing and feeder nodes

   B. A large network made up of multiple domains

   C. A network of peer nodes that communicate with all other nodes

Network type	Definition
Flat	C
Tiered	A
Structured	B

11 Which two of the following are not a function of the Cisco WAN Manager?

A. Provisioning user services
B. **Performing network monitoring of cell payload**
C. Collecting statistics from a single node or network-wide
D. Downloading software and firmware images to network nodes
E. **Providing SNMP management support for Cisco routers and LAN switches**
F. Providing real-time indication of network alarms on the topology map

Chapter 10

1 Which two of the following statements apply to the IGX 8410 node?

A. A booster fan assembly is required.
B. **The system will operate on 110 VAC power.**
C. The AC power tray holds six power modules.
D. **The AC power tray holds four power supplies.**
E. The backplane includes the utility bus as installed on the IPX switch.

2 When installing an IGX in a rack, which of the following two steps are always required?

A. Install the DC-PEM.
B. Install the AC power modules.
C. **Install the temporary mounting brackets.**
D. **Remove the card modules (if installed) from the card cage before lifting it into place.**
E. Install the multishelf ribbon cable between the upper and lower backplanes.

3 Mark the following statements as true or false.

A. SCMs should be installed in slot 1.   **True**
B. For an IGX 8410 with six cards, three power modules are required.   **False**
C. In an IGX 8430 node, redundant NPMs are installed in slots 1 and 17.   **False**
D. An IGX 8430 needs at least three power modules for N+1 redundancy.   **False**
E. When installing an SCM in an IGX 8410, the W6 jumper must be removed.   **False**

4 Which two cards support ATM trunks?

A. NPM
B. NTM
C. **UXM**
D. UFM-U
E. UFM-C
F. **ALM/B**

5 How many E1 ports are there on a UXM?

    A. 2 or 4
    B. 1 or 2
    C. 4 or 8
    D. 3 or 6

6 How many physical connectors are there on an UFM-U with a V.35 back card?

    A. 4
    B. 6
    C. 12
    D. 6 or 12, depending on the front card type

7 Which two devices could you attach to a CVM or UVM card?

    A. A digital PBX
    B. A Cisco LightStream 1010 ATM switch
    C. A Cisco 7000 router with a serial interface
    D. An IGX switch with a BTM or ALM/B trunk card
    E. A front-end processor with a synchronous interface

8 Match the card module in the table with its function in the list that follows.

Card Module	Answer
NPM	C
SCM	E
NTM	B
UFM/U	D
UXM	A

    A. Support for lines attached to ATM end-user equipment
    B. IGX to IGX trunks transporting FastPackets
    C. Central processor, software storage, and network management
    D. Serial lines, traffic policing, and ForeSight feature
    E. Local alarm notification, LAN port, and external clock port

Chapter 11

1 Which two of the following statements apply to the BPX 8620 node?

    A. A separate fan cooling tray is required.

    B. The AC power tray holds four power modules.

    C. The system does not operate on 110 VAC power.

    D. Redundant AC power supplies can have one or two AC feeds.

    E. The optional AC power tray can be installed above or below the card chassis.

2 Mark the following statements as true or false

    A. DC power supplies are optional equipment.   **False**

    B. All BPX front cards have card status LEDs.   **True**

    C. SONET APS is supported on single-mode fiber only.   **True**

    D. A BPX system can be mounted only in a Cisco cabinet.   **False**

    E. For a BPX 8620 with 15 cards, two AC power supplies are required.   **False**

3 Which three of the following elements are part of the BPX node?

    A. Fan assembly

    B. AC power shelf

    C. Crosspoint switch

    D. 32-card slot chassis

    E. Multishelf bus cable

    F. A standalone cabinet with front and back doors

4 Which card slots are reserved for the BCCs and the ASM?

    A. 1, 2, and 3

    B. 7, 8, and 1

    C. 7, 8, and 15

    D. 1, 2, and 15

5 Which card supports either lines or trunks?

    A. ASM

    B. BCC-4

    C. BNI-E3

    D. BXM-622

    E. ASI-155E

6 How many ports are on an ASI-E3?

    A. 2

    B. 3

    C. 8

    D. 12

7 Match the card module in the table with its functions from the list that follows:

Card Module	Answer
BCC	**B**
ASM	**D**
BNI	**A**
ASI	**C**

A. Trunks with STI cells, egress queuing, and physical-layer processing
B. Central processor, crosspoint switch, software storage, and network management
C. Lines attached to end-user equipment, traffic policing, ForeSight feature, and egress queuing
D. Local alarm notification, temperature measurement, power supply monitor, and alarm relays
E. Lines or trunks, traffic policing, standard ABR and ForeSight features, and physical-layer processing

8 Which two devices could you attach to a BPX node using an ASI card?

A. A Cisco 7000 router
B. A BPX node with a BXM trunk card
C. A Cisco LightStream 1010 ATM switch
D. An IGX node with a BTM or ALM/B trunk card

9 Which two devices could you attach to a BPX node using a BXM card in trunk mode?

A. A Cisco 7000 router
B. A BPX node with a BXM trunk card
C. A Cisco LightStream 1010 ATM switch
D. An MGX concentrator with a BNM trunk card
E. An IGX node with a BTM or ALM/B trunk card

Chapter 12

1 Which one of the following is not a valid choice of access method for a first-time installation?

A. StrataView Lite
B. Cisco WAN Manager
C. PC with terminal emulation
D. VT-100–compatible terminal
E. UNIX workstation with serial interface

2 Mark the following statements as true or false.

    A. When an abnormal boot sequence occurs, the power should be turned off.   **False**

    B. After a successful initial boot, the active BCC in a BPX node is always in slot 7. **True**

    C. Any trunk or line alarms must be cleared before the system will boot normally. **False**

    D. When an abnormal boot sequence occurs, the active BCC/NPM should be removed and reseated.   **False**

    E. When an abnormal boot sequence occurs, the power should be turned off, and the active BCC/NPM should be removed and reseated.   **True**

3 Which two of the following statements are true?

    A. The Esc key aborts a command.

    B. All commands have required and optional parameters.

    C. Most commands comprise an abbreviated verb and noun.

    D. A command is complete when all required parameters have been defined with appropriate values.

    E. The node prompts you for all required and optional parameters when you use the prompted entry mode.

4 What is the purpose of the help command?

    A. To teach you how to configure a node

    B. To identify the definition and syntax of a command

    C. To define the value range of the required parameters for a connection

    D. To provide you with a detailed description of the use of each command

5 Match each command in the table with its following primary function.

    A. Ends your CLI session

    B. Modifies your password

    C. Lists all cards in the node

    D. Modifies the temperature alarm threshold on a BPX node

    E. Shows the current IGX cabinet temperature

    F. Shows the status and the serial number of a card

    G. Shows the status of the BPX power supplies and fans

Command	Answer
bye	A
dspcd	F
dspcds	C
dsppwr	E
cnfasm	D
dspasm	G
cnfpwd	B

6 Mark each of the following statements as true or false.

A. The Delete key can be used to abort a command.   **True**

B. The abbreviation DIS means "display" on the CLI.   **False**

C. Cards can be in an active and failed condition at the same time.   **True**

D. All cards provide the same information when you use the **dspcd** command.   **False**

E. A user ID with a privilege level of 4 can perform all the commands available to a user ID with a privilege level of 5.   **True**

7 A card is reporting QRS as the revision when you use the **dspcds** or **dspcd** command. Match each letter in the table with the information it provides.

A. The hardware revision

B. The firmware revision, which is a variation on the model

C. The model, which determines the feature set available on the card

Revision Report	Answer
Q	C
R	A
S	B

Chapter 13

1 Which three of the following statements are true?

A. Node names must be unique.

B. Node names are case sensitive.

C. Node names must start with a letter.

D. A node name can contain up to 10 characters.

E. Any keyboard character can be used in a node name.

2 Which one of the following devices cannot be attached to the auxiliary port?

A. Serial printer

B. Dumb terminal

C. Dial-out modem

D. Router console port

E. Cisco WAN Manager LAN interface

F. PC running VT100 terminal emulation

3 Which two of the following statements are true?

A. All nodes must be in the same time zone.

B. You can Telnet to the LAN or IP relay address.

C. The cnfdate command changes the date and time on all nodes in the network.

D. A printer attached to a node's auxiliary port and configured to log events prints only the events for the local node.

4 Match the command in the table with its correct function from the following list:

A. Modifies the IP relay address

B. Configures the print mode

C. Modifies the control and auxiliary port application

D. Shows the IP address and the subnet mask of the LAN port

E. Shows the node numbers of the nodes in the network

F. Communicates with an external device on the control or auxiliary port

G. Shows the baud rate and the flow-control settings on the control and auxiliary ports

Command	Function
dspnds	E
window	F
cnfnwip	A
dsplancnf	D
cnfprt	B
dsptermcnf	G
cnftermfunc	C

Chapter 14

1 Which of the following card modules can terminate a trunk on an IGX node? (More than one answer could be correct.)

A. CVM

B. NPM

C. NTM

D. ALM/B

E. UXM

F. UFM/C

2 Which two of the following card modules can terminate a trunk from an IGX on a
BPX node?

A. BCC-4
B. BNI-T3
C. ASI-T3
D. BXM-E3
E. ASI-155E
F. BXM-622

3 Which three types of equipment can be attached to a node on a trunk?

A. A BPX node
B. An IGX node
C. A Cisco 7500 router
D. An MGX concentrator
E. A Cisco LightStream 1010
F. Another vendor's Frame Relay switch

4 What is the default size of the statistical reserve for a T3 trunk?

A. 600 cps
B. 992 cps
C. 1000 cps
D. 600 cps
E. 992 cps

5 How many virtual trunks can you terminate on a single port on a BXM-155 card?

A. 4
B. 11
C. 31
D. 32
E. 64

6 What is a virtual trunk?

A. A way to remotely log in to another node
B. An ATM connection that carries traffic for another switch network
C. A trunk that attaches a node to another vendor's ATM switch
D. A type of trunk that utilizes a public ATM service to trunk cell traffic to one
or more IGX and/or BPX nodes

7 Which three of the following statements are true?

A. Some trunk parameters do not apply to all trunk types.
B. Cell scrambling affects the alarm condition of an upped trunk.
C. The **addtrk** command must be issued before the **uptrk** command.
D. Configuration parameters are configurable when a trunk is added.
E. When deactivating a trunk, you must delete a trunk first before it can be
downed.

8 What information can you get using the **dspnw** command?

A. Node name
B. Node status
C. Node number
D. Number of connections
E. Available trunk bandwidth
F. Trunks terminating on the node

9 Match each trunk configuration parameter in the table with its function that follows.

Trunk Configuration Parameter	Answer
Loop clock	B
Statistical reserve	C
Frame scrambling	E
Transmit trunk rate	F
Connection channels	A
Receive impedance	D

A. The number of connections allowed on a virtual trunk
B. A way to use the receive clock in the transmit direction
C. A portion of the bandwidth that cannot be allocated to connections
D. Associated with E1 trunks
E. A standards-based method for rearranging the frame on a trunk
F. The maximum number of data cells permitted on a trunk per second

10 What information can you get using the **dspnds** command?

A. Node name
B. Node status
C. Node number
D. Number of connections
E. Available trunk bandwidth
F. Trunks terminating on the node

Chapter 15

1 Which two of the following statements apply to the MGX 8850 switch?

    A. A booster fan unit is required.

    B. Dual AC power sources are required.

    C. The AC power shelf holds up to six 875W power modules.

    D. The AC power shelf holds up to six 1200W power modules.

    E. High-speed service modules should be located in the upper bay.

    F. The backplane supports 1:N redundancy for all slots except 7 and 8.

2 Which one of the following statements applies to the MGX 8220 concentrator?

    A. Service modules always require a matching back card.

    B. LAN ports on redundant ASC modules should not be Y-cabled.

    C. Power modules deliver regulated 220 VAC to the shelf power bus.

    D. At least two AC power modules are required for a fully loaded shelf.

    E. The AC power shelf can supply full redundant power to four shelves.

    F. A booster fan is required if the number of shelves in a rack is two or more.

3 What is the total vertical space required in RMUs for an MGX 8850 switch with all optional modules?

    A. 21

    B. 19

    C. 20

    D. 16

4 Which card slots are reserved for the PXMs on the MGX 8850 switch?

    A. 1 and 2

    B. 1 and 3

    C. 3 and 4

    D. 7 and 8

    E. 15 and 16

    F. 31 and 32

5 Which card slots are reserved for the ASCs on the MGX 8220 concentrator?

    A. 1 and 2

    B. 1 and 3

    C. 3 and 4

    D. 7 and 8

    E. 15 and 16

    F. 31 and 32

6 Which card slots are reserved for the BNMs on the MGX 8220 concentrator?

   A. 1 and 2
   B. 1 and 3
   C. 3 and 4
   D. 7 and 8
   E. 15 and 16
   F. 31 and 32

7 Match the ASC and PXM back card port with its description.

   A. LAN port
   B. Control port
   C. Maintenance port

Description	Answer
A VT100 interface on the MGX 8850 switch for CLI access	B
An Ethernet interface for Telnet, TFTP, and SNMP access	A
A VT100 interface on the MGX 8220 concentrator for CLI access	C
A SLIP interface on the MGX 8850 switch for Telnet, TFTP, and SNMP access	C
A SLIP interface on the MGX 8220 concentrator for Telnet, TFTP, and SNMP access	B

8 How many E1 ports are on a CESM?

   A. 2
   B. 4
   C. 8
   D. 12

9 Match the card module in the table with its functions from the list that follows:

Card Module	Answer
PXM	**H**
ASC	**I**
BNM	**G**
SRM	**F**
RPM	**A**
CESM	**C**
FRSM	**B**
AUSM	**D**
IMATM	**E**

A. Layer 3 traffic router

B. AAL5 for Frame Relay traffic

C. AAL1 for T1 and E1 formatted traffic

D. CBR, VBR, ABR, and UBR ATM services

E. ATM inverse multiplexing for T3 or E3 lines

F. Service module redundancy, BERT, and optional line distribution

G. Trunk to ATM backbone network, synchronization, and local alarm reporting

H. Storage for configuration, network management, and shelf management on the MGX 8850 switch

I. Storage for configuration, network management, and shelf management on the MGX 8220 concentrator

10 If you had an MGX 8220 concentrator with the following requirements, which card module set would meet your needs?

— Redundant processors

— OC-3 trunk to the ATM backbone network

— BERT for access lines

— T3 line distribution

— Nine E1 circuit emulation lines

— Five T1 Frame Relay lines

— One HSSI Frame Relay line

— Two T1 ATM lines

A. 2 ASC, 1 BNM, 1 SRM-3T3, 2 CESM-8E1, 1 FRSM-8T1, 1 FRSM-HS1, 1 AUSM-T1

B. 2 ASC, 2 BNM, 2 SRM-T1E1, 1 CESM-8E1, 1 FRSM-8T1, 1 FRSM-HS1, 1 AUSM-T1

C. 2 ASC, 2 BNM, 2 SRM-3T3, 2 CESM-8E1, 1 FRSM-8T1, 1 FRSM-HS1, 1 AUSM-T1

D. 2 ASC, 2 BNM, 2 SRM-3T3, 2 CESM-8E1, 1 FRSM-8T1, 1 FRSM-HS1, 1 IMATM-T3T1

11 If you had an MGX 8850 switch installed with full redundancy (core cards and service modules), two RPMs, two FRSM-2T3E3, and two FRSM-8T1 cards, which of the following card slot configurations would be recommended?

Option	Card Slots
PXM	**7 and 8**
SRM	**15, 16, 31, and 32**
RPM	**9 and 10**
FRSM-2T3E3	**5 and 6**
FRSM-8T1	**21 and 22**

Chapter 16

1 Match the command-line access method in the table with its definition from the list that follows.

Command-Line Access Method	Definition
IP relay	**D**
LAN port	**B**
MGX 8850 control port	**C**
MGX 8220 control port	**A**

A. A SLIP port for Telnet access

B. A 15-pin AUI port connected to an Ethernet

C. The default CLI access using a VT100 terminal

D. A way to Telnet to a device inband through the BPX/IGX network

2 Which two of the following statements are true?

 A. The Esc key aborts a command.

 B. All commands have required and optional parameters.

 C. Many commands comprise an abbreviated verb and noun.

 D. The MGX CLI prompts you for all required and optional parameters.

 E. A command is complete when all required parameters have been defined with appropriate values.

3 What is the purpose of the **Help** command?

 A. To teach you how to configure an MGX device

 B. To identify the definition and syntax of a command

 C. To list all commands supported by a card type and user privilege level

 D. To provide you with a detailed description of the use of each command

4 Match the command in the table with its primary function from the list that follows.

Command	Primary Function
cc	D
bye	C
dspcd	E
dspcds	B
dspifip	F
cnfpwd	A

 A. Modifies your password on MGX 8220 and MGX 8850

 B. Lists all cards on the shelf

 C. Ends your CLI (and Telnet) session

 D. Logs in to another card on the concentrator

 E. Shows the status and the serial number of a card

 F. Shows the IP addresses configured for the shelf

5 Mark each of the following statements as true or false.

 A. The **dspshelfalm** command shows trunk and line alarms.   **False**

 B. The abbreviation "DIS" means "display" on the MGX CLI.   **False**

 C. You can check the shelf date and time by issuing the **cnfdate** and **cnftime** commands at the active ASC or PXM.   **True**

 D. A user ID with a privilege level of 4 can perform all the commands available to a user ID with a privilege level of 5.   **True**

Chapter 17

1 Which one of the following line formats cannot be used on the MGX 8850 PXM trunk?

   A. T1
   B. T3
   C. E3
   D. OC-3c
   E. STM-1
   F. STM-4
   G. OC-12c

2 Which four of the following line formats can be used on the MGX 8220 BNM trunk?

   A. T1
   B. T3
   C. E3
   D. OC-3c
   E. STM-1
   F. STM-4
   G. OC-12c

3 What is an MGX standalone concentrator?

   A. A homogeneous MGX 8850 switch network
   B. An MGX 8220 or 8850 device that is not attached to any other switch
   C. An MGX 8850 switch that is a feeder in an MGX/BPX tiered network
   D. An MGX 8220 or 8850 device used as a UNI feeder to any ATM backbone network
   E. An MGX 8220 concentrator that is attached directly to another MGX 8220 concentrator

4 Which two of the following BPX trunk cards can you attach to an MGX 8220 concentrator and have integrated network management using the WAN Manager station?

   A. BNI-T3
   B. BNI-155
   C. ASI-155
   D. BXM-E3 in line mode
   E. BXM-622 in trunk mode
   F. BXM-155 in trunk mode

5 Which two of the following BPX trunk cards can you attach to an MGX 8850 concentrator and have integrated network management using the WAN Manager station?

A. BNI-T3

B. BNI-155

C. ASI-155

D. BXM-E3 in line mode

E. BXM-622 in trunk mode

F. BXM-155 in trunk mode

6 What type of cell formats can you use between the following card modules (STI, UNI, NNI, or none)?

Card Module	Cell Format
PXM-T3 to ASI-T3	**UNI/NNI**
BNM-T3 to BNI-T3	**STI**
BNM-E3 to ASI-E3	**UNI/NNI**
BNM-155 to BNI-155	**None**
PXM-155 to BXM-155 in line mode	**UNI/NNI**
BNM-155 to BXM-155 in trunk mode	**NNI**

7 Which two of the following statements are true?

A. You must delete the shelf before downing the trunk on the BPX switch.

B. A mismatch in the payload scrambling configuration will cause the addshelf command to fail.

C. A mismatch in the payload scrambling configuration will cause the trunk to fail and report a LOS alarm.

D. The WAN Manager station can manage the MGX concentrator and any ATM backbone network to which it is attached.

8 Which four line characteristics can you modify with the **cnfln** command on the MGX 8850 switch?

A. Line loopbacks

B. Frame scrambling

C. Payload scrambling

D. The SONET framing

E. The ATM cell header type

F. The 1s density enforcement method

9 Which line characteristic can you modify with the **cnfbnmif** command on the MGX 8220 concentrator?

   A. Line loopbacks

   B. Frame scrambling

   C. Payload scrambling

   D. The SONET framing

   E. The ATM cell header type

   F. The 1s density enforcement method

Chapter 18

1 What is the meaning of a major alarm status on the lower-right corner of the node console screen?

   A. The local node has a major alarm.

   B. The network has at least one major alarm.

   C. All nodes in the network have major alarms.

   D. A major alarm has occurred in the last 5 minutes on a remote node.

2 Which two events will generate a major network alarm?

   A. Card self-test failure

   B. Loss of signal on a feeder trunk

   C. Loss of signal on a network trunk

   D. Missing processor in a redundant configuration

   E. Cabinet temperature above the configured threshold

   F. Loss of communication between an MGX feeder node and the WAN Manager station

3 Which one of the following statements is true?

   A. Use the resetcd slot f command to clear a self-test failure alarm on a card.

   B. Use the **resetcd slot h** command to clear a self-test failure alarm on a card.

   C. Use the **resetcd slot h** command to switch from the active to the standby processor.

   D. Use the **resetcd slot f** command to switch from an active to a standby Y-cabled card module.

4 Which two of the following statements are true?

   A. The ASC reports environmental shelf alarms.

   B. The dspalms command screen summarizes all alarms on a card module.

   C. The **dspshelfalm** command screen summarizes all alarms in the MGX device.

   D. The MGX alarm status is reported to the BPX wide-area switch in an integrated tiered network.

5 Match each command in the table with its function in the list that follows.

Command	Answer
dspcds	F
dspnds	E
resetcd	D
dspnode	A
clrcderrs	C
dspshelfalm	B

A. Verifies the alarm status of feeder shelves
B. Determines whether a fan has failed
C. Deletes card failure history without resetting card
D. Deletes card failure history and resets card
E. Determines which routing nodes have alarms
F. Determines which feeder service modules are in alarm

Chapter 19

1 Which of the following are not valid download options for new versions of software or firmware?

A. StrataView Lite for firmware download to an IGX or BPX node
B. StrataView Lite for firmware download to the MGX 8850 switch
C. A TFTP server for software and firmware download to all IGX, BPX, and MGX nodes
D. Cisco WAN Manager for software and firmware download to all IGX, BPX, and MGX nodes
E. Using the CLI on an IGX or BPX node to initiate software download from either a TFTP server or StrataView Lite

2 Which of the following best defines *version interoperability?*

A. Extension of the node-by-node upgrade feature to Release 9.1
B. Capability of PXM controller to retain slot-specific and generic firmware
C. Use of Cisco IOS to facilitate interoperation of RPM and PXM in the MGX 8850 node
D. Capability of network operation over an extended period of time with nodes at different software release levels
E. Capability of a node to operate with different software versions in its active and standby controller cards

3 Which of the three letters in the firmware release portion of the CCO filename identifies the release level?

The third letter. The first letter identifies the card type, and the second letter identifies the model.

4 Which two of the following statements are true?

A. **TFTP is the only valid download protocol for MGX nodes.**
B. New boot code is always downloaded into the standby ASC.
C. **You need to reboot the switch to invoke new boot code on an MGX 8850.**
D. The MGX 8850 retains a copy of service module boot code on the PXM hard drive.
E. The command sequence for a graceful firmware upgrade on an MGX 8850 is **install, newrev, commit, reboot.**
F. You cannot store both slot-specific and generic firmware files for a particular type of service module on the ASC hard drive.

5 Look at the following table containing output that would come from a **dspcd** command, and answer the questions that follow.

	Active	Updated
RAM ID	9.1	9.2
Flash EEPROM ID	9.2	9.1
BRAM ID	9.1	9.2

A. Which processor is in use by the node now?
    Active
B. How can you tell?
    BRAM status shows that 9.1 is running.
C. Which command was issued to get you to this point?
    loadrev
D. If the active module failed now, what version would be started by the standby module?
    Revision 9.2 because it is stored in BRAM

Look at the following table containing output for the same node that would come from a **dspcd** command, and answer the questions that follow.

	Locked	Active
RAM ID	9.1	9.2
Flash EEPROM ID	9.2	9.1
BRAM ID	9.1	9.2

E. Which processor is in use by the node now?

Active

F. How can you tell?

BRAM is updated to 9.2; only the active processor has Release 9.2.

G. Which command was issued to get you to this point?

runrev

H. If the active module failed now, what version would be started by the standby module?

9.1—it is in standby (locked) BRAM.

Symbols

Numerics

A

C

J-K

L

M

O

P

T

U

Cisco Career Certifications

Building Cisco Remote Access Networks
Cisco Systems, Inc., edited by Catherine Paquet
1-57870-091-4 • AVAILABLE NOW

Based on the Cisco Systems instructor-led course available worldwide, *Building Cisco Remote Access Networks* teaches you how to design, set up, configure, maintain, and scale a remote access network using Cisco products. In addition, *Building Cisco Remote Access Networks* provides chapter-ending questions to help you assess your understanding of key concepts and start you down the path for attaining your CCNP or CCDP certification.

Cisco Internetwork Troubleshooting
Cisco Systems, Inc., edited by Laura Chappell and Dan Farkas, CCIE
1-57870-092-2 • AVAILABLE NOW

Based on the Cisco Systems instructor-led course available worldwide, *Cisco Internetwork Troubleshooting* teaches you how to perform fundamental hardware maintenance and troubleshooting on Cisco routers and switches. If you are pursuing CCNP certification and anticipate taking the CCNP Support exam, this book is a logical starting point.

Cisco CCNA Exam #640-507 Certification Guide
Wendell Odom, CCIE
0-7357-0971-8 • AVAILABLE NOW

Although it's only the first step in Cisco Career Certification, the Cisco Certified Network Associate (CCNA) exam is a difficult test. Your first attempt at becoming Cisco certified requires a lot of study and confidence in your networking knowledge. When you're ready to test your skills, complete your knowledge of the exam topics, and prepare for exam day, you need the preparation tools found in *Cisco CCNA Exam #640-507 Certification Guide* from Cisco Press.

Interconnecting Cisco Network Devices
Cisco Systems, Inc., edited by Steve McQuerry
1-57870-111-2 • AVAILABLE NOW

Based on the Cisco course taught worldwide, *Interconnecting Cisco Network Devices* teaches you how to configure Cisco switches and routers in multi-protocol internetworks. ICND is the primary course recommended by Cisco Systems for CCNA #640-507 preparation. If you are pursuing CCNA certification, this book is an excellent starting point for your study.

www.ciscopress.com

CCIE Professional Development

Cisco LAN Switching

Kennedy Clark, CCIE; Kevin Hamilton, CCIE

1-57870-094-9 • AVAILABLE NOW

This volume provides an in-depth analysis of Cisco LAN switching technologies, architectures, and deployments, including unique coverage of Catalyst network design essentials. Network designs and configuration examples are incorporated throughout to demonstrate the principles and enable easy translation of the material into practice in production networks.

Advanced IP Network Design

Alvaro Retana, CCIE, Don Slice, CCIE, and Russ White, CCIE

1-57870-097-3 • AVAILABLE NOW

Network engineers and managers can use these case studies, which highlight various network design goals, to explore issues including protocol choice, network stability, and growth. This book also includes theoretical discussion on advanced design topics.

Inside Cisco IOS

Vijay Bollapragada, CCIE, Curtis Murphy, CCIE, and Russ White, CCIE

1-57870-181-3 • AVAILABLE JULY 2000

Inside Cisco IOS offers crucial and hard-to-find information on Cisco's Internetwork Operating System (IOS) software. Beyond understanding the Cisco IOS command set, comprehending what happens inside Cisco routers will help you as network designer or engineer to perform your job more effectively. *Inside Cisco IOS* provides essential information that will educate you on the internal aspects of IOS at this level.

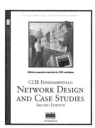

Cisco CCIE Fundamentals: Network Design and Case Studies, Second Edition

Cisco Systems, Inc.

1-57870-167-8 • AVAILABLE NOW

This two-part reference is a compilation of design tips and configuration examples assembled by Cisco Systems. The design guide portion of this book supports the network administrator who designs and implements routers and switch-based networks, and the case studies supplement the design guide material with real-world configurations. Begin the process of mastering the technologies and protocols necessary to become an effective CCIE.

www.ciscopress.com

Cisco Press Solutions

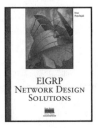

EIGRP Network Design Solutions

Ivan Pepelnjak, CCIE

1-57870-165-1 • AVAILABLE NOW

EIGRP Network Design Solutions uses case studies and real-world configuration examples to help you gain an in-depth understanding of the issues involved in designing, deploying, and managing EIGRP-based networks. This book details proper designs that can be used to build large and scalable EIGRP-based networks and documents possible ways each EIGRP feature can be used in network design, implementation, troubleshooting, and monitoring.

Cisco IOS Releases

Mack Coulibaly

1-57870-179-1 • AVAILABLE NOW

This book is the first comprehensive guide to the more than three dozen types of Cisco IOS releases being used today on enterprise and service provider networks. You will learn to select the best Cisco IOS release for your network and to predict the quality and stability of a particular release. With the knowledge, you'll be able to design, implement, and manage world-class network infrastructures powered by Cisco IOS software.

OpenCable™ Architecture

Michael Adams

1-57870-135-x • AVAILABLE NOW

Whether you're a television, data communications, or telecommunications professional, or simply an interested business person, this book will help you understand the technical and business issues surrounding interactive television services. It will also provide you with an inside look at the combined efforts of the cable, data, and consumer electronics industries' efforts to develop those new services.

Enhanced IP Services for Cisco Networks

Donald C. Lee, CCIE

1-57870-106-6 • AVAILABLE NOW

This is a guide to improving your network's capabilities by understanding the new enabling and advanced Cisco IOS services that build more scalable, intelligent, and secure networks. Learn the technical details necessary to deploy Quality of Service, VPN technologies, IPsec, the IOS firewall, and IOS Intrusion Detection. These services will allow you to extend the network to new frontiers securely, protect your network from attacks, and increase the sophistication of network services.

www.ciscopress.com

Cisco Press Solutions

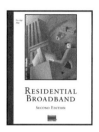

Residential Broadband, Second Edition
George Abe

1-57870-177-5 • **AVAILABLE NOW**

This book provides a comprehensive, accessible introduction to the topics surrounding high-speed networks to the home. It is written for anyone seeking a broad-based familiarity with the issues of residential broadband. You will learn about the services that are driving the market, the technical issues shapir the evolution, and the network with the home and how it connects to the acce network.

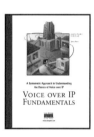

Voice over IP Fundamentals
Jonathan Davidson and Jim Peters

1-57870-168-6 • **AVAILABLE NOW**

This book will provide you with a thorough introduction to the voice and dat technology. You will learn how the telephony infrastructure was built and how it works today. You will also gain an understanding of the major concepts concerning voice and data networking, transmission of voice over data, and IP signaling protocols used to interwork with current telephony systems.

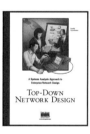

Top-Down Network Design
Priscilla Oppenheimer

1-57870-069-8 • **AVAILABLE NOW**

Building reliable, secure, and manageable networks is every network professional's goal. This practical guide teaches you a systematic method for network design that can be applied to campus LANs, remote-access networks, WAN links, and large-scale internetworks. Learn how to analyze business and technical requirements, examine traffic flow and Quality of Service require-ments, and select protocols and technologies based on performance goals.

CISCO SYSTEMS

CISCO PRESS

www.ciscopress.com